Social Justice

Social Justice has been a dominant concern of political philosophers, theorists and economists since the last century. *Social Justice: From Hume to Walzer* brings together leading theorists to discuss the latest thinking on this important area of study. The contributors explore:

- the origins of the concept
- the contribution of thinkers such as Hume, Mill and Rawls
- current issues such as international justice, economic justice, justice and the environment and special rights

By examining the latest applications of theories of justice with a discussion of origins, this book provides an excellent overview for students and specialists alike.

David Boucher is Reader in Politics at the University of Wales. **Paul Kelly** is Lecturer in Politics at the London School of Economics and Political Science.

Social Justice

From Hume to Walzer

Edited by David Boucher and Paul Kelly

London and New York

First published 1998
by Routledge
11 New Fetter Lane, London EC4P 4EE

Simultaneously published in the USA and Canada
by Routledge
29 West 35th Street, New York, NY 10001

Typeset in Baskerville by BC Typesetting, Bristol
Printed and bound in Great Britain by Clays Ltd., St. Ives

British Library Cataloguing in Publication Data
A catalogue record for this book is available from the British Library

Library of Congress Cataloging in Publication Data
Social justice: from Hume to Walzer/edited by David Boucher and Paul
    Kelly.
        p.   cm.
    Includes bibliographical references and index.
    ISBN 0–415–14997–5 (alk. paper). – ISBN 0–415–14998–3 (pbk.
alk. paper)
    1. Social justice.   I. Boucher, David.   II. Kelly, P. J. (Paul
Joseph)
    HM216.S5528   1998
    303.3′72–dc21   98-6009

ISBN 0–415–14997–5 (hbk)
ISBN 0–415–14998–3 (pbk)

Contents

Contributors

Richard Bellamy is Professor of Politics at the University of Reading. He previously taught at the Universities of Oxford, Cambridge, Edinburgh and East Anglia. He has published numerous works in political theory, the history of political ideas and jusriprudence. He is author of *Modern Italian Social Theory* (1988), *Liberalism and Modern Society* (1992) and with D. Schecter, *Gramsci and the Italian State* (1993). His edited books include *Victorian Liberalism* (1990), *Theories and Concepts of Politics* (1993) and, with D. Castiglione, *Constitutionalism in Transformation* (1997).

David Boucher was a Research Fellow and Senior Lecturer at the Australian National University and is currently a Reader at the University of Wales, Swansea. He is the author of *Texts in Context* (1985), *The Social and Political Thought of R. G. Collingwood* (1989), *A Radical Hegelian* (with Andrew Vincent, 1993), and *Political Theories of International Relations* (1998). Among his edited books are *The Social Contract From Hobbes to Rawls*, with Paul Kelly (1994) and *The British Idealists*, (1997).

Chris Brown is Professor of Politics at the University of Southampton, and currently Chair of the British International Studies Association. He is the author of *International Relations Theory* (1992), *Understanding International Relations* (1997), and numerous articles on international political theory. He has edited *Political Restructuring in Europe: Ethical Perspectives* (1994).

Joseph Femia is a Reader in Politics at the University of Liverpool. He has been British Academy Visiting Professor at the European University Institute in Florence, and a Visiting Fellow at Princeton and Yale Universities. He is the author of *Gramsci's Political Thought* (1981), *Marxism and Democracy* (1993), and *The Machiavellian Legacy* (1998). He is currently writing a book on the varieties of anti-democratic thought.

David Gauthier is Distinguished Service Professor of Philosophy at the University of Pittsburgh. His major publications include *Logic of Leviathan* (1969), *Morals By Agreement* (1986) and a collection of essays, *Moral Dealing: Contract, Ethics and Reason* (1992), as well as numerous papers in philosophical journals. His current research interests include contractarian moral and political theory, deliberative rationality and the thought of Thomas Hobbes and Jean-Jacques Rousseau.

Paul Kelly is Lecturer in Political Theory at the London School of Economics; he previously taught at the University of Wales, Swansea and was a visiting Research Fellow at the University of Chicago Law School. He is author of *Utilitarianism and Distributive Justice: Jeremy Bentham and the Civil Law* (1990) and is editor with David Boucher of *The Social Contract from Hobbes to Rawls* (1994) and editor of *Impartiality, Neutrality and Justice*, (1998). He is currently completing a book on Ronald Dworkin.

Rex Martin is Professor of Philosophy at the University of Kansas, Lawrence, and Professor of Political Theory and Government at the University of Wales, Swansea. Among his numerous publications are *Historical Explanation: Re-enactment and Practical Inference* (1977), *Rawls and Rights*, (1985) and *A System of Rights* (1993); he has edited *R. G. Collingwood, An Essay on Metaphysics* (1998) and with M. Singer, *G. C. MacCallum: Legislative Intent, and Other Essays on Law, Politics and Morality* (1993).

Kenneth Minogue is Professor of Political Science Emeritus at the London School of Economics and Political Science. He is author of numerous articles and chapters in edited books. His published books include *The Liberal Mind* (1961), *Nationalism* (1967), *Alien Powers, The Pure Theory of Ideology* (1984) and most recently, *A Very Short Introduction to Politics* (1995). He is also the editor of the Everyman edition of Hobbes's *Leviathan*.

Tariq Modood is Professor of Sociology, Politics and Public Policy at the University of Bristol. He was Gwilym Gibbon Fellow at Nuffield College, Oxford, and a Hallsworth Research Fellow at the University of Manchester before becoming Programme Director in the Policy Studies Institute, London. His recent publications include (co-author) *Ethnic Minorities in Britain: Diversity and Disadvantage* (1997), (co-ed.) *The Politics of Multiculturalism in the New Europe* (1997), and (ed.) *Church, State and Religious Minorities* (1997).

Carole Pateman is Professor of Political Science at the University of California, Los Angeles. She was President of the International Political Science Association 1991–94. Her publications include, *Participation and Democratic Theory* (1970), *The Problem of Political Obligation* (1985), *The Sexual Contract* (1988), *The Disorder of Women: Democracy, Feminism and Political Theory* (1989), and edited with Mary Lyndon Shanley, *Feminist Interpretations and Political Theory* (1991).

Raymond Plant was Professor of Politics at Southampton University and is now Master of St Catherine's College, Oxford and a Labour member of the House of Lords. He is the author of *Hegel* (1973), *Political Philosophy and Social Welfare* (with Harry Lesser and Peter Taylor-Goodby, 1980),

Equality, Markets and the State (1984), *Philosophy, Politics and Citizenship* (with Andrew Vincent, 1984) and *Modern Political Thought* (1991).

Jonathan Riley is Professor of Political Science at the Murphy Institute of Political Economy, Tulane University, New Orleans. In addition to numerous articles, his books include *Liberal Utilitarianism* (1988), the *Routledge Philosophy Guidebook to J. S. Mill: On Liberty* (1998), *Mill's Radical Liberalism* (1998), and the World Classics edition of *J. S. Mill: Principles of Political Economy and Chapters on Socialism* (1994). He is currently completing *Maximizing Security: A Utilitarian Theory of Liberal Rights* and working on aspects of American constitutionalism.

Andrew Vincent is Professor of Political Theory at the University of Wales, Cardiff. He was recently a Senior Research Fellow at the Australian National University. His books include *Theories of the State* (1987), *Modern Political Ideologies* (1995), *Philosophy, Politics and Citizenship* (with Raymond Plant, 1984) and *A Radical Hegelian* (with David Boucher, 1993). He is most recently editor of *Political Theory: Tradition and Diversity* (1997).

David West is a Senior Lecturer in Political Science at the Australian National University; he previously taught at the University of Liverpool. He is the author of *Authenticity and Empowerment: A Theory of Liberation* (1990) and *An Introduction to Continental Philosophy* (1996).

Acknowledgements

The editors would like to thank the Department of Political Theory and Government, University of Wales Swansea for its generous support of the conference at Gregynog in 1995 at which a number of the papers published here were presented. We are also indebted to Caroline Wintersgill and Patrick Proctor of Routledge for their encouragement and support of the project. One contribution has previously been published and we would like to thank John M. Rowehl for granting permission to include David Gauthier, 'David Hume: Contractarian', *The Philosophical Review*, 88 (1979). Copyright 1979 Cornell University. Reprinted by permission of the publisher and the author.

1 Introduction

David Boucher and Paul Kelly

This collection of essays in political theory and politics by an international cast of authors is united by a common theme, that of social justice. Social justice, under its pseudonym of 'distributive justice' has enjoyed a significant audience among academic political theorists since John Rawls' book *A Theory of Justice*[1] turned much of modern political theory in Britain and the United States of America into a discipline focused on issues of distribution. One could be forgiven for thinking that political theory is about how best to distribute the benefits of social cooperation and how one can justify such claims of justice to others. Such a perception would not be wholly accurate as the discussion of some of the essays in this book will show, but equally it would be forgivable.

Yet whilst political theorists are apt to see the world in terms of a dominant distributive paradigm that can be mined for policy prescriptions or else which must be challenged to allow alternative conceptions of the *political* to have a voice, the real world of politics at least during the 1970s and 1980s seemed to have given up the idea for dead. It was not uncommon for politicians and those academics who went over to political advocacy, to criticise the ivory tower preoccupations of political philosophers who could theorise about 'difference principles', 'basic income', 'equality of resources', etc., without any concern for how income and wealth (the primary objects of distribution) were produced or who might own them.

During the 1980s, whilst some political philosophers seemed to talk of nothing else, in the real world social justice seemed to have become deeply unpopular. Not only did 'supply side' theories, inflation and the claims about the 'fiscal crisis of the state' come to dominate discussions of political economy, but prominent politicians claimed 'there is no such thing as society'. If society does not exist, or is merely reduced to individuals and their families, then there did not seem to be much scope for social justice at all. Whatever else social justice meant – and in terms of substantive prescriptions it meant a whole variety of things – it was normally taken to imply that there are certain things individuals have an entitlement to merely by virtue of their membership of society. These things meant not only the traditional canon of liberal civil rights, but also economic rights to basic welfare provision. Even

a theorist as hostile to the idea of social justice as F. A. von Hayek was prepared to countenance a basic economic safety net below which no individual
should be allowed to fall.[2] Few thinkers of any significance were bold enough
to tolerate free markets allowing the weakest and most inadequate to starve
in the streets.

That even the most vociferous of new-right anti-state theorists rarely
contemplated the full rigours of a nineteenth-century Sumnerite 'social
darwinism'[3] in which only the fittest were really expected to survive, suggests
that the core ideas of social justice really do run deep, whatever may have
been the transformation of public political rhetoric. However many obitu-
aries were written for the concept it was never quite laid to rest. As the 1980s
gave way to the 1990s and new-right triumphalism started to collapse under
the weight of recession, growing unemployment and burgeoning welfare
budgets as governments tried to deal with the consequences of large scale economic restructuring, renewed interest in social justice started to be shown in
the public rhetoric of opposition and governing parties alike. The welfare
systems of the advanced industrial economies came under growing strain, as
they continued to respond to public demands and expectations, whilst at the
same time the same electorates showed no great propensity to vote for higher
taxation to relieve the fiscal burdens of the institutional manifestation of
social justice, the welfare state. This situation created practical problems for
governing parties, but more severe problems for opposition parties of the
centre and left. They could not simply advocate higher taxation to support
much needed welfare expenditure without confining themselves to the
oblivion of permanent opposition. The appeal to traditional justifications of
welfare policies in terms of social justice were not connecting with the popular
imagination. The demands of a new world of industrial restructuring and
globalisation as well as the continued need for welfare support for the economically dispossessed created a climate in which ideas of social justice came to
have a renewed significance, but also created a climate in which traditional
ideas of social justice and their policy implications came under review. In
1992 following yet another defeat in a British general election, the Rt Hon.
John Smith MP, then leader of the Labour Party, set up an independent
Commission on Social Justice. The task of this commission was to rethink the
foundations of the welfare state in Britain in as radical a way as Beveridge's
Report of 1945 which gave rise to the British Welfare State. Much of the
work of the new commission was to do with an analysis of the conditions of
deprivation, poverty, dependency and unemployment and policies to deal
with them. Similar inquiries, but with perhaps less grand titles, were undertaken in other countries with similar concerns about the burgeoning cost of
welfare along with the need to mitigate the human costs of economic restructuring. But an important consequence to the work of the Commission in the
British context was to raise again theoretical issues about the nature and justification of social justice.

The Commission itself played only a minor role directly advancing the discussion of social justice among political theorists, although two reports by the Commission, *The Justice Gap*,[4] and *Social Justice: Strategies for National Renewal*[5] address in a general way the philosophical underpinnings of the Commission's policy prescriptions. Nevertheless, the reports themselves and the philosophical bases of their analysis and prescription did provide an added impetus to make the study of social justice once again a central part of public political discourse to which political philosophers and political theorists could contribute.[6]

Our concern in bringing together this collection of essays was not to reflect directly on the current politics of social justice in light of the Commission's reports, though the essays by Ken Minogue and Lord Plant bear directly on this issue. Instead we set out to provide an overview of positive and critical perspectives on social justice which illustrate the variety of sources from which current thinking on issues of social justice emerges and the plurality of distributive issues which are brought under the heading of social justice. Some of the essays deal directly with particular historical thinkers such as David Hume or John Stuart Mill or groups of thinkers such as the British Idealists who have contributed to the vocabularies of contemporary debates. Other historical essays such as Joe Femia's on Vilfredo Pareto illustrate the historical resources of some contemporary assaults on the possibility of social justice. Contemporary theorists are dealt with, such as Michael Walzer, and contractarian theorists such as John Rawls, T. M. Scanlon and Brian Barry. Other essays set out to expand the scope of contemporary discussions or to recover neglected vocabularies, such as Carole Pateman's essay on rights which is influenced by the work of T. H. Marshall.

In substance each of these essays appears to have little in common other than the use of the vocabulary of social or distributive justice. Yet it is precisely this diversity that we deliberately set out to capture in these essays. In writing an adequate history of theories of social justice or study of the concept one has a choice; either one can impose a formal definition of the concept which results in a clearly identifiable narrative, but which will inevitably leave out much of the contested character of the concept; or, one can do what we have done which is to try to reflect adequately the contested character of the concept, its implications and historical sources, but at the cost of acknowledging that many of the debates about social justice are often about very different things. What we have deliberately chosen not to do is to try and show, as we did in our earlier book on the social contract tradition, that there is a relatively coherent tradition of argument at work here.[7] Also we have chosen not to provide a review of contemporary post-Rawlsian debates on distributive justice, though an overview of contemporary work on post-Rawlsian theories of distributive justice forms a later essay. Such debates are important and still, as mentioned earlier, exercise a dominant position in contemporary political theory – no adequate political theory text on the issue of social justice could neglect such debates – but equally we deliberately set out to show that whatever dominance Rawls type theorising still exercises there is yet more to the political theory of social justice. Furthermore, in light of a renewed public interest in the issue of social justice, coupled with a widespread recognition that traditional arguments and defences of social justice are no longer adequate or sufficient to cope with the full range of contemporary problems and expectations, it was all the more important that we should not confine our study merely to a review of contractarian or Kantian justifications of distributive or social justice.

In the remainder of this introductory chapter we have not set out to identify any unifying narrative or common set of themes. Instead we have confined our efforts to providing an overview of each of the subsequent chapters. This is not to say that there are no common themes and arguments running through the different essays. There certainly are themes that emerge in a number of them. However, our concern was to emphasise the variety rather than the uniformity of debates which fall under the heading of social justice.

SOCIAL JUSTICE: FROM HUME TO WALZER – AN OVERVIEW

In republishing David Gauthier's important essay on David Hume as a contractarian, our intention was to provide an account of Hume as a contributory source for contemporary theorising about social or distributive justice, and this is precisely what Gauthier provides. Ostensibly Gauthier is concerned with arguing that Hume despite being one of contractarianism's most famous critics was also at the same time a consistent contractarian theorist. In making this interpretative case Gauthier provides a useful distinction between the varieties of contractarianism, from 'original' contract theories of the origin of government – which Gauthier argues is Hume's real target – to hypothetical mutual advantage theories which he argues Hume used in his defence of private property and rules of justice.

It is this latter form of contractarianism and Hume's use of it to justify private property and justice which makes Gauthier's essay important for this collection. For the account of property and justice that Gauthier finds in Hume is akin to the mutual advantage theory which he develops in more detail in his own *Morals by Agreement*[8] which has become the main rival to impartialist contractarian defences of justice such as those advanced by John Rawls in *A Theory of Justice* and Brian Barry in *Justice as Impartiality*[9] and to utilitarian defences such as those offered by Bentham and John Stuart Mill (see Riley's chapter).

Unlike utilitarian theories, with which Hume's account of justice is often confused, Gauthier argues that for Hume the obligations of justice are not to be understood in terms of an interest in performing an act of justice. This would reduce all obligations of justice to the status of any obligation under act utilitarianism. However, Hume does not want to deny the connection between justice and interest for he wants a wholly naturalistic explanation of moral obligations such as those of justice. The solution is provided, for Gauthier, by a form of hypothetical contract argument which grounds the conventions and rules of justice in the mutual advantage of contributors and then moves to another level of explanation which shows that the obligatoriness of justice is based on an interest in maintaining the conventions which require specific acts rather than an interest in the specific act itself. Thus Hume does not have to show as do act utilitarians that there is always a natural convergence between individual and general interest to preclude defecting from the general interest. Hume can concede that in a particular case there may be grounds for saying the performance of the act is not in the person's interest, without conceding that the person ceases to be under an obligation.

A further crucial implication of Gauthier's argument is that it shows that a Humean conception of justice is one that confines the remit of social justice to maintenance of stable expectations in the distribution of property, and does not sanction the redistribution of property and income. As Gauthier was to show in his development of the idea in *Morals by Agreement*, a mutual advantage contract assumes that the only beneficiaries of justice are those who contribute to the production of the benefits of social cooperation. Those who are mere beneficiaries do not have a claim of justice on contributors because they do not contribute to that which the conventions of justice regulates. Thus Gauthier uses Hume to challenge the presumed egalitarian outcome of principles of distributive justice, and to support a different perspective on justice from that derived from the idea of impartiality.

Utilitarianism has a peculiar status among the sources of contemporary debates about social justice. Utilitarianism contributes to the growth of the idea of social justice through the social reforms advocated by historical utilitarians such as Jeremy Bentham, John Stuart Mill and their followers, and through the growth of modern welfare economics that in part developed from the utilitarian tradition. However, among contemporary political theorists and philosophers, at least since Rawls' *A Theory of Justice*, utilitarianism has been seen as one of the problems that theories of distributive justice are designed to deal with. For Rawls and his followers, utilitarians are unable to give an adequate account of justice because they apply a decision rule which denies the significance of the separateness of persons, and because they cannot provide a principled constraint on sacrificing the good of some to the majority's welfare. Utilitarianism violates what Rex Martin in his paper identifies as the root idea of economic justice 'that the arrangement of economic institutions requires, if it is to be just, that all contributors benefit or, at least, that none are to be left worse off'. It does this because it has no reason to deny making some social group economically worse off if the advantage to others is sufficient to outweigh that group's loss of utility.

Whilst some utilitarians are happy to accept this conclusion, arguing that Rawls type objections to utilitarianism apply equally to his 'original position' or else that they trade on unjustifiable intuitions, many other utilitarians have attempted to rebut these charges and show how utilitarianism can give rise to basic rights and justice. Similarly historians of utilitarianism[10] have argued that not only were historical utilitarians acutely aware of these charges but answered them. Jonathan Riley's essay on Mill, sets out to show that John Stuart Mill had not only recognised the problem of Rawls type criticisms, but had an answer for them based on his liberal variant of optimal rule utilitarianism. Riley's purpose, however, is not merely to defend the reputation of utilitarianism's greatest champion of justice and rights, but also show that the Millian strategy can form the basis of a viable utilitarian theory of justice, which is both superior to other variants of rule utilitarianism, such as those offered by John Harsanyi and Richard Brandt, but which is also a superior defence of a liberal theory of justice than Rawlsian contractarianism.

Riley argues that Mill offers a version of optimal rule utilitarianism, whereby actions are judged in terms of their conformity to an ideal code of rules. However, Mill's justification of optimal rule utilitarianism avoids the standard charge that rule utilitarianism collapses into act utilitarianism or else it ceases to be utilitarian on the grounds that the rules are not justified simply because of weaknesses of intellect and emotion, but because of the positive expectation effects of a system of rights and duties and the significance of these for individual freedom and character. For Mill the basic rights of liberal utilitarianism are not merely a response to weakness of motivation and character that would be lacking in a world of act utilitarian saints. What is distinctive about Mill's theory according to Riley, is that he defends a liberal constraint on the application of first order impartiality which is as robust as that which contemporary contractarian theories of distributive justice provide.

Riley's paper is also of interest for the way in which he defends the superiority of his reading of Mill's theory of justice to the theories of fellow rule utilitarians such as Harsanyi and Brandt as well as non-utilitarians such as Rawls. In this way his chapter is not concerned merely with the recovery of Mill's theory but with a direct contribution to debates about distributive justice.

Themes from Plato's seminal discussion of Justice are pursued and represented in this volume by Femia on Pareto and Boucher on the British Idealists. Thrasymachus's infamous equation of Justice with expediency and what serves the interests of the powerful is echoed in Pareto's contemptuous dismissal of the very idea of social justice. The starting point of Femia's exploration of Pareto's views is Justinian's restatement of Aristotle's definition of justice: that everyone should be rendered his due. This is another way of saying that justice is a matter of treating everyone equally, where equality is correlative with an equal entitlement to what is one's due. There is, of course, widespread agreement that justice certainly does have something to do with desert. David Miller, for example, identifies a just human condition with a society in which each individual has exactly the benefits and obligations due to him or her. Defining justice in terms of equality, or giving what is due to a person begs the question 'equal with respect to what', and exactly how do we determine what a person's due is.[11]

Pareto argues that judgements about what is a person's due are subjective and arbitrary. There can be no 'Archimedean point' from which we can arbitrate people's claims. Like Thucydides and Thrasymachus Pareto's focus is upon power and the uses to which it is put. Justice is a facade, an illusion perpetrated by the strong in their own interests. Femia compares Pareto with Marx and suggests that unlike the latter the former's critique of justice cannot be reduced to class interest. Thrasymachus, like many Classical Greek writers such as Protagoras and Glaucon who argued that justice is conventional, nevertheless believed it to be necessary for the purpose of social cohesiveness. Femia asks a similar question of Pareto. Despite the fact that justice is an illusion, can it be dispensed with completely in considerations of the distribution of benefits in society? Pareto's fanatical adherence to classical liberalism, outright condemnation of state intervention and trade union activity does not unequivocally, in Femia's view, rule out the implicit employment of a conception of social justice which depends upon some moral view of what a person's due is, or who should get what.

Plato's defence of justice based upon the principles of specialisation and subordination has a resonance in the views of the British Idealists. Like Plato, they are not advocating a rule-based conception of justice such as that of Cephalus who equates justice with the paying of one's debts, or that of Polemarchus who defines justice as giving what is owed, which translates into the good treatment of one's friends and doing harm to one's enemies. For Plato and the Idealists justice is a matter of knowing one's place in society and developing oneself to the best of one's capacity. For the Idealists the state removes the obstacles to self-realisation and facilitates that process. Boucher shows that the Idealists' argument is based upon equality of opportunity, and not equality of outcome. It acknowledges the inequality of talents, while acknowledging the equality of opportunity to develop whatever talents one has. This, of course, is the implication of Plato's view that the barriers between the classes in the Republic are permeable. While Plato does not rule out upward mobility, he is clearly more concerned that downward mobility be facilitated. Persons with talents unequal to the tasks of the class into which they are born commit an injustice against the state if they continue to occupy positions for which they are ill-suited. The Idealists, on the other hand, are much more concerned with upward mobility and the contribution of education to removing the obstacles to self-realisation. Boucher contends that the Idealists' view of social justice, of who should get what in society, cannot be separated from their metaphysics of the person, a definite view of the good, and a conception of the spiritual worth of individuals heavily influenced by religious beliefs. For them Christ is not transcendent, but immanent in every person – while the divinity of Christ is not denied, the divinity of every person is affirmed.

Amongst political philosophers the issue of social justice is most commonly dealt with in a domestic context applying to closed societies. Most contractarian theories such as Rawls' begin with the idea of the principles of justice applying to a closed society and with temporal constraints on the scope of those principles. However, in response to the growing debates that have followed the resurgence of interest in social justice in a domestic context theorists of justice such as Rawls, Brian Barry and Charles Beitz have begun to extend the discussion beyond the domestic realm into an international context and to take seriously issues of justice towards future generations and the environment. Two chapters deal specifically with these issues. Chris Brown's chapter examines the rival traditions within international relations theory and how these bear on social justice, and Andrew Vincent looks at the relationship between social justice and the environment.

Brown's review of the main theoretical approaches in international relations theory is particularly significant because it traces the complexity of extending ideas of distributive or social justice into an international context. On the one hand most of the more pressing issues of basic justice, such as starvation, poverty and hunger are issues that extend beyond the boundaries of states. However, there is a difficulty in extending the scope of distributive principles to such issues, because of the problem of transnational or universal obligations. What ties the members of one state to the poor and suffering of another, such that there is a relationship of justice and right and not merely one of charity? And what institutions can or ought to do the distributing? The international realm, whether viewed as a system or society challenges conventional social justice theory, precisely because of the ambiguity over where the actual society within which justice is to function begins and ends.

The different approaches that are adopted to issues of social justice within international relations are unsurprisingly related to the issue of whether the international realm is viewed as a global community or as a system of states. Similarly theorists who claim that the scope of obligations of 'justice' is set by the boundaries of nation states can be brought together under the heading of communitarians, whereas those such as Barry, Beitz and Onora O'Neill who argue that we have genuine obligations which extend beyond territorial boundaries are cosmopolitans. Brown also traces the subtle but significant differences between the participants of each tradition. Finally, Brown interestingly ties his review of mainstream international relations theory into a discussion of recent developments in political theory, in particular John Rawls in his Amnesty Lecture 'The Law of Peoples' and Martha Nussbaum's neo-Aristotelianism, to show how the scope of theories of social justice has been transformed by an engagement with the concerns of international relations theorists.

The second issue of social justice that has gained both theoretical and practical attention in recent years concerns the relationship between distributive principles and the environment. In his essay, Andrew Vincent explores the complex relationship between theories of distributive justice and concern for the environment. Vincent is not concerned with policies for sustainable growth, natural diversity or obligations to the future. Instead Vincent takes the more radical line of exploring the ways in which environmental theorists challenge the conceptual distinctions of modern theories of distributive justice. He argues that all the main contemporary variants of social justice theory are premised on anthropocentric concepts and distinctions and that this makes it impossible for contemporary theories of justice to take seriously the concerns of environmentalist thinkers. Whereas deep ecological theorists such as Aldo Leopold and Arne Naess argue that humankind is merely one part of the ecological system, Vincent sets out to show that all the major theories of justice privilege humans because of the central premise of agency in giving an account of value. As such, theories of distributive justice can only give the ecosystem an instrumental or derivative value, whereas the whole thrust of the modern ecology and green movement is to challenge the instrumentalisation of nature and the ecosystem. Though Vincent remains equivocal on the question of whether the completely non-instrumental accounts of the value of nature offered by ecological theorists can withstand critical scrutiny, he does argue that until contemporary theorists of justice can overcome their inherent anthropocentrism it is not possible for there to be a theory of environmental justice.

The argument of Rex Martin's 'Democracy, Rights and Distributive Economic Justice' forms part of an extension of his democratic theory of rights first developed in *A System of Rights*. In this essay Martin explores the role of economic justice within that theory, but without presupposing elaborate knowledge of that theory. The chapter opens with a sketch of the overall theory and his account of the democratic justification of basic rights. For Martin the justification of basic civil rights and democratic institutions go together and are mutually supportive, and in his system it is this connection between democratic institutions and civil rights and not some external or universal moral rule which grounds such basic civil rights.

In the context of this system Martin then discusses the issue of what place distributive principles of economic justice have in such a system. The answer to this question is given by an analysis of basic civil rights. Martin concludes that basic rights are those which are distributed in accordance with a rule that affects everyone in the same way. Then by looking at how principles of economic justice function in other theories, for example Rawls' account of the 'difference principle', Martin concludes that economic justice does not give rise to the same claim of rights. This is because in the case of economic redistribution the whole point is that the principles will affect individuals in different ways, such as maximising the position of the worst-off. Economic justice certainly benefits some individuals but not all individuals in the same way. Martin also argues that there are good reasons for leaving economic justice a matter of policy rather than of constitutional essentials, as these leave such issues open to democratic control and responsibility rather than to constitutional courts. Economic justice fits into the account of democratic institutions in a different way to basic civil rights. The remainder of the chapter is devoted to what Martin calls the root idea of distributive economic justice, which he describes as the view that a sufficient condition for a society being economically just is that 'every income group benefits or, at least, none is to become worse off' by any changes to the distribution of economic benefits and burdens. This root idea is, according to Martin, shared by a wide variety of theories falling under different ideological descriptions. Martin's argument is not intended to provide a fully developed defence of particular principles of economic justice, but rather to sketch an account of how economic justice fits into a democratic or political conception of rights.

Martin's theory is designed to provide an account of rights and justice through an account of the institutions of a democratic polity. As such his theory can be described as a political theory of rights. Despite this Martin's theory does not take the communitarian turn of restricting his theory to the particular substantive account of democracy found in one country or society. It is not a theory of the democratic institutions of the United States of America, though it will obviously have a bearing on how that country's democratic institutions are understood. A more communitarian democratic approach to justice is to be found in the work of Michael Walzer, the subject of Richard Bellamy's chapter.

Walzer is a major contemporary opponent of what might be called the dominance of the distributive paradigm associated with contractarian and Kantian defences of distributive justice. He rejects not only the tendency of contemporary theories of justice to answer the question 'equality of what?' with a universally valid list of 'primary goods' or equality of resources, he is also keen to abandon the 'top-down' conception of theorising about justice which is implicit in contractarianism and the 'distributive paradigm'. What the 'distributive paradigm' assumes is that all issues of justice turn into questions of challenging the monopolisation of certain goods. Certain classes or groups monopolise money or civil rights, which leaves other groups deprived and therefore unequal. The task of social justice becomes one of breaking these monopolies. In contrast Walzer argues that focusing on monopoly fails to address the issues of domination of groups over other groups which allows monopolies to form in the first place, and also that the standard prescriptions of theories of justice simply hand the issue of dominance from one social group to the state, leaving the beneficiaries of justice in the same subordinate position. Walzer is not merely arguing like some new-right theorists that institutions of justice such as the welfare state reinforce dependency (see Minogue's contribution): instead his concern is to show that the standard ways of theorising about social justice have a way of reinforcing such domination.

The solution Walzer offers is a pluralistic and democratic approach to justice and theorising about justice. Principles of justice are constructed within particular spheres of meaning and not imposed from some external perspective. Walzer's is an important challenge to much contemporary political theory about justice and Bellamy provides an important and lucid guide through the complexities of his argument. However, Bellamy is also concerned to show that despite his aspirations Walzer's argument is far less democratic than he suggests, and tainted with many of the failings of communitarian theories, that Walzer himself wishes to avoid.

Similar themes are taken up in Paul Kelly's review of contemporary contractarian defences of distributive justice. Despite the continuing debate between liberals and communitarians, Kelly argues that the contractualist form of contemporary theorising about social justice has shown itself to be particularly resilient in the face of challenges from neo-communitarians who emphasise the importance of identity. These thinkers include not only Michael Walzer, but feminists such as Iris Marion Young, and defenders of multicultural rights such as Will Kymlicka. Kelly's chapter also provides an overview of some of the debates within contemporary political theory about just how the contractarian component of theories of distributive justice should be interpreted. Kelly's conclusion is that the resilience of the distributive paradigm and contractarian justice is best explained by the inadequacy of theories of 'identity politics' to deal with the very issues they identify as so important, without appealing to the sort of universalist principles of distributive justice which contractarian theories provide.

In recent years Will Kymlicka has undoubtedly forced on to the agenda of social justice issues which go beyond rectifying the injustices suffered by economically disadvantaged groups. Injustice and economic disadvantage do not necessarily go hand in hand. Injustices associated with the denial of the development and expression of one's identity as a member of a national culture, or of one's participation in the dominant culture of a society if one belongs to an ethnic minority raises issues that go beyond those of distribution and may require special rights which go against contemporary conceptions of liberal universalism.[12] The issue of special rights is discussed by Carole Pateman and Tariq Modood in this volume. Pateman discusses them in relation to women, and adds the ironic twist that it is men who have enjoyed special rights which have enabled them to exclude women from many of society's benefits. Modood contends that special rights may not be the best way to deal with the injustices of racial discrimination.

Modood argues that in recent years there has been a change of focus away from universal theories of distributive justice to the justness of cultural rather than economic transactions, with the emphasis upon difference and diversity, pluralism and multiculturalism. It reflects the growing recognition that economic and material inequalities do not exhaust the spectrum of domination and oppression. Modood argues that economic and opportunity structures are constituted by the cultural norms and practices of those who occupy the positions of power and influence. Racial discrimination contributes to economic, social and political injustices, but the analysis of their extent and impact has been impeded by the simplicity of the racial categories used, such as black and white, which do not reflect the sophistication or the nuances of difference among, say, East African Asians and Bangladeshis. Categorising the victims of white racism as black served to forge a common identity in inequality, but the category of black fails to acknowledge the importance of ethnic pride in defining a person's mode of being as opposed to his or her mode of oppression.

Modood contends that even if discrimination were to disappear tomorrow, racial disadvantage, the cumulative effect of generations, would persist. Prejudice against ethno-religious groups has hardly begun to be addressed. Public recognition of minority cultures has been imperative to equality of citizenship, but at the same time the public recognition of religion is denied. Racial discrimination is not necessarily linked to racial disadvantage. An ethnic minority may have skills and talents which enable it to prosper despite discrimination. Prosperity should not, however, diminish our resolve to eliminate injustices. Conversely, we should not imagine that the elimination of racial discrimination necessarily eliminates racial disadvantage. The injustices of racial disadvantage, Modood argues, may be better dealt with by developing a strategy which is a broad class-based attack on socio-economic disadvantage, as opposed to special minority rights such as positive discrimination which may serve to generate racial and ethnic hostility.

Pateman highlights the proliferation of rights talk in recent years and its growing number of critics who suggest that it is a Western invention that threatens to undermine the integrity of other cultures. Even in Western cultures critics have suggested that rights talk has been taken too far. She maintains that if rights are to be separated from universalism, then rights discourse would become particularised and apply only to certain categories of people. These are what Pateman calls special rights which she closely allies to the idea of freedom. Many of these rights, however, serve to maintain power and domination and actually undermine freedom.

Welfare rights, for example, are special rights whose terms of reference in current discussions are very much those of the nineteenth century Poor Law, central to which is the idea of dependence which is understood as the antithesis of freedom. Following this logic independence is then identified with the capacity to engage in transactions in the labour market. Pursuing this line of thought social justice is equated with measures to promote independence and force welfare recipients to regain independence by being compelled to take low paid jobs. Following from this Pateman argues that men have traditionally enjoyed and exercised special rights which have persistently diminished the freedom of women.

Pateman argues that the common feature that unites the numerous disputes over special and equal rights, whether between feminists or between the protagonists in the more familiar wrangles about welfare rights, is that the terms in which they are conducted mean that a resolution to the disputes is impossible. The very notion of 'special rights' ensures that these rights must be seen as an addition to, and so occupying a different status from, equal rights. One side then claims that the addition is justified because of special circumstances, such as poverty or pregnancy; the other side claims that the addition cannot be justified because it confers privilege, and freedom is turned into dependence. Neither side pays any attention to the consequences for democracy of the special rights enjoyed by men. Pateman maintains that we need to search for a different conception of freedom, based on Marshall's ideas, which ceases to equate freedom with independence. When freedom is instead equated with autonomy welfare rights are the means by which individuals are protected from falling below a certain level of culture, and they are facilitated in their enjoyment of citizenship.

Like Carole Pateman's paper, David West's essay 'Beyond Social Justice and Social Democracy – Positive Freedom and Cultural Rights' makes use of T. H. Marshall's account of the three stages in the development of the concept of rights to challenge the sufficiency of contemporary understandings of the content of social justice. West extends Marshall's three stage picture by adding the notion of cultural rights as a way of securing individual flourishing as part of groups which are free from oppressive power structures and which are not dependent on the idea of states or other dominant political institutions as the provider of these benefits. Cultural rights provide an important component of any new emancipatory politics that is not subject to the domination of state institutions.

West's chapter draws on a broad literature from the left and 'new social movements' which challenges the sufficiency of the traditional social democratic agenda of social justice as the distribution of welfare benefits. Similarly, whilst rejecting the 'new right's' turn to the minimal state and the rejection of social justice (see Minogue's chapter) many critiques of the liberal–social democrat consensus on social justice accept much of the 'new right's' claims about the way welfare institutions and social justice create relations of dependency and disempowerment rather than emancipation and real freedom. In this respect, West's argument also converges with Michael Walzer's assault on the 'distributive paradigm' that has been the preoccupation of post-Rawlsian political philosophy. The difference between West and Walzer is that West is unhappy with Walzer's residual communitarianism and its reliance on conventional social practices and understandings to give content to the basic principles of justice and right that operate within given communities. Though Walzer is concerned both to democratise political theory and political practice, West is far more radical in terms of the types of identity-conferring institutions that should be protected and which should contribute to the debate over what kind of rights are necessary to expand and develop social justice beyond the dead end of 'negative' civil rights and minimal welfare rights. He draws on the ideas and experience of the 'new social movements' – feminism, gay liberation and other sources of 'identity politics' – to provide the content for a 'positive' conception of freedom and emancipation that can expand the scope of traditional discussions of social justice, and which does not confine itself to the pre-given understandings of traditional and conventional morality as in the case of Walzer.

West's essay concludes with a defence of 'cultural rights' against the charge that they fail to take seriously individuals. Though he builds his argument on the view that individual human identity is a complex social construction dependent on membership of groups, West does not want the idea of 'cultural rights' to create a potential tyranny over individual members of cultural and identity-conferring groups. He defends the value of cultural rights by showing that all rights, even traditional liberal rights, have a collective component, but more important the potential tyranny of cultures is diffused by recognising that personality is not constituted by membership of one homogeneous group and that only at the extreme do the obligations of cultural rights call on state power for enforcement. Human beings are members of different identity-conferring groups at the same time: indeed it is this which allows for the possibility of individuality not some pre-existing transhistorical notion of subjectivity. Recognising this is not to say that there will never be conflicts between group claims and the aspirations of group members, but such conflicts do not according to West vitiate the idea of 'cultural rights' any more than conflicts between the claims of freedom and equality vitiate the idea of liberal civil rights. (For the view that groups rights and the politics of identity reinforce the need for the impartial procedures of liberal distributive justice, see Kelly's essay.)

While both Pateman's and West's essays contribute to contemporary practical disputes and considerations of social justice, particularly in suggesting that the vocabulary and terms of reference need to be changed in order to advance the discussion and resolve the issues, the contributions by both Minogue and Plant engage directly with the modern day practical problems of social justice.

Minogue argues that the proponents of social justice advance it as a universal ideal for humankind, whereas in reality it is a remarkably particular and parochial doctrine, largely found among political activists in Western democratic countries. The whole concept, he argues, has an air of unreality about it. On the one hand it claims to have the whole of humanity as its domain, and on the other it concentrates upon the application of justice purely in terms of wealth redistribution. For all its talk about rights and utility there is scant concern for the economic costs and process of production of such redistributions.

In order to develop his argument against social justice Minogue turns his attention to providing a conjectural history of the concept. There are, he suggests two different conceptions of justice. The first is a posteriori derived from the fact of independence among subjects and responsive to their developing concerns. The second is a priori and despotic because even though in practice its workings are capricious, it entails a view of society as an inherently harmonious set of social roles, but which are subject to degenerating into chaos because of weaknesses in human nature. Social justice, Minogue argues, is an example of the a priori conception. It treats human beings as entities with needs which need to be controlled and managed. It is a project which is reactionary and tied up with social engineering. He argues that it has in fact no relation to justice. It employs the laudatory rhetoric of justice while employing the methods of a servile state.

Among Plant's concerns is the countering of some of the claims of the economic right. For example, adherents to the right argue that because the overall distribution of goods in the market is the result of no one's intention, and as long as the choices made are uncoerced, no moral approbation can be attributed to the outcomes. Plant argues that intention is not the only consideration where matters of justice are concerned. If we can forsee unequal and disadvantageous outcomes, irrespective of intention, we may wish to do something about them. Market outcomes are unlike acts of God in that they often can be foreseen. It is because we can anticipate them that moral considerations have some purchase. In addition Plant attempts to counter a claim made by both Pareto and Minogue, that social justice is illusory rhetoric and that there cannot be an objective reference point by which to choose between the competing principles for redistribution. Any such decision is both arbitrary and subjective. Plant takes on board the need for exponents of social justice to be much more specific about the different principles of distribution and their different outcomes. His justification of social justice does, contrary to Minogue's contention, try to link aspirations for the provision of services with economic realities and achievable levels of economic growth. This, he contends, can be achieved by employing the traditional approach delivering social justice through the tax and benefits system. The economic case has to be expounded in association with the moral case. The moral case is only likely to be persuasive if people are confident that their own ambitions and aspirations will not be impeded in the implementation of social justice policies.

The concept of social or distributive justice is one of the best examples – if there are any – of an essentially contested concept,[13] one that we hope to have shown is even more deeply contested than Rawls' attempt to order discussion under the categories of concepts and conceptions of justice suggests.[14] In bringing these essays together we hope to reflect some of that diversity of discussion, but we are aware that in making our selection of essays we have nevertheless had to exclude much more that we could have included.

NOTES

1 J. Rawls, *A Theory of Justice*, Cambridge, Mass., Harvard, 1971.
2 F. A. von Hayek, *Law, Lesiglation and Liberty*, 3 vols, London, Routledge, 1973–76.
3 W. G. Sumner, *What Social Classes Owe to Each Other*, New York, 1883.
4 *The Justice Gap*, London, IPPR, 1993.
5 *Social Justice: Strategies for Renewal, Report of the Commission on Social Justice*, London, Vintage, 1994.
6 See the essays in Jane Franklin ed. *Equality*, London, IPPR, 1997, for a series of reflections by prominent political and moral philosophers including Brian Barry,

Bernard Williams, G. A. Cohen and Anne Phillips on what social justice is about which was itself inspired by the reports of the Commission on Social Justice.

7 See D. Boucher and P. J. Kelly (eds), *The Social Contract: From Hobbes to Rawls*, London, Routledge, 1995.
8 David Gauthier, *Morals by Agreement*, Oxford, Clarendon Press, 1986.
9 Brian Barry, *Justice as Impartiality*, Oxford, Clarendon Press, 1995.
10 See P. J. Kelly, *Utilitarianism and Distributive Justice: Jeremy Bentham and the Civil Law*, Oxford, Clarendon Press, 1990, and F. R. Berger, *Happiness, Justice and Freedom*, Berkeley, University of California Press, 1984.
11 David Miller, *Social Justice*, Oxford, Clarendon Press, 1975, pp. 20 and 24; Aristotle, *The Politics*, Stephen Everson (ed.), Cambridge, Cambridge University Press, 1988, 1282b.
11 Will Kymlicka, *Multicultural Citizenship*, Oxford, Clarendon Press, 1995.
13 W. B. Gallie, 'Essentially Contested Concepts', in M. Black (ed.), *The Importance of Language*, Englewood Cliffs, N.J., Prentice Hall, 1962, pp. 121–46.
14 Rawls, *A Theory of Justice*, pp. 9–11.

2   David Hume, contractarian[1]

David Gauthier

I

David Hume's moral and political inquiries comprise three theories: a theory of moral sentiment, a theory of property and justice, and a theory of government and obedience. My concern is with the latter two, and my basic thesis is that, contrary to what may seem Hume's explicit avowals, these theories are both contractarian. In supporting this thesis I shall accept the following ground rules:

1   My interpretation will not contradict Hume's actual anti-contractarian avowals. I shall argue that he rejects – and for good reason – that understanding of contractarianism dominant in the Whig opinions of his time. But that rejection is inconclusive if there are, as I shall try to show, other, and deeper, ways of developing a contractarian position.
2   My interpretation will not question the evidently non-contractarian character of Hume's theory of moral sentiment. Thus I shall be committed to a distinction between that theory, which I shall usually call Hume's moral theory, and his theory of property and justice. Since Hume treats justice as a moral virtue, these theories must be connected, but connection is not identification.
3   Contractarianism is a species of normative conventionalism, but my interpretation will not reduce to triviality by identifying species with genus. In particular, utilitarianism may also be understood as a species of conventionalism, and my subordinate thesis is to refute the view that Hume is a proto-utilitarian.
4   My interpretation will rest on the *Essays, Moral, Political, and Literary*, and on the *Enquiry Concerning the Principles of Morals* (henceforth *Essays* and *Enquiry*). References to the *Treatise of Human Nature* will be subordinate, or comparative. Were my purpose either to glean from Hume an approach to contemporary issues in moral theory, or to place Hume in a history of contractarian thought, my reliance on his later works would be perverse, for, at least in my view, the *Treatise* is at once more profound and more contractarian. But my purpose here is to interpret Hume, and

in this endeavour I find myself bound by his explicit description of the *Treatise* as 'the juvenile work, which the Author never acknowledged', by his statement that he later corrected 'some negligences in his former reasoning and more in the expression', and most especially by his injunction that 'the following Pieces [which include the *Essays* and the *Enquiry*] may alone be regarded as containing his philosophical sentiments and principles'.[2] Others have chosen to disregard Hume's Advertisement on these matters; I shall prefer to establish that interpretation of his argument which Hume could not but find himself obliged to acknowledge.

II

Some terminological clarification is a necessary preliminary. Hume's understanding of *property* and *justice* are closely linked; indeed, he sometimes uses the terms interchangeably.[3] But I shall say that for Hume, property is determined by a system of rules for the possession and use of objects, so that my property is what, in accordance with the rules, I possess and use, and my exclusive property, what I alone possess and use. Justice, then, is the virtue determined by such a system, so that just behaviour consists in adherence to the rules governing the possession and use of objects. For Hume, a theory of property and justice explicates the rationale for systems of rules determining possession and use.

I shall use *government* (or *magistracy*) and *obedience* (or sometimes *allegiance*) in a manner parallel to property and justice. Government is determined by a system of rules for the enforcement of justice, that is, for Hume, rules for the enforcement of the system of rules governing the possession and use of objects. And obedience is the virtue determined by the system of government, so that obedient behaviour consists in adherence to the rules for the enforcement of the system of property. For Hume, a theory of government and obedience explicates the rationale for systems of rules for the enforcement of rules which determine possession and use.

Implicit justification for the controversial features of this usage will arise in the exposition of Hume's position. But the key assumption should be evident. Rules establishing property authorise certain modes of behaviour with respect to objects, and forbid other modes. Rules establishing government authorise certain modes of behaviour with respect to persons, and forbid other modes. But behaviour with respect to objects and behaviour with respect to persons are interdependent. The particular interconnection, assumed by Hume, requires the system of government to be dependent upon the system of property. Since my purpose is to interpret Hume's argument, and not to evaluate it, I am allowing that assumption to appear in the use of the primary terms, property and justice, government and obedience. And I shall give primary attention to the theory of property; only after exhibiting its contractarian character will I turn secondarily and more briefly to Hume's theory of government.

III

My interpretation of Hume requires an analysis of *convention*, and a distinction, within the genus of conventionalist normative theories, of several variants, including the *contractarian* and the *utilitarian*. About convention I must be dogmatic. My account owes much to reflection on the analysis offered by David Lewis, but I cannot explicate, much less defend, either the similarities or the differences in this paper.[4]

Very briefly, I propose to regard a convention as a regularity R in the behaviour of persons P in situations S, such that part of the reason that most of these persons conform to R in S is that it is common knowledge (among P) that most persons conform to R in S and that most persons expect most (other) persons to conform to R in S. What essentially distinguishes a convention from other regularities of behaviour among the members of groups is that almost every person's reason for conforming to the regularity includes his awareness and expectation of general conformity. Typically, this reason will relate to interest, and will include both a preference for general conformity, rather than the expected outcome of general nonconformity, and a preference for personal nonconformity unless there is general conformity.

If most persons do not prefer general conformity to R in S, or at least do not consider such conformity desirable, in relation to the expected outcome of general nonconformity, then R is a *pointless* convention, one which serves no purposes shared by the persons P. An account which treats property or government as a pointless convention may be *descriptively* conventionalist, but cannot be *normatively* conventionalist, since it denies that property or government has a rationale as a convention.

If most persons do not prefer personal nonconformity to R in S, or at least do not consider such nonconformity undesirable, unless others conform, then R is a *redundant* convention, in that most persons would have reason to conform to R even without the common knowledge that most persons do so conform and expect such conformity. An account which treats property or government as a redundant convention may again be descriptively conventionalist, but cannot be normatively conventionalist, since it affords a rationale for property or government as a nonconventional regularity.

There can be little dispute that Hume's theories of property and government are ostensibly conventionalist. Clear evidence is found in passages such as:

> if by convention be meant a sense of common interest, which sense each man feels in his own breast, which he remarks in his fellows, and which carries him, in concurrence with others, into a general plan or system of actions, which tends to public utility; it must be owned, that, in this sense, justice arises from human conventions.
>
> (*Enquiry*, App. III)

Reference to 'common interest' and 'public utility' makes clear that Hume does not suppose that justice arises from a pointless convention; reference to 'concurrence with others' suggests that Hume does not consider the convention redundant. I shall not have occasion to refer further either to pointlessness or to redundancy, since nothing in Hume's account suggests that either of these weaknesses affects his conventionalism. Henceforth, then, I shall take all mention of convention to exclude these possibilities.

To assist us in delimiting the sphere of contractarian theories, let us consider a favourite example in Hume. In the *Enquiry*, Appendix III, he writes: 'Thus, two men pull the oars of a boat by common convention for common interest, without any promise or contract. . . .'[5] The situation envisaged is very simple; each man has two possible actions, to row, or not to row. Each prefers the outcome if both row, that is, if each conforms to the convention of rowing, to the outcome if neither rows, or indeed, to any other possible outcome. Hence general conformity is preferred, not only to the expected outcome of general nonconformity, but to the expected outcome of conformity to any other possible convention – for example, that only the first man in the boat would row.

Each prefers not to row, unless the other rows. That is, each prefers personal nonconformity in the absence of general conformity. But also, each prefers to row if the other rows. (We assume that the boat will not move, or will move only in circles, if but one man rows.) Thus each prefers to row if and only if the other rows. Personal conformity to the convention of rowing is each person's most preferred response to conformity by the other, and each person's least preferred response to nonconformity.

To the extent to which R is not seriously dispreferred to any alternative regularity R' for behaviour in S by persons P, R is a *dominant* convention in S. If for certain situations there is a single dominant convention, the character of which is evident to the persons involved, then they may be expected to adopt it without any formal agreement, such as might result from a bargain among them. And to the extent that conformity to R is not seriously dispreferred to nonconformity, given conformity by others, R is a *stable* convention in S.[6] If a convention is stable, then persons who adopt it will have no need for a *covenant*,[7] that is, for assurance by each that he will do his part provided the others do theirs, since direct interest in conformity will provide a sufficient guarantee. A dominant, stable convention is a device which serves to coordinate the actions of two or more persons in situations in which their preferences converge on the choice of a mode of behaviour *and* on adherence to the mode chosen.

In Hume's example, rowing is both dominant and stable. By way of contrast, suppose that the two men were in a boat which required but one oarsman. Then if we suppose that each would prefer that the other row, no convention would be dominant. And if we suppose that the boat could be rowed, either by one or by both men, then a convention requiring one to row would be stable, but a convention requiring both to row would be unstable, in that each would prefer nonconformity assuming conformity by the other.

Since a dominant, stable convention requires neither bargain nor covenant, it affords no room for contract. Were the conventions establishing property and government similar to Hume's convention of rowing, then we should have to conclude that his theories were not contractarian. I shall argue that his accounts of property and government show that his example is insufficiently complex to capture the significant characteristics of just or obedient behaviour. But I shall argue more than this, for not all conventions which are either non-dominant or unstable are in fact contractual. If in some situations no possible convention is dominant, so that each regularity R is seriously dispreferred to some alternative R' by some persons, then we must consider how the opposed preferences of those concerned are reconciled, in deciding whether the resulting convention is contractual. And if conformity to a convention is not each person's preferred response to the conformity of others, then we must consider how adherence is assured, in deciding whether the convention is contractual.

Typically, contractual conventions are characterised by devices which have already been mentioned – bargain and covenant. Within the framework of this discussion, I intend by a *bargain* an agreement, entered into by each person on the basis of his own interests, which results in the selection of a convention. I intend by a *covenant* also an agreement, entered into by each person on the basis of his own interests, which assures, with or without enforcement, mutual adherence to a convention. What is common to bargain and covenant, and what is necessary to a contractual convention, is the appeal to each person's interests. Generalising, I shall use the phrase *interested recognition* to refer to any process such as bargaining, in which the resolution of opposed preferences necessary to select a convention is effected through an appeal to the interests of each. And I shall use the phrase *interested obligation* to refer to any device, such as a covenant, in which adherence to a convention against immediate interest is assured through an appeal to interest.[8] (The apparent paradox involved here will be discussed in Section VII.) Thus a convention is a contract if and only if either it is selected from alternatives by a process of interested recognition or it commands adherence on the basis of interested obligation.

Hume is frequently interpreted as a proto-utilitarian. But utilitarianism, insofar as it may be assimilated to moral conventionalism, appeals neither to interested recognition nor to interested obligation, although it introduces conventions which are neither dominant nor stable. Given opposed individual preferences among possible conventions, the utilitarian selects that one which maximises total utility or well-being. Although each person's interests are taken into account, and in one sense taken equally into account, in the selection of a convention, yet the process of selection involves, not interested recognition by each, but recognition of a single moral standard defined as a function of individual interests.[9]

Should the convention so selected prove unstable, in requiring some persons to conform against their own interests, given the conformity of others, then the utilitarian appeals to an obligation based directly on the standard of total well-being. He does not argue from the position of the individual who is required to act against his own interests, an argument typically contractarian, and which may be found in Hume.[10] Rather, the utilitarian insists that each person, having had his interests included in the determination of total utility, is now obligated without further appeal to those interests.

The utilitarian considers overall well-being a sufficient condition for the conventions of property. The contractarian considers the well-being of each individual a necessary condition for such conventions. This difference will play a decisive role in my interpretation of Hume, so I shall conclude these preliminary remarks by clarifying it. Suppose that we wish to ascertain if some convention of property and justice is acceptable among some group of persons. We evaluate each feasible set of circumstances in which this group may find itself in terms of the utility of each member. Then a utilitarian will consider a property convention acceptable if there is some feasible set of circumstances in which it affords the group a total utility greater than the total utility of any circumstances attainable in its absence. A contractarian, on the other hand, will consider a property convention acceptable only if there is some feasible set of circumstances in which it affords each member of the group no less utility, and some members more utility, than is afforded either by the existing circumstances, or than by any set of circumstances voluntarily attainable in the absence of any property convention. A sufficient condition of utilitarian acceptability is that a convention maximise total utility; a necessary condition of contractarian acceptability is that a convention increase the utility of some, and decrease the utility of none.

I shall argue that Hume's theories of property and government clearly reflect the latter condition for the acceptability of a convention. Only when everyone may reasonably expect to benefit, does Hume suppose that the circumstances of justice or of obedience obtain. His theories therefore have a starting point fundamentally different from those of a utilitarian, who supposes that the circumstances of justice or of obedience obtain whenever overall benefit may be realised even should this benefit be secured at the expense of some persons.

IV

Hume's explicit strictures on the original contract must be our next concern. For in showing Hume to be a contractarian, I do not intend to show him to be inconsistent, and so I must remove the apparent, but evident, stumbling block of his anti-contractarian views.

New discoveries are not to be expected in these matters. If scarce any man, till very lately, ever imagined that government was founded on compact, it is certain that it cannot, in general, have any such foundation.

(*Essays*, Part II, No. XII, *Of the Original Contract*)

But there are several species of contractarian theory. We should first distinguish *original contractarianism* – the theory that the origin of property and government is to be found in a contractual convention among human beings. This theory may extend to the claim that an original contract provides the rationale for existing society, but primarily it concerns the origin of society, and need not attempt either to explain or to justify present systems of property and government.

If the binding force of the original contract is called into question, the answer tends to introduce a second species of contractarian theory – *explicit contractarianism*. On this view the appeal to a contract serves, not to explain the origin or existence of systems of property and government, but rather to defend (or to attack) their legitimacy. Government is legitimated by, and only by, actual agreement, sometimes among all those who constitute political society, but more often between subjects and their rulers.[11] This agreement will reflect the actual abilities, aims, interests, and powers of those party to it. But for it to reflect a free choice between the existing system of property or government and possible alternatives, it must not be constrained by those powers institutionalised in actual social arrangements. Explicit contractarianism demands actual agreement, but not in circumstances which are weighted in favour of the existing order.

This is evidently an unrealistic requirement. And so the contractarian may be led to a further modification of his position – *tacit contractarianism*.[12] This view is also indifferent to questions of origin or explanation. It establishes the legitimacy of existing systems of property and government by contending that the acceptance, by anyone, of the advantages arising from enforced rules determining use and possession, implies his consent to the systems which uphold those rules. The rules confer benefits; the systems impose costs necessary to those benefits; accepting the benefits, then, one must accept the costs. The choice expressed in tacit agreement is thus between existing society, with its institutionalised powers, and either emigration or anarchy. Not only the actual abilities and interests of the members of society, but the existing social arrangements, constrain choice for tacit contractarianism. Thus if the explicit position fails to conform to the practice of the world, the tacit position conforms all too well, in sacrificing any real concern with free consent.

If this sacrifice is judged too great, then we are led to a fourth (and final) species of the theory – *hypothetical contractarianism*. On this view, systems of property and government are legitimated in terms of the consent they would receive from *rational* persons in a suitably characterised position of free choice.[13] The theory does not suppose that this choice is or ought to be expressed in actual agreement, and does not require that the choice enter into actual belief about the rationale of society. A system of property and government is justified if it *would* be the object of agreement among rational persons in a suitable choice situation, whether or not actual persons consider the system justified. Although such hypothetical agreement must reflect the real interests of those party to it, it abstracts not only from the existing institutional structures which constrain tacit consent, but also from the use, by individuals and groups, of force or fraud, and from the appeal against real interest to present desire, both of which would constrain explicit consent. Hypothetical contractarianism thus involves the resolution of opposed individual preferences by a process which depends solely on the interested recognition of those concerned.

With these four species of contractarian theory in mind, let us turn to Hume's arguments in the *Essay Of the Original Contract*.[14] He begins by granting the thesis of original contractarianism, insofar as it applies to the origin of government.

> The people . . . voluntarily, for the sake of peace and order, abandoned their native liberty, and received laws from their equal and companion. . . . If this . . . be meant by the *original contract*, it cannot be denied, that all government is, at first, founded on a contract, . . .

But this proves nothing about the origin of existing governments, or about the grounds of existing allegiance.

> Almost all the governments which exist at present, or of which there remains any record in story, have been founded originally, either on usurpation or conquest, or both, without any pretence of a fair consent or voluntary subjection of the people.

Hume proceeds to argue that the view

> that all men are still born equal, and owe allegiance to no prince or government, unless bound by the obligation and sanction of a *promise* . . . [which] is always understood to be conditional, and imposes on [them] no obligation, unless [they] meet with justice and protection from [their] sovereign . . . [which] advantages the sovereign promises . . . in return

is contrary to the views and practices of all the world. Although people consent to the authority of whomever they consider to be their lawful sovereign

> they never imagine that their consent made him sovereign. They consent, because they apprehend him to be already by birth, their lawful sovereign.

Hume does not

> exclude the consent of the people from being one just foundation of government. Where it has any place, it is surely the best and most sacred of any. I only contend, that it has very seldom had place in any degree, and never almost in its full extent; and that, therefore, some other foundation of government must also be admitted.

Explicit contractarianism is thus rejected by Hume. Although he accepts consent as a possible title, and as the best of titles, to government, yet he does not deny legitimacy to governments otherwise upheld. This conforms to the essentially empirical character of Hume's moral and political inquiries, to his assumption that what is required is to systematise and explain men's actual normative views, rather than to impose on theoretical grounds views which men do not in fact hold. Thus Hume insists that the direction of fit between consent and legitimacy is usually the reverse of what is required by explicit contractarianism, so that in fact legitimacy secures consent, rather than consent conferring legitimacy.

Tacit contractarianism fares no better in Hume's argument. He insists that one cannot infer that when a usurper succeeds in obtaining power

> the people, who in their hearts abhor his treason, have tacitly consented to his authority, and promised him allegiance, merely because, from necessity, they live under his dominion.

The tacit contractarian claims that the benefits of government cannot be had without acceptance of its costs – the duties of justice and obedience. But although this be true, it does not follow that acceptance of these benefits from the person who actually has *power* to confer them thereby commits one to consent to his *right* to confer those benefits, and hence to one's duty to obey him in return. No doubt Hume would agree that the person who willingly accepts the benefits of government must recognise an obligation to obey some authority, but not necessarily the existing claimant to that authority, even if de facto he be holder of the requisite power.

Finally, Hume insists that there is no

> necessity . . . to found the duty of *allegiance*, or obedience to magistrates, on that of *fidelity*, or a regard to promises, and to suppose that it is the consent of each individual which subjects him to government, when it appears that both allegiance and fidelity stand precisely on the same foundation, and are both submitted to by mankind, on account of the apparent interests and necessities of human society.

The justification for both allegiance and fidelity is the same so that an appeal to contract is as superfluous in theory as it is irrelevant in practice.

The explicit contractarian supposes that we are bound only by our own free consent. Hume replies that our consent binds us, only because of our interest in being thereby bound; consent obligates, because the stability of society requires that it should, and our interests require the stability of society. But we are bound to obedience for the same reason; the command of the magistrate obligates, because the stability of society requires that it should, and our interests require the stability of society.

Nothing in this argument is incompatible with hypothetical contractarianism. For this view agrees with Hume that government exists to serve the interests of the citizens, so that its legitimacy depends ultimately on its serving those interests, and their obligation to obey is founded in interest. The hypothetical contract gives precise expression to a particular way in which the conventions of property and government, and our obligations to conform to them, may be supposed to be founded in human interests. The question then is whether the connection between interest and government in Hume's thought is appropriately expressed by a hypothetical contract. Nothing in Hume's strictures against other species of contractarian thought serves to answer this question. The utilitarian equally expresses a particular way in which government may be related to human interests. Only Hume's positive account of the rationale for the conventions of property and government can show whether his thought is contractarian, or utilitarian, or neither.

Before turning to that positive account, we may pause briefly to remark that Hume's anti-contractarian arguments were of course addressed to the Whig doctrine current in his day, which supposed that the explicit consent of the people, or more correctly, of their elected representatives in the House of Commons, was the foundation of their duty of obedience to the sovereign. This doctrine may be viewed as an ancestor of the position that only democratic government is legitimate, since it alone rests on explicit consent. The practice of the world has in some ways come closer to embracing explicit contractarianism since Hume's time. Of course, the measures used to elicit consent have introduced the powers of existing society into the circumstances in which the choice among forms of society is made, and actual bargaining among groups has severely constrained individual participation in the process of agreement.[15] One might at least question whether the ideals of explicit contractarianism are better realised by liberal democrats in the twentieth century than by eighteenth century Whigs.

V

Hume's account of justice in the *Enquiry* begins with the claim: 'That public utility is the *sole* origin of justice, and that reflections on the beneficial consequences of this virtue are the *sole* foundation of its merit.' This claim may seem to pose an immediate challenge to a contractarian interpretation of Hume's theory of property and justice. For first, in insisting that public utility is the sole origin of justice, Hume may seem to be espousing the view that over-all utility is the measure of justice, and this is at least a quasi-utilitarian position. And second, in deriving the merit of justice from its beneficial consequences, Hume may seem to be equating the foundation of justice with the source of the morality of justice, so that his theory of justice would be merely part of his moral theory, which is unquestionably noncontractarian.

In reply to this reading of Hume's claim, I shall insist that public utility is to be understood as *mutual expected utility*, so that a rule or practice has public utility if and only if each person reasonably expects that rule or practice to be useful to himself. Thus in insisting that public utility is the origin of justice, Hume is not appealing to total utility, as would a utilitarian, but rather to mutual advantage, as befits a contractarian.

I shall also insist that beneficial consequences are not to be equated with public utility, so that the foundation of the merit of justice is to be distinguished from the origin of justice. Central to Hume's moral theory is the thesis that whatever has beneficial consequences receives moral approbation.[16] Whatever, then, is generally useful, or useful on the whole, receives overall moral approbation, and so may be denominated a virtue. Since justice has mutual expected utility, it must be generally useful, and so receives moral approbation. We may thus say, with Hume, that the beneficial consequences of justice establish its moral merit.

But to say that justice has public utility, or is mutually advantageous, is to say more than to say merely that justice is generally useful, or that justice has beneficial consequences. It is, of course, to say that each person may expect beneficial consequences *for himself* from justice. This additional factor does not enter into the moral approbation accorded to justice. That beneficial consequences extend to each person does not affect our moral sentiments, except insofar as overall, more beneficial consequences arise. However, it is this additional factor which is essential to *justice*; it is not the beneficial consequences themselves, but the expectation of benefit by each person, that is just-making. Thus we may again say, with Hume, that public utility, understood as mutual expected advantage, is the origin of justice.

Hence we distinguish public utility as the origin of justice, from general utility, or overall advantage, as the basis of our moral approbation of justice. Arrangements may be expected to be useful to each person; therefore they are just. These arrangements may also be expected to have beneficial consequences; therefore they receive moral approval, and justice is a virtue. In this way Hume's contractarian theory of justice may be clearly distinguished from his noncontractarian theory of morality. His initial claim should then read, with words added [thus]: 'That public utility [i.e. mutually expected advantage] is the *sole* origin of justice, and that reflections on the generally beneficial consequences of this virtue are the *sole* foundation of its merit [i.e. moral approbation].'

But so far this is mere assertion, not argument. I have set out the interpretation which I intend to establish by an appeal to Hume's texts. First, however, it is worth noting that if my interpretation is sound, then Hume's theory occupies in some important respects a middle ground between the theories of Hobbes and of Locke. For all three, government is contractarian in its rationale. For Hobbes and Hume, but not for Locke, property and justice are also contractarian. For Hobbes, but not for Hume or Locke, moral approbation is contractarian in rationale. Hume and Locke of course differ in their accounts of the basis of morality, since Locke derives it from divine natural law, whereas Hume, who like Hobbes is a conventionalist about natural law, bases morality on natural sentiment.[17] What is perhaps most controversial about these comparisons, and so about my interpretation, is that with respect to property and justice, Hume is in essence a Hobbist.

In examining Hume's text, we shall consider first whether mutual advantage is a necessary condition for the convention of property or whether overall advantage is sufficient. Hume develops his account of justice in the *Enquiry* by distinguishing six sets of circumstances in which justice would be useless, and no rules determining property would arise, or be maintained. Analysis of these situations will show how he is to be understood.

The first two sets of circumstances lend themselves equally to contractarian or utilitarian interpretation. Hume first supposes a situation of natural super-abundance, in which the objects of all of our desires are provided without need for our efforts. He next supposes a situation of universal fellow-feeling, in which each person has the same concern for the interests of all of his fellows as for his own. In both of these circumstances, Hume insists, there would be no rules of property. In the first situation, maximum overall satisfaction would result from each person seeking his own; in the second situation, each person's own satisfaction would be maximised by the common pursuit of over-all satisfaction. Conventions would serve purely to coordinate the endeavours of different individuals, and would be both dominant and stable.

In the second set of circumstances, human beings are natural utilitarians, directly motivated by concern for overall well-being. But that natural utilitarians would have no use for property and justice does not show that actual human beings, who are not natural utilitarians, accept the conventions of property on utilitarian grounds. Hume's natural utilitarians may represent a moral ideal, but we can make no direct inferences from that ideal to our own situation.

After considering circumstances in which abundance or benevolence makes justice superfluous, Hume turns to circumstances in which extreme scarcity or excessive rapaciousness leads each individual to a concern with his own self-preservation which must override all conventions. Hume's treatment of these situations strongly suggests that mutual advantage is the necessary condition of justice. Consider his argument:

Suppose a society to fall into such want of all common necessaries, that the utmost frugality and industry cannot preserve the greater number from perishing, and the whole from extreme misery; it will readily . . . be admitted, that the strict laws of justice are suspended, . . . and give place to the stronger motives of necessity and self-preservation. . . . The use and tendency of that virtue is to procure happiness and security . . . but where the society is ready to perish from extreme necessity, no greater evil can be dreaded from violence and injustice; and every man may now provide for himself by all the means, which prudence can dictate, or humanity permits.

(*Enquiry*, Sec. III, Pt I)

What Hume is saying, I suggest, is that in conditions of extreme scarcity, the institution of property ceases to be mutually advantageous, and the rules of justice are then suspended. However, morality does not lapse altogether, for even in these circumstances humanity may lead us to moderate our treatment of our fellows, so that we do not press small gains for ourselves at the expense of their lives.

A defender of the utilitarian interpretation might reply that in the circumstances envisaged, no *overall* advantage is secured by the institution of property, so that justice lapses. But Hume's argument proceeds from the standpoint of each individual; when the social order maintained by justice becomes useless to him, then he must seek his own survival by whatever means are prudent and humane.

However, we cannot rest our case on these examples. For when Hume considers a man fallen among thieves, among whom 'a desperate rapaciousness' prevails, he supposes that

> his particular regard to justice being no longer of use to his own safety or that of others, he must consult the dictates of self-preservation alone, without concern for those who no longer merit his care and attention.

We should want Hume to tell us what this man should do, were his regard to justice of no use to his own safety, but of some use to the safety of others. If he should still adhere to the dictates of justice, then mutual advantage cannot be necessary to the rationale of justice. If he should consult the dictates of self-preservation, then total advantage can be sufficient.

The fifth set of circumstances concerns the relation between human beings and inferior creatures. Hume's position here is decisively against total advantage, and for mutual advantage.

> Were there a species of creatures intermingled with men, which, though rational, were possessed of such inferior strength, both of body and mind, that they were incapable of all resistance, and could never . . . make us feel the effects of their resentment; the necessary consequence . . . is that we should be bound by the laws of humanity to give gentle usage to these creatures, but should not . . . lie under any restraint of justice with regard to them, nor could they possess any right or property, . . . as no inconvenience ever results from the exercise of a power, so firmly established in nature, the restraints of justice and property, being totally *useless*, would never have place in so unequal a confederacy.

There is no reason to suppose that a convention of property would not be of substantial benefit to the inferior creatures who find themselves among us, and no reason to suppose that this benefit might not outweigh the costs to us. We could certainly contrive a convention of which this would be true. But we should have no basis for establishing it, since there is no advantage *to ourselves* in so doing. If total advantage were sufficient, then justice might enter into our relation with these inferior creatures. But it does not. Mutual advantage is necessary, and its absence rules out conventions of property and justice.

Morality is not ruled out. Hume insists that humanity requires us to use inferiors gently; 'compassion and kindness [are] the only check, by which they curb our lawless will.' Since moral approbation extends to whatever is generally beneficial, we approve what benefits them, but this is sharply distinguished from considerations of justice.

Finally, Hume considers the situation of persons who have neither the desire nor the need for society. Did

> each man . . . love himself alone, and . . . depend only on himself and his own activity for safety and happiness, he would, on every occasion, . . . challenge the preference above every other being, to none of which he is bound by any ties, either of nature or of interest.

Property and justice could have no place among such men. But, Hume argues, the conjunction of the sexes in fact gives rise to the family, and thereby to those rules

> requisite for its subsistence . . .; though without comprehending the rest of mankind within their prescriptions. Suppose that several families unite together into one society, . . . the rules . . . enlarge themselves to the utmost extent of that society; but becoming then entirely useless, lose their force when carried one step farther.

And the process continues. Justice extends as far as, and no farther than, mutual convenience and advantage are recognised. Human history represents the progressive but slow

> enlargement of our regards to justice, as we become acquainted with the extensive utility of that virtue.

Hume's discussion of justice proceeds negatively, by exhibiting the circumstances in which it would be of no use. The circumstances Hume selects are those in which some of those involved could not reasonably expect to benefit from adherence to conventions of property. This is not sufficient to confirm a contractarian interpretation of Hume, since the positive features of a contractarian position – interested recognition and obligation – have yet to be identified in his account. But his reliance on mutual advantage, the advantage of all those concerned – as necessary to conventions of property and justice – is consistent with, and indeed suggestive of, a contractarian position, and inconsistent with utilitarianism.

VI

In Section III I defined a convention as a contract if and only if either it is selected from alternatives by a process of interested recognition or it commands adherence on the basis of interested obligation. In this section and the next, I shall consider whether Hume's theory of property and justice satisfies either or both of these contractarian requirements. First, how are the conventions or rules which constitute a system of property selected?

Hume's basic supposition is that the need for rules determining rights in use and possession is sufficiently strong and evident that it effectively overrides opposed preferences among different rules, dictating the simplest form of agreement.

> Public utility is the general object of all courts of judicature; and this utility too requires a stable rule in all controversies; but where several rules, nearly equal and indifferent, present themselves, it is a very slight turn of thought which fixes the decision in favour of either party.
>
> (*Enquiry*, App. III)

To this passage Hume appends a long footnote in which he discusses the grounds for choosing among different rules.

> That there be a separation or distinction of possessions, and that this separation be steady and constant; this is absolutely required by the interests of society, and hence the origin of justice and property. What possessions are assigned to particular persons; this is, generally speaking, pretty indifferent; and is often determined by very frivolous views and considerations. We shall mention a few particulars.

The particulars include present possession, labour, inheritance, accession, precedent, analogy. All of these involve a connection of the imagination; some relationship connects a person with an object, and this relationship 'naturally draws on the relation of property'.

Hume's argument, then, is that the expected benefit, to each person, of a system of property, in comparison with no system, is very great, so that each has a strong interest in reaching and maintaining agreement with his fellows on some system. On the other hand, the expected differential benefit, to any person, between any two systems of property, is comparatively small, so that each is much more concerned with agreement on some system, than with the choice among possible systems. This concern then results in acceptance of 'the most obvious rule, which could be agreed on'. What is obvious turns on 'connexions of the imagination', so that the basis for agreement among persons is to be found in that feature, which is a member of the set of possible circumstances each of which picks out a particular rule, and which has a stronger effect on the imagination of those concerned than any other member of this set.

Elsewhere, I have characterised the appeal to such a feature as the appeal to *salience*.[18] A rule is required to connect objects as property to persons in situations of type S. Each possible rule appeals to some feature of S. Among these features, we suppose that there is one, f_1, which establishes a stronger imaginative connection between particular objects and particular persons than any other feature, at least for most individuals. Each person, then, whether or not he shares this direct imaginative apprehension, will expect most others to respond to it, and so the feature f_1 provides the salient basis for agreement on that rule which appeals to it.

Salience is a coordinating device. Hume conceives the problem of selecting among rules as one of coordination, rather than bargaining. Bargaining, the typical contractarian device, is a relatively costly procedure for reaching agreement, suitable only when our differential preferences among possible conventions are strong in comparison with our interests in the selection of some convention rather than none. But the absence of bargaining does not affect the fundamentally contractual character of the procedure. For selection by salience, as Hume employs it, is based on interested recognition. Each person, given his own interests, recognises that salience is relevant to the possibility of agreement on conventions of property. Each regards the appeal to present possession, to labour, to precedent, and so forth – the appeal, that is, to the various specific salient features which determine particular rules of possession and use – as in his own interest, insofar as it resolves opposed preferences among ways of affording 'a separation and constancy in men's possessions' at less expected cost than any other form of appeal.[19]

It will be noted that the use of salience to select among possible conventions and rules is highly conservative in its effects. This conservatism, of course, reflects Hume's insistence that, while a system of property is essential, the choice among systems is of much less importance. In a critical discussion of Hume's theory we might wish to question this insistence. We might question whether present possession, inheritance, precedent, would command the interested recognition of all concerned. But such questions would only express our doubt that Hume has chosen the appropriate contractarian device to select among systems of property and justice. The basis in interested recognition, essential to contractarian thought, would only be confirmed by this critique.

VII

In the preceding two sections we have established, first, that Hume supposes that property and justice are determined by conventions accepted in the expectation of mutual advantage, and second, that he supposes that the particular choice among conventions is accomplished through the interested recognition of those salient features which discriminate among the several possibilities. Next, then, we must consider the grounds of adherence to the conventions so chosen. This will lead both to an examination of Hume's account of the obligation to be just, and to a consideration of his theory of government, which to this point has been largely neglected in our argument.

Hume begins his account of the need for government by considering our interest in being just:

All men are sensible of the necessity of justice to maintain peace and order, and all men are sensible of the necessity of peace and order for the maintenance of society. Yet, . . . such is the frailty or perverseness of our nature! it is impossible to keep men faithfully and unerringly in the paths of justice. Some extraordinary circumstances may happen, in which a man finds his interests to be more promoted by fraud or rapine, than hurt by the breach which his injustice makes in the social union. But much more frequently, he is seduced from his great and important, but distant interests, by the allurement of present, though often very frivolous temptations. This great weakness is incurable in human nature.

(*Essays*, Pt I, No. V, *Of the Origin of Government*)

In Section III I defined a convention as stable if, given conformity by others, one's own conformity is not seriously dispreferred to nonconformity, and I argued that a stable convention, as such, is not contractual, and does not require the support of obligation. The passage just quoted suggests that Hume supposes that for the most part, the conventions of property and justice would be stable, were men to be guided by consideration of their real overall interests. But this would be too much to expect from human nature. Thus Hume is led to consider both obligation and enforcement, as supports for our real interest in justice.

Two species of obligation enter into the argument of the *Enquiry* – moral obligation and interested obligation.[20] Were Hume consistently to maintain the view that only extraordinary circumstances cause our real interests to diverge from the dictates of justice, then we might expect the latter to suffice. Given the real benefits of just behaviour, one is obligated, against present temptation, to conform to the conventions determining property. But Hume's actual discussion of our interested obligation to be just reveals a rather different picture.

Treating vice with the greatest candour, and making it all possible concessions, we must acknowledge that there is not . . . the smallest pretext for giving it the preference above virtue, with a view of self-interest; except, perhaps, in the case of justice, where a man . . . may often seem to be a loser by his integrity. And though it is allowed that, without a regard to property, no society could subsist; yet . . . a sensible knave, in particular incidents, may think that an act of iniquity or infidelity will make a considerable addition to his fortune, without causing any considerable breach in the social union . . . That *honesty is the best policy,* may be a good general rule, but is liable to many exceptions; and he, it may perhaps be thought, conducts himself with most wisdom, who observes the general rule, and takes advantage of all the exceptions.

(*Enquiry*, Sec. IX, Pt II)

Hume's sensible knave, like Hobbes' Foole,[21] perceives the fundamental instability involved in justice. Each person prefers universal conformity to the conventions of property, to the expected outcome of general non-conformity. But each person also prefers, in many particular situations, not to conform, even if others do conform. Each expects to benefit from the just behaviour of others, but to lose from his own; hence, whenever his own injustice will neither set an example to others, nor bring punishment on himself, his interests will dictate that injustice.

Recognising the force of the sensible knave's argument, Hume continues the passage quoted above:

> I must confess that, if a man think this reasoning much requires an answer, it would be a little difficult to find any which will to him appear satisfactory and convincing.

His further remarks constitute an appeal to our moral sentiments, tacitly admitting that there is no sufficient interested obligation to justice.[22]

But before concluding that Hume's theory of property does not provide a contractarian ground for just behaviour, we should consider whether the moral obligation to justice has a basis in interest. The *Enquiry* contains only brief references to this obligation, but these relate it clearly to public utility.

> These reflections are far from weakening the obligations of justice, . . . ; or what stronger foundation can be desired or conceived for any duty, than to observe, that human society, or even human nature, could not subsist without the establishment of it; and will still arrive at greater degrees of happiness and perfection, the more inviolable the regard is, which is paid to that duty?
>
> *(Enquiry,* Sec. III, Pt II)

Hume is then led to the strong claim that the obligation to justice is proportionate with its utility. For he says that when we consider the relations of societies:

> The observance of justice, though useful among them, is not guarded by so strong a necessity as among individuals; and the *moral obligation* holds proportion with the *usefulness.*
>
> *(Enquiry,* Sec. IV)

If we are to interpret Hume's view of moral obligation correctly, we must attend carefully to this reference to usefulness. Clearly it is not the usefulness of the particular action, performance of which is obligatory, which is in question. This is the sphere of interested obligation, which we have seen to be insufficient. Rather, what Hume must intend is the usefulness of the convention which gives rise to the obligation. Insofar as it is useful, so that general conformity to it is preferred to the expected outcome of general nonconformity, then there is a moral obligation to conform to it. This interpretation may be confirmed by Hume's discussion in the *Essay of the Original Contract*:

> The *second* kind of moral duties are . . . not supported by any original
> instinct of nature, but are performed entirely from a sense of obligation,
> when we consider the necessities of human society, and the impossibility
> of supporting it, if these duties were neglected. It is thus *justice* or a regard
> to the property of others, *fidelity* or the observance of promises, become
> obligatory, . . . or as . . . every man loves himself better than any other
> person, he is naturally impelled to extend his acquisitions as much as pos-
> sible; and nothing can restrain him in this propensity, but reflection and
> experience, by which he learns the pernicious effects of that licence, and
> the total dissolution of society which must ensue from it. His original
> inclination, therefore, . . . is here checked and restrained by a subsequent
> judgement or observation.

Each person reflects, not on the consequences of his own failure to conform to
the conventions of property, but on the consequences of general failure. And
this reflection gives rise to a judgement, representing conformity as obligatory, which checks the inclination not to be just. Both the obligation and the
inclination, it should be noted, rest on interest. The inclination not to be just
rests on the interest, expressed by the sensible knave, in taking advantage of
'the exceptions' – in violating the rules of justice when violation would go
uncopied and unpunished. The obligation to be just rests on the interest,
which each man shares with his fellows, in maintaining the rules of justice
rather than abandoning all conventions of property. Although in the absence
of any checks the former interest will tend to dominate the latter, Hume
supposes that reflection will lead us to weigh our interest in maintaining
society more heavily than our interest in pursuing direct advantage.

But this account does not explain why our obligation to be just is denominated *moral*. Somewhat speculatively, I suggest that moral obligation, for
Hume, arises from a coincidence between an object of our moral sentiments
and an object of our reflective interests. A convention which is generally
useful receives our moral approbation. Insofar as an individual has himself
an interest in general conformity to such a convention, this interest combines
with his moral approbation to give rise to a sufficient moral ground for his
own adherence to the convention, provided others adhere as well. If the individual also has a direct interest in violating the convention, this moral
ground represents itself as an obligation, overriding such contrary considerations. The force of this moral obligation is then proportionate, not to the
degree of moral approbation, which depends only on the total utility of the
convention, and not to the extent of his particular interest in performing the
obligatory act, which may be negative, but to the extent of his interest in
upholding the convention requiring the act, so that as this latter interest
diminishes, the moral obligation diminishes correspondingly.

Justice is the virtue necessary to the maintenance of the conventions of
property. Insofar as property is generally useful, justice receives everyone's
moral approbation. Insofar as an individual has an interest in maintaining

the system of property, his interest combines with his approbation to make justice morally obligatory for him. The force of this obligation varies with the utility, to him, of the conventions of property. Insofar as he finds these essential within his own society, but only convenient in relations among societies, he is strictly obligated to respect the rights and possessions of his fellows, but only weakly obligated to respect the rights and possessions of strangers.

On this interpretation, moral obligation differs from any strictly interested obligation, in appealing to our moral sentiments. However, it differs from moral approbation, in appealing also to the interests of the person obligated. And this appeal is not to his interest in performing the act to which he is obligated, but to his interest in maintaining the conventions which require the act. Such an appeal is typical of contractarian theory.

Since moral obligation combines an appeal to interest with an appeal to moral approbation, Hume, after admitting that there is no sufficient interested obligation to justice, reintroduces an appeal to moral sentiment. Recognising that the maxim: Follow the general rule but take advantage of all the exceptions, cannot strictly be refuted, he shifts his ground and considers the man of moral feeling, saying:

> If his heart rebel not against such pernicious maxims, if he feel no reluctance to the thoughts of villainy and baseness, he has indeed lost a considerable motive to virtue; and we may expect that his practice will be answerable to his speculation.
>
> (*Enquiry*, Sec. IX, Pt II)

Hume's account of our obligation to be just, to conform to the conventions of property, is thus not purely contractarian, insofar as it reflects his theory of moral sentiment. But insofar as it also reflects his theory of property, it has a strong contractarian component. Although justice is not sufficiently upheld by a directly interested obligation, it is upheld by an obligation which, in a larger sense, conforms to the contractarian requirement, in being the effect of moral sentiment on what is acknowledged from the standpoint of individual interest.

VIII

Hume's theory of government supplements and parallels his theory of property. A brief sketch will therefore suffice. As we noted in the preceding section, Hume singles out the inability to resist the temptation of immediate desire as a weakness incurable in human nature. 'Men must, therefore endeavour to palliate what they cannot cure.' (*Essays*, Pt I, No. V). The palliative is government. Men

> must institute some persons under the appellation of magistrates, whose peculiar office it is, to point out the decrees of equity, to punish trans-

gressors, to correct fraud and violence, and to oblige men, however reluctant, to consult their own real and permanent interests.

Thus to the interested and moral obligations which we have examined, Hume now adds a further obligation, effected by countering the allurement of present temptation with the laws and punishments of authority.

> In a word, OBEDIENCE is a new duty which must be invented to support that of JUSTICE; and the tyes of equity must be corroborated by those of allegiance.

We may ask, with Hume, how the introduction of a new duty will help. If justice does not motivate us, then why should obedience? Interest and temptation may overcome both. But Hume replies that the institution of government affords men the opportunity to exercise power, an opportunity which they eagerly seize, and so obedience, unlike justice, easily finds partisans determined to maintain it, because they serve their immediate interests thereby. And ordinarily, those who wish to secure the obedience of their fellows can best do so by 'the impartial administration of justice'. Hence those who exercise power tie men to obedience, and in order to exercise power, they in turn are tied to justice.

The visible interest of the magistrate in securing obedience leads to a visible interest in his subjects in offering obedience, since the magistrate has power to enforce conformity to his commands. But the relation of magistrate and subject is not conceived by Hume as resting solely on power, even though it begins with power.

> Habit soon consolidates what other principles of human nature had imperfectly founded; and men, once accustomed to obedience, never think of departing from that path, in which they and their ancestors have constantly trod, and to which they are confined by so many urgent and visible motives.

Since government exists to uphold property, and obedience exists to enforce justice, we need not hesitate to interpret Hume's theory of government in the same manner as his theory of property. The convention determining property rests on mutual benefit. But it is insufficient to confirm men in the advantages of settled possession, without a further convention establishing magistracy or government. The mutual interest men have in establishing property thus extends also to a mutual interest in establishing government. Corroboration of this interpretation is easily found; witness the continuation of the discussion of moral duties in the *Essay of the Original Contract*:

> The case is precisely the same with the political or civil duty of *allegiance*, as with the natural duties of justice and fidelity. Our primary instincts lead us, either to indulge ourselves in unlimited freedom, or to seek dominion over others: And it is reflection only, which engages us to sacrifice such strong passions to the interests of peace and order. A small degree of

experience and observation suffices to teach us, that society cannot possibly be maintained without the authority of magistrates, and that this authority must soon fall into contempt, where exact obedience is not paid to it.

But there are costs to government which make it, for Hume, very much a second-best arrangement. Only because men are unable to act steadfastly in their real interests, is it necessary. In the *Essay of the Origin of Government* Hume represents the costs of magistracy in terms of

> a perpetual intestine struggle . . . between AUTHORITY and LIBERTY; . . . A great sacrifice of liberty must necessarily be made in every government; yet even the authority, which confines liberty, can never, and perhaps ought never, in any constitution, to become quite entire and uncontroulable.

Absolute authority, a Hobbist authority, would be purchased at too great cost; men can secure the benefit of a settled distinction of possessions without subjecting themselves to a ruler able to override all such distinctions at mere pleasure.

Hume argues that the constraints of justice are to be overridden when the conventions of property cease to be mutually advantageous. Similarly, we should want the constraints of obedience to be overridden when the conventions of magistracy cease to be mutually advantageous. But magistracy, unlike property, has power to enforce its rules, and obedience, unlike justice, becomes habitual and less easily ignored by men. Hence Hume concludes his brief discussion of the struggle between authority and liberty with the remark

> that a circumstance [authority], which is essential to the existence of civil society, must always support itself, and needs be guarded with less jealousy, than one [liberty] that contributes only to its perfection, which the indolence of men is so apt to neglect, and their ignorance to overlook.

IX

The last major questions which confront a contractarian interpretation of Hume concern the role of interested recognition in choosing among possible conventions of government and the role of interested obligation in insuring adherence to the particular convention selected. About the latter I have little to say. It is evident that the power of magistracy will give rise to a more direct obligation to conform, based solely on interest, than is found in the case of justice. Otherwise, we may suppose that the same coincidence of moral approbation and individual interest in the maintenance of conventions, which gives rise to the moral obligation of justice, will equally give rise to the moral obligation to obedience. I turn, then, to the choice among possible conventions of government.

In the *Essay of the First Principles of Government*, Hume maintains that opinion, not force, must be the ultimate basis of the magistrates' authority.

I interpret his view to be that the opinion of the many (the governed) is the essential condition for the force of the few (the magistrates) to be effective in society. Three forms of opinion are relevant – opinion of interest, of right to power, and of right to property.

Hume says little about the last, which is peripheral to our concerns. Opinion of interest includes

> the sense of the general advantage which is reaped from government; together with the persuasion, that the particular government, which is established, is equally advantageous with any other that could easily be settled.
>
> (*Essays*, Pt I, No. IV)

But the advantageousness of the established order is by no means the only ground for our opinion that we are obliged to uphold it. Hume holds that we suppose ourselves obliged to obey certain persons, and not others, because we suppose those first persons to have a right to command our allegiance, a right to power.

> What prevalence [this] opinion . . . has over mankind, may easily be understood, by observing the attachment which all nations have to their ancient government, and even to those names, which have had the sanction of antiquity. Antiquity always begets the opinion of right; . . .

In the *Essay of the Coalition of Parties,* Hume outlines the argument of the monarchical party at the time of the civil war. Although he is not speaking in his own person, but rather in the person of a seventeenth-century royalist, his statement that 'according to the established maxim of lawyers and politicians, the views of the royalists ought . . . to have appeared more solid, more safe, and more legal' may permit us to suppose that he endorses the argument, which, I should hold, is of the first importance to an appreciation of his own political thought. Here is the crucial passage:

> The only rule of government . . . known and acknowledged among men, is use and practice: Reason is so uncertain a guide that it will always be exposed to doubt and controversy: Could it ever render itself prevalent over the people, men had always retained it as their sole rule of conduct: They had still continued in the primitive, unconnected state of nature, without submitting to political government, whose sole basis is, not pure reason, but authority and precedent. Dissolve these ties, you break all the bonds of civil society, and leave every man at liberty to consult his private interest, by those expedients, which his appetite, disguised under the appearance of reason, shall dictate to him. The spirit of innovation is in itself pernicious, however favourable its particular object may sometimes appear. . . .
>
> (*Essays*, Pt I, No. IV)

And one further excerpt is essential:

> The true rule of government is the present established practice of the age. That has most authority, because it is recent: It is also best known, for the same reason.

The ultimate appeal, in determining right to power, and so the choice among conventions of government, is the present established practice.

An appeal to antiquity may appear to conflict with an appeal to present practice. What connects them is the key term 'established'. Opinion of right to power is not determined by an antiquarian appeal to practices which prevailed in the distant past but have fallen into desuetude. Opinion of right to power is equally not determined by what prevails at the present moment without regard to what has occurred previously. Rather, this crucial opinion is determined by present practice which is established, and which therefore can be traced back to antiquity. In the absence of such established practice, no government can possess a clear and unquestionable title to the exercise of power, and no person can possess a secure title to the use and possession of land and goods.

But where, in Hume's account, is there place for the selection of governments or governors on the basis of interested recognition? If opinion of interest supports the established government as equally advantageous with any realistic alternative, then is not existing authority founded on a dominant convention, one not seriously dispreferred to any other? And if there is a dominant convention, then there are no opposed preferences to resolve, no real selection to make among possible governments or governors.

Hume was well aware of the existence of controversy over the determination of the right to power. The passages quoted above, in support of the claim that opinion of right rests primarily on established practice, are found in a discussion of political conflict in England. And Hume was of course aware that such conflict reflected opposed individual interests and preferences. When he argues that governmental authority must be established on the opinion that the existing government is equally advantageous with any realistic alternative, he does not set aside the existence of conflict and contention. Rather, he holds that government must be supported by the opinion that no alternative would afford greater mutual advantage – that the established government is, at least from a practical point of view, optimal. But different individuals will still have clear preferences for alternatives, although they will not agree on any one alternative. In such a situation, Hume supposes that opposed individual preferences are best resolved by an appeal to salience. Established authority captures the imagination. The actuality of past obedience carries the imagination to accept the duty of future obedience.

Each person has a strong interest in effective government. Different persons have differing preferences with respect to the forms of authority, or the persons who exercise authority. But most persons will grant that no alternative to the existing government would be mutually preferable. The appeal, then, of long standing authority to the imagination provides a focal point for the convergence of men's preferences for some authority, despite their differing individual preferences concerning that authority, so that all can agree that the established government has the right to power. Prescriptive title commands interested recognition.[24]

Thus we find the contractarian appeal to the mutual advantage of conventions, and to the interested recognition of established conventions, underlying Hume's theory of government. Mutual advantage requires the settled distinction of possessions, or property, and the orderly enforcement of that distinction, magistracy or government. Interest leads to the recognition of present established practice, as that way of resolving questions about the rules of property and government which most readily commands acceptance. But as we have seen, neither the content nor the binding force of the conventions of property and government is founded directly on advantage. We adhere to what is established because of its practical salience. In considering what we should do, we are led by the exercise of imagination to the memory of what we have done, and associate future decision with past action.

We may admit the value of Hume's prescriptive appeal without fully accepting its accompanying conservatism. In effect, he supposes that the utility of upholding established practice takes precedence over the utility of the practice itself. Although he suggests that changes in the conventions of property or of government would afford no gains sufficient to outweigh the costs of abandoning settled rules and procedures, we may associate his defence of the *status quo* with the limited horizon of his own social position. And so we may hold that the admittedly disruptive effects of change can and should be neutralised by accommodating change to tradition, so that alteration is represented as development. Present practice may be established, not by conceiving it as the unchanged heir of past tradition, but by showing it as the development of that tradition in changing circumstances. If human institutions are viewed as shaping and altering man's world, then present practice may be considered as the adaptation of past practices to the changes which those practices themselves effected in the world. In this way, a continuing modification of practice, guided by criteria of mutual advantage, may be accommodated to the requirement that practice be legitimated, not by its utility but by its establishment.

X

Hume's men, like those of Hobbes and Locke and Bentham, are possessive individualists.[25] They are, no doubt, among the more civilised and humane representatives of that tradition, exhibiting benevolence as well as self-love, although, as Hume happily reminds us, 'the present theory, . . . enters not into that vulgar dispute concerning the *degrees* of benevolence or self-love, which prevail in human nature.' (*Enquiry*, Sec. IX, Pt I).

The world of possessive individualists is not benign. Their natural condition is marked by great inconveniences. The overcoming of these inconveniences, the emergence of possessive individualists from their wanderings in the wilderness of the state of nature into the promised land of civil society, is the great theme of moral and political thinkers in the developmental era of our capitalist society. Central to that theme is the role of self-interest.

This paper was first presented to a conference honouring the bicentenary of Hume's death together with the bicentenary of the publication of Adam Smith's *The Wealth of Nations*. That juxtaposition serves to remind us that, when Hume wrote, the Invisible Hand had yet to place its fingerprints on economic and social thought. Were all the world a perfectly competitive market, then self-interest would pose no problem, and the early utilitarian thinkers whose enthusiasm led them to embrace this wondrous belief were able to rejoice in the perfect coincidence of the happiness of each with the happiness of all.

But Hume is sensibly aware of men's interest in curbing interest. It is this awareness which makes his thought contractarian, for the essence of the social contract is found in the mutual advantage of restraining the pursuit of advantage. In the world outside the marketplace, where the Invisible Hand is powerless to direct self-interested men to a stable competitive optimum, the social contract is the conceptual constraint necessary to prevent a society of possessive individualists from being overcome by externalities and return-ing to the chaos of the state of nature. But how shall the contract prevail?

Hume's illustrious predecessors offer answers which are comfortless to us. Hobbes:

> Covenants being but words, and breath, have no force to oblige, contain, constrain, or protect any man, but what it has from the publique Sword; that is, from the untyed hands of that Man, . . . that hath the Soveraignty.[26]

Locke:

> Promises, covenants, and oaths, which are the bonds of human society, can have no hold upon an atheist. The taking away of God, though but even in thought, dissolves all.[27]

Either the public sword or the divine power is required to turn the headlong rush of possessive individualists from competitive chaos. But if, as Hume insists, the public sword rests on opinion, and if the deity, too, is the creature of opinion, then what can make mutual advantage prevail? What is the basis of right?

Although a Scot, Hume's answer is peculiarly English, finding in the resources of common law and history the forces which promote our mutual well-being. If all is opinion, then Hume will embrace opinion itself. Mutual advantage prevails through our opinion of right, formed by 'authority and precedent. Dissolve these ties, you break all the bonds of civil society, . . .' (*Essays*, Pt II, No. XIV).

Property and government are the greatest of the creatures of opinion. Brought into being by the historical acts and speeches of men, they exist subject to all the vicissitudes of the temporal. The realm of generation is the realm of corruption, but also of duration. Settled possession endures, and becomes property; orderly regulation endures, and becomes magistracy. The politics of interest endure, and become the politics of right. Opinion is all; there is and can be no appeal against the present established practice of the age.

NOTES

1 The first version of this paper was read to a Conference commemorating the bicentenary of the death of Hume and of the publication of Adam Smith's *The Wealth of Nations* at Dalhousie University in 1976. I am grateful for comments made on that occasion, and especially for the remarks of Virginia Held, who replied to the paper. I am also grateful for comments from my colleagues at Toronto, in particular John Hunter and Robert Imlay.

2 *Advertisement* from *Essays and Treatises on Miscellaneous Subjects*, Vol. II, posthumous edition of 1777.

3 E.g., 'what rules of justice or property would best promote public interest' (*Enquiry*, Sec. III, Pt II).

4 See David K. Lewis, *Convention: A Philosophical Study*, Cambridge, Mass., Harvard, 1969, esp. pp. 42, 78.

5 The same example appears in the *Treatise*, Book III, Pt II, Sec. III.

6 See my paper, 'The Social Contract as Ideology', *Philosophy and Public Affairs*, 1977, vol. 6, no. 2, pp. 141–4. As distinguished there, a *type I* situation permits a dominant, stable convention. In a *type II* situation, there is no dominant convention; in a *type III* situation, any stable convention is not optimal.

7 My use of *covenant* is taken from Hobbes, *Leviathan*, ch. 14.

8 My use of *interested obligation* is less restricted than that of Hume, as will be seen in Sec. VII infra. For discussion of this dual relation to interest, see my papers, 'Morality and Advantage', *Philosophical Review*, 1967, vol. LXXVI, no. 4, pp. 460–75, and 'Reason and Maximization', *Canadian Journal of Philosophy*, 1975, vol. IV, no. 3., esp. pp. 421–33.

9 One can provide a decision-theoretic grounding for average utilitarianism which in effect assimilates the utilitarian position to contractarianism. See, for example, John C. Harsanyi, 'Can the Maximin Principle Serve as a Basis for Morality? A Critique of John Rawls' Theory', in *Essays on Ethics, Social Behavior, and Scientific Explanation*, Dordrecht, Nijhoff, 1976, pp. 37–63, and other papers in Part A of this volume. But of course, not all utilitarians would accept this grounding (which seems to me to fail for reasons which I hope to discuss in another paper).

10 Hume's argument may be found in his discussion of the *natural obligation* to justice in the *Treatise*, Book III, Pt II, Sec. II. The crucial passage is:

> 'Tis certain, that no affection of the human mind has both a sufficient force, and a proper direction to counter-balance the love of gain, and render men fit members of society, by making them abstain from the possessions of others. . . . There is no passion, therefore, capable of controlling the interested affection, but the very affection itself, by an alteration of its direction. Now this alteration must necessarily take place upon the least reflection; since 'tis evident, that the passion is much better satisfy'd by its restraint, than by its liberty, and that in preserving society, we make much greater advances in the acquiring possessions than in the solitary and forlorn condition, which must follow upon violence and an universal licence.

11 The two forms of agreement distinguished here correspond to the distinction between the social contract proper and the contract of government; cf. J. W. Gough, *The Social Contract*, Oxford, Oxford University Press, 1957, 2nd edn pp. 2–3.

12 See John Locke's distinction between express and tacit consent, *Second Treatise of Government*, Sec. 119.

13 The idea here is of course based on John Rawls' conception of the original position; see *A Theory of Justice*, Cambridge, Mass., Harvard, 1971, esp. pp. 17ff.

14 Hume's earlier criticism of contractarian theory in the *Treatise*, Book III, Pt II, Sec. VII does not differ in any essential respects.

15 See my paper 'The Social Contract as Ideology' (referred to in n. 5 above) for discussion of the place of contractarianism in our thought about social relationships.

16 See, for example Hume's discussion in *Enquiry*, Sec. V, Pt I:

> Usefulness is agreeable, and engages our approbation. . . . But, *useful*? For what? For somebody's interest, surely. Whose interest then? Not our own only: For our approbation frequently extends farther. It must, therefore, be the interest of those, who are served by the character or action approved of; and these we may conclude, however remote, are not totally indifferent to us.

17 See my paper 'Why Ought One Obey God? Reflections on Hobbes and Locke', *Canadian Journal of Philosophy*, 1977, vol. VII, no. 3, for discussion of some of the differences between Hobbes and Locke; on Hobbes on natural law, see especially pp. 436–7.

18 See my paper 'Coordination', *Dialogue*, 1975, vol. XIV, no. 2, pp. 207–13, for a discussion of salience. See also the discussion of focal points in Thomas C. Schelling, *The Strategy of Conflict*, Cambridge, Mass., Harvard, 1960, in chs 3 and 4.

19 Note that under some circumstances, total utility might be considered the most salient feature differentiating possible conventions, so that under such circumstances, an appeal to total utility would accord both with Hume's arguments and with the contractarian requirement of interested recognition. But this appeal would not be utilitarian in spirit, for total utility would not be supposed to justify the selection of a convention, but rather to permit easiest agreement on a convention.

20 Interested obligation is discussed in the *Enquiry*, Sec. IX, Pt II. The phrase 'moral obligation' occurs, I believe, but once in the *Enquiry*, in Sec. IV, and is quoted later in this section of my paper.

21 See Hobbes, *Leviathan*, ch. 15.

22 In the *Treatise*, Hume discusses an obligation to justice based on interest, which he there calls *natural obligation*, and which in effect covers the interested part of moral obligation, as I characterise it here. See n. 9 above.

23 Hume's main concern in considering right to property is to deny that right to property and right to govern coincide; although there is a strong connection between the system of property and the choice of magistrates, the one does not fully determine the other.

24 Those puzzled by 'prescriptive' may be aided by this definition from the *Shorter Oxford English Dictionary*, Oxford, Oxford University Press, repr. 1964, p. 1573: Derived from or founded on prescription or lapse of time, . . . and the definition of 'prescription', 'The action of prescribing or appointing beforehand'.

25 Possessive individualists are, of course, creatures of C. B. Macpherson *The Political Theory of Possessive Individualism*, Oxford, Oxford University Press, 1962.

26 Hobbes, *Leviathan*, ch. 18.

27 Locke, *Letter Concerning Toleration*.

3　Mill on justice

Jonathan Riley

I INTRODUCTION

J. S. Mill argues, in chapter V of his classic essay on utilitarianism, that 'justice is a name for certain moral requirements, which, regarded collectively, stand higher in the scale of social utility, and are therefore of more paramount obligation, than any others . . .'[1] He associates social utilities of this higher kind with 'security, to every one's feelings, the most vital of all interests'.[2] Security emanates from a network of individual rights and correlative obligations assigned by social rules, including laws, customs, and common dictates of conscience. By distributing and sanctioning rights to things deemed essential to the right-holder's welfare, such rules create a degree of general security of expectations for those essentials. But different codes of rules will evidently give rise to different degrees of general security, depending on the content of rights, how broadly rights are extended, whether different persons' rights are equal, and so on.[3] To *maximise* general security, Mill seems to suggest, an *ideal* code is needed which gives *equal* rights *to all* (excluding children, mental defectives, and the like), and which also fosters substantial material equality.[4] That ideal code is not yet feasible for actual societies, however, for want of the requisite mass education if for no other reason, and there is no prospect of remedying existing intellectual and moral disabilities overnight, through some form of revolution. In the meantime, general security is so valuable that society must establish and require compliance with some non-ideal code of justice which, given the constraints of the present imperfect state of education, is an *optimal feasible* code. By doing so, society provides 'the very groundwork of our existence':

> [S]ecurity no human being can possibly do without; on it we depend for all our immunity from evil, and for the whole value of all and every good, beyond the passing moment; since nothing but the gratification of the instant could be of any worth to us, if we could be deprived of everything the next instant by whoever was momentarily stronger than ourselves . . . [Security] cannot be had, unless the machinery for providing it is kept unintermittedly in active play. Our notion, therefore, of the claim we have

on our fellow-creatures to join in making safe for us the very groundwork of our existence, gathers feelings around it so much more intense than those concerned in any of the more common cases of utility, that the difference of degree (as is often the case in psychology) becomes a real difference in kind. The claim assumes that character of absoluteness, that apparent infinity, and incommensurability with other considerations, which constitute the distinction between the feeling of right and wrong and that of ordinary expediency and inexpediency.[5]

At the same time, society should encourage its members to voluntarily undergo a process of self-development essential for the attainment of an ideal code.

Mill's focus on rules of justice has not escaped the attention of modern rule utilitarians such as Richard Brandt and John Harsanyi, who also tend to interpret him as an optimal rule utilitarian (although they do not distinguish between optimal and ideal ones not yet feasible under the present state of mass education).[6] That there is considerable evidence for such a reading is undeniable, despite the traditional view of the classicals as act utilitarians. Consider, for example, how Mill elaborates his doctrine in a letter to George Grote in 1862. If we conceive the general happiness 'as composed of as many different units as there are persons', he says, 'all equal in value except as far as the amount of happiness itself differs', then at least three related conclusions can be drawn about how to promote it. 'First, it requires that each shall consider it as his special business to take care of himself: the general good requiring that one individual should be left, in all ordinary circumstances, to his own care, and not taken care of for him, further than by not impeding his own efforts, nor allowing others to do so.'[7] Unusual circumstances aside, the general happiness is promoted by giving each person control over his particular affairs, free from undue interference by others. 'The good of all can only be pursued with any success by each person's taking as his particular department the good of the only individual whose requirements he can thoroughly know; with due precautions to prevent these different persons, each cultivating a particular strip of the field, from hindering one another.'[8]

Second, the way to give each person due control over his own affairs is to jointly commit to a code of rules which distributes reciprocal rights and obligations:

[H]uman happiness, even one's own, is in general more successfully pursued by acting on general rules, than by measuring the consequences of each act; and this is still more the case with the general happiness, since any other plan would not only leave everybody uncertain what to expect, but would involve perpetual quarrelling: and hence general rules must be laid down for people's conduct to one another, or in other words, rights and obligations must . . . be recognized; and people must, on the one hand, not be required to sacrifice even their own less good to another's greater, where no general rule has given the other a right to the sacrifice; while, when a right *has* been recognized, they must, in most cases, yield to that right even at the sacrifice, in the particular case, of their own greater good to another's less. These rights and obligations are (it is of course implied) reciprocal.[9]

Such moral rules promote the general happiness by making known to each person how others may reasonably be expected to act with respect to his personal affairs. Only when he knows which sorts of interferences in his affairs by others are permissible and which are impermissible under the rules, for example, can the individual know the sense in which he can reasonably expect to be free from *undue* interference. 'What each person is held to do for the sake of others is more or less definite, corresponding to the less definite knowledge he can have of their interests, taken individually; and he is free to employ the indefinite residue of his exertions in benefitting the one person of whom he has the principal charge, and whose wants he has the means of learning the most completely'.[10]

A third conclusion is that supererogatory acts can be recognised as praiseworthy without being prescribed as obligatory for promotion of the general happiness. The first two conclusions 'are consistent', Mill claims, 'with recognising the merit, though not the duty, of making still greater sacrifices of our own less good to the greater good of others, than the general conditions of human happiness render it expedient to prescribe'.[11] He implies that act utilitarian morality, because it cannot accommodate this distinction between supererogatory and obligatory acts, may be appropriate for 'the "perfect" (the saints)' but is too demanding for mankind.[12]

I propose to interpret Mill as an optimal rule utilitarian of a distinctive liberal brand. I begin by arguing that he endorses rule utilitarianism over act utilitarianism for utilitarian reasons similar to those emphasised by Harsanyi in particular, and that rule utilitarianism thus understood has considerable appeal as a theory of liberal justice (Section II). The argument for rule utilitarianism is then given more precision in terms of a game-theoretic model (Section III). The next two sections highlight some differences between Mill and modern optimal rule utilitarians. His rule utilitarianism is quasi-Rawlsian, I suggest, in the sense that it assigns lexical priority to a set of basic rights over competing considerations of social value, whereas Harsanyi and Brandt are hostile to the notion of absolute priorities within an optimal moral code (Section IV). Moreover, his view of security has remarkable implications for a liberal utilitarian process of social reform not sufficiently appreciated by moderns (Section V). In particular, given that society's assessment of an optimal code changes such that the existing code ceases to be optimal, the absolute priority assigned to security of existing legitimate expectations implies that any progress toward the ideal must be slow and gradual rather than sudden or revolutionary.[13]

II MILL AS AN OPTIMAL RULE UTILITARIAN

J. O. Urmson insisted more than forty years ago that Mill is properly inter-preted as a rule utilitarian, although he was subsequently criticised for failing to make clear whether for Mill moral obligations are determined by an opti-mal code or by existing non-optimal rules.[14] The latter issue is surprisingly complicated because, as I interpret him, Mill imagines an ideal egalitarian code that is not yet feasible, and for the moment prescribes a distinct feasible code which he recognises will cease to be optimal if the present state of educa-tion improves. As a result, the possibility cannot be dismissed that existing rules, though no longer optimal, can determine moral duties. But discussion of the issue is best deferred (see Section V). Confining our attention for now to the usual optimal rule utilitarian interpretation (which ignores non-feasible codes), it is still necessary to ask what reasons Mill can have to adopt that form of utilitarianism rather than act utilitarianism.[15] In this regard, it is instructive to examine the reasons offered by Brandt and Harsanyi, especially since these leading modern proponents of optimal rule utilitarian-ism regard Mill as a precursor.

Brandt argues that an optimal rule utilitarian code will not be extensionally equivalent to act utilitarianism because of the values of simplicity and publi-city in an optimal system of rules. To reduce to act utilitarianism, a rule utili-tarian code would have to be extremely complex, allowing deviations from its general rules whenever deviations are maximising in act utilitarian terms, such deviations being prescribed by myriad exceptional rules that override the more ordinary ones in the relevant special circumstances. But complexity should be restricted in an optimal code because otherwise the costs of learning it will become prohibitive for individuals like us, with our limited intellectual and emotional capacities. Even if an elite among us is capable of overcoming the problem of complexity to know when it is best to deviate from general rules, knowledge which the elite might secretly act upon so that the rest of us are not discouraged from sticking to the rules, the proscriptions of an ideal code ought to be public so that all adults have assurance of their joint commit-ment to the same rules. Although he also mentions the valuable coordination and incentive effects of a network of rights and correlative obligations, simpli-city and publicity seem to be the main utilitarian reasons stressed by Brandt for adopting an optimal code that is distinct from act utilitarianism.[16]

Brandt's reasons are persuasive as far as they go, and there is no reason to suspect that Mill would reject them. Nevertheless, the reasons suggest that optimal rule utilitarianism is superior to act utilitarianism only because humans lack the intellectual and emotional capacities needed to effectively implement act utilitarianism.[17] But then, in a theory such as Mill's, where the possibility of indefinite improvement in human capacities is allowed for, it seems to follow that the optimality of rule utilitarianism would eventually vanish. As individuals developed their capacities, society would converge on an ideal act utilitarian code. Although such an ideal cannot be discounted altogether, it does not seem to be what Mill has in mind when he imagines what a utilitarian society could become in the foreseeable future.

As I have argued elsewhere, Mill seems to imagine an ideal *liberal* utilitarian society, whose members have developed liberal characters involving dispositions to exercise certain universal equal rights and satisfy correlative obligations.[18] In short, the best form of utilitarianism of which humans might prove capable is a liberal rule utilitarianism, such that individuals internalise an ideal liberal code and invariably act in accord with their dictates of conscience, without any need for external sanctions. Thus, it is not that humans necessarily lack the intellectual and emotional capacities required to implement act utilitarianism. Rather, even for humans with the requisite capacities, an optimal rule utilitarianism promotes an even higher level of general utility. Why might this be so? Harsanyi suggests two reasons.

One is that act utilitarianism has '*intolerably burdensome* negative implementation effects' for beings with the natures we seem to have.[19] Act utilitarian morality is simply too demanding for humans as opposed to gods or saints. Its 'rigidly universalistic principles' would require 'a complete suppression of our natural inclinations', which are 'particularistic' in the sense that an agent gives 'greater weight to the interests of himself, his family and friends than to the interests of other people'. Such suppression 'could be done, if it could be done at all, only by extreme efforts and at extremely high psychological costs'.[20] Thus, an optimal code will duly recognise the utility of personal freedom to make choices contrary to the demands of act utilitarianism. A rule utilitarian code that distributes and sanctions individual rights becomes privileged over act utilitarianism for people like us.

Unlike act utilitarianism, rule utilitarianism can permit the individual 'to relax' and choose freely in at least some situations, even though his choices do not maximise social utility in act utilitarian terms. Suppose, for example, that person k has a moral duty to choose act f_k rather than act f_k' to maximise an act utilitarian social utility function w^{au}, that is, $w^{au}(f_k) > w^{au}(f_k')$. 'But a rule utilitarian moral code could assign a *procedural utility* g to free moral choice'.[21] If person k freely chooses f_k' rather than f_k, for example, a rule utilitarian code m^{ru} can suitably recognise the value of individual freedom such that:

$$w^{ru}(f_k') \geq w^{ru}(f_k),$$

where $w^{ru}(f_k') = w^{au}(f_k') + g$, and $w^{ru}(f_k) = w^{au}(f_k)$. As Harsanyi also remarks, rule utilitarianism can thereby recognise what act utilitarianism cannot, namely, 'the traditional, and intuitively very appealing, distinction between merely doing one's *duty* and performing a *supererogatory* action going beyond the call of duty'.[22] For, under m^{ru}, the individual does his duty if he freely chooses either f_k or f_k', given that g will be added to the act utilitarian moral value of whatever action he chooses. But he performs a supererogatory action by choosing f_k rather than f_k', given $w^{au}(f_k) > w^{au}(f_k')$.

This sort of libertarian argument for rule utilitarianism is highly reminiscent of Mill's elaboration of his doctrine in his letter to Grote discussed earlier. The argument claims that social value attaches to the individual's freedom to make his own choices, provided precautions are taken to prevent different persons from unduly harming one another. People like us will experience higher general utility under an optimal rule utilitarian code that gives us such freedom than under an act utilitarian code that gives us no such freedom. Unlike Harsanyi, however, Mill does not tie the value of freedom to particularistic natural inclinations. Rather, he links it to self-development: the freedom to choose is said to be essential to the development and maintenance of our intellectual and emotional capacities.[23] It follows that, for him, the optimality of rule utilitarianism does not vanish as society approaches an ideal state of education in which, among other things, our particularistic inclinations might be replaced by rigidly impartial attitudes. Since freedom remains necessary to the maintenance of our capacities, its value does not diminish if our capacities undergo indefinite improvement. Thus, for any given situation, an ideal code will continue to specify a permissible set of acts among which it is generally expedient for the individual to choose freely, and then assign universal equal rights and correlative duties accordingly.

A second general reason identified by Harsanyi for choosing an optimal rule utilitarian code, in addition to its more reasonable implementation costs for people like us, relates to the positive 'expectation effects' associated with its system of rights and duties. More specifically, a rule utilitarian code can produce positive 'incentive effects' and 'assurance effects' that cannot be realised by act utilitarianism. For example, such institutions as laws and customs of private property (including contract) 'provide socially desirable *incentives* to hard work, saving, investment, and entrepreneurial activities' and 'also give property owners *assurance* of some financial security and of some independence of other people's good will'.[24] Act utilitarianism cannot recognise these expectation effects of entire moral codes. It can consider only the expectation effects of individual actions, which are 'normally . . . negligibly small'.[25]

As Harsanyi admits, however, act utilitarian saints would not miss the expectation effects of optimal rule utilitarian codes. The relevant incentives and assurances are really only socially useful for people of liberal temperament who value the freedom associated with a network of rights and correlative duties. At the same time, some of the rights recognised by an optimal code in the present state of education clearly are tied to our particularistic inclinations. Such rights would disappear from an ideal code if particularistic inclinations are replaced by rigidly impartial attitudes during the course of social improvement. Given our particularistic inclinations, for example, we have little incentive to engage in socially useful production in the absence of a suitable system of private property rights and correlative duties. Highly developed persons with suitably impartial attitudes could behave essentially like socialist saints, however, and dutifully perform any acts of work and saving required to maximise social utility in act utilitarian terms, independently of any rights to own the fruits of their labour and saving. Similarly, given our particularistic biases, we are hardly likely to lend money to relatively poor people unless we have the assurance that promissory obligations will be enforced. But highly developed humans without our biases would not care if the poor individual breaks his promise to repay a debt when he has greater need for the funds, and, just like act utilitarian saints, 'will shower further wealth upon him until each has the same marginal utility for one dollar more or less'.[26]

Nevertheless, this tendency of highly developed persons to mimic act utilitarian saints has definite limits from a Millian perspective. Specifically, universal equal rights to liberty with respect to what Mill calls 'purely self-regarding' choices will not disappear from an ideal code.[27] Highly developed humans, unlike gods or saints, will need at least that core of liberty to maintain their highly developed capacities, including their emotional capacities to remain rigidly impartial in other-regarding matters (where harm to others is implicated). Thus, rather than reduce to act utilitarianism, an ideal Millian utilitarian code will continue to distribute and sanction universal equal rights to choose as one likes in one's purely self-regarding affairs, even if private property and other familiar liberal rights tied to our particularistic inclinations vanish from the code.[28]

III GAME THEORETIC MODEL OF RULE UTILITARIANISM

It emerges that, for Mill, an optimal rule utilitarian code yields more general utility than act utilitarianism not so much because humans are plagued by intellectual and emotional shortcomings but because people capable of self-development place a peculiar value on freedom, and on a network of rights and correlative obligations which provides incentives and assurances for the reasonable enjoyment of that freedom by all. The term 'security' as used by Mill (as well as Bentham) is synonymous with freedom in this sense. Both terms imply rights to choose without interference by others among options permitted by a social code of rules. This is 'ordered freedom', not licence, the same thing as 'justice', as Burke puts it, 'ascertained by wise laws, and secured by well-constructed institutions'.[29]

Indeed, an optimal rule utilitarian code places rather severe intellectual demands on those committed to it, demands no less imposing, perhaps, than the counterparts of act utilitarianism. The point can be illustrated in terms of Harsanyi's two-stage n-person game of rule utilitarianism, where all players are assumed to be committed rule utilitarians with complete information.[30] The first stage is a cooperative game in which the players agree to maximise social utility by jointly establishing an optimal moral code m^{ru} from some given set M of all feasible moral codes. Any moral code $\in$ M gives rise to a permissible strategy set P(m) which is the same for all utilitarian agents.[31] The second stage is a non-cooperative game in which each player k chooses a (pure or mixed) personal strategy s_k from his feasible strategy set S_k so as to maximise his personal utility, subject to the requirement that for all k:

$$s_k \in P(m^{ru}),$$

where $P(m^{ru})$ is the permissible strategy set associated with the optimal code m^{ru} chosen at the first stage. Any person's rights and obligations are included among his permissible strategies. The idea of equal rights for all is reflected in the fact that $P(m^{ru})$ is the same for everybody. Every person also has a general obligation not to make impermissible strategy choices.

To choose an optimal code m^{ru} at the first stage, the players must predict an equilibrium point $\bar{s} = (\bar{s}_1, \ldots, \bar{s}_n)$ of the non-cooperative game which will be played at the second stage. Different non-cooperative games will emerge for different codes and their respective permissible strategy sets. Even under a given code and its permissible strategy set, distinct non-cooperative games will emerge as we vary the given set of players' preferences over the options. Given an appropriate non-cooperative solution concept (some refinement of Nash equilibrium, for example), a 'predictor function' p may be defined that selects, for every possible non-cooperative game $g(m)$, an equilibrium point $\bar{s} = q(g(m))$.

Harsanyi supposes that any person k's utility function u_k takes the form $u_k = u_k(\bar{s}, m)$. He includes m as a variable 'because the players may derive some direct utility by living in a society whose moral code permits a considerable amount of free individual choice'.[32] Thus, a player's utility may vary with different degrees and types of freedom permitted by distinct moral codes, as well as with distinct equilibrium strategy combinations selected by the players. Since a social utility function w is defined in terms of the personal utility functions $u_1, \ldots, u_n$, however, we must have:

$$w = w(\bar{s}, m) = w(q(g(m)), m).$$

Social utility maximisation is achieved by joint commitment to an optimal code m^{ru} such that each person k chooses a permissible personal strategy $s_k \in P(m^{ru})$ which is a best reply to the given permissible strategy choices of his fellows.

The implementation effects of an optimal code are represented in the model 'by the fact that the players' strategies will be restricted to the permissible set $P(m^{ru})$ defined by this moral code m^{ru}'. That restriction 'will produce both utilities and disutilities for the players and, therefore, will give rise both to positive and negative implementation effects'.[33] Compared to act utilitarianism, which gives the individual no freedom to depart from the acts which it defines as obligatory, m^{ru} produces utilities for the players by distributing equal rights. At the same time, the obligations correlative to those rights are less burdensome than act utilitarian obligations. They also produce less disutilities for the players than would be produced by an Hobbesian state of nature, in which no obligations are recognised.

The expectation effects of an optimal code m^{ru} are represented 'by the fact that some players will choose different strategies than they would choose if their society had a different moral code – not because m^{ru} directly requires them to do so but rather because these strategies are their *best replies* to the other players' expected strategies, on the assumption that these *other players* will use only strategies permitted by the moral code m^{ru}'.[34] If he has assurance that his fellows will respect his property rights, for example, a player with particularistic motivations may choose to work and invest in ways that he would not choose if he had no such assurance. Or if he has assurance that borrowers will satisfy their obligations to repay their debts, he may choose to lend funds to a degree that he would otherwise refuse to risk. Even highly developed players without particularistic inclinations will have distinctive expectations under an optimal code. If he has assurance that his rights to choose as he likes in purely self-regarding concerns will be respected, such a player may choose to experiment with radical ideas or eccentric personal life-styles which he would refuse to consider under a different code, including act utilitarianism, that offered no such freedom.

Evidently, the players in this rule utilitarian game must display remarkable intellectual capacities to identify an optimal code, even if we agree that their commitment to such a code involves less stringent emotional demands than those of act utilitarianism. In particular, these agents must be able to predict how people's interactions will change across distinct codes and associated net-works of rights and obligations, in order to calculate which code maximises social utility. Moreover, those interactions can be extremely complicated, necessitating consideration of highly intricate systems of rules involving many exceptional elements, higher-order rules to settle contradictions among more basic rules, and so on. Even Brandt, despite his focus on the need for simplicity to facilitate learning, admits that optimal codes may have to be complex. As he emphasises against Hare, for example, an optimal code must include higher-order rules that set priorities among the lower-order rules in cases of conflict: 'long-range utility will be maximised if agents are taught that, in case of conflict of intuitive principles, they must try their best to find a *principle* they themselves, as utilitarians, would want to see prevail for the type of case at hand'.[35] Such higher-order principles 'may not be . . . easy to teach everyone, but we should not underestimate the capacities of the beings who are able to master English grammar and vocabulary'.[36]

As well, when only partial compliance with a code can be reasonably expected, it seems necessary to build exceptions into an optimal code which avoid serious harm yet at the same time encourage more widespread accep-tance of, and full compliance with, the code. Brandt argues for the inclusion of 'disjunctive rules . . . , with the first part of the disjunct having prior force, such as: "Treat everyone equally, without regard to race, religion, or sex;

but in case such conduct would produce serious social harm because of massive disagreement, then perform that [type of] act which [in situations like this] is benefit-maximizing, for all of society, for you (your group) to do, as a *means to social change in the direction of equal treatment*''.[37] But, as he recognises, the addition of the latter sorts of clauses to otherwise optimal rules can result in a daunting complexity, sufficient, perhaps, to preclude at least some of us from learning the code. Still, he does not despair of 'the possibility of learning such a morality', despite its 'complications when we try to work out the details in a realistic way'.[38]

Given the requisite intellectual capacities, rational individuals with a love of freedom can, by jointly committing themselves to comply with an optimal code m^{ru}, gain a significant advantage over act utilitarians. Such a commitment does not merely prevent individuals from lowering social utility by deviating from the optimal code so as to increase their own personal utilities at the expense of their fellows. As Harsanyi stresses, 'the players' commitment to the jointly adopted moral code will [also] prevent them from violating the other players' rights or their own obligations in order to *increase social utility*' in some temporary situation.[39] Act utilitarian deviations from an optimal code are no less impermissible than selfish deviations. They equally detract from the valuable security and freedom made possible by the optimal code.

As to the substance of the rights distributed by an optimal code, this depends on the set of preferences assumed for the players. Given broadly liberal democratic preferences, for example, the code would distribute and sanction familiar liberal democratic rights. Harsanyi emphasises that an optimal code 'would have to be simply a *more humane* and *more rational* version of our conventional moral codes'.[40] But that emphasis might assign too much importance to our contemporary codes, especially if (as seems likely) preferences are largely shaped by the present state of general education (including existing moral rules). If preference possibilities are constrained by states of education, we might imagine ideal preferences attainable only in highly advanced states of education. As education improves and possibilities expand, we could then refer to a series of optimal codes, one code for each state of education, converging ultimately on an ideal code of egalitarian justice. Some such approach seems to have been adopted by Mill and even Bentham.

IV LIBERAL JUSTICE AND LEXICAL PRIORITY RULES

Modern rule utilitarians take seriously the familiar liberal or libertarian claim that individuals have moral rights which generally ought to prevail over competing social values. As Harsanyi puts it:

> Only rule utilitarianism can explain why a society will be better off if people's behaviour is constrained by a network of moral rights and moral obligations which, barring extreme emergencies, must not be violated on

grounds of mere social expediency considerations. Prior to the emergence of rule-utilitarian theory, utilitarians could not convincingly defend themselves against the accusation that they were advocating a super-Machiavellistic morality, which permitted infringement of all individual rights and all institutional obligations in the name of some narrowly defined social utility.[41]

Despite their liberal perspective, however, even Brandt and Harsanyi seem unreceptive to liberal theories of justice, including rule utilitarian theories, which involve lexical priority rules within a moral code. Brandt, for example, suggests that 'moral motivations must be of finite strength' and that 'the moral motivation expressed by rights language', though justifiably stronger than 'marginal . . . [or] even substantial increments to the general welfare', probably does not take absolute priority over all conflicting moral consider-ations.[42] He leans toward the conclusion that 'all rights . . . are only *prima facie*, not only in the sense that they may be overridden by other rights in certain circumstances, but also that they may be overridden by other moral considerations that are not matters of rights at all'. Nevertheless, he does not deny the possibility, however improbable, that 'one small set of [basic] rights that cannot conflict with each other' might take absolute priority over com-peting considerations.[43]

Harsanyi insists that 'the hope that such rigid principles of absolute priority can work is a dangerous illusion'.[44] 'Common sense' rebels against John Rawls' reliance on lexical priority rules in his theory of justice, for example, including the rule that gives a set of equal basic liberties absolute priority over other moral considerations: 'Surely, there will be cases where common sense will tell us to accept a *very small* reduction in our liberties if this is a price for a *substantial* reduction in social and economic inequalities.'[45] Even if we cannot calculate precisely the tradeoffs which would maximise social utility, he insists, taking this more flexible utilitarian approach 'will focus our attention in the right direction'. By implication, we should accept that all rights are effectively non-basic in an optimal code: any right may have to be sacrificed at times in favour of some competing moral values.

Contrary to Brandt and Harsanyi, Mill seems to agree with Rawls that a set of moral rights properly has absolute priority over other considerations.[46] Recall his statement that the feelings associated with security seem different 'in kind' than those concerned in cases of 'ordinary expediency', and that the difference has the quality of 'absoluteness, . . . infinity, and incommensur-ability'.[47] In short, the feelings associated with justice and rights seem *higher in kind* than those of mere general expediency, in the sense that the one class of utilities has absolute priority over the other. It is true that he speaks of other social duties being occasionally so important that they 'overrule any one of the general maxims of justice'. As he also notes, however, we label these as *extraordinary* duties of justice itself, to avoid speaking of 'laudable injustice'.[48] The duties are made correlative to extraordinary rights, such as a right in certain circumstances of a dying man to steal medicine necessary to save his life, and are absorbed into the network of rights and duties distributed by an optimal moral code, where they are viewed as exceptional considerations *of justice* that override the more general ones in special types of circumstances. Thus, 'the character of indefeasibility attributed to justice is kept up', and nothing can override rights except other more valuable rights.[49] Whatever is counted as a moral right takes priority over other moral considerations, so that the permissible strategy set $P(m^{ru})$ associated with an optimal code has the appearance of a layer cake, in which an upper layer of rules distributes permissible strategies called moral rights whereas lower layers distribute other sorts of permissible strategies that never rise to the status of rights. The latter may include charitable obligations (which are not correlative to rights), for example, and moral permissions or liberties (defined by the absence of obligations on all parties).

Even within that upper layer of the code which may be termed the rules of justice, Mill seems to prescribe absolute priority for one basic right (strictly speaking, a set of basic rights which cannot conflict), namely, the equal right of all to choose as they like in their respective 'purely self-regarding' affairs: 'In the part [of his conduct] which merely concerns himself, his independence is, of right, absolute. . . . No society . . . is completely free in which [these rights] do not exist absolute and unqualified.'[50] Thus, according to his theory of justice, such basic rights can never properly be overridden even by other rights. I have elaborated elsewhere a Millian rule utilitarianism which provides a solid foundation in social utility for rigid liberal rights.[51] An optimal Millian code maximises a vector of heterogeneous social utility functions, as opposed to a single homogeneous social utility function, related to each other by lexical priority rules. The highest kind of social utility function represents a moral evaluation of outcomes with respect to features which are regarded as moral rights.[52]

It is another question whether such a Millian rule utilitarianism is superior on liberal utilitarian grounds to the more flexible utilitarianisms of Brandt and Harsanyi. The question deserves further study. Rawls, for example, arguably needs a comprehensive approach such as Millian utilitarianism, rather than the 'freestanding' political theory which he now endorses, to provide a solid foundation for the *priority* of liberal rights. Even he now seems to admit that his theory, though it may be associated with a reasonable overlapping consensus relating to the 'political values' of liberal justice, cannot provide any guarantee for the priority of these political values over competing elements within any plural admissible comprehensive doctrines. In short, diverse reasonable people may jointly affirm something like 'justice as fairness' as a political conception yet also assign more weight to 'non-political values' that conflict with the political values of justice and right. Nothing in liberalism itself can suitably privilege the political over the non-political. That sort of priority, he admits, could be *guaranteed* only by a suitable comprehensive moral philosophy. He merely hopes that liberal political values will 'normally' outweigh the others: 'we hope that citizens will judge (by their comprehensive view) that political values are normally (though not always) ordered prior to, or outweigh, whatever non-political values may conflict with them'.[53] Though he goes on to indicate why he thinks such a hope 'may not be . . . unrealistic', any absolute priority of basic rights over competing moral considerations has become contingent. Indeed, as his caveat 'though not always' suggests, he might wish no longer even to defend absolute priority.[54] In that case, his approach would differ little in this respect from the rule utilitarianisms of Brandt and Harsanyi.[55]

V REFORM IN ACCORD WITH LIBERAL UTILITARIAN IDEALS

Another difference between modern rule utilitarians and their classical predecessors relates to an optimal process of social reform. Brandt's suggestion that an optimal code will include disjunctive rules that both encourage full compliance and remain optimal as compliance varies from minimal ('perhaps a minority of one') to maximal is ingenious.[56] But it does not seem to capture certain elements of the approach shared by Mill and Bentham, in particular, the normative force accorded to existing non-optimal rules. Suppose for convenience that existing rules were at one time optimal given the sets of preferences possible under a former state of education. Because of a general improvement in intellectual and emotional capacities, however, possible preference configurations have expanded such that the existing code is no longer optimal. Even so, the lexical priority of general security – the rights and obligations distributed and sanctioned by the existing code – over competing moral considerations implies that reform in the direction of an optimal code – and the higher level of security associated with it – must be gradual and piecemeal, or so I will now argue by way of conclusion.

To capture the spirit of Mill's approach, consider an ideal code $m^{ru} = m^*$ which distributes universal equal rights and also promotes substantial (if not perfect) material equality. Stipulate that the level of general security is perfected under m^*, in the sense that it reaches its supreme value at a most advanced state of education where (unlike the present) there are no restrictions on feasible codes or possible sets of preferences. More precisely, confining attention to security as the most valuable kind of utility, we can define any person k's ideal utility function u_k^* as a *supremum* (or finite upper bound) of his utility function u_k such that:

$$u_k^* = u_k^*(\bar{s}) = u_k^*(\bar{s}, m^*) = \sup_M u_k(\bar{s}, m),$$

where u_k is defined over all feasible codes (and thus all possible states of education), m^{ru} can vary across states of education (because feasible sets of codes and preferences expand as education improves), and m^* is a parametric ideal code which becomes feasible only at a highly advanced state of education. Then society can maximise an ideal social utility function w^* such that:

$$w^* = w^*(\bar{s}, m^*) = \sup_M w(q(g(m)), m).$$

But w^* is attainable only if m^* is jointly accepted, and such acceptance can be expected only if the players are inculcated with the relevant norms of equal justice.

In the meantime, given the present imperfect state of education, m^* is not feasible. Rather, a code in the neighbourhood of the existing code must be accepted as optimal because, among other things, the existing laws and customs largely shape what most conceive their preferences can and should be.[57] Without loss of generality, assume that the existing code is conceived as the only feasible code in the existing state of education, in which case it must be accepted as an optimal code m_{t1}^{ru} for the given time t1. Then suppose that the state of education improves such that, at a later time t2, the set of feasible codes expands to include another element, namely, m_{t2}^{ru}. Moreover, m_{t2}^{ru} yields a higher level of general utility (security) than m_{t1}^{ru} does at t2, leading to cries for reform of the existing rules. What moral constraints (if any) does the existing code place on utilitarian reform? More generally, if society progresses towards m^* through an indefinite series of optimal codes $m_{t1}^{ru}, m_{t2}^{ru}, \ldots$, one for each distinct state of education, the question arises at any time tn+1: Which code determines moral obligations? The existing code m_{tn}^{ru}, which was optimal at tn but is no longer optimal at tn + 1? Or a new code m_{tn+1}^{ru}, which is optimal at tn + 1 but will cease to be optimal at tn + 2? Or an ideal code m^*, which is not feasible at tn + 1 but is predicted to become optimal at some point in the future if society continues to improve?

Mill's answers can be inferred, I suggest, from his assessment of capitalism versus socialism.[58] Leaving open whether an ideal code will distribute private property rights or rights to equal participation in socialistic enterprises, he associates the increase of general welfare (and its chief ingredient, security) with egalitarian reform of existing laws and customs of private property:

> We hold with Bentham, that equality, although not the sole end, is one of the ends of good social arrangements; and that a system of institutions which does not make the scale turn in favour of equality, whenever this can be done without impairing the security of the property which is the product and reward of personal exertion [labour and saving], is essentially a bad government – a government for the few, to the injury of the many.[59]

More specifically, he advocates egalitarian reform in accord with an 'equitable principle' of desert upon which he thinks the justification of private ownership of productive assets rests, namely, the principle (also apparently endorsed by Bentham) that individual producers deserve the fair market fruits of their own labour and saving.[60] Existing rules of property deviate from that desert principle in important respects and, to that extent, are unjustified from the perspective of capitalism itself. Capitalism reformed in conformity with the principle would not recognise individual rights to own natural resources *per se*, for example, so that any rents associated with mere possession of resources could in principle be taken by the community through the tax system.[61] Nor would capitalism thus understood recognise a right to acquire unlimited wealth by gift or inheritance. Instead, any surplus which a person acquired above some limited 'amount sufficient to constitute a moderate independence' would properly be confiscated, in which case givers would have a strong incentive to spread the wealth among various recipients.[62] These and other reforms of the existing idea of property would tend to promote a far more egalitarian distribution of wealth without subverting capitalism itself.[63]

Equal property rights based on the desert principle are necessary for predominantly self-interested producers to feel as secure as possible that they can provide for their own subsistence (and that of their dependents) through their own exertions. Such rights guarantee the producer the fruits of his own labour and saving, where society takes steps to minimise (without pretending to remove altogether) inequalities of opportunity by, for example, limiting inheritance and ensuring reasonable access to natural resources. Moreover, while private property might eventually become dispensable if producers develop moral sentiments that suitably constrain their material self-interest, it is 'at present [the] sole reliance for subsistence and security' and is likely to remain so for an indefinite period.[64] By implication, to increase the level of general security and advance toward an ideal liberal utilitarian code, egalitarian reform of capitalism must preoccupy reformers for the foreseeable future.

Given that general security would be perfected under a system of equal rights accompanied by substantial economic equality, progress toward that ideal must nevertheless be gradual rather than immediate. A time-consuming process of mass education is needed, for example, to inculcate essential moral and aesthetic dispositions, in particular, habits of mutual cooperation and respect together with a love of equal justice. Of crucial importance in facilitating this development process is social recognition of the basic right to experiment as one likes with respect to purely self-regarding concerns, including one's thoughts and ideas on all subjects, for example, as well as one's choices of lifestyle with other consenting adults.[65] Even apart from the time required for learning by trial and error, however, security itself is a value that can only be increased in a gradual manner.

Starting from any non-ideal position, where rights and wealth may be distributed in a highly unequal way, Bentham and Mill both insist that legitimate expectations formed around the existing rules of property must not be disappointed by any egalitarian reform of those rules if security is to increase.[66] It is not sufficient to justify reform that security takes on its supreme value under an ideal egalitarian code. Society is not yet ready to accept such a code. In the meantime, reform must not destroy even the imperfect degree of security achieved to date under the existing rules. That imperfect security, associated with the existing system of rights and holdings, has priority such that a reduction of security cannot be balanced or offset by increases in other values. Thus, if existing rules of property are reformed to abolish slavery, for example, or to terminate any other sort of recognised property right, then persons whose expectations were formed prior to the reform ought to receive fair market compensation for the taking of their property to avoid arbitrary disappointment of their plans of life. Such compensation tends to perpetuate existing economic inequalities for a certain period of time, until the relevant generations of persons pass away and are replaced by new generations whose expectations have been formed after the reform.[67] Similarly, although sharply progressive taxation of estates and resource rents would foster diffusion of wealth, protection of existing expectations requires that those special taxes must not be applied retroactively. The present market values of inheritances and resources should thus be exempt from new special taxes.[68]

In effect, general security can really only be maximised by a gradualist strategy of egalitarian reform. Any reform must protect the existing pattern of expectations associated with rights in place prior to the change, while simultaneously introducing a new pattern associated with a more egalitarian system of rules. That new pattern of expectations is inculcated in generations whose expectations are formed after the change. Moreover, the original right-holders have no reason to oppose the reform because they are not taxed retroactively and are fairly compensated for any taking of their property: the old pattern of expectations associated with their rights has not been upset *for them*. A gradualist strategy of this sort is essential because there is no other feasible way to increase general security. Any attempt at egalitarian reform through retroactive special taxation or through non-payment of fair compensation would tend to reduce security, by disappointing the legitimate expectations of existing right-holders. Such attempts can only signal to the holders of new rights that those rights are also insecure. Violation of even a single person's existing rights is sufficient to reduce security and thereby render the reform self-defeating in liberal utilitarian terms since other considerations of value cannot make up for that reduction of security. In short, raising the present level of general security requires egalitarian reform of the existing rules together with absolute protection for any individual's legitimate expectations formed under the existing system.

It deserves emphasis, however, that social recognition of any individual's right to alter his purely self-regarding affairs as he likes gives rise to no legitimate claims by other persons for legal compensation or other forms of public consolation. According to Mill, harm to others is not involved in these cases. Such licence ought to be tolerated if not welcomed, he emphasises, because it is the main engine of the social development process, however gradual.

Given the gradualism characteristic of an optimal reform process, not only because of the need for mass education but also because of the need to protect the expectations of existing right-holders as reforms are implemented, it follows that Mill does not insist on equal rights to self-manage economic and political (as opposed to purely self-regarding) matters during the social development process. Otherwise, he would advocate a socialist revolution and immediate imposition of some form of radical participatory democracy, rather than gradual egalitarian reform of existing arrangements. He certainly highlighted the possibility that equal rights to participate in economic and political decisions might be characteristic of an ideal code. In the meantime and for the foreseeable future, however, he defended in principle greater economic and political voices for the more industrious (e.g., profit-sharing in proportion to private capital contribution) and the more educated (e.g., plural voting). Yet, consistently with this, each person capable of self-development ought to retain an equal basic right to liberty in his purely self-regarding concerns. Only then might progess toward an ideal code of equal justice be reasonably expected.

NOTES

1 J. S. Mill, 'Utilitarianism', in *Collected Works of John Stuart Mill* [henceforth, *CW*], J. Robson (gen. ed.), Toronto and London, University of Toronto Press and Routledge & Kegan Paul, 1963–91, vol. X, p. 259. Mill goes on to admit that 'particular cases may occur in which some other social duty is so important, as to overrule any one of the general maxims of justice' (p. 259). It can be a duty to steal medicine or kidnap a doctor to save a life, for example. As he also says, however, we keep up 'the character of indefeasibility attributed to justice' by speaking of exceptional rules of justice that override the ordinary maxims in the special cases.
2 Mill, 'Utilitarianism', p. 251.
3 Strictly speaking, general security depends not only on the nature of the rights assigned and sanctioned by a code, but also on the level of enforcement of the code. To simplify matters, I will usually assume that any given code is perfectly enforced, that is, non-compliance does not occur. Mill himself distinguishes the identification of optimal rules of justice from their expedient enforcement ('Utilitarianism', pp. 244–6). In this regard, laws, customs and dictates of conscience are rules which can be distinguished in terms of their implicit enforcement mechanisms ('Utilitarianism', pp. 227–33). Laws are rules backed by society's announced threat to use government officials to punish violators. Customs are rules enforced by social stigma, that is, by organized displays of popular contempt for deviants. Dictates of conscience are rules backed by internal enforcement mechanisms, for example, the violator's own feelings of shame or dishonour. A rule can fall into more than one of these categories simultaneously, of course. Moreover, it seems generally expedient that a law, for example, also be a custom and a dictate of conscience. This suggests that laws ought to be suitably transformed customs and dictates of conscience. But it does not follow that a dictate of conscience or custom should always be enforced as a law.
4 Admittedly, Mill is not very clear on this point in 'Utilitarianism', despite his suggestive remarks at pp. 257–9. For further argument that he has such an ideal code in mind, see, for example, Riley, 'J. S. Mill's liberal utilitarian assessment of capitalism versus socialism', *Utilitas*, 1996, vol. 8, pp. 39–71. Bentham seems to have endorsed a similar ideal rule utilitarianism. See, for example, Paul J. Kelly, *Utilitarianism and Distributive Justice: Jeremy Bentham and the Civil Law*, Oxford, Oxford University Press, 1990.

5 Mill, 'Utilitarianism', p. 251.

6 See, for example, Richard B. Brandt, 'Some merits of one form of rule-utilitarianism', in his *Morality, Utilitarianism, and Rights* [henceforth, *MUR*], Cambridge, Cambridge University Press, 1992, pp. 119-36; Brandt, 'Fairness to indirect optimific theories in ethics', in *MUR*, pp. 137–57; Brandt, 'The concept of a moral right and its function', in *MUR*, pp. 179–95; Brandt, 'Utilitarianism and moral rights', in *MUR*, pp. 196–212; John C. Harsanyi, 'Morality and the theory of rational behavior', in *Utilitarianism and Beyond*, A. K. Sen and B. Williams (eds), Cambridge, Cambridge University Press, 1982, pp. 30–1; and Harsanyi, 'Rule utilitarianism, equality, and justice', *Social Philosophy and Policy*, 1985, vol. 2, p. 119. For a detailed discussion of Harsanyi's doctrine, see Riley, 'Interpreting Harsanyi's utilitarianism, typescript.

7 'Letter of January 10, 1862, to G. Grote', in *CW*, vol. XV, p. 762.

8 'Letter to Grote', p. 762.

9 'Letter to Grote', p. 762, emphasis original.

10 'Letter to Grote', p. 762.

11 'Letter to Grote', p. 763.

12 Mill remarks that 'the Catholic theologians have recognized' the distinction between supererogatory and obligatory acts, 'laying down a lower [rule utilitarian] standard of disinterestedness for the world and a higher [act utilitarian] one for the "perfect" (the saints): but Protestants have in general considered this as Popish laxity, and have maintained that it is the *duty* of every one, absolutely to annul his own separate existence' ('Letter to Grote', p. 763, emphasis original).

13 I do not mean to suggest that these are the only differences between Mill and modern rule utilitarians. Brandt and Harsanyi disagree between themselves, for example, over the importance of hedonism, Harsanyi rejecting it as 'naive' whereas Brandt seems inclined to support it – at least against theories which conceive utility as desire-satisfaction or preference-satisfaction. See Brandt, 'Two concepts of utility', in *MUR*, pp. 158–75; Harsanyi, 'Utilities, preferences and substantive goods', Working paper 101, Helsinki, UNU World Institute for Development Economics, 1992; and Harsanyi, 'Expectation effects, individual utilities, and rational desires', *Rationality, Rules, and Utility*, B. Hooker (ed.), Boulder, Westview, 1993, pp. 115-26.

14 J. O. Urmson, 'The interpretation of the moral philosophy of J. S. Mill', *Philosophical Quarterly*, 1953, vol. 3, pp. 33–9. For a thoughtful critique of Urmson's argument, see Ernest Sosa, 'Mill's Utilitarianism', in *Mill's Utilitarianism: Text and Criticism*, J. M. Smith and E. Sosa (eds), Belmont, Wadsworth, 1969, pp. 157–61.

15 Sosa concludes, for example, that 'it is not at all clear whether Mill was in any interesting sense a rule utilitarian' ('Mill's Utilitarianism', p. 160). That conclusion seems to be based largely on a claim that Mill gave no reasons to limit 'the complexity of the allowable rules', in which case there is no reason to think that an optimal rule utilitarian code is distinct from act utilitarianism: 'If there is no limit to the complexity of the ideal rules, it would seem that some such set of rules is one that requires all acts that in fact are optimific and no others . . . If no other set could improve on this, it would seem that Mill's presumed rule utilitarianism does reduce to simple act utilitarianism' (p. 160).

16 Brandt, 'Some merits of one form of rule-utilitarianism', p. 136; 'Fairness to indirect optimific theories in ethics', pp. 140, 142–6, 150–7; 'Utilitarianism and moral rights', pp. 200–6.

17 Such a perspective, stressing our bounded rationality and/or limited capacity to sympathise with fellow creatures, is common in the literature. See, for example, Richard Hare, *Moral Thinking: Its Method, Levels, and Point*, Oxford, Oxford University Press, 1981; and Russell Hardin, *Morality Within the Limits of Reason*, Chicago,

University of Chicago Press, 1988. Whereas Hardin's approach can be construed as a version of optimal rule utilitarianism, Hare proposes a two-level theory in which the higher level of moral thinking is act utilitarian. By implication, only 'proles' without the time or capacities for careful and impartial deliberation at the higher level are rule utilitarians.

18 Riley, *Liberal Utilitarianism*, Cambridge, Cambridge University Press, 1988.

19 Harsanyi, 'Game and decision theoretic models in ethics', in *Handbook of Game Theory*, vol. I, R. J. Aumann and S. Hart (eds), Amsterdam, North-Holland, 1992, p. 688, emphasis original.

20 Harsanyi, 'Game and decision theoretic models in ethics', pp. 675, 688.

21 Harsanyi, 'Game and decision theoretic models in ethics', p. 689, emphasis original.

22 Harsanyi, 'Game and decision theoretic models in ethics', p. 689, emphasis original.

23 J. S. Mill, 'On liberty', in *CW*, vol. XVIII, pp. 260–75.

24 Harsanyi, 'Game and decision theoretic models in ethics', p. 690, emphasis original. He also suggests that 'widespread property ownership' yields 'a kind of assurance effect benefiting society as a whole', to wit, enhanced 'social stability' and 'personal and political freedom' (p. 690).

25 Harsanyi, 'Game and decision theoretic models in ethics', p. 690. Among other things, act utilitarians cannot credibly precommit to follow a given pattern of acts into the future. If conditions change to make any act of deviation from the pattern generally expedient, act utilitarians must break the pattern.

26 Ken Binmore, 'Evolution in Eden', draft chapter two of his *Just Playing*, Cambridge, The MIT Press, forthcoming, p. 20.

27 See Mill, 'On liberty'. For further discussion, see Riley, 'Rights to liberty in purely private matters, parts I–II', *Economics and Philosophy*, 1989–90, vols. 5 and 6, pp. 121–66, 27–64; Riley, 'One very simple principle', *Utilitas*, 1991, vol. 3, pp. 1–35; Riley, 'Individuality, custom, and progress', *Utilitas*, 1991, vol. 3, pp. 223–50; and Riley, *Philosophy Guidebook to J. S. Mill: On Liberty*, London, Routledge, 1998.

28 I do not mean to imply that rules of private property, constitutional democracy, and the like would *necessarily* vanish from an ideal Millian code. Mill leaves open whether society can ever advance to a stage where private property is replaced by a form of socialism in which the members of cooperative enterprises behave essentially like act utilitarian saints with respect to economic production and distribution. See, for example, Riley, 'J. S. Mill's liberal utilitarian assessment of capitalism versus socialism'.

29 Burke's letter of November 1789 to Depont, in *The Correspondence of Edmund Burke*, A. Cobban and R. A. Smith (eds), Chicago, University of Chicago Press, 1967, vol. 6, p. 42.

30 Harsanyi, 'Game and decision theoretic models in ethics', pp. 694–7. The game can be elaborated in different ways, by dropping the assumption of complete information, for example, as well as the assumption of full compliance. For further discussion of such extensions, see, for example, Peter J. Hammond, 'Incentives and allocation mechanisms', in *Advanced Lectures in Quantitative Economics*, R. van der Ploeg (ed.), New York, Academic Press, 1990, pp. 213–48; and Hammond, 'Social choice of individual and group rights', in *Social Choice, Welfare, and Ethics*, W. A. Barnett, H. Moulin, M. Salles, and N. Schofield (eds), Cambridge, Cambridge University Press, 1995, pp. 55–77.

31 Harsanyi assumes that, for all $m \in M$, $P(m)$ is a non-empty compact subset of the feasible strategy set S which is conveniently assumed to be the same for every player, i.e., $S = S_1 = \ldots = S_n$. The latter assumption could easily be dropped to permit each player to have a distinct strategy set, however, in which case $S = \prod S_k$.

32 Harsanyi, 'Game and decision theoretic models in ethics', p. 693.
33 Harsanyi, 'Game and decision theoretic models in ethics', p. 693, notation altered.
34 Harsanyi, 'Game and decision theoretic models in ethics', pp. 693–4, emphasis original, notation altered.
35 Brandt, 'Utilitarianism and moral rights', p. 209, emphasis original.
36 Brandt, 'Utilitarianism and moral rights', p. 209. Brandt makes a compelling case that Hare's reversion to act utilitarian thinking in particular contexts threatens to collapse his two-level theory into simple act utilitarianism, and leaves his theory open to the objection (pressed by David Lyons) that it cannot recognize the peculiar normative force of rights. Unlike Hare's theory, an optimal rule utilitarianism seems immune from Lyons' sort of objection. There is thus no need to choose between utility and rights, despite received opinion to the contrary. See Brandt, 'Utilitarianism and moral rights', pp. 200–12; Brandt, 'Fairness to indirect optimific theories in ethics', pp. 143–54. A powerful expression of the received opinion in the context of classical utilitarianism is provided by H. L. A. Hart, 'Natural rights: Bentham and John Stuart Mill', in his *Essays on Bentham*, Oxford, Oxford University Press, 1983, pp. 79–104.
37 Brandt, 'Fairness to indirect optimific theories in ethics', p. 156, emphasis original.
38 Brandt, 'Fairness to indirect optimific theories in ethics', p. 157.
39 Harsanyi, 'Game and decision theoretic models in ethics', p. 694, emphasis original. For related discussion, see also Harsanyi, 'Some epistemological advantages of a rule utilitarian position in ethics', *Midwest Studies in Philosophy*, 1982, vol. 7, pp. 389–402; Harsanyi, 'Rule utilitarianism, equality, and justice', *Social Philosophy and Policy*, 1985, vol. 2, pp. 115–27; and Harsanyi, 'A theory of prudential values and a rule utilitarian theory of morality', *Social Choice and Welfare*, 1995, vol. 12, pp. 319–33.
40 Harsanyi, 'A defence of utilitarian ethics', WIDER Institute Discussion Paper, 1994, p. 9, emphasis original.
41 Harsanyi, 'Morality and the theory of rational behavior', p. 41.
42 Brandt, 'The concept of a moral right and its function', pp. 184–5, 194.
43 Brandt, 'The concept of a moral right and its function', p. 185, emphasis original.
44 Harsanyi, 'Game and decision theoretic models in ethics', p. 696.
45 Harsanyi, 'Game and decision theoretic models in ethics', p. 696, emphasis original. The later version of Rawls' theory is presented in his *Political Liberalism*, New York, Columbia University Press, 1993. Certain political rights are given a special place within his principle of liberty in the sense that they (unlike other basic rights) must have roughly equal worth (or 'fair value') for all persons (pp. 5–6, 324–31, 356–62). The rationale for this special treatment seems to be the allegedly essential role that exercise of the political liberties plays in 'preserving the other liberties' (p. 299). Thus, individuals must have a fair opportunity to exercise their basic political rights 'because it is essential in order to establish just legislation and also to make sure that the fair political process specified by the constitution is open to everyone on a basis of rough equality' (p. 330).
46 Rawls himself interprets Mill in this fashion. See, for example, Rawls, *A Theory of Justice*, Cambridge, Harvard University Press, 1971, pp. 42–3, n. 24.
47 Mill, 'Utilitarianism', p. 251.
48 Mill, 'Utilitarianism', p. 259.
49 Mill, 'Utilitarianism', p. 259.
50 Mill, 'On liberty', pp. 224, 226.
51 Riley, *Liberal Utilitarianism*; Riley, 'Rule utilitarianism and liberal priorities', in *Justice, Political Liberalism, and Utilitarianism*, to be published; and Riley, M. Salles and J. Weymark (eds), Cambridge University Press, Cambridge, *Security of Rights: A Liberal Utilitarian Theory of Liberal Rights*, to be published.

52 In principle, a complete and transitive social preference can be constructed from the lexical hierarchy of heterogeneous social utility functions. Moreover, it is even possible to construct a single ideal social utility function that validly represents this social preference ordering and also conveys some (but not all) of the richer utility information contained in the lexical hierarchy of distinct types of social utility functions. Thus, the modified approach is monist yet at the same time allows for plural basic values (or dimensions of utility) some of which are incomparably (in the sense of indefinitely or infinitely) more (less) valuable than others.

53 Rawls, 'Reply to Habermas', *Journal of Philosophy*, 1995, vol. 92, pp. 147–8, n. 29.

54 It is not entirely clear what Rawls means by the caveat. He might be thinking of extraordinary emergencies where the moral or political rules are temporarily suspended, perhaps because something like a state of war is unavoidable in any case. If so, he can still defend absolute priorities within the code itself.

55 For further discussion of this potentially remarkable turn in Rawls' theory of justice, see Riley, 'A difficulty in Rawls' conception of political liberalism', typescript.

56 Brandt, 'Fairness to indirect optimific theories in ethics', pp. 154–7.

57 For further discussion of the tendency of an existing code to perpetuate itself by suitably constraining most persons' conceptions of preference possibilities, see Mill, 'On liberty', pp. 260–75; and, in an American context, Cass Sunstein, *The Partial Constitution*, Cambridge, Harvard University Press, 1993.

58 For more complete discussion, see Riley, 'Mill's liberal utilitarian assessment of capitalism versus socialism'; Riley, 'Introduction', in *J. S. Mill: Principles of Political Economy and Chapters on Socialism*, J. Riley (ed.), Oxford, Oxford University Press, 1994, pp. i–lii; and Riley, 'Mill's political economy: Ricardian science and liberal utilitarian art', in *Cambridge Companion to Mill*, J. Skorupski (ed.), Cambridge, Cambridge University Press, 1998, pp. 293–337.

59 Mill, 'Vindication of the French Revolution of February 1848', *CW*, vol. XX, p. 354. See also his discussion of an ideal 'society between equals' in 'Utilitarianism', pp. 231–3, 243–4, 257–9; and in 'The Subjection of Women', *CW*, vol. XXI, pp. 293–5, 324–40.

60 Mill, 'Principles of Political Economy' [henceforth, POPE], in *CW*, vols. II–III, pp. 208, 215. Bentham, in passages quoted by Kelly, mentions a guarantee only for the fruits of labour (*Utilitarianism and Distributive Justice*, pp. 112–3). Kelly seems to interpret this to imply that, for Bentham, there was no right to a return on capital: '[I]n the long term all unearned benefits [might be redistributed], *even those which are a return on capital*' (p. 127, emphasis original). But Bentham may not have meant to exclude a legitimate reward for capital, given that capital goods are themselves the fruit of labour. Indeed, in his *Defence of Usury* [1816], he agrees in effect with Mill that a return on capital is legitimately earned for abstinence, risk, and/or managerial efforts on the part of investors.

61 Mill, *POPE*, pp. 227–32, 819–22, 868.

62 Mill, *POPE*, vol. III, p. 755. See also *POPE*, vols. II–III, pp. 218–26, 887–95.

63 For further discussion of the desert principle of distributive justice associated with capitalism in its best form, see J. Riley, 'Justice Under Capitalism', in *Markets and Justice: Nomos XXXI*, J. Chapman and J. R. Pennock (eds), New York, New York University Press, 1989, pp. 122–62.

64 'Chapters on Socialism', in *CW*, vol. V, p. 750. See also Mill's letter to Charles Elliot Norton dated June 26, 1870, reprinted in *CW*, vol. XVII, pp. 1739–40.

65 See Riley, 'Individuality, custom, and progress'.

66 For Bentham's view, see Kelly's discussion of what he calls Bentham's 'disappointment-preventing principle' (*Utilitarianism and Distributive Justice*, pp. 168–206). Kelly emphasizes that the 'disappointment-preventing principle . . . is largely

concerned with extending access to property . . . , while protecting those expectations which are derived from the existing distribution of property rights . . . [It] enables the Benthamite legislator to pursue a policy of the substantial equalization of property holdings while also respecting the pattern of expectations embodied in the existing distribution of property' (pp. 8–9). Mill clearly recognizes a similar principle. See, e.g., 'Utilitarianism', pp. 242–3, 247–8, 256; *POPE*, pp. 230–3; and 'Chapters on Socialism', p. 753.

67 Fair compensation is due to an owner for any taking of her property by the state but, as Mill makes clear, every legal reform does not amount to a taking. Individuals do not hold title to 'confessedly variable' general taxes or tariffs, for example, and thus cannot claim compensation for changes in those institutions (with the caveat that such changes cannot apply retroactively). The line between a taking of property and a reform with incidental effects on the distribution of property is not always easy to draw, however. If the state has never exercised its power to tax estates or resource rents, for example, or has left taxes fixed for generations, then existing property owners may have some moral claim for compensation if taxes are reformed. See Mill, *POPE*, pp. 217–8, 230–3, 819–22.

68 See, e.g., Mill, *POPE*, pp. 819–22, 868. More generally, for Mill's principles of fair taxation, see *POPE*, pp. 805–72. With the caveat that all persons should be legally guaranteed a basic income exempt from taxation, he generally argues for proportional taxation of any surplus income earned from one's own labour and saving under competitive conditions, and for sharply progressive taxation of all unearned surplus income including gifts, inheritances, resource rents, and the like.

4   Pareto and the critique of justice

Joseph Femia

Justinian defined justice as the constant and perpetual will to render to every-one his due. Most people would agree with this general definition, but such agreement is purchased at the price of indeterminacy – for how do we decide what is 'due' to any given person or group? Pareto's answer is that there is no 'Archimedean point', no neutral ground from which we can make such deci-sions. They will always reflect the biases of those who are doing the deciding. Justice, that is to say, is an 'essentially contested concept',[1] representing 'nothing real', and 'designating nothing more than indistinct and incoherent sentiments'.[2] It is therefore vain to inquire what, objectively, is justice. In what follows, I shall make some effort to elucidate Pareto's argument, assess its cogency, and consider its implications for recent speculation about justice. Casting Pareto as a protagonist in the debate on justice might seem odd. He is of course famous for his economic analysis and for his theory of elites. But no one, to the best of my knowledge, has ever examined what Pareto had to say about justice. My contention is that this neglect is due to ignorance. His contribution to political philosophy – as distinct from political sociology – remains more or less unexplored for one simple reason: hardly anyone takes the trouble to read his works. Even as an economist and sociologist, he is more often alluded to than read. A proud positivist who set his face against abstract verbiage, a man of the Right who actually welcomed the advent of fascism in Italy – Pareto is someone whose image is bound to repel the arbiters of modern academic fashion. There is perhaps an irony here, since his ethical relativism and fierce hostility to metaphysical systems might be considered fashionably (and precociously) 'post-modern'.

As a thinker, Pareto was firmly within the tradition of Italian 'realism', which can be traced back to the writings of Machiavelli. According to the notorious Florentine, men hunger for constants, and this leads them to create an illusory world which is then treated as if it were real. Emotionally frail, and given to imaginative make-believe, they prefer the security of a false world to the anxieties of the real one. This escapism may take a reactionary form of clinging to age-old habits or traditions, but at the opposite extreme are the types of illusion arising from man's tendency to project a world dis-torted by his own excessive hopes – this often results in the creation of ideals wholly untested by experience. Man, in short, is a spinner of fancies and myths concealing the true nature of events. For Machiavelli, living in a period of rapid change, there seemed to be little point in continuing the ancient quest for an immutable polity, be it reactionary or visionary in its content. His writings signalled a marked shift away from questions of legitimate authority, with their connotations of a stable political order, to questions of power, the ability to control a variable complex of dynamic forces. It was time to base knowledge on the 'verità effettuale delle cose' (the effective truth of things) rather than 'cose immaginate' (imagined things). And, in Machiavelli's opinion, the 'effective truth' was that the state was a form of concentrated power, grounded in violence. Despite protestations to the contrary, the chief role of the political actor is to dispense violence, because politics is inevitably plagued by the dilemma of limited goods and limitless ambitions. Beneath superficial differences, all political systems are dominated by the clash of particular interests, by the never-ending struggle for brute advantage. Machiavelli understood, however, that the psychological impact of power is softened if it is made to appear the agent of an objective good. Consciously or not, we weave our elaborate veils of euphemism to hide the ugly fact of violence.

For Pareto, as for Machiavelli, the purpose of the political sphere is to impose peace and security in a world governed by the conflict of interests and insatiable desires. But Pareto follows his illustrious mentor in acknowledging that human beings love to cover their conduct with a logical varnish; very beautiful theories have been evolved to show why a person ought to do the things that his sentiments or appetites would prompt him to do anyway. The practical effect of such theories is 'virtually nil', for power is what counts in the final analysis.[3] Pareto thinks that all talk of justice – especially when it refers to the distribution of the benefits and burdens of social cooperation – must be understood in this context. 'Justice' is a euphemistic fiction, enabling the dominant groups in society to seize the goods of others with a clear conscience; it may even encourage those who are despoiled to accept their fate with equanimity. 'The strong exact what they can, and the weak make the best of it.' So said Thucydides – and Pareto describes this remark as a 'sound experimental observation, true for all times and places'.[4] What 'justice' cannot do is to determine the success or failure of any particular cause. To believe otherwise is the equivalent of believing, as did the ancient Greeks, that the fortunes of war were presaged by solar or lunar eclipses, which reflected the favour or disfavour of the Gods.[5]

Pareto could make such a comparison because he regarded the apotheosis of justice as a theological residue, a search for divine law divorced from its agent. He interpreted Kant's categorical imperative in the same light: it appealed to those who wished 'to retain their customary morality and yet be free of the necessity of having it dependent upon a personified deity'. As Christianity progressively loosened its grip on the minds of philosophers and other intellectuals, they increasingly took refuge in the realm of metaphysics, not realising that they were merely exchanging one set of woolly abstractions for another.[6] Divine revelation was replaced by 'Reason' – the touchstone for the two most potent fictions of modern metaphysical thought: natural law and social contract. In demolishing these fictions, Pareto was ipso facto demystifying all those conceptions of justice that depended on them. And his criticisms remain relevant today. For John Rawls' contractarian theory of justice,[7] as well as Robert Nozick's rights-based theory (which implicitly invokes a doctrine of natural law),[8] both testify to the enduring attractions of Enlightenment rationalism, with its prescriptive logic and elaborate thought experiments.

Pareto's critique of natural law displays the corrosive sarcasm that made him such a formidable polemicist. Like previous critics, he laments the tendency of natural law thinkers to extract moral imperatives from arbitrary assertions. Their method, Pareto argues, is two-fold: (1) they use indefinite words, which 'do not correspond to anything exact'; and (2) they employ circular reasoning, defining one unknown concept by another unknown concept.[9] Discourses on natural law – he repeatedly tells us – are full of vague terms: nature, divine will, right reason. Even if we wished to use one or more of these as our guides, we could not say for certain what they require us to do. For example, metaphysicians of religious persuasion insist that natural law originates in God's will; though we are not told whether He be the God of the Christians, the God of the Moslems, or some other God: 'God has made a natural law common to all men, who, however, do not have the same God! It all sounds like a puzzle.'[10] As for 'right reason', it is never explained how the reason worthy of this exalted epithet is to be distinguished from the reason which has to go without it.[11] Undaunted by the imprecision of their terms, the natural lawyers proceed to define one by another. The dictates of right reason, we learn, are equivalent to the dictates of nature, for reason is inherent in human nature. If we are still baffled we may be informed that the dictates of nature are identical to the commands of God, as the Lord of the Universe created the natural world. Those who, after scanning the heavens, remain uncertain about the content of divine will are then referred back to right reason, a gift of God, allowing us to discover the propositions of natural law. All this swaying back and forth – so typical of the metaphysical mind – betrays the fact that the conclusions do not follow from the demonstration; rather, the demonstration is selected for the purpose of obtaining the conclusions.[12]

Pareto maintains that bogus theories of natural law spawn equally bogus theories of natural rights. Why say simply that you want something when, by devising sophistries, you can claim 'a right' to it?[13] But from which indeterminate source do such rights derive? from nature? from God? or merely from right reason? Defenders of natural rights find it difficult to make up their minds, and often contrive ingenious, if meaningless, combinations of all three concepts.[14]

Pareto attempts to illustrate the fallacy of affirming a natural right to property through a discussion of Bastiat's celebrated parable on the use of a carpenter's plane:

> It is a story of two imaginary carpenters, James and William by name. James makes a plane; William borrows it, and in return for such 'service' agrees to give James one of the boards he makes with it.[15]

Bastiat notes that without the plane, William would not be able to make any boards at all. Moreover, the plane is a product of James' labour, which he could use to advantage himself alone. James, by depriving himself of the use of his own property, enables William to produce many boards.

Surely it is right, then, for James to demand that the beneficiary of his property give him something in return – say, one board out of every twenty made with the borrowed tool. Bastiat concludes that interest on capital is perfectly legitimate. Pre-eminent in his mind is the notion that a person who renders a 'service' has a natural right to remuneration. To deprive him of it would be 'unjust'. But, on Pareto's analysis, Bastiat begs crucial questions. When he has James and William make a contract for the use of the plane, he implicitly assumes that they are free to make the contract, whereas the very question at issue is whether they should or should not have that freedom. At a deeper level, Bastiat assumes that James has a 'natural right' to ownership of the plane; but the existence or non-existence of property rights is a matter of dispute, which cannot be resolved by mere assertion. According to Pareto, such question-begging is typical of attempts to 'prove' the 'justice' of capitalist transactions – buying, selling, lending, bequeathing.[16] His argument here obviously applies to Nozick's theory, whose point of departure is the inviolable freedom of the person and the absolute right to property in the self and its possessions. In common with Bastiat, Nozick effectively takes these propositions for granted. But – if we pursue the implications of Pareto's argument – all his rigorous logical deductions count for nought, since they are founded on an arbitrary (and indefinite) premise.[17]

Pareto's attack on social contract theory is less original, though no less compelling, than his attack on natural law. Among the many thinkers who have represented human society as originating in some pact, or contract, Pareto reminds us, some have talked as though they were describing a historical incident: certain human beings not as yet living in society came together somewhere one fine day and organised human society, much as people in our day get together and form a business corporation. The obvious absurdity, not to mention irrelevance, of this idea persuaded later contractarians to desert the field of history. The contract came to be seen as a hypothetical device, specifying the relationships that would obtain if people could scrape away the 'muck of ages', clear their minds of inherited prejudices or special interests, and build a society based on pure justice. For Pareto, though, the social contract remains a ridiculous notion – whether one locates it at the beginning of human society or at the end. To compare political obligation with the contractual duties of a businessman is to reveal a shocking lack of insight into the nature of the social bond. He claims, in a manner similar to Burke, that human society is held together by deeply rooted sentiments, by inbred affection and customary loyalties. Neither calculations of rational interest nor contractual obligations conjured up by speculative philosophy can possibly serve as a substitute. Surprisingly, for a theorist who is often accused of atomistic individualism, Pareto insisted that 'man is a social animal', moulded by the values and institutions of his birthplace. Contract theory must neutralise empirical individuals to make them free and equal agents, capable of reaching decisions impersonally and sub *specie aeternitatis*. Individuals, that is to say, must be stripped of their personal identity. But why, asks Pareto, should these etiolated creatures, who little resemble human beings as we know them, be permitted to determine the distribution of social goods? Anyway, how can abstract individuals without personal identity or social reference points possess the linguistic and symbolic resources required for decision-making? In fact, the choices of these imaginary individuals always coincide with the convictions held by the contract theorist before he conducted his thought experiment. This is no accident, in Pareto's opinion. One might take such inane speculation more seriously if all (or even most) of its practitioners arrived at the same conclusion. But in actuality they arrive at a wide variety of contradictory conclusions, which seem to reflect extraneous cultural factors. Pareto suggests that Rousseau's version of contract theory 'is in vogue today because we are living in a democratic age', but 'Hobbes's theory might again prevail tomorrow if a period favourable to absolutism should recur'.[18]

Pareto's critique of contract theory is applicable to Rawls, who imagines a group of rationally self-interested people coming together in order to formulate principles which will govern the allocation of social benefits and privileges. In this hypothetical congress (the 'original position'), men and women must choose behind a 'veil of ignorance' – i.e. they are temporarily ignorant of their tastes, talents, ambitions, convictions, and future status in society. Only such unreal individuals, argues Rawls, could reach a fair and binding agreement. But he makes not the slightest attempt to meet the realist and historicist criticisms of contractualism, all of which would seem to undermine his theory. Small wonder that he stands accused of abstracting his own moral code, and giving it a universal status. As Pareto asserts, every single contract theorist has done precisely this. Instead of arguing from the 'perspective of eternity'[19] they merely rationalise their own sentiments.

From what has been said so far, the reader might be struck by the similarities between Pareto's critique of 'justice' and that of Marx, who also inveighed against metaphysical speculation and 'eternal' principles. After all, Pareto does proclaim, in Marxian fashion, that 'at all times the dominant class has sought to make justice serve its ends'.[20] Moreover, his statement that 'most men make convictions of their interests' is remindful of Marx as well as Machiavelli.[21] While the affinities are certainly there, one must also register some fundamental differences. These stem, I submit, from Pareto's rejection of economic reductionism. Indeed, Pareto objects to all forms of reductionism. Borrowing from general systems theory, he saw society as a system of mutually interdependent phenomena, moving from one state of equilibrium to another. According to this mechanical model, the 'form of society is determined by all the elements acting upon it and it, in turn, reacts upon them. We may therefore say that a reciprocal determination arises.'[22]

Marx, he thought, had gone astray in substituting relationships of cause and effect for relationships of interdependence.[23] Belief systems do not simply mirror economic interests. On the contrary, it often happens that the latter are defined in terms of the former. Not all men 'make convictions of their interests'. Pareto also highlighted the importance of sentiments, or (to use his jargon) 'residues' – underlying psychic states that manifest basic human instincts and form a permanent substratum in human psychology.[24] He goes so far as to say that these residues are 'the main factors'[25] in social life. While it may be true that 'the dominant class has sought to make justice serve its ends', it is also true, in Pareto's estimation, that disquisitions on justice express, and satisfy, profound psychological needs, which are by no means reducible to material interest. One residue discussed by Pareto is the powerful urge to transform personal feelings into objective realities.[26] This, he believes, goes a long way towards explaining the phenomenon of natural law:

> In the minds of vast numbers of persons the concepts of certain relationships between human beings are welcomed as agreeable, whereas the concepts of certain other relationships are rejected as disagreeable. Concepts of the former type do not differ very widely from certain other concepts that are commonly designated by the adjectives 'good', 'honest', 'just', whereas they conflict with the concepts designated by the opposite adjectives, 'bad', 'dishonest', 'unjust'. Now there is nothing wrong in designating that first group of concepts, vague as they are, by the expression 'natural law', nor in describing the situation by the statement that the concept of natural law 'exists in the minds of men'. But from that point people go on to conclude that the thing called natural law must necessarily *exist*, and that the only question is to discover what it is, and define it accurately.

Subjective existence – the presence of the idea of natural law in human minds – is confused with objective, or real existence.[27] For Pareto, glib references to bourgeois ideology do not succeed in describing the psychological imperatives at work here. People feel a need to objectify their likes and dislikes, regardless of whether these serve any rational social function.

He also relates our ideas about justice to a class of residues that he labels 'Integrity of the individual and his appurtenances and possessions'. Criminal or deviant activity, he notes, often elicits a ferocious response from the community out of all proportion to the direct threat posed by the offenders.

Still, their behaviour does cause a disturbance to the social equilibrium, and –
on Pareto's mechanisitic model of society – compensating forces necessarily
come into play. Such forces take the form of popular revulsion, engendered
by a vague fear that discordant actions, if unresisted, would sooner or later
bring about the dissolution of society, thus endangering our safety and possessions. The actions in question – theft, assault, civil disobedience, damage to
property, etc. – are then called 'unjust'. But what this really means, Pareto
reasons, is that they are offensive to our sentiments. Again, to dismiss such
invocations of 'justice' and 'injustice' as bourgeois ideology betrays an
impoverished understanding of human motivations and needs. Even workers
have an instinctive preference for social stability.[28]

Yet, as an opponent of one-sided causality, Pareto was keen to stress that
cultural and economic circumstances could help to determine the types of
sentiments prevalent in a society. The residual substratum of human attitudes
may be invariant, but different events and traditions will encourage some
residues to flourish and others to lie dormant. For example, the natural
human attachment to habitual ways of doing things might be overwhelmed
by more anti-social traits of human nature during periods of economic dis-
location. Our ideas and behaviour cannot be explained by universal psychological responses alone.[29] Amongst the other explanatory variables Pareto
includes 'interests'. True, his observations about how ideas like justice are
manipulated to suit the interests of the powerful sound downright Marxian.
But only if we neglect to delve beneath the surface. He opposed Marx's
simplistic 'two-class' model of society. While the bipolar division between
'exploiters' and 'exploited' may be useful as a broad historical generalisation,
it certainly fails – from Pareto's perspective – to capture the complexity of
the modern social order, where exploitation takes place within classes and
not just between them. In this connection, Pareto gave vent to his obsessive
hatred of trade unions. Organised workers, he argued, use their collective solidarity as a weapon to create inflationary wage pressures; the resultant rise in
consumer prices amounts to the robbery of poor pensioners living on fixed
incomes and of non-union workers who lack the bargaining power to inflate
their own wages. Likewise the state subsidies enjoyed by some manufacturers
mean higher taxes for those manufacturers who are not favoured by political
largesse. Further examples would not be hard to find.[30] Surveying this
complicated system of corruption and selfishness, Pareto detects the curious
phenomenon of 'mutual spoliation': i.e. groups in society that despoil other
groups are often themselves despoiled in turn. As he wryly remarks: 'One
could draw up a sort of balance sheet for each group.'[31] What is more, these
groups need not be economically defined. Along these lines, he comments on
the oppression of women, especially amongst primitive peoples. Nationality
is another factor that underlies conflict over scarce resources: 'In our own
day the struggle of the Czechs and the Germans in Bohemia is more intense
than that of the proletariat and the capitalists in England.' Nor, says Pareto,
should we ignore the social cleavages based on race and religion. The

American subjugation of blacks, to take an obvious example, fits uneasily into the rigid categories of Marxist analysis. Capital – Pareto concludes – is *a* means of exploitation, not *the* means of exploitation.[32]

The upshot of all these criticisms is that concepts of justice – while context-dependent and intrinsically variable – cannot be reduced to class interests in the Marxist sense. But, if Pareto's understanding of justice is substantially different from Marx's, is it not, for all intents and purposes, identical to that of the utilitarians? Thinkers like Hume and J. S. Mill did not ask what justice 'really' is – in common with Pareto, they sought to explain it by reference to social and psychological needs. Justice issues from human conventions: we perceive that rules that confer rights and protect property are indispensable to the general welfare, and develop an affinity for them. Their claim to obedience rests solely on their utility. The utilitarian antipathy to metaphysical speculation was positively Paretian – before Pareto. The reader may therefore be surprised to learn that he treated utilitarianism with the same contempt that marked his treatment of every other philosophy.

His critique focused on the ambiguity of the concept of 'utility'. How can we claim that justice promotes 'the greatest happiness of the greatest number' when we cannot reach a consensus on the meaning of 'happiness'?[33] Evidently, Bentham and Mill could not even agree between themselves on this crucial matter. For the former, happiness simply meant a preponderance of pleasurable sensations over painful ones; for J. S. Mill, on the other hand, happiness incorporated all kinds of admirable, if vague, qualities: truth, rationality, virtue. Pareto points out that arguments from utility beg a central question: what value-coefficients will we use to render the diverse utilities of different social actors homogeneous and therefore amenable to utilitarian calculation? An admirer of aristocracy and a champion of equality are likely to arrive at very different conclusions concerning the utility of a particular distribution of power and wealth. Would a Marxist agree with Hume on the utility of private property? And what criterion, apart from sentiment, would enable us to choose between the different value-judgements embodied in their respective calculations?[34] Pareto also draws our attention to the internal complexity of the concept of utility. We can aim to maximise either the 'utility *of* a community' or the 'utility *for* a community'. The former arises when the community is considered as a unit. The latter refers to the community understood as a collection of individuals. Take the matter of population increase. This will undoubtedly be a good thing if we measure the utility *of* the community with respect to international prestige or military power. If, however, we desire the maximum of utility *for* the community, we will concern ourselves with the living standards of individual citizens, which might be diminished by overcrowding or rising unemployment.[35]

Pareto's suspicion of utilitarianism as a mode of explanation (or justification) seems valid. The concepts various individuals have of what is good for them and good for others are essentially heterogeneous, and there is no objective way of reducing them to unity. Strangely, J. S. Mill concedes this very point in presenting his utilitarian case for justice, yet fails to see how it undermines his argument. He first acknowledges that there is 'much difference of opinion' about what is just:

> Not only have different nations and individuals different notions of justice, but, in the mind of one and the same individual, justice is not some one rule, principle, or maxim, but many, which do not always coincide in their dictates, . . .[36]

Now, if (as Mill says) justice is explained by utility, and if, furthermore, there are conflicting versions of justice, then it would seem to follow that utility is an uncertain standard, interpreted differently by different persons. Mill agrees: justice, we are told, 'bends to every person's idea of social expediency'.[37] In that case, social expediency is too indefinite to offer authoritative guidance on which principle or principles of justice to accept. We are left with the proposition that different ideas of utility give rise to different ideas of justice. But the variability of the key concepts in this analysis raises the possibility that, contrary to Mill's conclusion, the different standards of justice determine the different versions of utility. Pareto comes close to endorsing this chain of causation when he observes that the meaning of 'happiness' is contentious because each individual defines it in terms of whatever values he holds dear, including those inherent in his particular conception of justice.[38] That much granted, it is evident that if the 'happy' society is the 'just' society, the 'just' society is the 'happy' society. We thus go round and round in circles. If Pareto's observation is correct, the Humean/Millsian analysis of justice misses the point: justice does not bring about happiness; rather, it is an integral component of happiness. And neither concept admits of objective definition.

Was Pareto right to claim that justice is not only a contested concept, but an *essentially* contested one, whose meaning is inevitably a matter of controversy? As we have seen, he produced powerful reasons for rejecting rights-based, contractarian, and utilitarian theories of justice. In essence, his argument is that all these theories are irreducibly value-laden, and that there is no rationally compelling case for adhering to one set of values rather than another. Since neither fact nor logic can provide definitive answers, questions like 'What is Justice?' are, in Pareto's words, 'meaningless, inconclusive, fatuous'.[39] I would like to supplement his argument by briefly reflecting on Rawls and Nozick.

At various points in his magnum opus, Rawls lays it down that the distribution of natural abilities is a 'collective asset', as no one actually deserves the talents that nature has bestowed upon him. Why, then, should he be a privileged recipient of the advantages they bring? An apparent reply is that natural endowments are worthless unless cultivated, and that those who are industrious and responsible surely do deserve the fruits of their labour. Rawls will have none of this, because, in his eyes, a person's 'character depends in large part upon fortunate family and social circumstances for which he can claim no credit'. Therefore, I do not deserve to benefit from my capacities and endeavours. This, Rawls adds, is an intuitively obvious truth, relying as it does on 'fixed points of our moral judgements'.[40] Really? One might query the use of the word 'our' here. Pareto makes the point that it is a staple of metaphysical argument to appeal to the universal consensus of mankind.[41] When it is protested that many people disagree with this supposed consensus, the response seems to be that it is a consensus of the good and the wise only. This being so, it would be appropriate for Rawls to change the word 'our' to 'my'. At any rate, he deduces, logically enough, that the resources generated by our collective efforts are themselves common assets available for redistribution. As Alan Ryan comments: 'The thought that we come into the world with natural rights in ourselves and our capacities is not argued against, so much as ruled out by the starting-point.'[42] The 'starting-point' is Rawls' notion of a pure self, totally detached from its attributes. On this conception, nobody owns 'his' empirical characteristics (talents, skills, etc.) because they are randomly distributed products of nature rather than essential constituents of the self. (A distinction is being made here between ownership and mere possession.) But natural proprietorship of one's physical and mental endowments lies at the very heart of the rights-based theory of justice. Nozick finds Rawls' distinction between a person and his characteristics unsustainable, since by removing the empirically-given features of the personality and categorising them as contingent, we are in effect reducing the self to an abstract consciousness, an empty shell.[43] Rejecting the Rawlsian idea of a radically disembodied self allows Nozick to claim that each person is sovereign over himself and his material possessions, always assuming that he has acquired them in a legitimate way. Resources in society are therefore not available for redistribution in accordance with some guiding principle – desert, needs, or whatever might be dreamed up by hypothetical contractors. Hence Nozick's opposition to 'patterned' or 'end-state' conceptions of justice.

It should be clear that there is no way of resolving this dispute between Rawls and Nozick. No amount of logical deduction or empirical investigation can possibly determine which thinker is right on the nature of the self – a metaphysical issue if ever there was one. Both thinkers implicitly admit this, for they appeal only to 'our' intuitions – and draw precisely opposite conclusions.

But if Pareto's 'realist' analysis of justice is essentially correct, does it follow that we can dispense with the concept altogether when considering the apportionment of benefits in society? Before answering this question, we should note that Pareto, a classical liberal, himself denounced every deviation from free market principles as 'theft', 'spoliation', 'robbery', 'exploitation' – all words that presuppose a moral entitlement to goods or property.[44] Much like Marx, Pareto pretended to be a pure scientist, who refrained from making evaluative judgements about the objects of his analysis.[45] This self-description was not even remotely tenable. His condemnation of state intervention and trade union activities exuded moral outrage; he assumed that every strike, every subsidy, every protective tariff involved a seizure or destruction of rightfully acquired wealth. Thus, when curbs on imports lead to higher prices, the consumers have been 'robbed'; when social legislation causes higher taxes, the tax-payers have been 'fleeced' – and so on. Although he ostentatiously avoided using the language of justice, there is no doubt that his arguments were informed by an implicit conception of justice, or – to use a term he detested – social justice. He was torn between his moral commitment to *laissez-faire*, which probably required a doctrine of natural rights as its foundation, and his theoretical commitment to ethical relativism, which precluded any such doctrine. Contemplation of Pareto's predicament suggests an awkward dilemma. On the one hand, we appear to have no rational way of determining which of any two contradictory statements about justice is correct; on the other, intelligent reflection on the distribution of social goods would seem to depend upon some moral view (implicit or explicit) of who should get what. Could it be that justice is 'void of all meaning' (Pareto's words)[46] but nevertheless indispensable to political discourse?

Straightaway we must challenge Pareto's assumption that the essential contestability of a concept renders it meaningless. For it is necessary to distinguish between different levels of meaning. At the highest level of abstraction, the definition of justice is uncontroversial: i.e. giving each person his due, in conformity with proper principles and procedures. Exactly what these principles and procedures should be is open to conflicting interpretations, however. 'Empty' rather than 'meaningless' would seem to be a more accurate way of describing the concept. Given that nature abhors a vacuum, it would be futile to expect people to refrain from 'filling' this emptiness with their subjective feelings and values ('intuitions'). Nor is this undesirable, as a widespread attachment to justice – however conceived – is a kind of bulwark against arbitrary power. 'Take away justice', declared St. Augustine, 'and what is a state but a large robber band?'[47]

NOTES

1 Pareto himself did not use this exact terminology, though it accurately conveys what he had in mind. The expression 'essentially contestable' was coined and first applied to concepts by W. B. Gallie. See 'Essentially Contested Concepts', *Proceedings of the Aristotelian Society*, vol. 56, 1955–6, pp. 167–98.

2 V. Pareto, *The Mind and Society* (henceforth MS), trans. A. Bongiorno and A. Livingston, London, Jonathan Cape, 1935, paras 1551, 1513. The Italian title was *Trattato [Treatise] di sociologia generale*. Originally published in 1916, and divided into four volumes with consecutively numbered paragraphs, it is regarded as Pareto's master-work.

3 Pareto, *The Mind and Society*, para. 1146.

4 Pareto, *The Mind and Society*, para. 2345. *Cours d'Economie Politique* (1896), in V. Pareto, *Sociological Writings*, trans. D. Mirfin and ed. S. E. Finer, Oxford, Basil Blackwell, 1966, p. 120; *Les Systèmes Socialistes* (1902), in Pareto, *Sociological Writings*, p. 140.

5 MS, para. 2440 n.

6 MS, para. 1514.

7 J. Rawls, *A Theory of Justice*, Cambridge, Mass., Harvard University Press, 1971.

8 R. Nozick, *Anarchy, State and Utopia*, Oxford, Basil Blackwell, 1974.

9 MS, para. 442.

10 MS, para. 430.

11 MS, para. 422.

12 MS, para. 412.

13 MS, para. 1689.

14 MS, paras 405, 417, 1509.

15 MS, para. 2147.

16 MS, para. 2147.

17 To Pareto, this is a characteristic error of what he calls 'metaphysical reasoning':

> The premises contain terms altogether devoid of exactness, and from the premises, as from mathematical axioms presumably trustworthy, conclusions are drawn by strict logic. They serve, after all, to probe not things but the notions that given individuals have of things.
>
> (MS, para. 872)

18 MS, paras 1146, 1505–7.

19 Rawls, *A Theory of Justice*, p. 587.

20 *Cours d'Economie Politique* (1896), in Pareto, *Sociological Writings*, p. 120.

21 *Les Systèmes Socialistes* (1902), in Pareto, *Sociological Writings*, p. 141.

22 MS, para. 2060.

23 MS, para. 255.

24 His terminology in this area is slightly confusing. When explicitly defining 'residues' in his Treatise, he says that these 'constant' elements in human thought 'are the manifestations of sentiments and instincts just as the rising of the mercury in a thermometer is a manifestation of the rise in temperature' (MS, para. 875). Residues are thus the verbal or symbolic expression of psychic states, not the states themselves. Throughout the work, however, he tends to use the terms 'residue' and 'sentiment' interchangeably, claiming to do so 'for the sake of brevity' (MS, para. 1690).

25 MS, para. 875.

26 MS, para. 1069.

27 MS, para. 1689.

28 MS, paras 1207–16.

29 MS, paras 1091, 1690; *Les Systèmes Socialistes* (1902), in Pareto, *Sociological Writings*, p. 124; and *Manuel d'Economie Politique* (1909), in Pareto, *Sociological Writings*, pp. 148–9.

30 *Les Systèmes Socialistes* (1902), in Pareto, *Sociological Writings*, pp. 140–1; *Trasformazione della Democrazia* (1921), in Pareto, *Sociological Writings*, pp. 314–15.

31 *Les Systèmes Socialistes* (1902), in Pareto, Sociological Writings, p. 141.

32 *Les Systèmes Socialistes*, p. 140; and *Cours d'Economie Politique* (1896), in Pareto, *Sociological Writings*, p. 120.

33 MS, para. 1898.

34 MS, paras 439, 2135.

35 MS, paras 2133–5, 2143. Anthony Quinton highlights a similar distinction between 'maximisation of utility' and 'maximisation of output of typically utility-bearing things'. The latter is equivalent to the utility *of* a community, in Pareto's sense. For example, unqualified enlargement of GNP can be seen as an absolute good if we view the community as an organic whole. But 'maximisation of utility' requires us to look at the satisfaction-patterns or utility-schedules of the individuals in the community. The manner of distribution therefore becomes relevant. An

increase in GNP, if accompanied by a reduction in living standards for certain sectors of the community, may – because of the law of diminishing marginal utility – actually decrease utility *for* the community. *Utilitarian Ethics* (London: Duckworth, 1989), pp. 71–81.

36 'Utilitarianism', in *Utilitarianism, Liberty, and Representative Government*, London, Dent, 1910, p. 51.

37 Mill, *Utilitarianism, Liberty, and Representative Government* Ibid., p.59.

38 MS, paras 1898, 1904.

39 MS para. 471.

40 *A Theory of Justice*, pp. 12, 15, 101–4, 179, 310–13.

41 MS, para. 402.

42 'Introduction', in *Justice*, A. Ryan (ed.), Oxford, Oxford University Press, 1993, p. 14.

43 *Anarchy, State and Utopia*, p. 228.

44 MS, paras. 2231, 2255, 2313, 2316; *Cours d'Economie Politique* (1896), in Pareto, *Sociological Writings*, pp. 117, 119–20; *Les Systèmes Socialistes* (1902), in Pareto, *Sociological Writings*, pp. 140–1; and *Trasformazione della Democrazia* (1921), in Pareto, *Sociological Writings*, p. 315.

45 '. . . my wish is to construct a system of sociology on the model of celestial mechanics, physics, chemistry'. MS, para. 20. See, also, paras 5, 6 and 69. In his last major work, a withering analysis of liberal 'democracy', he emphatically denied having a moral or political agenda: ' . . . we abstain entirely from making judgements about the facts we are expounding, from awarding praise or blame'. (*Trasformazione della Democrazia*, (1921) in Pareto, *Sociological Writings*, p. 324).

46 *Manuel d'Economie Politique* (1909), in Pareto, *Sociological Writings*, p. 149.

47 St. Augustine, *The City of God*, BK. IV, Harmondsworth, Penguin, 1984, p. 139.

5   British Idealism and the just society

David Boucher

For the British Idealists the scope of social justice is much broader than the question of the redistribution of benefits and wealth. The purpose for which redistribution takes place is not to uphold principles of fairness, impartiality, mutual benefit, desert or entitlement, the most common justifications, but instead to secure the minimum conditions for the promotion of self-realisation. Their concern for physical well-being is a condition of the much more important emphasis upon spiritual development. It is a theory that rests upon a metaphysics of the person and a definite conception of the good. It is a theory that explicitly seeks to transform individual self-interest into social virtue by making all institutions, including factories, mines and the state itself into educative entities. Social justice for them is promoted and sustained within the context of a system of rights. Such rights are justified by the social purpose they uphold.

Idealism fulfilled a number of purposes in a society that was experiencing the consequences of rapid industrialisation and the expansion of world trade. Idealism was a philosophy that was responsive to the crucial concerns of Victorian and Edwardian Britain. It was opposed to excessive individualism and acted as a counterbalance to the individualism of utilitarianism, offering a philosophy that gave a much needed emphasis to social cohesiveness and to the closeness of the relation between individual and collective responsibility. It is true to say that when the British Idealists were writing during the latter part of the last century issues about social or redistributive justice became particularly acute because of the barely conceived and ill-prepared for implications of rapid industrialisation and the consequent urbanisation of a displaced rural population. Disease, squalor, deprivation, appalling working conditions, drunkenness and social and moral disintegration gave rise to social unrest accompanied by calls for state intervention to alleviate social problems and for the greater democratisation of society. Bernard Bosanquet, one of the leading British Idealists, saw the appeal for social reform as urgent and one which went 'straight to every human heart'.[1] It was the large cities, faced with the consequences of rapid industrial growth, Caird argued, that had to confront the issue of the extent to which the community should 'interfere' in order to ameliorate the plight of the disadvantaged.[2] With a few exceptions, notably Bradley and McTaggart, British Idealist philosophy was integrally related to practical life and was directed to the improvement of the condition of society.[3] At a time when religion was under attack from the scientific orthodoxy of evolution, Idealism was able to provide a rational basis for belief, which together with its emphasis upon the unity and development of human potential, provided a philosophical basis for social legislation.[4] It was an intensely moralistic and judgmental philosophy, condemning all social evils, including the evils of drink. It emphasised both the responsibilities of individuals to seize the opportunities to make themselves more virtuous, and of the owners of capital to transform their workshops into exemplars of virtue. They also gave their practical support to projects which sought to alleviate injustice.

In this paper I intend to argue that the Idealists could not conceive of a theory of social justice independently of their metaphysical theories of the socially constituted person. In the first section I will demonstrate how what the Idealists argue arises from assumptions regarding the nature of philosophy and the unity of experience. In the second section I will show how the British Idealists understood the person as significantly socially constituted, but who nevertheless had certain capacities which to some extent are independent of particular societies. Third, I will show how the Idealists necessarily saw a positive role for the state in removing the obstacles to individual self-realisation. And lastly, I will show how their so-called particularism was not incompatible with a universalism which envisaged the extension of the moral community beyond state borders.

IDEALIST ASSUMPTIONS

Much of what the Idealists argue is based upon metaphysical assumptions that they do not attempt to prove, but without which, they say, the universe would be ultimately unintelligible.

Dualisms of any kind, including those posited by Descartes and Kant, rest upon abstract one-sided accounts of experience which fail to acknowledge or take into account what is posited in its antithesis. The British Idealists maintain that all reasoning must rest upon hypotheses. A hypothesis is more than a guess: it is suggested to the intellect by the world whose intelligibility we seek, and is held 'only so long as the realm of reality seems to support it'.[5] Contrary to what is often asserted about Idealists, they did not think that reality is a product of mind. The universe did not come into being as a consequence of thinking about it. The world of reality is intelligible only by mind and in this respect reality and mind are mutually inclusive, a unity rather than a dualism. Hypotheses are never ultimately proven, but always in the process of being proved. All forms of enquiry require 'working hypotheses'[6] before any advance can be made in understanding experience. An hypothesis, while lacking certainty, 'commends itself to our notice by the range and clearness of the light it seems to throw on the manifold data of our experience'.[7]

Individualistic hypotheses that postulate the knowing subject as the starting-point of philosophy have in their view proved unsustainable. In Hegel the British Idealists found the idea of the unity of experience. Henry Jones had consistently maintained that the Hegelian hypothesis of unity must be the starting-point of all Idealist philosophy.[8] Unity, or the idea of 'a One in the Many',[9] does not deny the differences of which it is comprised, but refuses to rest content with abstract dualisms of any kind.[10] From this starting point the question of how the unity becomes differentiated into all its various modes becomes the central issue. Caird sums up Hegel's position thus: the highest aim of philosophy 'is to reinterpret experience, in the light of a unity which is presupposed in it, but which cannot be made conscious or explicit until the relation of experience to the thinking self is seen – the unity of all things with each other and with the mind that knows them'.[11]

Metaphysically, of course, the Idealists go to elaborate lengths to formulate hypotheses about the ultimate purpose of the universe and the relation between God, nature and man. Against the degradation of man and God in naturalistic theories of evolution they offered an elevated view of the relation between Spirit and Nature. For many of them God was immanent in the development of freedom in the world and expressed Himself through the finite centres of individual lives. They contend that the individual is potentially free and that he or she has capacities the realisation of which contributes to the good of all, and which it is the role of the state to facilitate. This is a normative conception of human nature in two respects. It is a moral criterion in that it offers a standard by which to judge the performance of actual states and, in addition, it implies a qualitative ranking of human capacities as is clear from Green's emphasis upon realising the best in oneself and Bosanquet's emphasis upon the real will of the person.[12] For many of the Idealists God is immanent in the world. The Divine and the human constitute the inseparable spiritual unity of the world. For Green and Ritchie, Christ is incarnate in the world reflecting the unity of God and man. For Ritchie, God is not merely the Creator, but reveals Himself in man.[13] Green contended that the test of the morally worthwhile existence is the extent to which the individual attempts to do God's work in the world by achieving his or her own potential and contributing to the common good.[14] Green, for example, argues that human knowledge depends upon the existence of an eternal consciousness or mind present in man which makes him conscious of perfect knowledge, and that his own progressive knowledge of the universe of experience is the manifestation in him of the eternal consciousness. Green's epistemology is closely allied to his moral philosophy. In seeking his self-satisfaction it is the presence of the eternal consciousness or mind in man that makes him aware of his true self-satisfaction or moral perfection and that the gradual moralisation of man is the manifestation of the eternal consciousness in him.[15] As Ritchie argues, however, we can dispense with the metaphysics of the person because 'for the purposes of *practical ethics and politics* it is sufficient to recognise that personality is a conception meaningless apart from society'.[16] Society and the individual are a unity, they are mutually inclusive. Unlike individualists, then, both utilitarian and organic, the Idealists did not view the state and the individual as opposed.

SOCIAL JUSTICE AND RIGHTS

Like Aristotle the British Idealists hold that justice 'is a sort of equality' and that it requires that equals be treated equally. But as Aristotle acknowledged this begs the question, equal in respect of what?[17] The Idealist answer is complex, but basically it relates to a conception of the person whose spiritual fulfilment is self-realisation, or the realisation of the good self. All individuals in society have a capacity for self-realisation, but they do not have it to the same degree. Different persons will attain different levels of self-realisation. The aim of social justice is to remove as far as possible the impediments to such attainment. This may often involve active state intervention. The condition of such intervention is that it must empower people, and not diminish individual responsibility.

It is a theory, then, that is concerned with equality of opportunities, and which sanctions inequalities of outcomes. As long as the impediments are removed to the legitimate realisation of one's capacities, the inequality in natural capacities is condoned. No one should be disadvantaged by their sex, race, or social circumstances. Inequalities of income can be justified if the competition for offices and their consequent benefits can be shown to be fair. The inequalities of social goods are justifiable if they are the result of merit, that is if they are deserved. It is a theory which primarily attempts to exclude undeserved inequalities due to social circumstances. Idealists are egalitarians, not in equating equality with the redistribution of resources, but with opportunities.

There is no equivalent in the Idealist theory to Rawls' difference principle which attempts to take account of other undeserved inequalities. Inequalities in natural talents or capacities are for Rawls equally undeserved. For the Idealists disproportionate advantages which acrue to those of greater natural capacities do not have to be justified on the grounds that they benefit the least well off. It is the condition that such disproportionate distributions of resources contribute to the Idealist conception of the common good which acts as the justification. Because of their conception of the person formulations of the common good which diminish the individual's capacity for self-realisation would be excluded. The least well off must enter the competition on a level playing field.

Modern polarities, such as moral absolutism versus moral relativism, justice versus virtue, communitarianism versus cosmopolitanism, and universalism versus particularism, about which much has been written in recent years, fail to capture the complexity of Idealism. Idealists rejected all dualisms as false abstractions. Although the source of justice and morality for the Idealists is community based they did not think it completely relativistic, nor did they envisage the community and its morality ending at the state's borders, nor, unlike many modern theorists of justice, did they separate the right from the good, justice from virtue.[18] The Idealists do not offer a coherent theory of distributive justice, independent of what it means to be a person within a society premised upon a conception of the common good, and ultimately the good life.

The question of social or distributive justice for the British Idealists resolves itself into what social arrangements are best suited to securing the best possible good of all citizens. The good is defined in terms of self-realisation and the role of the state is to maximise the conditions in which each citizen can develop or fulfil his or her potential capacities and talents. The appeal is not to any conception of a pre-civil individual with natural rights against an unjust set of social arrangements, but to a higher form of society to which we should aspire, a form which incorporates a system of rights justified by the ends it maintains.

On the principle of the unity of experience the Idealists cannot conceive of an isolated individual as theories of social justice based on social contract and natural rights require us to do. The cause of social progress, Ritchie maintains, is not helped by invoking the bad arguments of natural rights and abstract justice.[19] Idealists are critical of hedonist and utilitarian theories because they equate morality with the aggregate of pleasurable feelings, as if feelings have an existence independent of the person and society. There cannot be unencumbered selves independent of society. This is not to say that they totally dismiss either social contract or natural rights theories without acknowledging that they contain an element of truth.

Green argues that rights cannot be conceived independently of society, or as existing prior to society. The old doctrine of natural rights related to individuals in a state of nature, and which are transformed or retained in society by means of a social contract is a fiction. Rights are the creature of society and develop according to the needs of individuals in society. The justification of rights in terms of social ends is for Green teleological. Here he acknowledges that utilitarianism is able to avoid the defects of social contract by offering a justification of rights in terms of the ends which they sustain, but it ultimately fails because of its hedonism in refusing to acknowledge that there can be any other object of desire than pleasure.[20] It fails to account for moral actions which cannot be reduced to the pursuit of pleasure or happiness. Like Rawls the Idealists would exclude utilitarian interests which violated the principle of justice. In a situation where each individual has his or her fair share of resources it is unreasonable and offends against the utilitarian principle of equal consideration to expect others to subsidise my tastes on the grounds that it would make me happier. In fact, the inclusion of such preferences offends against the utilitarian principle of equal consideration. This is not to say that utilitarianism has nothing useful to contribute. Ritchie, for example, acknowledges that utilitarianism posits a good for the whole community and in terms of which political institutions were to be evaluated. Its individualistic basis, however, is its own undoing. In thinking that society is no more than an aggregate of individuals it retains an aspect of the natural rights doctrine that it intended to refute. He argues that: 'The practical value of the theory remains if we interpret the common good as the well being of the social organism of which the individual is a member.'[21]

The Idealist theory of rights consciously attempts to overcome the deficiencies in the individualism of both social contract and utilitarian theories. Idealists explored not individuals as such, but the relations of individuals which they saw as essential to, or even constitutive of, individuality.[22] Rights belong to individuals as members of a community. They are justifiable claims recognised as rational and necessary for the common good of society. What is presupposed in the general liberal account of the individual is that human nature is universal. The constitutive theory of the British Idealists, on the other hand thinks human nature circumstantial. Human nature is significantly a product of the different social formations in which people find themselves. The common good is inconceivable apart from membership in a society,[23] and the self that is to be realised through moral activity is 'determined, characterised, made what it is by relation to others'.[24]

For the Idealists rights are not always trumps. Because of their emphasis upon the individual developing within a community rights may have to be foregone in the interests of the common good. Bosanquet, equates justice with impartiality. The advantages and disadvantages in society have to be distributed impartially. It relates to individuals who have claims, and in this respect it is individualistic. It relies on comparisons between individuals regarding their relative circumstances. One person is rich, another poor, why? And what should be done to adjust it? Justice, for Bosanquet, has two components. First there is the justice of keeping a rule, that is, unalikes are not to be treated the same and likes treated differently. There should be no arbitrary exceptions to the rule. The second component is the rule itself which if it fails to take adequate account of different circumstances may break down in its application. There are, he argues, many rules which achieve different degrees of adequacy in taking account of individuals' different circumstances. But the principal point is that they relate to individual claims which when placed in the context of society as a whole may break down. In other words the recognition of an individual's claim may be contrary to the interests of society as a whole. Justice, then, may not be the highest of social ideals, but in its emphasis upon the individual's claims it is the basis of all social life. Bosanquet argues that, 'individual human beings have to be taken account of; each is one among others, having bodily and spiritual life of his own, which cannot even be genuinely sacrificed or surrendered unless it is first his own to sacrifice or to surrender'.[25] The demand of ordinary justice to treat each person equally, or treating everyone alike does in practical terms, however, often stand in opposition to the collective notions of the common good, public safety, love of mercy that is anything in which the individual has become absorbed. The demands of the ultimate sacrifice, patriotism, or strong community responsibility are what Bosanquet describes as Ideal Justice the call of which may not be manifest in equitable treatment. It is to move beyond claims and rights to the notion of obligations to the whole.

The basic structure of any social system has to recognise the claims of individuals on the grounds of justice, while at the same time afford minimum scope for undermining these claims with the tyrant's plea of public safety. It must also be recognised, however, that there are more elevated claims than those of simple individual justice and circumstances when the individual may forgo a claim, or even repudiate his or her separate existence for a higher good. What justice requires is the impartial development of individual capacities along with social stability secured by the prudent management of the necessary social performances of individuals.[26]

Rights are nevertheless important in the overall theory. For the Idealists the common good is necessarily entailed in making the best of oneself in one's station or social role and working towards the same for others. This necessarily involves the distribution of goods and benefits within a society to ensure that each can contribute fully to the common good. Securing rights for citizens, recognising and giving them the backing of law – civil rights – are the way to achieve this distribution. The opportunities for self realisation and the pursuance of the common good have to be secured through a socially constituted framework of rights, including property rights, which in the modern European state have assumed legal status. Rights are themselves associated with the common good. Rights secure for the individual the conditions for self-realisation. The Idealists reject, however, any notion that rights naturally inhere in the subject or that they pre-exist society. They are the result of the social situation and become rights in being recognised. Individuals do not possess rights in themselves, only as persons or members of a community embodying in themselves the larger collectivity.[27] All persons possess wills and equally have the right to develop their personalities, but not to the detriment of others. The opportunities for self-realisation must be shared by all members of society and must not be parasitic upon or entail degrading any part of it.

Among the rights to secure these opportunities, Green argues, is the right to private property which is imperative for moral development and self-realisation. The labourer without property is in the unenviable position of living from hand to mouth, and is denied the opportunity of developing the sense of responsibility associated with the possibility of permanent possession. Such men are morally defective because they recklessly squander the money they have without making provisions for the future. They lack the education and self-discipline to plan for the future or to pursue the ideal objects they could will. To some extent the institutional structure of society beyond the control of the individual is responsible for hindering these people from owning property.[28] Green places severe conditions on the ownership of property on the grounds of the promotion of human personality. Unlimited acquisition and utmost destitution would be unacceptable. Everyone must have a share in property as a necessary corrolary of self-realisation. Society has a responsibility to ensure the fair distribution of material resources so that none of its members are denied the opportunity to realise the good self. No right is unconditional in the sense that it cannot be overridden by the principle of personality which forbids the exercise of rights which adversely affect the rights of others. Hence there are restrictions on the exercise of ownership rights. No employer can use his or her advantage to bargain for low wages with an employee who has no choice, and taxation is permissible not only to enhance public services but also to remove obstacles to and provide opportunities for the self-realisation of the disadvantaged.

What then determines rights? The British Idealists basically follow the same pattern. The idea of recognition is crucial to their arguments. Ritchie, for example, closely follows Green in distinguishing between legal rights and moral rights. A legal right is a claim that the individual has on others, and is recognised by the State. The correlative obligations are, then, enforceable. A moral right is a claim that a person has on others which is recognised by society irrespective of recognition by the State.[29] That is not to say that Idealists endorse relativism. They certainly see some rights as more fundamental than others, and these they are prepared to call natural rights, not because they exist independently of the power of society to enforce them, but 'because they are necessary to the end which it is the vocation of human society to realise'.[30] This denial of relativism is further reinforced by a developmental view of human reason and morality. What Onora O'Neill says of Hegel is equally true of the British Idealists. She contends that Hegel embeds his particularistic theory of the stages of development in 'a more inclusive universal reason'.[31] For Bradley one's station gives content to duty, unlike the one-sided contentless bare duty of Kant. It is not a fixed and final duty. Its content develops over time, but at any particular time it is an objective fact of the moralised world. He at once denies that there is anything that is right in itself independent of time and place, but also denies that morality is relative to time and place; such a morality would be no morality at all. Bradley emphasises the historical dimension to morality. The brute nature of man is humanised by being a member of a society and realising himself in the gradually developing stages of a higher life. The notion that moral ideals fell fully fledged from the heavens is contrary to all of experience. Morality is 'relative' but it is nevertheless a reality in being the accomplished will and an objective fact of the past and present manifest in the world so far moralised: 'It comes to me as the truth of my own nature, and the power and the law, which is stronger and higher than caprice or opinion of my own.'[32]

Onora O'Neill has argued that modern writers on ethics have tended to sever the traditional connection between justice and virtue. She associates cosmopolitans, or universalists, with arguing the case for justice and a rights based culture, and communitarians or particularists with propounding a constitutive and embedded view of the virtues. What is crucial for her is the distinction between perfect and imperfect obligations. O'Neill's distinction rests upon the idea that perfect obligations are those which have determinate correlative rights and right holders, whereas imperfect obligations differ in structure in that they have no correlative rights attached to them. In her view this makes them no less obligatory. Those theories that make rights the fundamental ethical category and which therefore rely heavily upon the notion of acts of recipience find it difficult to justify as good or obligatory other act-types which cannot be claimed as of right. Thus the virtue of charity which has attached to it no correlative right is deemed supererogatory, that is beyond what is regarded obligatory, and is therefore in the realm of discretion. The virtue of charity has therefore almost become a pejorative term in the vocabulary of rights based ethical theorists. This is the case with David Gauthier. From the point of view of justice as mutual advantage, he contends that the rational choice for bargainers who are aware of their various talents and who are concerned to allocate the surplus of goods resulting from cooperation is constrained maximisation. Those people who have nothing to bargain, however, have no right to a just share in this surplus and are appropriately potential recipients of charity or philanthropy, not by right, but by the generosity of those whose gifts are supererogatory to justice and obligation.[33] It is a theory which fails adequately to provide for those very people most in need of social justice. In O'Neill's view justice is a matter of perfect obligation. Its requirements fall upon everyone and are matched by correlative rights. Virtues, on the other hand are a matter of imperfect obligation. Their requirements fall upon everyone, but specify no one as their recipients. Can principles of virtue, like principles of justice, also be inclusive or are they always embedded in situations? As with justice there must be certain princples of virtue which connect, or act as a manifold, for the different spheres of activity in which an agent moves in the world: 'The spheres of action must be linked not only by public institutions that co-ordinate or subordinate them, but by continuities of character which support continuities of activity, including feeling, relationships and community.'[34] Without some consistency of character in different situations life would be erratic and unpredictable, and the basis for trust and sustainable relationships would be eroded.

O'Neill's point is that virtues are inextricably related to justice and must be embodied not only in individuals but also in institutions, traditions and the common culture of social groups. Institutions established on principles of justice cannot be sustained for long if they operate in a culture of corruption. The virtues of justice such as fairness, reciprocal respect, truthfulness, probity and fidelity are essential to the maintenance of just institutions.

This is a position that is very close to that of the British Idealists. Justice for them could not be separated from the virtues of character displayed in the discharge of one's duties and the realisation of the self. This is partially because of our ability to cooperate, through the institutions of society, including the family, church, local communities, and trade unions. Charity was for Bosanquet not a gift to be bestowed beyond one's moral duty. He saw it instead as a right of the individual which brought with it certain obligations. Not only did the community have a duty to minister charity, the individual had the responsibility to submit to the casework methods of voluntary organisations and more or less follow their suggestions.[35]

In essence, the Idealists place a great deal of moral significance on the social community, or what they generally refer to as the nation. It provides for us the terms of reference in relation to which we identify our rights and duties to others and fulfil our obligations. Caird argues that 'the highest really organic society, the greatest actual ethical union that exists is the national state.'[36] The self, for both Bosanquet and Bradley, is realised in the social organism, not as an abstract individual but in relations with other individuals in society. It is only in our relations with others that we become more complete persons, and it is only because of these relations that we are able to abstract ourselves from others and establish what is distinctive about ourselves.[37] Bradley argues that what a person realises, or 'has to do depends on what his place is, what his function is, and that all comes from his station in the organism'.[38] This is not, in Bosanquet's view, merely one's occupation but includes the family, neighbours and the nation.[39] Bosanquet argues that our external life is itself the product of dominant ideas in which we participate as persons living in communities.

The constitutive theory of Idealism finds various forms of expression in contemporary philosophy. Michael Sandel expresses the difference between liberal individualism and communitarianism when he contends that communities are constitutive of the shared identities and self-understandings of those who participate in them. Our membership of a community shapes what we are and what we take to be morally significant, and what is significant finds expression in the institutional arrangements of that community. We are simply not autonomous individuals capable of constructing or choosing a morality for ourselves.[40] The role of politics in the formative process of individuality is much more pronounced in constitutive theory than in liberalism. For constitutive theorists a political structure and a system of rights are part of the social fabric that shapes individuals.

This is not to say that there are no wider obligations, but our humanitarian principles upon which we act, or which are acted upon on our behalf by the state, are universalised from the point of view of the community in which we first recognise these principles in relation to fellow citizens. This is a view which Walzer follows in distinguishing between thick and thin morality. Thin morality, or the universal principles of ethics and justice, derive from the thick morality of communities.[41] In many important respects the Idealist position, without the theological metaphysics, has recently been reiterated by David Miller. The idea of nationality, he contends, may legitimately be taken to constitute part of a person's identity. The nation is not a mere figment of the imagination and exists as a real community to which it is not irrational to appeal for self-identity. It does not exist in the same sense that a mountain exists. With a nation a people's own beliefs have a bearing on the definition. A national identity differs from other identities in that national communities are constituted by belief; they exhibit historical continuities; the identity is active in that common goals are pursued; often through authoritative agents or representatives; there is a geographical attachment that most other identities do not have, and finally the people who share a national identity must have something in common, what used to be called a national character and which Miller calls a 'common public culture'.[42] What distinguishes modern nationality from previous forms of national identity is that the people become elevated to the status of the bearers of sovereignty and capable of conferring authority on political institutions whose policies are seen as somehow expressive of a national or popular will.

Nations are more than just communities, they are ethical communities. Miller contends that: 'The duties we owe to our fellow-nationals are different from, and more extensive than, the duties we owe to human beings as such.'[43] Miller contends that the particularist as opposed to an universalist justification of nationality assumes that membership and other forms of attachment such as the family, college and local community give rise to properly acknowledged obligations to the members of these groups which do not extend to people in general. A national community, because of the closeness of the relations that hold among its members, ought to be able collectively to make decisions that affect it. It has a justifiable claim to self-determination, although not invariably through the state.

Bradley's theory of my station and its duties has been described as an extreme version of holism opposed to the liberal individualist view that all duties can be accounted for by showing that they arise out of the actions of individuals.[44] Bradley does not, however, want to suggest that the whole content of one's morality comes from one's station in life. The fact that morality is evolving means that it is not always entirely consistent. We must step back from these inconsistencies and try to resolve them. The consequence is that we conclude that the world is not all that it should be and enter into a process of trying to improve it. The person is assisted in this process by cosmopolitan morality. By this Bradley means that we are aware these days of what is thought right and wrong in other communities, and what people have thought in different times. From this arises an idea of goodness that stands apart from particular communities and a moral ideal of a good man who realises himself in any community and who is not fully realised in any station. The doctrine of my station and its duties gives us the external content of morality, but in Bradley's view this needs to be supplemented with an internal content. Bradley modifies his theory by articulating two demands of morality. First, he argues that the moral domain is coextensive with human activity. In whatever a person does his or her action is subject to moral appraisal. And second, every person has a moral duty to realise the best self. This is an unattainable ideal of perfection, but what it means is that in all a person's activities, both social and solitary, he or she must strive to realise the best self and suppress the bad self. The content of this ideal self cannot be fully supplied by my station because the duties it offers are often not ideal and are limited to the social. So it does not prescribe all duties, but it does supply the largest part of them. This is why Bradley believes the theory of my station and its duties to be largely, but not wholly, correct. My station offers ideals by which I aspire to live and they are therefore manifest in the world. In addition to the demands of my station, which are the expectations the world has of me, the content of the ideal self is supplied for some individuals by higher considerations by which they judge the prevailing moral standards offered by one's station. This is what Bradley refers to as the ideal of the social self, but this also needs to be supplemented with a non social ideal. The activities of the artist or scientist, for example, are not exhausted in duties to others. The content they aim at may not necessarily be for the good of other people. The moral consciousness acknowledges this and any theory of morality must take account of it.[45]

SELF-REALISATION AND THE COMMON GOOD

For the Idealists the enabling state should provide the conditions for the development of character, or self-realisation. They associate morality with self-realisation, which unlike pleasure, is the object of moral action. Morality is fundamentally social, and acting morally entails a reciprocal concern for others, and not merely a desire to achieve a private state of mind, namely happiness. Bradley, for example, argues that self-realisation is a moral duty. We have a duty to realise our best self. They also associate self-realisation with the common good. Religion is an inextricable part of the process of self-realisation.

In O'Neill's terms of reference one may think of this common good as particularistic. Green's particularism, like that of all of the British Idealists, however, is always developed against a background of universalism. In this respect Green identifies moral action with the true good which is not the good of any particular society. It is the tendency in all those who are participators in the good and who communicate with each other as 'I and Thou' to implicate a wider and wider common good until the whole of humanity is included in 'a universal human fellowship'.[46]

Green's idea of the true good is notoriously ambiguous and has been a focus of considerable criticism. It is essentially an assault upon the tendency within British philosophy to view individuals as utility maximisers whose ultimate end is to aggregate the greatest pleasure. The authentic end of human activity is for the British Idealists, as we have seen, the development or self-realisation of the capacities exclusive to man. The pursuit of this true good entails man being an active participant rather than a passive recipient. It is a good shared with other members of a community and it is therefore common.[47] The common good for Green is 'a good in the effort after which there can be no competition between man and man; of which the pursuit by any individual is an equal service to others and to himself'.[48] For Green self-realisation is attained by willing the common good, a doctrine quite distinct from public interest theories. As Peter Nicholson suggests, Green invests the common good 'with all the special meaning derived from the long tradition of the supreme good as a social life of virtue and of the State as a moral institution devoted to the pursuit of that good'.[49]

It is nevertheless the case that Green never systematically lays out what the content of this good is and what exactly the capacities are that humans must realise and what it means for individual conduct. This is because when it comes to ideals the details of required conduct can never go more than a certain distance beyond the prevailing conditions of the time.[50] What is already realised in human endeavour is indicative of what may yet be attained, the true good. The essential structure of Green's moral theory rests upon the idea of a personal good which is divorced from the pursuit of pleasure. Personal good, the idea of a possible better self, can only be conceived by the individual as a member of society. In Green's view each person's personal good is not only good for himself or herself, but must also be good for society. It must be a common good.

THE ENABLING STATE

David Miller has recently argued that the obligations of nationality are strengthened when they coincide with state boundaries. Miller contends that: 'Where this obtains, obligations of nationality are strengthened by being given expression in a formal scheme of political cooperation; and the scheme of cooperation can be based on loose rather than strict reciprocity, meaning that redistributive elements can be built in which go beyond what the rational self-interest of each participant would dictate.'[51] When the Idealists refer to the state they mean by it all of the social relations and associations encompassed by a community, including the political apparatus which acts as the sustainer of the moral world in which they all act. The state is a self-sustaining, self-complete, comprehensive unity or organised whole. Such an organised whole encompasses within itself the customs, law and common sympathy, or experience necessary to sustain a moral community. It is the highest form of social organisation we know capable of effectively maintaining moral relations. It is the total social environment which affords opportunities for the development of character. In the sense that it is all that stands between us and a barbarous brutal nature we are indebted to it for everything.[52]

Much of contemporary literature on social or distributive justice centres upon establishing the procedures for the just allocation of benefits and resources within or between societies, with particular emphasis upon economic justice. O'Neill argues that such theorists, including Rawls, have tended to assume that all obligations have correlative rights. A great deal of attention is given to procedural justice which requires a minimal or thin conception of the good and which claims to be neutral between competing substantive or thick conceptions of the good. The outcome of certain redistributions may not be predictable, but as long as the procedure is impartial and one upon which rational people can reasonably agree the result must be accepted as just. In this respect the state provides the conditions for differing conceptions of the good to be pursued by its citizens. Rawls, Gauthier and Barry present us with different versions of this style of argument and each tries to jettison metaphysics and ally the principles of justice to rational agreement.

The British Idealists do not conform to O'Neill's distinction between universalists who focus on rights based justice and communitarians who focus on embedded virtues. They were definitely communitarians, or constitutive theorists, for whom the virtues of character were crucial to the spiritual development of the self. Jones maintained that a person's will is directed towards virtue, and that the state is nothing less than the accumulated and consolidated result of this moral endeavour.[53] At the same time, however, while they rejected the very idea of natural rights, they nevertheless emphasised the importance of a system of rights valid claims that citizens have on each other – acknowledged and promoted by the state in ensuring that individual potential is not hindered from flourishing.

Following Plato the British Idealists give a broadly similar answer to the question 'what is Justice?'. The best arrangement of a society is one in which each individual fulfils a station best suited to his or her talents and for which he or she is adequately prepared and furnished with the necessary means to discharge the responsibilities. This must be the guiding principle even though it may be unattainable in a large modern state, but in so far as it is not attained some injustice remains. The state may not be able to place every citizen in the place where he or she is best suited according to talent, but it can endeavour to remove obstacles that would prevent the citizen discovering that talent and realising his or her potential.[54] In other words, the duty that a citizen has to society is to fulfil his or her potential through self-realisation. In doing so the individual contributes to the common good. Society in turn has a duty to remove any obstacles to self-realisation.

The role of Liberalism in the common view of the Idealists was to raise all members of society to a civilised condition, and this necessarily entailed positive state intervention, although they disagreed among themselves about the desirable level. The Idealists did not believe that there was any ready made formula for state intervention. Each social problem had to be approached on its merits. The test was to be the enhancement of individual freedom and responsibility, the provision of opportunity but not at the expense of individual initiative. As Green suggests: 'It is enough to point out the directions in which the state may remove obstacles to the realisation of the capacity for beneficial exercise of rights, without defeating its own object by vitiating the spontaneous character of that capacity.'[55]

Green and Bosanquet were much less state interventionist than Ritchie, Jones or Haldane. Their disagreements on this issue really amount to a question of the right balance between individual and collective responsibility. Bosanquet, for example, endorses the desirability of civilised society exercising its will through the state to encourage progress in the condition of its members, but not to the extent that it weakens the character of the individual by transferring responsibility to the state. It is the point at which individual responsibility might be undermined by too much interference over which they differ. Bosanquet and Green give a great deal of emphasis to self-reliance. Improved housing conditions in themselves do not improve moral character. People have to will self-improvement. Whereas Green and Bosanquet took a hard line on Poor Relief because of the possibility of undermining individual character, other Idealists such as Jones and Muirhead were much more sympathetic to its extension. As Muirhead remarked: 'What the State could do was to remove hindrances to the free action of what for lack of a better name moralists call "conscience" – a faculty that might be deadened rather than quickened by a hasty ill-considered collectivism . . .'[56]

THE DEMOCRATIC STATE

The Idealists were cautious enthusiasts of democracy and sought to emphasise that with the added responsibility of political participation came the obligation of society to eliminate gross inequalities which fuelled class antagonisms. Green argued that enfranchisement could not be an end in itself. It was only through citizenship that a person could become truly moral and attain self-respect which is the basis of respect for others.[57] Education and democratic reform had to go hand in hand. Knowledge for the Idealists is power, the capacity for self-realisation through personal development, and hence they put a high premium upon educational reform. Education was freedom from ignorance. The Idealists, particularly Green, Caird, Haldane and Jones, like Matthew Arnold explicitly and fervently linked democratic reforms with the need for educational reform. For Green the great social leveller was education. Idealists maintained that at all levels access to knowledge was a concomitant of the extension of democracy. Only an educated enfranchised electorate could exercise the duties of citizenship responsibly. Enjoyment of the higher pleasures, Green argues, if they are not somehow pertinent to social reform cannot be condoned, 'while the mass of men whom we call our brethren, and whom we declare to be meant with us for eternal destinies, are left without the chance, which only the help of others can gain for them, of making themselves in fact, what in possibility we believe them to be'.[58]

On the broader front education was conceived in the widest possible sense. Like Plato, Aristotle and Hegel the British Idealists believed that the best education a person could have was to be a citizen in a good state. Men and women of integrity set the examples of conduct and virtuous living that were to be put before the ordinary person. In this respect, every place of work was to act as a school of virtue in which, as Henry Jones put it, relations would be moralised as they stood. The state itself was an educational institution charged with teaching only one thing, that is, 'the nature of the good'.[59] Educational opportunities, however, presuppose the material conditions in which individuals can develop the civic virtues requisite for enjoying the benefits and discharging the duties of citizenship.

Freedom and individuality was for most of the Idealists inextricably linked to citizenship, that is, to the idea of self development within a civilised state. Freedom was not therefore associated with the absence of constraints, but with acting in accordance with the higher good, or general will of the community. Freedom is associated with choice, and to act rationally is to make the right choices in conformity with one's higher interests. The existence of poverty, social deprivation and appalling conditions of work were simply incompatible with these ideals. Economics had to be made subordinate to morality, and the state as the sustainer of the moral community had to take an active role providing the conditions in which this transformation could take place.

For the Idealists morality presupposes freedom of choice. Necessity might produce results that could be condemned as wrong, but they could not be immoral if the actor is deprived of the element of choice. The State cannot make men moral, but in the words of Green it can remove the obstacles to self-realisation, or hinder the hindrances as Bosanquet famously put it. For Green and Muirhead social improvement was dependent upon the individual's power of seizing and making the most of external conditions. State action could not be ruled out or ruled in *per se*, but instead had to be judged on its merits. The criterion of state action for Henry Jones, for example, was the contribution that legislation could make to moralising existing social relations.

BEYOND THE STATE

A great deal of contemporary political theory has tried to change the focus of traditional concerns about social justice away from the state and the obligations of the citizen. The question of justice within borders has been extended to justice beyond borders. Any notion of justice and ethics at a global level, whether the subjects are individuals in their relations with each other as members of a common humanity, or whether states are the main bearers of rights and duties, requires some conception of a moral community without which questions of justice and redistribution could have little purchase. This is what Rorty refers to as a sense of solidarity. Walzer has suggested that there is a minimal code of universal morality constituting cross cultural requirements of justice, such as the expectation not to be deceived, treated with gross cruelty or murdered.[60] Walzer in fact posits the idea of an international society which he grounds, not on a natural or a hypothetical contract in a Rawlsian original position, but on ideals and principles that have become commonly accepted by leaders of states and their citizens. This is because he at once wants to endorse difference while subscribing to a 'thin' universalism. This is something like Mervyn Frost's explicitly secular Hegelianism in which he uses Dworkin's idea of settled norms and applies it to international relations. There are, he contends, settled norms among nations relating to the international system of sovereign states and human rights. Such norms are reconciled not by the background theories of natural rights, utilitarianism, nor contractarianism, but instead by the constitutive theory of individuality posited by Hegel. When rights are seen to arise within the context of institutions and practices, and individuals constituted by them, individual rights and state sovereignty are no longer at odds. Individuals within a state are not fully free until the state itself has full recognition within the sovereign society of states.[61] The universalism of both Frost and Walzer is not prior to, but instead a distillation of, the 'thick' morality associated with communities. This is what Walzer calls reiterative universalism because it is at once particularist and pluralist in orientation. This version of universalism is to be found in some aspects of Jewish history. The liberation of oppressed peoples, such as the Israelites, Philistines and Syrians, did not occur with one act of redemption. Instead each has its own experience of liberation under the same God who finds oppression universally deplorable.[62] The main point of reiterative universalism is the acknowledgement that subject to minimal universal constraints there are many different and valuable ways of life that have equal rights to flourish in their respective locations, and deserve equal respect to our own. This is quite different from what he calls covering law universalism. Here we have a universal standard for all of humanity to which all societies must conform if they are to be redeemed. There is one law, one justice, and one conception of the good life.

In answer to the question are universalism and particularlism in ethics incompatible British Hegelians provide the key to reconciling the duties of men and citizens. Morality and the higher ideals of humanity do not preexist in a realm outside the state awaiting apprehension and application. They cannot be forced or contrived and imposed upon an unreceptive world by means of a legal framework. A legal framework may promote a common sympathy, but the sympathy is itself a prerequisite of its success. The British Hegelians maintain that our conception of the good life and of the highest ideals of civilisation are derived from our participation in a community which is itself a partial realisation of these ideals. Our nation provides and sustains for us the standards we project upon humanity. As we have seen the purpose of the state is to enhance human freedom by providing the conditions for self-realisation, and ensuring that all are participators in the common good. The good, cannot be mean, demeaning, sectional, or harmful to anyone with the capacity for a good life. This includes the whole of humanity. Each state may travel a different path, and all seek to emulate the best that they find in the representatives of civilisation they admire most.

Patriotism and humanitarianism are not for the British Hegelian antagonistic principles. The nation or state is the instrument through which we make our contribution to humanity. It is by being a good citizen and ensuring that the state is genuinely committed to its purpose that the way is opened to contribute what is best in the state to the cosmopolitan ideal. Sectional interest and privilege, the causes of external and internal antagonism, will wither away in the face of the patriotism of the good citizen. 'The royal road to peace', Bosanquet suggests, 'is to do right at home, and banish sinister interests and class privileges from the commonwealth.'[63] In general, then, the British Hegelians are suggesting that the cause of humanity is furthered by putting one's own house in order, and this requires moralising the institutions and relations of the state as they stand. The good citizen is at once a patriot and an internationalist.

Patriotism and humanitarianism are for the Idealists not incompatible because what Walzer calls the thick morality of the community gives rise to a thin universalism. In other words humanitarian ideals emanate from communities. In this respect the British Idealists envisage and acknowledge the desirability of a broadening of the ethical community beyond states in which a general will can flourish. The British Hegelians would not want to deny that there is a basis for obligation in international relations, and that this obligation must rest upon the existence of a wider community. Where they differ amongst themselves is not over the question of the possibility of a world community, but over the question of the extent to which it already exists. Even Hegel believed that the shared religious and cultural heritage of states in close proximity gave rise to customary behaviour and agreements, some of which were articulated in international law and which served to constrain states in their relations with each other. When he makes reference to the Germanic peoples he is talking about a states system the members of which 'form a family with respect to the universal principle of their legislation, customs, and culture . . .'[64]

The British Idealists all believed, in their different degrees, that there was the possibility of a General Will developing out of the already existing attempts at international cooperation such as the Empire, or in the relations which Canada, the United States of America and Great Britain enjoy with each other.[65] For these Idealists there is no opposition between the obligations of a citizen and the obligations of the person towards humanity, that is between political right and cosmopolitan right, because it is through the state that we most effectively contribute to the development of higher ideals and the establishment of a general will among nations. It is true that Bradley and Bosanquet were rather pessimistic about the extent to which international law could develop given the lack of an organised moral community in the international sphere, but they did not rule out the state being superseded by a higher organised and more inclusive moral community. Bosanquet argued that any unity of nations must rest upon a common will, and any arrangement that entails the subordination of one to another rests on a relation of force, that is, the imposition of an external law. Such an arrangement is justifiable only in terms of a potential end in which the people attain that level of freedom requisite for choosing to go its own way or to incorporate itself into the larger unity of empire.[66]

Modern communitarians reject idealist metaphysics but retain the distrust of anything like the liberal idea of an unencumbered self. And even if there is a coincidence of values at a very abstract level, in what way can this be said to constitute a moral community which has claims on us as individuals? A resemblance of attributes, whether moral or physical, may be sufficient for the purposes of classification, identifying us as human beings or certain types of human beings, but something more is required to designate something a society or community, a collection of people with which we feel a certain solidarity. Rorty, for example, argues that our sense of solidarity, our sense of being one of us, with its associated beliefs, is historically specific and does not transcend time and institutions. Such beliefs, even when those who hold them are conscious of their contingency, are capable of regulating action, and even of inspiring people to die for them. He denies that a sense of identity centred on humanity as the relevant focus can have the same power to move an individual as solidarity with co-religionists, co-nationals, revolutionary comrades, etc. He argues that 'our sense of solidarity is strongest when those with whom solidarity is expressed are thought of as "one of us", where "us" means something smaller and more local than the human race. That is why "because she is a human being" is a weak, unconvincing explanation of a generous action.'[67]

Much of current international relations normative theory – I have in mind such writers as Chris Brown, Mervyn Frost, Janna Thompson and Andrew Linklater – carry forward the Idealist aspiration of extending the moral community to become more and more inclusive of people we are willing to acknowledge as our neighbours. The Idealist aspiration, however, had its dangers. The Idealists tended to be more like what Walzer calls covering law than reiterative universalists, although they did make concessions to the latter. Their conception of the person as self-determining and free to realise the best self of which he or she is capable precludes many types of society structured on principles of caste, hierarchy, or subordination. Taking the ideas of freedom and individual choice as central to human development, from the vantagepoint of the present, and viewing any impediments to self-realisation as regressive historical tendencies they were able, despite being communitarians, to eschew relativism. But in doing so they were affirming a way of life as right and desirable for world moral progress.

Many of the British Idealists justified imperialism on the grounds that the more civilised nations had a duty to raise the lower nations to the level of being capable of self-government. Ritchie was certainly uncompromising in this respect, but other Idealists such as Muirhead and Bosanquet, and to a lesser extent Jones, come closer to a version of reiterative universalism as described by Walzer. They would all acknowledge universal values, such as independence, individual responsibility, self-determination and freedom as universal values, but at the same time they acknowledge that the implications are particularistic and admit of a plurality of forms. The universal values which emanate from the advanced civilised nations should, they believed, also be realised in those nations where a community or general will had hardly developed, but their realisation could not simply be an imposition. Each of the values and virtues should be developed within the context of the traditions already in existence.

NOTES

1 Bernard Bosanquet, 'Three Lectures on Social Ideals: Lecture 1 – Justice', in *Social and International Ideals*, London, Macmillan, 1917, p. 195. I would like to thank Andrew Vincent for his generous comments on this chapter.
2 Edward Caird, 'The Present State of the Controversy Between Individualism and Socialism', *The British Idealists*, D. Boucher (ed.), Cambridge, Cambridge University Press, 1997, p. 173.
3 Henry Jones, for example, believed that the practical purpose should be broad enough to make the universe an accomplice in the plot. Henry Jones, 'Francis Hutcheson', a discourse delivered in the University of Glasgow on Commemoration Day, 18 April 1906, Glasgow, Maclehose, 1906, p. 20.
4 See A. M. Quinton, 'Absolute Idealism', *Proceedings of the British Academy*, vol. LVII, 1971, pp. 305–6.
5 Henry Jones, 'The Immortality of the Soul in the Poems of Tennyson and Browning', a lecture, London, 1905, p. 32. Jones argues that: 'Except for hypotheses, facts and events would seem to us to stand in no relation of any kind to one another'. Henry Jones, *A Faith That Enquires*, London, Macmillan, 1922, p. 93.
6 Henry Jones, 'The Present Attitude of Reflective Thought Towards Religion', *Hibbert Journal*, vol. 1, 1902–3, p. 233.
7 H. Jones, 'The Nature and Aims of Philosophy', *Mind* N.S., vol. 6, 1893, p. 164.
8 See Jones, 'Mr. Balfour as Sophist', *Hibbert Journal*, vol. III, 1904–5, p. 452; Henry Jones, 'Divine Immanence', *Hibbert Journal*, vol. V, 1906–7, p. 761.
9 Henry Jones, *Working Faith of the Social Reformer*, London, Macmillan, 1910, p. 205.
10 Jones, 'Idealism and Epistemology', p. 292.
11 Edward Caird, 'Metaphysic', *Essays on Literature and Philosophy*, Glasgow, Maclehose, 1892, vol. 2, p. 442.
12 See Andrew Vincent and Raymond Plant, *Philosophy, Politics and Citizenship*, Oxford, Blackwell, 1984, p. 169.
13 David G. Ritchie, *Philosophical Studies*, London, Macmillan, 1905, p. 241.
14 M. Richter, *The Politics of Conscience: T. H. Green and His Age*, London, Weidenfeld and Nicholson, 1964, p. 143.
15 See I. M. Greengarten, *Thomas Hill Green and the Development of Liberal-Democratic Thought*, Toronto, University of Toronto Press, 1981, p. 29.
16 David G. Ritchie, *Natural Rights: A Criticism of Some Ethical and Political Conceptions*, London, Allen and Unwin, 1894, p. 102.
17 Aristotle, *The Poltics*, Stephen Everson (ed.), Cambridge, Cambridge University Press, 1988, 1282^b.
18 These are the terms of reference of O'Neill's, *Towards Justice and Virtue: A Constitutive Account of Practical Reasoning*, Cambridge, Cambridge University Press, 1996.
19 Ritchie, *Natural Rights*, p. 107.
20 Green, *Prolegomena to Ethics*, Oxford, Clarendon Press, 1899, 4th edn, §373, and *Principles of Political Obligation*, London, Longman, 1917, §23.

21 D. G. Ritchie, 'Ethical Democracy: Evolution and Democracy', in *British Idealists*, Boucher (ed.), pp. 81–2.
22 Henry Jones, 'The Social Organism', in *British Idealists*, D. Boucher (ed.), pp. 3 and 25.
23 T. H. Green, *Prolegomena to Ethics*, London, Logmans Green, 1899, 4th edn, sec. 183.
24 F. H. Bradley, *Ethical Studies*, Oxford, Clarendon Press, 1927, 2nd edn, p. 116. Cf. Green, *Prolegomena to Ethics*, sec. 184.
25 Bosanquet, 'Three Lectures on Social Ideals', p. 198.
26 Bosanquet, 'Three Lectures on Social Ideals', p. 229.
27 William Wallace, 'Natural Rights', *Lectures and Essays on Natural Theology and Ethics*, Oxford, Clarendon Press, 1898, p. 289.
28 See Nicholson, *British Idealists*, p. 99.
29 David G. Ritchie, *Natural Rights*, pp. 82–5 and Green, *Principles of Political Obligation*, §9.
30 Green, *Principles of Political Obligation*, §9. Cf. Ritchie, *Natural Rights*, 87.
31 O'Neill, *Towards Justice and Virtue*, p. 29.
32 Bradley, *Ethical Studies*, p. 190.
33 David Gauthier, *Morals By Agreement*, Oxford, Clarendon Press, 1986.
34 O'Neill, *Towards Justice and Virtue*, p. 185.
35 See A. W. Vincent, 'The Poor Law Reports of 1909 and the Social Theory of the Charity Organization Society', *Victorian Studies*, vol. 27, 1984, p. 350.
36 Edward Caird, 'The Nation as an Ethical Ideal', in *Lay Sermons and Addresses*, Glasgow, Maclehose, 1907, p. 110.
37 See William Sweet, 'Was Bosanquet a Hegelian?', *Bulletin of the Hegel Society of Great Britain*, No. 31, Spring/Summer, 1995, p. 42.
38 Bradley, *Ethical Studies*, p. 173.
39 Bernard Bosanquet, 'The Kingdom of God on Earth', in *Science, Philosophy and Other Essays by the late Bernard Bosanquet*, J. H. Muirhead and A. C. Bradley (eds), London, Macmillan, 1927, pp. 121–2.
40 M. J. Sandel, *Liberalism and the Limits of Justice*, Cambridge, Cambridge University Press, 1982, pp. 173, and 179.
41 Michael Walzer, *Thick and Thin*, Notre Dame, Indiana, University of Notre Dame Press, 1994.
42 David Miller, *On Nationality*, Oxford, Oxford University Press, 1995, p. 25.
43 Miller, *On Nationality*, p. 11.
44 Jonathan Wolff, *An Introduction to Political Philosophy*, Oxford, Oxford University Press, p. 200.
45 Bradley, *Ethical Studies*, 'Ideal Morality', ch. VI. Reprinted in *British Idealists*, Boucher (ed.). My account here owes much to Peter Nicolson, *The Political Theory of the British Idealists*, Cambridge, Cambridge University Press, 1990, pp. 33–9.
46 Green, *Prolegomena to Ethics*, sec. 209.
47 Green, *Prolegomena to Ethics*, sec. 377.
48 Green, *Prolegomena to Ethics*, sec. 283.
49 Nicholson, *Political Philosophy of the British Idealists*, pp. 63–4.
50 Green, *Prolegomena to Ethics*, sec. 268. Also see Greengarten, *Thomas Hill Green*, p. 41.
51 Miller. *On Nationality*, p. 73.
52 Cf. what the Laws say to Socrates in Plato's *Crito*, 50A: 'since you have been born and brought up and educated, can you deny, in the first place, that you were our child and servant, both you and your ancestors?'
53 'Philosophy and Modern Life: Professor Jones's final lecture', *Sydney Daily Telegraph*, 29 July, 1908. This lecture concluded the series of six at Sydney, but he delivered a further lecture at Sydney on his way to Melbourne after speaking in Brisbane and Newcastle. The lecture was delivered on 7 August and the theme

was 'Are the Ideals of the Poets and Philosophers more than Dreams'. See 'Idealism Vindicated', and 'Smart but not Sane'. Both articles appeared in *Sydney Morning Herald*, 8 August, 1908, pp. 9 and 13 respectively.

54 J. S. Mackenzie, *Outlines of Social Philosophy*, London, Allen and Unwin, 1918, p. 156–9.

55 Green, *Principles of Political Obligation*, sec. 210.

56 J. H. Muirhead, *Reflections by a Journeyman in Philosophy*, London, Allen and Unwin, 1942, p. 160.

57 See Andrew Vincent and Raymond Plant, *Philosophy, Politics and Citizenship*, Oxford, Blackwell, 1984, p. 1.

58 See, for example, Green, *Prolegomena to Ethics*, sec. 70.

59 Henry Jones, *The Principles of Citizenship*, London, Macmillan, 1919, p. 117. Cf. '. . . the State itself is, in the last resort, an educational institution'. Jones, *Working Faith of the Social Reformer*, p. 58.

60 Michael Walzer, 'Interpretation and Social Criticism', *The Tanner Lectures on Human Values*, vii, S. M. McMurrin (ed.), Salt Lake City, University of Utah Press, 1988, p. 22.

61 Mervyn Frost, *Ethics in International Relations*, Cambridge, Cambridge University Press, 1996.

62 Michael Walzer, 'Nation and Universe', *The Tanner Lectures on Human Values*, xi, G. B. Peterson (ed.), Salt Lake City, University of Utah Press, 1990, p. 513.

63 Bosanquet, 'Wisdom of Naaman's Servants', p. 309. Also see MacCunn, 'Cosmopolitan Duties', p. 160; Caird, 'Nation as an Ethical Ideal', p. 110; and Hetherington and Muirhead, *Social Purpose*, p. 215.

64 Hegel, *Philosophy of Right*, §339.

65 Caird, 'Individualism and Socialism', 28; John Watson, *State in Peace and War*, Glasgow, Maclehose, 1919, pp. 273; and, J. B. Haldane, 'Higher Nationality: A Study in Law and Ethics', in *The Conduct of Life*, London, Murray, 1914, pp. 97–136.

66 Bosanquet, 'Function of the State in Promoting the Unity of Mankind', p. 294.

67 Richard Rorty, *Contingency, Irony and Solidarity*, Cambridge, Cambridge University Press, 1989, p. 191. For a critique of this position see Norman Geras, *Solidarity in the Conversation of Humankind*, London, Verso, 1995.

6   International social justice

Chris Brown

INTRODUCTION

The idea of 'international social justice' is problematic in a number of different ways.[1] As is always the case when justice is under consideration, what ought to be the substantive *content* of principles of international social justice is contestable and fiercely contested, but what is distinctive about discourse at the level of international relations is that the very idea that there is an international 'society' to which principles of social justice might be applied is also contested. To get some idea of what is at stake here, consider the frequently-made distinction between *formal* or *procedural* as opposed to *social* or *distributive* justice. Within a domestic context it is quite possible to argue that the second category ought to be empty – this, for example, is the position of Oakeshottians who argue that '. . . no performance is "just" or "unjust" in respect of being a wish to achieve an imagined satisfaction or in respect of its actual outcome, but only in respect of its relationship to a moral practice understood as a composition of rules'.[2] As will be seen below, some opponents of international distributive justice develop a similar argument, but a more radical position is that of so-called 'realists' who argue not that the category should be empty, but that it does not exist in the first place, that there is no social formation at the international level that has the characteristics of a 'society'.[3] Nor is this simply an argument deployed by moderns – in so far as a continuous tradition of speculation about justice can be said to begin with Plato's *Republic*, it is worth noting that in that dialogue there is virtually nothing said that bears directly on 'international' relations. What this means is that, in principle, any argument about international social justice has to begin by facing a higher level of incredulity about the very existence of the topic than its domestic equivalents are accustomed to face.

Nor is this the only meta-problem faced by international political theorists in their inquiries into international social justice. An even more basic – and unavoidable – problem concerns the very term 'international'. The word itself was coined by Jeremy Bentham in the context of a discussion of 'international law', his replacement for the more traditional 'law of nations'; in this original form it clearly meant 'inter-state' − a confusing substitution since most states are not nations, but useful since for Americans 'inter-state' refers to relations between, say, California and New York (as in Interstate Highways, and the Interstate Commerce Commission). The problem here is not so much whether we are to think of the nation or the state (or, in Plato's case, the *polis*) as the constituent unit of 'international' society, but whether we are to think of our subject matter as being ineradicably composed of separate units at all. 'International' as a term implies that what we are dealing with here is relations between entities which have some kind of privileged ontological status before they enter into relations with each other. This is certainly the way the existing practices of international law and diplomacy sees things, and inter-state bodies such as the United Nations rest on precisely this assumption. However, any serious account of international social justice has to examine this assumption very closely, and insist that those who rely upon it give good reasons for their decision to do so. We might well wish to argue, for example, that humanity as such ought to be given the privileged status international law assigns to states, in which case rather than *international* social justice we should think of *global* social justice, or even, more radically, simply of *social justice* without any qualification, on the principle that, contrary to our normal assumption, it is the application of principles of justice at any level *other* than that of humanity as a whole which requires to be explained. Given these considerations, it might be thought more appropriate for this chapter to be entitled 'Global Social Justice', thereby signalling that the focus is to be upon humanity rather than upon its constituent parts. However, the obvious problem with this is that it would prejudge the issue in the other direction. The key point is that there is no neutral descriptive term here. Any theorist of the 'international' is continually faced with a tension between universalist and particularist readings of his or her subject.[4]

This unavoidable tension shapes the argument of this chapter. In the first part − 'Social Justice in a World of States' − the working assumption will be that humanity is divided into morally relevant political communities, and the focus will be on the kind of rights and duties these communities owe each other, and, in particular, on whether these rights and duties can be given an explicitly 'social' colouring. The second part − 'Global Social Justice' − relaxes this working assumption and explores approaches to international social justice which frame the question in terms of the rights and duties that individuals have to one another by virtue of their common humanity. A final preliminary point should be made: these issues may seem at times to be quite abstract, but in fact the way we understand 'real-world' issues of great significance such as international inequality, human rights, and environmental degradation depends in large part on how we set up these problems, which approach to international social justice we adopt.

SOCIAL JUSTICE IN A WORLD OF STATES

The 'realist' critique of international justice deploys some powerful arguments; none the less, it need not delay us for long, because some of these arguments can be met without too much difficulty, others can be incorporated in a different kind of discourse, while yet others simply act to bring about a closure in ways we are not obliged to accept. The latter is the case with the arguments deployed by 'amoral' realists who simply deny the relevance of any kind of moral argument to international politics, and, indeed, to politics in general, and therefore have no place in their scheme of things for any notion of justice. A paradigmatic figure here might be Thrasymachus in the *Republic* for whom 'justice' was simply a word used to conceal the rule of the powerful; Hitler obviously thought in this way, and the, inaccurate, impression that they also were amoralists could be drawn from some of the less judicious formulations of Morgenthau and other postwar American realists.[5] As Socrates discovered in the *Republic*, there are no compelling arguments that oblige such folk to acknowledge that they are wrong – when Socrates shows what an impoverished view of human potentiality his position entailed, Thrasymachus simply leaves the conversation rather than accept the weakness of his arguments – but equally there is no compelling reason why we should follow them in their extreme moral scepticism. We can simply acknowledge that it is, indeed, sometimes the case that the rich and powerful use the rhetoric of justice to cloak their interests without accepting, as the amoralists would have us believe, that this is the *only* use for such rhetoric, that all talk of justice has this function. Perhaps paradoxically, it is every bit as difficult to believe that all talk of justice is hot air as it is to believe that all talk of justice is in good faith, indeed more so.

A more serious objection is raised by 'prudentialist' realists. They accept that a concern for justice is often expressed in good faith, but worry that, if pursued too enthusiastically, the consequences of this concern could be large-scale international disorder, dysfunctional conflict and violence. This, rather than amoralism, is the position of classical American realists such as Niebuhr, Morgenthau and Kennan; it rests on an Augustinian awareness of the limits of political action in the earthly city, the essential unperfectibility of the human condition. Hedley Bull, the 'English School' theorist of international society – a figure on the margins of realism – was equally clear that order is a more basic value than justice and that if it can only be sustained by means that are palpably unjust, so be it.[6] The problem with this position is that it is not clear why we should accept *as a general rule* that order without justice is preferable to disorder generated by the search for justice; we might agree that this will *sometimes* be the case – but, then again, is this not a statement of the obvious? Only the most obdurate deontologist *actually* believes that justice should be done even if the heavens fall, seductive though that slogan may be. It may only rarely be the case that an injustice will be so extreme that no action taken to remedy it could possibly make things worse –

one thinks of Hitler's extermination programme where, in retrospect we can see that even a bombing campaign directed at the camps and their rail links would have saved lives regardless of how many it took – and equally there may be circumstances where effective action to right an obvious injustice would have disastrous consequences, but, most of the time, the trade-off between order and justice is much less clear cut.

A third realist position gets to the heart of the matter. This is the view that while social justice is indeed a virtue, it is, by definition, a virtue appropriate to societies, and the international system is not, at least not in this sense, a society. It is, instead, composed of separate societies each of which has its own principles of social justice. These principles may not be compatible one with another, and it is a mistake to think that some kind of reconciliation of these different principles is available at the international level. It is at this point that realist thinking as expressed by, for example, Robert Gilpin, shades towards the thought of English School writers such as Bull, international political theorists such as Mervyn Frost and Terry Nardin, and communitarian political theorists such as Michael Walzer.[7] In each case what is on offer is an account of the world in which the right of different societies to assert and defend the ways in which they are different is taken to be primary, and whatever work the idea of international justice can do has to be done within this context. There are clearly two basic issues raised by this position; first, we must ask what reasons can be given for asserting the primacy of a particularist, local, account of justice as opposed to a universal perspective. Second, we must explore what account of international justice, if any, might still be defensible, assuming that the case for particularism can be sustained.

Why should a full account of social justice be restricted to particularistic entities – states, nations, communities or whatever – as opposed to applying at a universal, global level? There are a number of reasons which might be offered here, some rather bad, others more promising. We can exclude immediately the ethno-nationalist position that a group is enjoined to promote its own interests by establishing a justly arranged society – and correspondingly entitled to disregard the interests of others – simply by virtue of common descent. There are (virtually) no ethnonations left in the world today,[8] and even if there were it is difficult to see how common descent on its own could establish any kind of moral reason for particularism. Equally unsatisfactory, and for similar reasons, is the view, associated with John Rawls, that it makes sense to treat societies for certain purposes as self-contained cooperative ventures for mutual advantage, whose members therefore have obligations to each other – as fellow cooperators – that are qualitatively different from those they have to everyone else.[9] This does not work, first because (virtually) no society is self-contained in this way, and, second, because even if they were it is by no means clear why this should necessarily limit the scope of justice in ways that Rawls suggests.

There are, however, two rather more plausible reasons why we might think that a richer, thicker, notion of justice ought to apply at a local rather than a global level. While we certainly should not accept that 'nation-states' are descent groups, we might wish to argue that they are groups of fellow *citizens*, engaged in a political association and developing common projects.[10] This variety of nationalism clearly does not rely upon the fiction of a descent group; it has more in common with the idea of a cooperative venture for mutual advantage, but without relying on an arbitrary curtailment of the international division of labour to produce a self-contained cooperative scheme; instead it rests on political divisions in the world which are not fictional, and which, although ultimately arbitrary in the sense that there are no 'natural' borders, undoubtedly, in some cases, correspond to 'social facts'. Political cooperators in a civic nationalist conception of the state are self-governing and this self-government can entail the citizens of one state developing projects that differ from those developed by the citizens of other states. 'Difference' arises out of the free choices made by particular civic 'nations', and, so the argument goes, these nations are entitled to make such choices and thereby to develop different conceptions of social justice.

Before going further into this it may be helpful to introduce the second plausible defence for particularism which, in effect, generalises the civic nationalism argument. This is the notion that a world of states allows for the existence of plural conceptions of the Good.[11] Whereas the civic nationalism model is tied to notions of self-determination and self-government, this argument contains no such political baggage. Instead the case is made that 'difference' of whatever kind – cultural, religious or whatever – ought to be allowed to flourish, and that only a conception of justice which is explicitly not universal can achieve this aim. Local communities ought to have the right to develop their own conceptions of the good life free from external domination, the 'ought' in this proposition being derived either from a relativism that refuses as a matter of principle to judge the value of different ways of life, or from a pragmatic consciousness that any such judgement will be fallible.

Since the whole of the second half of this paper is, in effect, a critique of these two positions, it seems sensible at this point to move on and ask what kind of notions of justice are appropriate in an international order composed of autonomous states? Realist writers may suggest that there is no concept of justice that is appropriate here, but others believe that there is an international 'society' in the sense that relations between states are norm-governed and not simply the product of power and interest, and thus that some notion of justice is appropriate. Amongst these latter writers, there is a wide consensus that it is formal or procedural justice that is appropriate, while social or distributive justice is not.

This point is elaborated by the foremost of modern, contractarian, theorists of justice, John Rawls; in Rawls' account the principles of social justice are determined by contract under ideal conditions, but *international* justice emerges out of a second contract, made by representatives of justly-constituted societies in a second Original Position, and is characterised by an emphasis on the equal rights of states, self-determination, non-intervention, a right of self-defence, and so on.[12] These are the characteristic rules of international law as it has developed over the last three centuries – the 'settled norms' of the modern international system as described by Mervyn Frost, the basis for the Legalist Paradigm' that Michael Walzer employs in his account of *ius ad bellum*.[13] The general idea in each case is that while we should look for 'just' relations between states in the sense that we should expect states to obey international law and act peacefully towards one another, we should not expect them to act together in pursuit of common projects; for example, we should not expect them to develop schemes for international redistribution between rich and poor – Rawls himself is quite clear that his 'difference' principle for regulating arrangements within a society does not apply as between societies.[14]

Terry Nardin in *Law, Morality and the Relations of States* makes this general point in a very clear way. His account of international society is based on the Oakeshottian distinction between 'enterprise' and 'civil' association, which Nardin renames 'purposive' and 'practical' association respectively. Enterprise/purposive associations are dedicated to the pursuit of the common goals of their members all of whom have actually chosen to co-operate in this activity; at the international level, bodies such as the European Union, or the World Trade Organisation are clearly purposive, the equivalent of clubs whose rules one must follow if one wishes to be a member, but which one is under no obligation to join.[15] In civil/practical association, on the other hand, membership is not optional. All states must abide by the practices of international society, as instanced by conventional international law, if they are to be recognised as states by other states – but the corollary to this involuntary membership is that the nature of practical association rules out the pursuit of any purposes other than that of living in peace and justice. Practical association is the basis for an ethics of coexistence which precludes any common project; it is only the lack of such a project that makes it tolerable for states to be obliged to be part of an international society whose rules they had no hand in shaping – which, of course, is the position of the 'Southern' states who have been obliged to join international society and accept its rules as a precondition for the recognition of their post-decolonisation independence. International society understood as a practical association is based on impartial rules, impartially applied. These rules do not distinguish between rich and poor, powerful and weak – they allow each state to develop its own sense of individuality, its own conception of the Good, but by the same token they stand in the way of the development of any *international* conception of the Good. Thus, on Nardin's account, it was a mistake – perhaps a category error – for the United Nations General Assembly to engage in the project of constructing a New International Economic Order in the 1970s.[16] That this project failed is unsurprising; a project which attempted to reshape the world's economy for the benefit of the poor (or at least of poor states – not quite the same thing), was obviously suitable only for a purposive association and could not be taken on by a practical association without causing considerable strain – as, indeed, it did.

In summary, on this account and that of Rawls, Walzer, Frost and most English School theorists, to behave justly in international relations means to act in accordance with the rules and practices of international society. Social justice – in the sense of a concern not simply for rules but for social outcomes, for the distribution of 'goods' in a society – is not appropriate internationally. For some, this is precisely because it *is* appropriate in domestic society. Individual societies may well be committed to the production of particular social outcomes; part of the reason why international society should not be committed in this way is because, if it was, its activities could easily override local initiatives. The norm of non-intervention, if adhered to, allows poor and weak societies the same kind of ability to develop their own projects as the rich and powerful – but with the corollary that they do so on their own, without a right to demand assistance. Does this mean that all forms of assistance from rich to poor, powerful to weak are ruled out? Clearly not – there is nothing wrong with voluntary forms of aid. Moreover, even within the terms of practical association, there may be reasons why international society should assist its weaker members, namely in order to enable them to be good 'international citizens' – much in the same way that some domestic opponents of distributive justice will support measures which involve redistribution if the aim is, for example, the education of fellow citizens, or even the relief of extreme hardship, rather than the creation of any planned distribution of wealth.

This latter point involves a slight blurring of the distinction between practical and purposive association, or at least of the consequences of this distinction. A not too-dissimilar blurring can be found in the work of some of the younger members of the English School – in particular, Timothy Dunne and Nicholas Wheeler.[17] Their account of international society stresses the way in which the English School has always attempted to steer a middle way between, on the one hand, a realist dismissal of the notion of society, and, on the other, a commitment to universalism. However, they argue that within this middle way there are distinctions to be made between a more 'pluralist' account which comes close to realism in its prescriptions if not in its mode of reasoning, and a more 'solidarist' account which begins to approach universalism in its sensitivity to non-pluralist values. They argue that there is a tension here in the work of Bull between these two approaches, and that in the late 1990s the more solidarist account of international society – which they link to a 'Grotian' tradition of thinking about international relations – may be more relevant than the pluralist.

These thoughts are interesting in so far as they offer the beginnings of a bridge between 'justice in a world of states' and 'global social justice', and they will be returned to briefly in this context in the conclusion to this chapter. However, the basic notion that justice in a world of states will be procedural rather than social stands. If we start from the proposition that individual societies are the basic building blocks of the international order, and that international society is secondary to these primary institutions, then it follows that a full account of social justice is only to be found at the particularistic level, while the international level is likely to offer, at best, a more restrictive sense of just relations. The key question, of course, is whether conventional thinking on international relations is right to take individual societies – states – as primary in this way.

GLOBAL SOCIAL JUSTICE

One of the problems with the thinking outlined in the previous section of this chapter is that a certain amount of sleight of hand is necessary if the principles which might justify assigning moral primacy to the state are to be applied not to ideal-typical political communities but to the actual members of the present system of states. The notion of civic nationalism makes a certain amount of sense when applied to constitutional, 'republican', political systems whose members identify with the polity because they perceive themselves to be engaged with their fellow citizens in a common project. The Scandinavian social democracies might well be cases in point, and it is, indeed, noticeable that while these countries can point to a commendable record of obedience to international law and general international 'good-citizenship', they have been markedly reluctant to take steps which would prejudice their political sovereignty and capacity for self-government.[18] However, the number of such polities in the world is quite small; at best, perhaps a quarter of the members of the United Nations could with some degree of plausibility claim to be this kind of 'civic nation'. What of the remainder? On what moral basis can their claim to sovereignty rest? Perhaps on some other 'conception of the Good', but even a cursory examination of the current world order suggests that quite a number of states are little more than complicated protection rackets – sometimes actually quite simple protection rackets – rather than anything so grand as the expression of a conception of the Good.

These practical objections to a notion of international justice that takes the state as the primary category clearly have some force, but they do not conclusively make the case that cosmopolitan critics of communitarian thought wish to make. Most supporters of the idea of an international society would acknowledge that, in practice, most members of that society do not uphold values that deserve to be upheld, that only a minority of 'actually-existing' states can claim to be civic nationalist or, in some other way, an expression of a way of life. The point is, such supporters value pluralism for its own sake, on the principle that it is good that different ways of being human are explored and good that communities should have the opportunity to determine their own way in the world. The fact that most communities either do not use – or, worse, actively misuse – this opportunity is neither here nor there; the value of international society, a world of states, is that the opportunity is there, which it would not be in a world that was not established on these lines. Supporters of global justice must address this argument; it is not sufficient simply to demonstrate that the practice of the present world order does not live up to the ideals of communitarian theory.

Fortunately, on the other hand, it is not necessary for cosmopolitan thinkers to attack all forms of 'difference' in the name of some kind of bland uniformity – although this is often the charge made against this kind of thought by supporters of diversity and pluralism. The question is not whether a particular form of difference is valuable as such, rather it is whether a particular form of difference ought to be regarded as of such moral significance as to justify its protection in an independent political entity – or, indeed, whether such protection is required. To give a concrete example, many people, and not just the inhabitants of Wales, might think it good that the identity, language and distinctive way of life of the Welsh people be preserved, and for that reason would oppose policies of the British state which would have the effect of undermining this good. The same people might go further, and agree that some kind of self-government in Wales is required if this good is to be preserved – the record of recent English 'Governors-General' lends support to this conclusion. However, and here is the crux of the issue between an essentially global and an essentially international vision of justice, it does not necessarily follow that the protection of Welsh identity requires the creation of a sovereign Welsh state. Perhaps it does, and this is the goal of some Welsh Nationalists – but others look to a world in which the state-form as such is undermined, and the Welsh nation takes its place as one of the many components of a world community composed of communities, a goal which may be compatible with, indeed supportive of, universalist, globalist notions of justice.[19]

A plausible account of global social justice requires of its advocates that they have good reason(s) to think that the appropriate focus of a moral understanding of world politics is humanity taken as a whole rather than the division of humanity stressed by those who prefer to see justice expressed via a world of states. What kind of reasons might these be? As in the previous section it may be helpful to eliminate some candidates for this role. First, the fact that humankind forms a distinct species in a biological sense certainly provides us with a reason for believing in human equality at some fundamental level, but it does not give us a good reason for regarding this equality as something that mandates a cosmopolitan approach to global justice.[20] On similar lines, the fact that contemporary international politics is characterised by quite high levels of global interdependence does not in itself make the case for cosmopolitanism. Both of these arguments involve a shift between an essentially descriptive proposition about the world and a moral evaluation of this proposition; there is no need to get into the wider issue of whether one can derive an 'ought' from an 'is' in order to make the point here that some reason has to be given for this shift. A simple statement of the fact of inter-dependence, or of human equality, will not do.

A paradigmatic example of such a reason is offered by Kant, which is why he is so often taken to be a central figure in cosmopolitan discourse.[21] On Kant's account the human race is united not just by biology but by the moral law. The Categorical Imperative is, as it were, wired into the brains of all thinking beings, and forms the basis upon which 'judgements' of appropriate conduct are made. By applying maxims such as 'act in such a way that your action could be willed to form the basis of a universal law' or 'never treat others solely as means, but rather as ends in themselves',[22] we all possess the intellectual and moral wherewithal to reach the right decision in difficult circumstances, and, particularly to the point in this context, this means to reach the *same* decision. Customs and mores may differ from locality to locality, but the requirements of morality are the same always and everywhere and it is this feature of our make-up that means that notions of justice ultimately must reach beyond the parochial to the universal. In Kant's writings on international relations, and in particular in *Perpetual Peace: a Philosophical Sketch*, this point is made quite specifically.[23] We need to live in a legal, constitutional order – our will to follow the dictates of morality is weak and requires to be buttressed by a political authority – and that order must have three components covering our relations with our fellow citizens (*ius civitas*), the relations of states one with another (*ius gentium*), and 'a constitution based on *cosmopolitan right* in so far as individuals and states, coexisting in an external relationship of mutual influences, may be regarded as citizens of a universal state of mankind (*ius cosmopoliticum*)'.[24]

Kant's specific account of the demands of cosmopolitan right seems quite thin; the third Definitive Article of a Perpetual Peace states that 'Cosmopolitan Right shall be limited to Conditions of Universal Hospitality', glossed as the right of a stranger not to be treated with hostility when he arrives on someone else's territory.[25] However, this is a little misleading; Kant holds that the Moral Law requires of us that we create political orders that he calls 'republics' – constitutional states based on the separation of powers and the rule of law – and republicanism is required for membership of a system of peaceful international relations. What this means is that before the issue of cosmopolitanism is formally raised, it is already the case that many (perhaps most) of the differences we might expect to find between communities have been declared invalid. In the system of international relations that Kant believes we are enjoined to create, human rights will be, in effect, universal because only states that respect civil rights will be eligible for membership.

In any event, later Kantians have expanded the notion of cosmopolitanism beyond simple hospitality. Kant does not address issues of distributive justice directly, but O'Neill takes the requirements of the Categorical Imperative to include a duty to act towards all human beings on the basis of truth, respect and beneficence and sees this as entailing obligations towards the poor that are not limited by considerations of space – assuming we have the ability to do something about it, distant hunger creates obligations as surely as does deprivation closer to hand.[26] The moral significance of political boundaries is strictly limited and the right of states to exclude non-citizens must be highly restricted.[27] Other Kantians have suggested that one of their number, John Rawls, was mistaken in his account of two contracts, described in the first section of this paper. Charles Beitz argues that there can be no reason why Rawls' 'difference principle' – which states that social and economic inequalities are legitimate only if they are arranged to provide the greatest benefit to the least advantaged – should be applied only within discrete societies; on the contrary, because of the unity of the human race under the moral law no such restriction can be allowed.[28]

Although influential, these Kantian arguments are by no means the only basis for a case for global justice. Those who think within the broad church of utilitarianism can also find good reasons for taking a broad view of the requirements of 'justice' – although strict utilitarians are unhappy with the latter term. Certainly, any sense that states or other particularistic entities are the *necessary* building blocks of world order would be contested by utilitarians who subject any such argument to an assessment of its consequences – and if a consequence of the principle of state sovereignty is that avoidable suffering is incurred, a plausible enough inference, then this principle cannot be accepted. Even if a cosmopolitan writer such as Peter Singer is not in a strict sense a 'justice' theorist, others who adopt a broadly consequentialist although not utilitarian viewpoint are producing theories of international justice.[29] Brian Barry is one such; he has published a number of papers on international justice in the past, and his current project, a *Treatise on Social Justice* will move into the international arena in later volumes.[30]

Along with Rawls, and as against O'Neill or Singer, Barry is a contractarian, holding that justice is the product of a particular kind of agreement amongst contractors, but his focus is on 'justice as impartiality', resting heavily on Scanlon's formulation, which assumes the desire for reasonable agreement and asks of any system of rules whether it could be rejected by those so motivated.[31] When it comes to issues of global justice, Barry argues that the rules of the current international order with their emphasis on state-sovereignty should, indeed, be rejected as clearly not impartial in their outcomes; these rules legitimate a world in which there are dramatic inequalities, in which some countries have massive food surpluses while in others millions starve, in which environmental degradation is a fact of life, and in which the blatant exercise of military power by the strong over the weak is a regular occurrence.[32] Given these circumstances, he argues that it would be perverse to suggest that notions of social justice apply only within particular societies and have no purchase on international relations. The practices of international society may involve impartial rules, impartially applied in some formal or procedural sense of impartiality, but it would be absurd to suggest that impartiality in any substantive sense is achieved by these rules. Instead, he argues that the demands of justice in the world today involve dramatic changes in the lifestyle of the peoples of the rich world, the adoption of a form of global basic income and curtailment of the ability of states to employ military force in pursuit of national objectives; such changes could not be achieved in a world in which it was accepted that norms of sovereignty should be applied.

Writers such as Charles Beitz have argued for 'moral' cosmopolitanism, in which institutional change is less important that a change in attitude. Barry is more willing to think in terms of the emergence of a confederal global government. He is not alone in this; utilitarians such as Robert Goodin suggest that the time may be ripe for some such move.[33] Richard Falk's World Order Models Project has always seen this as a possibility, and, more recently, David Held's work on democracy and global order also involves a search for new democratic forms which would operate at a global level.[34] It may be that the time has come for the issue of global institutional reform to shake off the stigma of utopianism which realist writers attached to it in the 1940s and 1950s.

If it is the case that the achievement of global justice does require institutional reform and the emergence of some kind of global government, then the issue of 'difference' with which this section began re-emergences with some force. Consider, for example, the self-governing Wales envisaged above; would this community have the right, say, to prevent outsiders from buying up property in villages in the highly scenic parts of the country, on the grounds that such purchases of holiday homes undermine the way of life of the locals? Most cosmopolitans support a right of 'free movement' and would oppose such restrictions – but it is not clear how meaningful self-government would be in the absence of such elementary powers.[35] This example is relatively low-key – no-one actually needs a holiday home in Wales – but there will be other cases where more important values are at stake. If the example is shifted to the case of the rights of communities of aboriginal bands in Canada, then the possibility that such rights might infringe more serious values becomes real. The ability to prevent the sale of land belonging to the band is one thing, but would such groups have the right to institute non-democratic, patriarchal forms of rule?[36] It quite quickly becomes apparent that global notions of justice have rather more difficulty in coping with 'difference' than was, provisionally, suggested above. Whether or not this is to be held against such notions depends, of course, on how highly the ability to be different is valued, but it cannot be denied that there is, at least potentially, a real issue here.

CONCLUSION: BEYOND THE COSMOPOLITAN–COMMUNITARIAN DIVIDE OR BEYOND 'JUSTICE'?

A case can be made for both viewing justice globally and from the perspective of a world of states; both positions appeal to intuitions about the human condition that are quite widely shared, and that most people are reluctant to abandon. Are there, as it were, intermediary positions which allow us to hang on to at least part of both sets of intuitions? One such position was referred to in the first section of this chapter – the 'solidarist' account of international society offered by Vincent and, more recently, Dunne and Wheeler. This account while still embedded in a 'world of states' approach does pay more than lip-service to the values promoted by globalist cosmopolitans. Another cognate position is to be found in embryo in the later work of John Rawls, and in particular in his aforementioned Amnesty International lecture on 'The Law of Peoples'.

Rawls in this paper reiterates his earlier position that, as between just societies/states, the law of peoples is governed by principles, produced in a second contract, such as non-intervention and non-aggression – the classic proceduralist account of international justice. In such relations, principles such as universal human rights applying cross-nationally would be redundant because rights would be guaranteed separately by each society in so far as its arrangements were constructed justly.[37] What, however, of relations between a society that is just in Rawls' sense and one that is not? Here Rawls makes a distinction which is potentially very important, between states that are simply tyrannies, to whom no duties are owed and with whom relations of justice are, effectively, impossible, and societies which while not 'just' in his, liberal, sense of the term are, none the less, 'well-ordered'. As it happens, his account of a 'well-ordered' society is rather strange – such societies differ from liberal societies because a state religion is allowed, freedom of expression in religious matters curtailed, and representative institutions are not mandated, but other civil rights are maintained[38] – but the general idea is good; it is, indeed, sensible that even within the perspective of justice in a world of states, we make distinctions between different kinds of states. It is right to hold that relations between, say, Britain and Singapore, will be qualitatively different from relations between Britain and Iraq, even if Singapore is not in any full sense a liberal state, neither is it a personal tyranny, and it makes sense to recognise this fact.

However, neither a solidarist account of international society nor a distinction between well-ordered and tyrannical states can actually bridge the conceptual gap between justice in a world of states and global social justice, although, combining the two, a solidarist account of relations between well-ordered societies might come close in practice to what a global approach required. Probably there is no middle way between these two conceptions of the world, or at least no middle way that starts from the desire to produce an account of international/global *justice*. Perhaps the only feasible way of advancing this discussion would be to change the line of approach here, and move away from thinking about relationships in terms of justice, and towards a different kind of ethics. This is too big a topic to address here in any depth, but there are two or three bodies of work which it is worth drawing attention to, as a way of signalling that they may, over time, succeed in changing the agenda.

One such is the small but growing body of literature that approaches international ethics from a post-positivist perspective.[39] The authors here draw on a variety of sources including versions of an 'ethic of care' and of Levinas's ethic of responsibility in order to argue that a concern with justice in the sense of adherence to a system of impartial rules does not exhaust the possibilities of ethical discourse, and may actually undermine our ability to understand 'difference'.[40] On this account, sensitivity to particular cases may be more important than the development of impartial rules and procedures. In 'Human Rights, Rationality and Sentimentality', the American pragmatist philosopher Richard Rorty develops a non-dissimilar line, although one more supportive of the *content* of notions of justice, even if the *form* of conventional arguments about justice is rejected.[41] He resists the idea that rights can be rooted in foundational claims, arguing instead that advocates of universal human rights should promote the way of life associated with adherence to human rights in explicitly cultural terms. The only terms under which the 'human-rights culture' of the West can be defended or promoted are that it creates societies that are less cruel than their alternatives; this promotion can only take place via a 'sentimental education' based on the telling of edifying stories rather than on the elaboration of rules of conduct or principles of justice.

Equally – perhaps more – promising is the neo-Aristotelian approach to these issues typified by the work of Martha Nussbaum. Nussbaum is a classicist by training who has become engaged in work on the ethics of development for the UN University, and in the process has felt it necessary to combat the relativism she perceives to be rampant in much current thinking on the subject. Her approach is to argue that there are certain human capabilities which all societies ought to allow to develop and that this requirement allows us to determine which forms of 'difference' are acceptable, and which are not.[42] The obvious objection to this procedure is that it rests upon an unacceptably essentialist account of human nature; Nussbaum's response is that her universalism rests upon the existence of certain common situations that all human beings must face rather than on Aristotelian biology as such. It remains to be seen whether this defence will stand; if it does, her work offers the prospect of breaking open the debate between cosmopolitans and communitarians outlined above.

The 'critical' theoretical, Habermasian, approaches to international ethics of writers such as Andrew Linklater may also pay dividends by providing cosmopolitan, globalist arguments with supports that are less overtly Western and rationalist than is usually the case.[43] These writers wish to see International Relations contributing to the 'emancipatory project' of critical theory by virtue of its inherited concern with the politics of bounded communities and with issues of inclusion and exclusion. Although unwilling to give priority to the virtue of justice, preferring, as they would put it, to privilege the 'good' rather than the 'right', these critical theorists none the less make space for both proceduralist and distributive notions of justice in their project for moral evolution towards an ever more inclusive sense of community. What is yet to be established is how a concern with justice fits into this wider agenda

It would be a mistake to suggest that any of these latter approaches has yet reached a level of development equivalent to that of the two main lines of the argument discussed in the substantive sections of this paper. None the less the current stalemate in the debate between particularists and globalists is creating a space for new kinds of thinking about international ethics to emerge. It seems quite likely that in the longer run one or other of these newer approaches will establish itself as a viable alternative to the present debate. In the meantime, contestations between cosmopolitans and communitarians will continue; the number of normative issues in which questions of international justice loom large continues to grow, and the importance of these issues is not such that they can be put aside until such time as greater intellectual clarity has been achieved. These issues will not go away – we will have to handle them as best we can with the tools currently available to us, even though we can envisage their replacement in the not too distant future.

NOTES

1 This chapter draws upon, reworks and extends ideas which were first examined in 'International Relations Theory and International Distributive Justice' *Politics*, vol. 16, 1996 and 'Review Article: Theories of International Justice' *British Journal of Political Science*, vol. 27, 1997.

2 Michael Oakeshott *On Human Conduct*, Oxford, Oxford University Press, 1975, p. 69.

3 The paradigmatic 'realists' are usually taken to be, in Britain, E. H. Carr *The Twenty Years Crisis*, London, Macmillan, 1939, in the United States, H. J. Morgenthau *Politics Among Nations*, New York, Knopf, 1948. Ken Booth '75 years on: rewriting the subject's past – reinventing its future', in Booth, Steve Smith and Marysia Zalewski (eds) *International Theory: Positivism and Beyond*, Cambridge, Cambridge University Press, 1996 and A. J. Murray 'The Moral Politics of Hans Morgenthau' *Journal of Politics*, 1996, vol. 58 argue that neither figure actually lives up (or down) to their realist reputation, but it is the reputation that has been influential rather than the more nuanced reality. The distinction between an 'international system' (the term favoured by realists) and an international society is examined in Chris Brown 'International theory and international society: the viability of the middle way?' *Review of International Studies*, vol. 21, 1995.

4 This disagreement is sometimes cast in terms of a debate between 'cosmopolitans' (universalists) and 'communitarians' (particularists). See, for example, Chris Brown *International Relations Theory: New Normative Approaches*, Hemel Hempstead, Harvester Wheatsheaf, 1992; Janna Thompson *Justice and World Order: A Philosophical Inquiry*, London, Routledge, 1992; Molly Cochran 'Cosmopolitanism and Communitarianism in a Post-Cold War World', in Andrew Linklater and John Macmillan (eds) *Boundaries in Question*, London, Pinter Press, 1995; and Andrew

Linklater *Men and Citizens in The Theory of International Relations*, London, Macmillan, 1982 (2nd edn 1990).

5 For a good recent account of why this characterisation is inaccurate see A. J. Murray 'Moral Politics' and 'Reconstructing Realism', Edinburgh, Keele University Press, 1997.

6 See Hedley Bull *The Anarchical Society*, London, Macmillan, 1977, p. 91 and, for a slight softening of the position, *Justice in International Relations: The 1983–4 Hagey Lectures*, Ontario, University of Waterloo, 1984; on the English School, see Timothy Dunne *Inventing International Society*, London, Macmillan, 1998.

7 Robert O. Gilpin 'The Richness of the Tradition of Political Realism', in Robert Keohane (ed.) *Neorealism and Its Critics*, New York, Columbia University Press, 1986; Bull *Anarchical Society*; Mervyn Frost *Ethics in International Relations*, Cambridge, Cambridge University Press, 1996; Terry Nardin *Law, Morality and the Relations of States*, Princeton, Princeton University Press, 1983; Michael Walzer *Just and Unjust Wars*, (2nd edn) New York, Basic Books, 1992; *Spheres of Justice*, Oxford, Martin Robertson, 1983.

8 North and South Korea and Iceland are sometimes suggested as 'genuine' nations in this ethnic sense.

9 John Rawls *A Theory of Justice*, Oxford, Oxford University Press, 1971, p. 4. For a more overtly Hobbesian version of a similar contrast between the obligations we have to fellow contractors and those to non-contractors, see David Gauthier *Morals by Agreement*, Oxford, Clarendon Press, 1986.

10 I take it that the kind of nationalism espoused by David Miller *On Nationality*, Oxford, Oxford University Press, 1995, and Michael Walzer *Spheres of Justice* is essentially of this variety, even if this is not always entirely unambiguous. Although, as a neo-Hegelian, Mervyn Frost does not use nationalist language, his argument bears some similarity to that described here (Frost *Ethics*).

11 This is a view associated with the English School, but given clearest articulation by Terry Nardin *Law, Morality and the Relations of States*, Princeton, NJ, Princeton University Press, 1983.

12 *A Theory of Justice*, pp. 378ff. For reasons of space the standard Rawlsian mechanisms of the 'original position' and the 'veil of ignorance' are here taken as read. In *Political Liberalism*, New York, Columbia University Press, 1993, and, especially, his essay 'The Law of Peoples', in Stephen Shute and Susan Hurley (eds) *On Human Rights: The Oxford Amnesty Lectures*, 1993 New York, Basic Books, 1993, Rawls attempts to rethink some of his ideas on international justice, but without abandoning the basic mechanism of the two contracts. These later works are discussed in the final section of this chapter.

13 Frost *Ethics*, chapter 4. A norm is defined as settled when 'it is generally recognised that any argument denying the norm (or which appears to override the norm) requires special justification' (p. 105). Walzer *Just and Unjust Wars*, p. 58 for the 'Legalist Paradigm' which is based on the existence of a society of states the independent members of which are entitled to territorial integrity and political sovereignty.

14 As will be apparent below, it is not clear that Rawls ought to reach this conclusion given his starting point, but, in any event, he does.

15 In practice it may be quite difficult to avoid being a member of some purposive associations; if, for example, a state wishes to be an active participant in the world economy membership of the WTO and the International Monetary Fund is difficult to avoid. The point is that some – very few, but some – states do not wish so to participate and, crucially, they are not obliged to do so.

16 *Law, Morality*, chapter 10.

17 Nicholas Wheeler 'Pluralist and Solidarist Conceptions of International Society: Bull and Vincent on Humanitarian Intervention' *Millennium*, 1992, vol. 21; Timothy Dunne 'The Social Construction of International Society' *European Journal of International Relations*, vol. 1 1995; Dunne and Wheeler 'Hedley Bull's pluralism of the intellect and solidarism of the will' *International Affairs*, vol. 72, 1996.

18 Norway has refused to join the European Union; Denmark and now Sweden and Finland are members, but have always adopted a sceptical approach towards economic and political union, holding instead the Anglo-Gaullist notion of a Europe of the Nations. It is noteworthy that it is the people of these countries rather than their elites who display this scepticism, which rather reinforces the point about the value of self-government.

19 This example draws on the author's experience of frequent trips to the Department of International Politics at Aberystwyth, and, in particular, on conversations with Richard Wyn Jones, who, however, should not be held responsible for an Englishman's interpretation of his views.

20 As Hegel puts it, '*a Human being counts as such because he is a human being*, not because he is a Jew, Catholic, Protestant, German, Italian, etc. This consciousness, which is the aim of thought, is of infinite importance, and it is inadequate only if it adopts a fixed position – for example, as *cosmopolitanism* – in opposition to the concrete life of the state.' G. W. F. Hegel *Elements of the Philosophy of Right*, trans. H. B. Nisbet, Cambridge, Cambridge University Press, 1991 p. 240 (emphasis in original).

21 See Brown *International Relations Theory*, chapter 2, and, for example, Charles Beitz 'Cosmopolitan ideals and national sentiment' *Journal of Philosophy*, 1983, vol. 80, Onora O'Neill *Faces of Hunger*, London, Allen and Unwin, 1986.

22 These maxims are treated as equivalents by Kant, but the details here need not concern us. See H. J. Paton *The Moral Law: Kant's groundwork of the metaphysics of morals*, London, Hutchinson University Library, 1948.

23 In H. J. Reiss (ed.) *Kant's Political Writings*, trans. H. B. Nisbet, Cambridge, Cambridge University Press, 1970.

24 *Perpetual Peace*, p. 98 (emphasis in original). It is noteworthy that Kant prefers interdependence here ('mutual influences') but not as a sufficient grounding for cosmopolitanism.

25 *Perpetual Peace*, p.106.

26 O'Neill *Faces of Hunger*.

27 Onora O'Neill, 'Justice and Boundaries', in Chris Brown (ed.) *Political Restructuring in Europe: Ethical Perspectives*, London, Routledge, 1994.

28 This is the argument of 'Cosmopolitan ideals', in *Political Theory and International Relations*, Princeton, Princeton University Press, 1979. Beitz makes the same case on the basis of global interdependence, an argument he withdrew in 'Cosmopolitan ideals'.

29 Peter Singer's most famous paper in this area is 'Famine, Affluence and Morality' *Philosophy and Public Affairs*, vol. 1, 1972.

30 For past papers see 'Humanity and Justice in Global Perspective' and 'Justice as Reciprocity', in Brian Barry *Democracy, Power and Justice*, Oxford, Clarendon Press, 1989.

31 Brian Barry, *Justice as Impartiality*, Oxford, Oxford University Press, 1995; Thomas Scanlon 'Contractualism and utilitarianism', in Amartya Sen and Bernard Williams (eds) *Utilitarianism and Beyond*, Cambridge, Cambridge University Press, 1982.

32 These comments are based on a number of unpublished papers as well as the works cited above; I am grateful to Brian Barry for the opportunity to read this material.

33 See, for example, 'Government house utilitarianism', in Robert E. Goodin *Utilitarianism as a Public Philosophy*, Cambridge, Cambridge University Press, 1995, pp. 60–77, where locating 'Government House in UN Plaza' (p. 67) is seen as a potentially desirable strategy, albeit after substantial reform of the UN.

34 Richard Falk *On Humane Governance*, Cambridge, Polity Press, 1995; David Held *Democracy and the Global Order*, Cambridge, Polity Press, 1995.

35 One cosmopolitan who does not support complete free movement is Brian Barry: see 'The quest for consistency: a sceptical view', in Brian Barry and Robert E. Goodin (eds) *Free Movement*, Hemel Hempstead, Harvester, 1992. His reasoning is precisely that given above, that there are impartial reasons to think that free movement taken as an absolute would undermine any community's capacity to pursue projects; however, as the majority of the essays in that collection reveal, most cosmopolitans would disagree in principle, even though they might reach the same result in practice.

36 The many Canadian political theorists who have addressed these issues – including James Tully, Charles Taylor, and Will Kymlicka – characteristically end up caught between a desire to endorse liberal values and an unwillingness to criticise local customs; thus in Kymlicka's *Multicultural Citizenship*, Oxford, Oxford University Press, 1995, the rights of local communities to be different are first asserted and then undermined by the assumption that members of these communities will still possess the rights guaranteed them by the Canadian equivalent of the 'Bill of Rights'.

37 Justly, that is to say in terms of the principles agreed under the Veil of Ignorance in the first Original Position, the first of which is as extensive as possible a system of rights and duties.

38 If these criteria are taken literally, then this is a null category; there are no well-ordered states that are not also liberal. If the criteria are interpreted loosely then one could imagine a society such as Saudi Arabia might qualify – but it is difficult to see why we should privilege religious sources of difference in this way, especially since there are other non-liberal societies which are much less authoritarian, perhaps precisely because they do not rest on a religious conception of the good (Singapore, for example).

39 A good survey, although somewhat polemical in tone, is Jim George 'Realist "Ethics", International Relations and Post-Modernism: Thinking Beyond the Egoism-Anarchy Thematic' *Millennium: Journal of International Studies*, vol. 24, 1995.

40 See David Campbell *Politics Without Principle: Sovereignty, Ethics, and the Narratives of the Gulf War*, Boulder, Lynne Reinner, 1993 and the exchange between Campbell and Daniel Warner 'The Ethical Implications of Otherness', vol. 25, *Millennium*, 1996.

41 In Shute and Hurley *On Human Rights*.

42 See 'Non-Relative Virtues: an Aristotelian Approach', in Martha Nussbaum and Amartya Sen (eds) *The Quality of Life*, Oxford, Clarendon Press, 1993 and 'Human Capabilities, Female Human Beings', in Martha Nussbaum and Jonathan Glover (eds) *Women, Culture and Development*, Oxford, Clarendon Press, 1995.

43 See, for a kind of prospectus here, Andrew Linklater 'The Question of the Next Stage in International Relations Theory' *Millennium*, vol. 21, 1992.

7 Is environmental justice a misnomer?

Andrew Vincent

One key intuition informs this essay, namely, that justice has been, and, by and large still is, focused on the social, political and economic relations that hold between human beings – something that environmentalists would link with anthropocentrism – whereas environmental theory has been critical of the central role of human beings *qua* nature. If justice (in theory and practice) is tied closely to an anthropocentric position, then it cannot rest easily with environmental theory. Before justice can take effect with regard to nature, the human/nature relation needs to be worked out at another level. Justice, as yet, has little or nothing to say on nature. To some this contention may be startlingly obvious, to others it may be mildly therapeutic. To avoid any misunderstanding, this paper neither criticises present justice theory, nor promotes environmental theory. It is *not* a partisan essay. Rather, it is concerned, from a sceptical standpoint, to suggest that the notion of environmental justice may be a misnomer. This essay will, first, briefly review the question whether there is any immediate reason for environmental theory to be concerned with justice; second, it will present an outline of the main elements of environmental theory; it will then turn to the central question as to what theoretical impediments there are within justice theory in dealing with environmental issues.

SHOULD ENVIRONMENTALIST THEORY BE INTERESTED IN JUSTICE?

On one level, one might register immediate doubts about the relation between justice and environmental awareness. It is theoretically feasible to have a pollution free, environmentally friendly society, with a faultless environmental record, which is inegalitarian and unjust. In this reading, there seems to be no necessary relation between justice and the environment. There may, indeed, be a very simple solution to this whole issue. Environmental justice may be simply a non-starter. Justice is bound up with the constraints on politics. It does not apply outside this sphere. This might account for why the bulk of mainstream theorising on justice over the last two decades has found scant place, except tangentially, for the environment issues. This lacuna may, of course, be purely fortuitous and need not imply anything about the ability of justice theory to encompass environmental issues.

On the other hand, it is clear that some theorists and environmental practitioners are concerned with environmental justice. Books are written about the topic. As Peter Wenz notes in his book *Environmental Justice*, 'theories of justice are tested most thoroughly for their comprehensiveness when they are applied to environmental matters'.[1] The lack of attention to 'environmental justice' might, however, still look curious on a very practical level. In the run up to the millennium, if there are two very practical problems which press upon most states, it is the issue of sustaining the global environment (if only on pragmatic self-survival grounds), and second, the question of alleviating global poverty. Some would see these as related issues. Thus, to address the issue of world poverty would go some way to meeting some of the problems of the environment, particularly issues like the destruction of rain forests or agricultural degradation. Poverty is, therefore, seen to have a direct relation to the environment. In this context, justice (particularly distributive justice) would seem to be deeply relevant. In this sense, the issue of environmental justice is of both theoretical and practical interest. Prima facie, there is, therefore, a rudimentary case to be made out for the fact that environmentalists should be concerned about justice. A quick argument résumé would demonstrate something of this point. The argument would go as follows: a society is constituted by human agents. Human agents are subjects of worth, respect and moral considerability. There are certain necessary conditions for any society to exist and flourish. Given that society is constituted by agents, then these necessary conditions are involved in the flourishing of human agency. In short, these conditions have value only and in so far as they provide the groundwork for the well-being and flourishing of human agency. If a healthy and clean environment is one of the conditions (necessary or sufficient) for society and thus human agency, it acquires a derivative value from the significance of human agency. Therefore, if social or distributive justice contributes to conditions for the well-being and flourishing of human agency, in such a way as to, directly or indirectly, improve environmental conditions (by altering for example the economic or social conditions of citizens), then social justice could be said to incorporate, indirectly, environmental concerns.

There are fairly obvious theoretical examples of this more abstract argument. Thus, Marxist commentators might deny that nature has any real independence from political or economic arrangements. At root, capitalistic conditions form the causal nexus within which inequality, poverty and exploitation subsist. Not only does capitalism manipulate, instrumentally, the natural surroundings of human beings, but it is also premised on the exploitation and alienation of human beings themselves. Capitalism fosters an underclass, the attitude of acquisitiveness and both, directly and indirectly, degrade the natural environment. Thus, in sum, environmental

problems are in essence political and economic problems. To rectify environmental problems entails political and economic action. If it is the case that
social justice can address the fundamental political and economic problems,
then it follows that social justice has direct links with environmental concerns.
Although many classical Marxists would be definitely chary of speaking positively of the methods of justice, rights or equality – being more concerned
with emancipation than bourgeois tinkering – they would, none the less, still
see political and economic emancipation as the crucial *precondition* for a clean
environment.

In developmental terms, arguments on population control reveal a similar
basic rationale. There is some division of opinion now, in global environmental debate, as to whether controlling birth-rates directly, or, alternatively, improvement of economic and social conditions (in developing
societies) is the preferred policy. Both views presuppose (particularly the
latter) that it is the social/human conditions which are essential to environmental health. Whilst, for example, there is no acceptable distribution of
burdens and benefits in society, in terms of basic health, education, sanitation,
housing, and the like, there will be little change in population levels and
social conditions. Population growth, in poverty-stricken situations, entails
excessive and unbridled demand for finite natural resources, leading to
heavy burdens on the natural environment – the classic case being the
diminishing rainforests in developing societies. Greater social justice, in this
perspective, would raise incomes, increase expectations, control family size
and eventually moderate poverty. This, in turn, would diminish environmental degradation. Social, economic and political conditions are thus
envisaged as the necessary prerequisite to environmental improvement.
Thus, social justice can incorporate environmental concerns. An environmental theory of justice could also address itself to the division of resources
between the poor and affluent nations. To redistribute wealth from North to
South, via, say, carbon taxes in highly developed industrialised societies,
which would be used for aid programmes, would (so the argument goes) go a
long way to addressing environmental problems. Thus, there is a strong intuition, in some quarters, that environmentalists should be concerned, in some
way, about distributive justice.

ENVIRONMENTAL THEORY

Before focusing more intensively on the relation between the environment and
justice, a brief exegetical account needs to be given on the various dimensions
of environmental theory, in order for the background of the arguments to be
grasped. Environmental theories can be distinguished in terms of pliant
anthropocentric, intermediate axiology and ecocentric theories.[2] Pliant
anthropocentric arguments stress, to varying degrees, the point that human
beings are the criterion of value. The value of nature is thus usually quasi-
instrumental in character, namely, that the natural world, including animals,

has value for humans. It is certainly not the case here that nature is low on the priority of such valuing. In fact, it can, paradoxically, be more intensely valued and preserved more successfully than by many who profess deeply eco-centric values. Nature, though, without humans is still largely valueless. One can go beyond this latter idea into a much harder-edged anthropocentrism, asserting that nature in general can be destroyed, manipulated or polluted, as long as it serves humans. This, however, by definition goes off the scale of environmental thought. One way of accommodating these senses of anthro-pocentrism would be to draw a distinction between deep and pliant anthropo-centrism. Deep anthropocentrism would be the harder-edged variant and pliant anthropocentrism would try to accommodate itself to nature and environmental concerns.[3]

In the ecocentric view, the locus of value is the whole ecosphere (or *Gaia* in some readings). Value here is usually embedded (sometimes intrinsically) in the whole ecosphere. It is not given by humans and therefore it cannot be used instrumentally for human ends. This is the most controversial eco-philosophy wing whose inspiration came, initially, from the North American writer, Aldo Leopold's, *A Sand County Almanac*, and later from the philosopher Arne Naess. For Leopold, a thing is right when it tends to preserve the integrity, stability and beauty of the biotic community. As Leopold stated 'a land ethic changes the role of Homo sapiens from conqueror of the land . . . to plain member and citizen of it'.[4] There is one proviso that should be added to this ecocentric view, and that is the attempt, in some recent ecocentric theory, to transcend ethical and value-based discussion altogether.[5]

In between the pliant anthropocentric and ecocentric components is a broad intermediate category, which can be usefully subdivided into two further tendencies. The formal position of the intermediate view is not to accept either anthropocentrism or ecocentrism. It is committed to environ-mental axiology. The bulk of contemporary environmental *ethics* subsists in this category. The two subtendencies of the intermediate position can be called 'moral extensionism' and 'reluctant holism'. A rough and ready dis-tinction between these subtendencies is that the former leans uncertainly towards pliant anthropocentrism, whereas the latter leans reluctantly toward ecocentrism. The clearest examples of moral extensionism are the various animal liberation and rights arguments of figures like Peter Singer or Tom Regan.[6] This might be subdivided legitimately again between Singer's more consequentialist utilitarian ethics of 'sentientism' and Regan's more deontological right-based approach. Singer, for example, argues that 'sentience' is the real locus of value. Animals are sentient, therefore animals are of value. It follows that non-sentient life does not possess value. We extend value to creatures because we can reasonably see that they possess the faculty of sentience. Thus plants, rocks or rivers are ruled out. As Singer puts it bluntly: 'There is a genuine difficulty in understanding how chopping down a tree can matter to the tree if the tree can feel nothing.'[7] The 'reluctant holism' wing consciously extends arguments concerning value beyond sentience to notions like the biosphere, including plants. Most reluctant holists, like Baird Callicott and Holmes Rolston, are, in other words, prepared to go much further than the moral extensionists in locating value well beyond humans and in some cases even beyond animals. This is the formal defining feature of reluctant holism. Some theorists would contend that 'wholes', like the biotic community, have intrinsic value. This can be called life-centred ethics. Life-centred ethics, broadly, decentres humans and animals, insists upon the inherent worth of all living (biotic) systems, and stresses their systematic interdependence with each other. This position leans well towards holism. However, life-centred ethics still keeps a critical distance from the ecocentric holism of thinkers like Arne Naess, George Sessions and Warwick Fox. Reluctant holists, though keen to extend value well beyond humanity and higher primates, definitely do not want to 'think like mountains'.

If there is one inference which can be drawn from this brief outline sketch of environmental theory, it is that the ontological centrality of human agency is seriously in doubt for the majority of environmental theorists. The thrust of the bulk of the above theories is to extend value beyond human interests.

DIMENSIONS OF JUSTICE

In analysing the relation of justice to environmental concerns two points need to be made: first, concerning the complexity of the term justice; second, that certain areas of justice discussion never engage with environmental issues. This effectively controls the range of any discussion.

The first point to note is that justice is not one thing. The genus justice is usually subdivided between certain species. The most significant species of justice in the twentieth-century literature are distributive and retributive justice. Twentieth-century discussion of distributive (social) justice has been concerned largely with the formal principle 'to each according to his or her due', or, more simply, the fair allocation of burdens and benefits in society (with the important proviso that certain harder-edged procedural theories, like those of Hayek, deny the need of any distributional framework). The fine-tuning of the distributive idea arises with the interpretation of what *is* the more substantive principle which determines 'due'. There are a wide range of such principles and they can broadly be subdivided between desert and non-desert-orientated principles. Desert theory contends that if someone has performed a merit-worthy activity or possesses a valuable quality then they should be rewarded in relation to that activity or quality. In the last few decades, the bulk of attention has fallen to non-desert orientated principles, with some recent exceptions in the literature.[8] The formal claim of non-desert theories is that distribution is justified via an agreement or consensus on a rational procedure, empirical assumption, principle or a pluralistic combination of these, which forms the basis for distributing burdens and benefits. Non-desert principles vary widely. One convenient way of typologising them is to distinguish between two forms of non-desert orientated distributive principles, namely, the rationalist (basically contractarian claims) and the more empiricist claims (like need). The latter is concerned to establish an uncontested empirical ground for distribution.[9] The former is concerned with the conditions in which individuals come to a decision or agreement about the manner of distribution in society. This latter theme has dominated justice literature over the last three decades. The contractarian claims can be further subdivided between what Brian Barry has called 'justice as mutual advantage' and 'justice as impartiality' arguments.[10] In the former, justice is seen as the outcome of a mutual bargaining process among individuals (James Buchanan and David Gauthier). In the latter, justice is seen to be the process and outcome of rational agreement (John Rawls, Brian Barry, Thomas Scanlon).

Second, any discussion that does take the place of justice in relation to the environment tends to focus on distributive justice. Retributive notions never figure. In addition, the contractarianism of David Gauthier or James Buchanan, the rights-based entitlement theories of Nozick and the commutative procedural justice claims of Hayek are alien to environmental interests. There are two key reasons for this. The first is that the ontology of such writers tends to prioritise human interests above all other concerns – this runs against the sceptical more holistic and inclusive ontology of the environmental movement (whether the environmentalist position is defensible I leave to later). Second, theorists like Hayek are quite explicit in thinking that any justice beyond human agents is a category mistake.

Thus, Gauthier's *Morals by Agreement* is underpinned by a hard-edged metaphysics of the human self. For Gauthier, economic man is 'the natural man of our time'.[11] Justice is instrumental to the pursuit of human self-interest. Self-interested agents agree to cooperate for mutual advantage. Only bargains which derive from a fair initial position (minimax relative concessions) will be acceptable to all agents. Voluntary compliance eliminates the need for many costly social institutions. Thus, when Gauthier insists that every individual justifiably engages in 'indefinite appropriation, seeking to subdue more and more of the world to his power', the strong anthropocentric (and anti-environmental) message comes through loudly.[12] No environmental writer could subscribe to Gauthier's strong anthropocentric position, neatly encapsulated in his assertion (paraphrasing David Hume) 'that it is not contrary to reason to prefer the destruction of the world to the scratching of one's finger'.[13]

Friedrich Hayek does not take as fierce an abstracted tone on individualism as Gauthier. He also has no truck with rational choice contractarianism or entitlement theory. However, his first premise, again, is that all social actions must be understood via human agents. The only genuine propositions about society are those reducible to propositions about individual actions and volitions. In Hayek's work, methodological individualism is intimately linked to economic and moral individualism.[14] Injustice is intentional acts of interference or coercion. The outcomes of a market order are neither just nor unjust, since they are not the result of intentional actions.[15] If impersonal market behaviour causes environmental collapse, this is emphatically *not* an issue of justice.[16] Hayek is quite explicit on this point, remarking 'Strictly speaking, only human conduct can be called just or unjust. . . . To apply the term just to circumstances other than human actions or the rules governing them is a category mistake . . . Nature is neither just nor unjust. Though our inveterate habit of interpreting the physical world animistically or anthropomorphically often leads us to such a misuse of words.'[17] It is only where someone *intentionally* destroys the environment that justice might arise and even then it would be considered indirectly under the rubric of property rights.

Another way of conveying the above position is by asking the following question: can we (from a Hayek or Gauthier perspective) be just or unjust to the natural environment? The most straightforward answer is 'no'. The reason is that the environment is *not* something that one can be just or unjust to. One can only be just or unjust to entities worthy of moral consideration. The point can be reformulated in the distinction 'justice for' and, the possible misnomer, 'justice to' the environment. 'Justice for' focuses on justice between human beings which may indirectly benefit the environment. Humans, out of concern for their own self-interest, preference satisfaction, self-realisation or property, might protect or improve the environment. Yet, 'justice to' implies that we *owe* moral consideration to, or, that the environment morally requires, a just response from us – as independently valuable. The Hayekian and Gauthier model of justice theory thus denies the latter, seeing it as a category mistake. Justice is about security of *human* life, liberty and property.

In environmental writings the above accounts are often considered under the rubric of the tragedy of the commons argument. The gist of the argument is that a finite world can only support finite demands for certain resources. In common land, which can only support grazing for a finite number of animals, it is rational (in the above arguments) for each herdsman to keep as many cattle as possible. As Garrett Hardin remarks: 'Each man is locked into a system that compels him to increase . . . without limit – in a world that is limited.' Each is 'pursuing his own interest in a society that believes in the freedom of the commons. Freedom in the commons brings ruin to all'.[18] Thus, 'the individual benefits as an individual . . . though society as a whole, of which he is a part, suffers'.[19] For Hardin, it is a mistake to think that individual freedom can be controlled by appeals to rationality. People come armed to any controversy with variable resources and powers and will use those resources to acquire maximal satisfaction. The only liberty individuals actually have in the commons is 'to bring on universal ruin'.[20] It is thus hardly surprising to find James Buchanan, addressing the environmental degradation caused by the modern motorist in the following terms: '[the motorist's] behaviour produces . . . harm only as a by product of his straightforward utility maximisation, given the choices that confront him . . . in his private capacity through which he must act there may be no means for the individual to influence the behaviour of others. . . . Hence, it remains rational for the individual to do the best that he can under the circumstances. And since this is simultaneously true of all persons . . . the aggregate result is pollution, deterioration in environmental quality.'[21] The upshot of this section is, therefore, to leave to one side the proceduralist theory of Hayek and the contractarianism of Gauthier *et al.* when discussing the environment.

ENVIRONMENTAL JUSTICE?

Having narrowed the focus, the discussion now turns to the more promising area of justice for environmental concern – distributive justice – and the question as to whether there are any fundamental inhibitions to linking distributive justice with environmental theory. The focus will be on some recent 'justice as impartiality' exponents.

Is distributive justice (in the justice as impartiality mode) concerned in any fundamental way with human agency or value theory? Is there a similar anthropocentric moral ontology at work, as in the Hayek and Gauthier positions?[22] For environmental writers, as argued, moral individualism and anthropocentric value theory are envisaged as risky metaphysical theses.[23] They conflict with one of the most cherished views of environmentalism, namely, that humans are integral with nature. Environmental theory thus insists on a more relational understanding of humanity and nature. In the environmental perspective, unless humanity works out its relation to nature, all the speculation in the world about just social and political arrangements will not be worth a bean. Environmental attitudes thus come prior to any consideration of justice (of whatever kind). Environmental collapse is no respecter of persons, liberty or property. In this sense, 'environmental justice' looks like a category mistake, this time from the environmental perspective.

One immediate, if equivocal response, is to note that justice is often described as, first and foremost, a political or institutional virtue. For some it is the *basic* virtue of politics, which forms a presupposition to the existence of society. Some modern impartiality theorists have made much of this point. Justice is not derived from any foundational moral beliefs or self-interested prudence. Thus, if environmental theorists criticise the moral individualism and anthropocentric value theory within some liberal theory and justice arguments (qua Hayek or Gauthier), it has no bearing upon the impartiality theories, since justice is *political* not moral or metaphysical. In other words, the environment argument misfires. Human agency, human valuation and morality are thus *not* crucial for understanding justice. In addition, (and this is important in environmental terms) human agency is not necessarily privileged. There is also no evidence that political justice is necessarily instrumentalist or could not take account of the environment.

However, the term 'politics' here is ambiguous. Rawls' reputation as a thinker and probably his greatest achievement was to separate issues of justice from those of the moral beliefs and personal aspirations of individuals.

His early *A Theory of Justice* offers a viable solution to the problem of uniting a diversity of distinct individuals within a coherent public system of justice. Reasonable individuals, within a veil of ignorance, make decisions which carry them forward to principles of a just order. That is until a swathe of critics asked the questions: what is 'reasonable' and are not certain cultural and moral beliefs built into Rawlsian 'reasonableness'? Further, what of the fact of pluralism within liberal societies? Given peoples' diverse constitutive beliefs and attachments what reason would they have for considering the original position and hypothetical contract?

Rawls, over a number of years, has gradually responded to these points, especially in his *Political Liberalism*, by suggesting he had never advanced any universalist claims concerning justice. He was neither offering a *modus vivendi* (Hobbesian and Gauthierian) thesis, premised on untrammelled rational choice, nor a comprehensive morally-based liberalism. Conversely, he was reading off and examining what reasonable citizens of liberal democratic states tend to value. Practical reason achieves an overlapping consensus through the embeddedness of liberal values, like freedom, tolerance and equality, within the institutions of liberal democratic societies. This overlapping consensus is addressed to the political problem of pluralism. It implies an intuitive consensus on values, like toleration, which are implicit in the comprehensive moral beliefs themselves. Since it is highly unlikely, in a plural liberal society, that consensus on a comprehensive doctrine could be reached, it is necessary to have an overarching prior political agreement on issues like tolerance. This makes political justice, for Rawls, 'free-standing'. To avoid conflict in a democratic society, citizens have good reason to opt for political justice and the contractarian imaginative device. However, the important point is that political justice is still not derived from any comprehensive moral standpoint, but it still provides a clear reason for individuals within various comprehensive standpoints to opt for it. This is clearly offering some comfort to his communitarian critics, where justice takes on a more situated character.

In Brian Barry there is, though, a quite explicit repudiation of this more limited communitarian-inclined notion of 'politics'. For Barry, apart from a few articles after the publication of Rawls' *A Theory of Justice*, 'everything [from Rawls] since then has tended to weaken the theory'. Barry continues to believe in the 'possibility of putting forward a universally valid case in favour of liberal egalitarian principles', which he also considers is what Rawls' *A Theory of Justice* was really about. For Barry, contra the later Rawls and communitarians, mass political culture is 'labile' and there is 'no such thing as a set of underlying values waiting to be discovered'. Deriving any conclusions from such a bogus political culture is 'tendentious'.[24] For Barry, justice must go beyond single societies.

Principles of justice, to Barry, are impartial because they capture a kind of equality which is also embodied in reason. Reasonable agreement, to Barry, (without the trappings of the original position) can suffice. Impartial reason does not evaluate outcomes. It is a second order impartiality which acts as a test to be applied to moral and legal rules.[25] Justice as impartiality is not though a view from nowhere. It can arise from the most earthy ethics imaginable.[26] Thus Barry claims to 'draw upon ordinary beliefs'.[27] Justice as impartiality 'entails that people should not look at things from their point of view alone, but seek to find a basis of agreement that is acceptable from all points of view', namely, putting oneself in another's shoes.[28]

How does politics appear in these various impartialist arguments and is it clearly demarcated from morality? In the earlier Rawls and Barry's work, justice is something which transcends particularistic interests, in fact it appears in universalist apparel. Obviously, this is 'political', in one sense. Yet, politics also doubles-up as 'diverse partial interests' over which justice rises in a universalistic impartial manner (at least in Barry's reading). These partial interests would also include moral beliefs and, as Barry remarks, 'It is . . . a great mistake . . . to suppose that justice as impartiality is intended to constitute a complete, self-sufficient moral system'. Justice as impartiality is *not* designed to tell us how to live. Rather, it addresses how we are to live together with different ideas on how to live.[29] However, this does not mean that justice is apolitical, rather it is the most basic political virtue. Justice, as read through the medium of politics, becomes a rational process of negotiation over private interests, but under implicit moral constraints. This is then a moral conception, but worked out for a specific political subject. Thus, justice is universalistic, relative to morality (or the methods of morality), but constrained by politics. Politics, thus, works on two levels here: first, implying particular interests, which also include moral beliefs; second, it implies the institutions embodying justice which resolve or provide impartial conditions for partial interests to rub along together.

In the later Rawls, justice is again not derived from any comprehensive morality. It refers to particularistic communities or individuals. It is not universalistic – which is the major difference to Barry – although it is particularistically political. Finally, it deals with a pluralism of diverse interests which need some process of agreement to rub along – which is roughly the same as Barry. 'Politics', in this reading (given that we are dealing with justice which is political not metaphysical) is, first, a description of the situated pluralistic interests, second, a situated institutional structure which resolves matters impartially, and, third, the separate comprehensive moral beliefs (although they are, somehow, formed separately outside politics). In both Rawls and Barry, justice is a notion which remains unaffected by the pluralism it regulates. It also bears little or no relation to a politics of power or manipulation (which is the more immediate intuition that many have had about politics) or a politics of group interests in the work of Iris Marion Young or Bill Connolly. It is, oddly, essentially benign. It is also premised on airy 'intuitions' concerning what is latent in democratic culture or, more broadly, everyday perceptions of morality. Yet, it is still separate from morality. Morality seems to refer to comprehensive beliefs which are, once again, articulated outside, or independent of politics, although, at the same time, they constitute the pluralism of one sense of politics and, yet, also act to constrain political justice.

In this utterly baffling scenario of justice, politics and morality, it is hardly a significant criticism of environmental theory to say that it has misfired in its critique of moral beliefs, since justice is purportedly a political virtue. The fact of the matter is that there is little or no clarity *at all* in the distinctions drawn by Rawls and Barry.[30] Nothing significant comes out of this discussion except one point. Those who claim that there are clear distinctions made by theorists like Rawls and Barry between justice, morality and politics need to seriously think again. At most, one could criticise the hypothetical environmentalist for assuming there might be some clarity in justice theory over these issues, which, in fact, there is not.

Moving away from the more negative discussion above, the argument now turns to more substantive points concerning anthropocentrism and value theory. Two key questions occupy this next section of the paper: first, is it the case that justice as impartiality is actually limited to human beings? Second, can environmental theories of value withstand critical scrutiny ?

On the first question: does Rawls, like Hayek or Gauthier, envisage that humans are the only subjects of justice? For Rawls, only moral persons are entitled to equal justice. Moral persons, for Rawls 'are capable of having . . . a conception of their good (as expressed by a rational plan of life); and second they are capable of having . . . a sense of justice, a normally effective desire to apply and to act upon the principles of justice'. Thus, justice is *only* applicable 'to those who have the capacity to take part in and to act in accordance with the public understanding of the initial situation'. Overall, Rawls remarks, 'it does seem that we are not required to give strict justice . . . to creatures lacking this capacity'. Rawls does not think that this gives us licence for cruelty to animals. However, in general, such questions as treatment of animals, 'are outside the scope of the theory of justice, and it does not seem possible to extend the contractarian doctrine so as to include them in a natural way'. Rawls continues that:

> A correct conception of our relations to animals and to nature would depend upon a theory of the natural order and our place in it. One of the tasks of metaphysics is to work out a view of the world which is suited to this purpose; it should identify and systematize the truths decisive for these questions. How far justice as fairness will have to be revised to fit into this larger theory it is impossible to say.[31]

Rawls' answer to the initial question, concerning the anthropocentric focus of justice as impartiality, is, thus, clearly affirmative. However, Barry is much more open to extensionist arguments. Most significantly, for Barry, justice as impartiality gives no special weight to interests and treats them all in the same way – including (with some reservations) ecocentric interests.[32] The impartialist theory, thus, does not necessarily confine itself to human beings. For Barry, there is 'no reason in principle why we could not derive protection for the interests of non-human animals by using the machinery of the original position. All we have to do is to extend its scope to include . . . all sentient beings'. There are differences in species which are inevitable, but once, for example, 'we concede that bears suffer from bear-baiting we have the basis for condemning the practice'.[33] All that needs to be done is to weigh non-human interests to human interests. This emphatically does not entail that one becomes or imagines oneself to be a bear.

The only puzzle here is that justice, for Barry, is a rational agreement the content of which 'should be reached by rational people under conditions that do not allow for bargaining power to be translated into advantage'. Further, 'it is inherent in this conception that there is a distinctively moral motive, namely, the desire to behave in accordance with principles that can be defended in oneself and others in an impartial way'.[34] The fundamental components of this argument are *people* who can *reasonably assess*, make *judgements*, form *motives*, be personally *morally* motivated, and, most significantly, make *agreements*. Kymlicka has noted, on this issue, that if someone is incapable of being a party to an agreement, that certainly should not mean we lack any moral motive for considering their interests. Agreement, within impartiality, creates the same dilemmas that the emphasis on bargaining power produces. Certain individuals will stumble beyond the reach of morality.[35] Kymlicka's solution (which focuses on human beings) is not to look to *agreement*, but rather to respond to *legitimate interests*. If something has a good and can flourish then its interest should be seen as legitimate. Justice is thus about equal consideration of legitimate interests.

As we have seen, Barry does have an answer of sorts to Kymlicka, namely, all that needs to be done is to weigh interests (sentience being the focus of moral considerability). However, how does this square with the fact that *only* humans are involved in all the other elements of Barry's discussion, only humans can make rational assessments, can be morally motivated and, most importantly, make *agreements*. It is all very well saying that impartiality arguments can extend to ecocentric or biotic entities, but what happens, in this scenario, to *agreement* and, more importantly, the idea of *contractarianism*? Surely, once you move to weighing the interests of bears, cockroaches or river systems (not that Kymlicka moves in this direction), ideas on rational agreement and contract go out of the window? Further, what *motive* would one have to do so, given the importance of mutual rational agreement? It is also fairly certain that, for Barry, despite the weighing of interests, in the final analysis, it is humans who do the weighing and it is human interests which are primary in any weighting.[36] The argument which might carry Barry's point forward is the one that agreement is not crucially necessary, since one can in the end coerce. This is a quite legitimate point; however, it is no solution to the trickier theoretical issue of interests in general and is also problematic on the wider relevance of justice to human interests. Thus, in general terms, it is clear that impartiality arguments are also committed, in one form or another, to anthropocentrism, unless, of course, one abandons totally the relation between justice and rational agreement. This does emphatically *not* entail that a theorist could not believe in non-anthropocentrism or intrinsic value *outside* of justice theory. However, *within* justice theory (as it is presently constructed) such theorists appear committed to an anthropocentric agenda. This is not a criticism of any theoretical inadequacy in such theory, rather it is simply a statement of fact which environmentalist should take note of.

It might be wise, for a moment, to move from high theory to consider the actual practice of distributive justice. In this area, it is arguable that distributive justice is, in practice, both unremittingly anthropocentric and possibly inimical to the environment. What distributive justice does, in practice, is to bring more of the dispossessed human beings into the market as consumers. Thus, when developing countries become more prosperous and distribute more fairly, then bicycles will be replaced by cars, more consumption will take place, more energy will be used and further depletion of finite natural resources will occur. In this sense, distributive justice is the handmaiden of further environmental problems. In addition, distributive justice, in practice, is often premised on a background preoccupation with an expanding stock of wealth and continuous economic growth to meet growing expectations. Yet, can such growth be environmentally sustained? Thus, distributive justice might well be in partial conflict with the environmental icon of sustainability. Because of its reliance on economic growth, its relative indifference to what is consumed, distributive justice is as remote from environmental concern as the more market-orientated proceduralism. It might though be replied that there is nothing intrinsically wrong with distributive justice *becoming* interested in what is consumed; however, whether this could be called environmental justice is questionable.[37]

Another difficulty with distributive theory is the fact that the environment, unlike the bulk of justice theory, does not correspond with the 'political' boundaries of states. It might be pleasant to contemplate international justice; however, the relation between domestic law and international law, remains contested. Yet, the environment remains doggedly global. Thinning of the ozone layer is an international issue. Distributive justice (with its more common domestic focus) can make only marginal (if still important) contributions. The argument against this would draw attention to the need for justice across boundaries. Rawls has acknowledged this issue in his Amnesty lectures. He notes, for example, in the beginning of the lecture, that the law of peoples could apply to future generations, the poor and 'what is owed to animals and the rest of nature'. However, this is the first and last reference that we have to 'nature' in the whole lecture. It would have been interesting to have considered how the difference principle might work for the ecosphere. Nearer the end of the lecture Rawls makes a frank admission, that 'there is no reason to think that the principles that apply to domestic justice are also appropriate for regulating inequalities in a society of peoples . . . the basis of the duty of assistance is not some liberal principles of distributive justice. Rather, it is the ideal conception of the society of peoples.'[38] In other words, distributive justice, as we are accustomed to think of it in the domestic sphere, cannot function on a global scale.

Shifting focus to the second main theoretical question of this section: can environmental arguments withstand critical scrutiny? If there is one theme which unites environmental theorists, of most shades, it is that value is not something which can be considered solely in relation to human interests or values. The precise opposite of this would be Gauthier, where values always relate to individual human preferences. Value is 'not something existing as part of the ontological furniture of the universe'. There are, therefore, no objective or intrinsic values. For Gauthier, even the idea of objective value is seen as ontologically queer. Thus a legitimate question would be: don't value arguments presuppose the human valuer? Moral and legal philosophers have largely divided over this issue. Some have focused on human beings, whilst others have adopted forms of extensionism, particularly some deep ecology writers (some of the forms are outlined in the earlier section on environmental theories). John Rodman, for example, has moved (in his terms) beyond extensionism, arguing that anything which has an end (*telos*) is objectively valuable. This objective value is not only characteristic of individual things, but also systems and communities in nature. To see this with any clarity involves, for Rodman, a paradigmatic psychological shift in human consciousness towards an 'ecological sensibility'. Yet, to conceive of a river system's interests is surely to humanise nature? Writers, like Rodman, appear to be illegitimately anthropomorphising nature. Non-anthropocentrism is thus anthropocentrism in a different guise.

There is a tautological sense to this claim, namely, that all human statements are equally human statements, which is true by definition (depending on what is meant by human). Thus, any statement is a human-based and human interest statement. Therefore, a moral statement about nature (even about objective value in nature) is by definition a 'human-based-interest' statement. However, there is another level, in which, whatever the substantive claim I make in a statement, can only refer to the fact that I am, say, a white European male. These latter facets constitute my humanity – humanity without such facets would be an empty shell. This might then translate – which is a point made by a diverse range of critics – into the claim that whatever I might say, would involve implicitly my whiteness, maleness and Eurocentrism. Does this then entail that every statement I make will be racist, sexist and imperialist? The fundamental question critics have to ask themselves is this – does the fact that my humanity forms a basis to my statements about the world entail that none of my statements about the world have any independence or informative content outside the fact of my humanity? Thus, in making a statement about non-anthropocentric value or quantum physics, does the informative and truth-content of this statement entail that this must relate to the fact that I (a human) thought it? What is surely happening here is a conflation by the critic of the trivial tautological fact of my humanity with a more serious substantive point about human instrumentalism and human-moral-centredness, *vis à vis* nature.

Another perspective on this question is to ask what makes us human? One answer is our genetics – which goes down well with sociobiologists. But, are our moral judgements about how we treat our fellow humans simply based upon genetics? One of the perspectives pursued by animal liberationists is that there are moral (non-biological) facets which constitute what we call humanity. It is not humans *per se*, but actual or potential 'persons' of whom we are thinking. Persons are constituted by morally relevant features. Agency is one of these crucial features and, as intermediate 'sentient' environmental theorists remind us, agency is not necessarily linked to genetic human beings.[39] There can thus be *non-human persons*. 'Agency' – including creatures with desires, perception, memory, emotions and a capacity to suffer – transcends *anthropos*. Agency widens the sphere of value outside humans. In this sense, to remark that humanity is a crucial premise, becomes more ambiguous if we translate this into all creatures with actual or potential agency. In sum, critics who claim that non-anthropocentric value is really anthropocentrism in disguise are committing some basic logical fallacies: first, conflating factual tautologies with substantive claims; and, second, assuming what they are trying to prove. Thus, the notion of non-anthropocentrism cannot simply be refuted by the bland assertion that humans are necessary for the making of such statements.

Yet, do intrinsic moral values in nature make sense? To recognise a value surely requires some degree of conscious human awareness, which surely undermines the idea of intrinsic value. Recognition itself of an intrinsic value might also leave one completely indifferent when it comes to action? Thus, does intrinsic moral value provide any reason for actions?

The first point to note is that there are different types of intrinsic moral value argument. There are philosophers who see intrinsic value in objects in the world. Others identify intrinsic value with 'states of affairs' which contribute towards the flourishing of something.[40] Some see intrinsic value as *the* moral trump card, others use it in the sense of a significant description of an entity or state of affairs which might be trumped by, or weighed against, other good reasons. My own understanding refers to the fact that something can be described as having intrinsic moral value if it is an end in itself. Entities which are ends in themselves have interests in sustaining themselves and a good of their own and therefore possess an intrinsic reason for being valued. An entity having a good of its own is morally considerable (again this does not necessarily imply that intrinsic value trumps other reasons, but it does maintain that the reasons for value are internal to the entity). Further, there is no reason why one should not hold that the ecosystem as a whole is intrinsically valuable, at the same time as holding that a human organism might take moral priority in certain circumstances. Trade-offs would be required; there seems nothing insuperably difficult here.

However, is conscious awareness always crucial to having an interest and being valued? Someone in a coma, a human baby, plants and ecosystems have interests in survival and maintaining themselves. Biological entities, in general, have basic concerns – biochemical and self-regulatory systems tied to survival and self-regeneration – which carry on regardless of awareness. Plants and ecosystems heal and maintain themselves and strive, in some way, to remain alive without the additive of direct conscious awareness. Thus, why do we have to add awareness to having an interest? Why this mentalistic partiality? What, in other words, is the argument for *awareness* being essential to *interest*, other than stipulation? What sentience and awareness, in fact, describe are classes or types of interest, not interests *per se*.[41] In sum, interests *per se* and value are not necessarily primarily located with human beings and do not necessarily need human recognition.

Second, does any form of intrinsic value exist? Minimally, the critic must accept one form of intrinsic value, although it does not get us very far. If reason – as Rawls and Barry, amongst others, deploy it – is the basis for the assessment of value, then reason must in some manner be objectively (or non-derivatively) valuable, prior to the assessment. [42] Even subjectivists and sceptics must accept the notion of objectively valuable reason to make their case. It is, thus, a necessary postulate of reason that it must be respected intrinsically. Without the non-derivative value of reason, no value could exist.[43] What is interesting about this argument is that anyone who reasons must accept, logically, that reason is *intrinsically* valuable and that therefore non-derivative independent intrinsic value exists. Whether this persuades anyone that further intrinsic value exists is a moot point.

Third, do intrinsic values provide any reasons for action? The first point to note is that the conferral of value is distinct from the recognition of value. It is a crucial point in the non-anthropocentric argument that values are *recognised*, not *conferred*, by humans. Yet, even recognition of an intrinsic value might leave one completely indifferent. However, even if human interests need to be engaged for recognition of intrinsic value, this does not imply (as argued above), either that human awareness is crucial for the existence of such values or that statements about intrinsic values might not have truth value. Further, if intrinsic value can be defined as that which embodies an internal reason to value, then recognition of intrinsic value would create the ground for action. If moral obligations are dependent upon what there is most reason to do, and some intrinsic values provide strong internal reasons, then there is an internal connection between intrinsic value and obligations. The reason for acting in accordance with intrinsic value would therefore be the recognition of the reasonableness of life-based or intrinsic value. If one, therefore, accepts that something can have a good, independent from the *human* conferral of a good, and then asserts that one can remain indifferent or can deny moral consideration, then one is actually denying any possibility of rational ethical discussion at all, that is, unless there is another body of reasons which might direct one to another action or obligation. In effect, the critic arguing that there are convincing reasons for recognising x (intrinsic value) and performing y (obligation) and, then, saying that there are no grounds to act, is committing a complete self-contradiction.

Before concluding this section on value it is worth remarking that a number of environmental writers do not rely on intrinsic value arguments (or indeed ethics) at all. They argue that the question of how we treat nature moves beyond the question of ethics towards what Rodman called 'ecological sensibility'. As Arne Naess remarks: 'Academically speaking, what I suggest is the supremacy of environmental ontology and realism over environmental ethics as a means of invigorating the environmental movement.'[44] Ethics does not determine our consciousness or our experience, rather the broader our consciousness and experience, the more we are likely to act in an unwitting ethical manner. In a Spinozist ontological vein, Naess notes, 'if your "self" in the wider sense embraces another being, you need no moral exhortation to show care . . . You care for yourself without feeling any moral pressure to do it.'[45] The self is, in effect, seen as a locus of identification and the wider the identification the wider the self.[46] Levels of identification are taken to indicate psychological and ecological maturity. As another deep ecology thinker states, 'the "ultimate norm" is living in . . . a state of being that sustains the widest possible identification'.[47] Wider identification is the means by which one deepens environmental consciousness. The identification is not literal, conversely, the psychological sense of self expands, even though the 'I' remains physically separate. The self is, thus, 'as comprehensive as the totality of its identifications'.[48] In consequence, the diminution of the river, forest or mountain becomes my diminution. Ethical behaviour follows from the level of maturity, in sum, character, of the human self. As John Rodman notes, in his claims for ecological sensibility: 'It is worth asking whether the ceaseless struggle to extend morality and legality may now be more a part of the problem than its solution.'[49] Thus, psychology is seen to take priority over ethics in considering our attitude to the environment. This throws a different light again on the whole argument, which it is impossible to deal with in the present discussion, although it does draw attention to the metaphysical changes envisaged by many in the deep ecology movement.

None of the above arguments are conclusive by any means. However, there is enough force in them to enable us to have doubts about the claims that non-anthropocentrism is simply a veiled anthropocentrism and that intrinsic value makes no sense. In this context, the critical arguments of the non-anthropocentrist, including claims to intrinsic value, even if not decisive, are none the less plausible and might make us pause for thought.

CONCLUSION

Whereas justice theory and practice, in the main, does presuppose the pivotal role of human agency (and thus anthropocentrism), environmental theory is premised on serious misgivings about such agency. Environmental theory retains a diversity of views on the question of value; however, minimally, even the most pliant of environmental theories still sees nature as more than just an instrument of anthropocentric value. The only area of justice theory which is clearly relevant to the environment is distributive justice. Theorists, like Barry, definitely widen the reach of justice and the consideration of interests, although what ultimate effect it has on the overall theory remains unpredictable. Once impartialist theory widens its ambit to biotic communities and ecosystems, then notions like rational agreement and contract begin to look distinctly odd. It is clearly *possible* for justice to widen its ambit, but I would follow Rawls in suggesting that this could only really be achieved by a much larger metaphysical change, or, as some deep ecologists would have it, a paradigmatic change in ecological sensibility. On the other hand, it might be the case that justice has simply *nothing* to do with the environment whatsoever, and to think it does is to commit, as Hayek put it, a category mistake. Indeed, it might be the case that justice is irremediably a human political virtue and will remain so, whilst sensitive environmental issues can be effectively dealt with outside its ambit. My conclusion would be that, at the present moment, it seems reasonable to remain sceptical about the very idea of environmental justice, which is a misnomer waiting upon a metaphysical change.

NOTES

1 Peter S. Wenz, *Environmental Justice*, Albany, State University of New York Press, 1988, p. xii.
2 For an attempt at a more comprehensive typology, see Andrew Vincent, 'The Character of Ecology' *Environmental Politics*, vol. 2, no. 2, 1993, pp. 248–76.
3 Many contemporary environmental writers, like John Rodman, Warwick Fox, Max Oelschlaeger, Richard Sylvan, John Passmore and Robyn Eckersley, subdivide the above pliant anthropocentric concerns into 'conservation' and 'preservationism'. On the one hand, the ethic of conservation entails 'wise use' of nature to prevent reckless exploitation. On the other hand, preservation groups, like the famous North American Sierra Club, have a much stronger sense of the interrelation of humanity and nature, and a wider concern for the whole ecosystem, often expressed in religious and aesthetic terms. Although both are pliant anthropocentrist in orientation, conservation is committed to a slightly stronger anthropocentrism, whereas preservationism is much weaker and more qualified. In preservationism humans are clearly not the only supreme locus of value.
4 Leopold in D. Scherer and T. Attig (eds) *Ethics and the Environment*, New York, Prentice Hall, 1983, p. 7.
5 This will be briefly examined later in the discussion.
6 For a detailed rendering of further subdivisions here, see Vincent, 'Character of Ecology'.
7 Peter Singer, *The Expanding Circle: Ethics and Sociobiology*, Oxford, Oxford University Press, 1983, p. 123.
8 G. Sher *Desert*, Princeton NJ, Princeton University Press, 1987 and W. Sadurski, *Giving Desert its Due*, Dordrecht, D. Reidel, 1985.
9 I am not suggesting that need *is* definitely an empirical claim, but rather that part of its initial appeal and force in argument has been its empirical 'tag' (see ch. 5,

'The Claim of Need and Politics', in Raymond Plant, *Modern Political Thought*, Oxford, Blackwell, 1991).

10 See Brian Barry, *Theories of Justice*, London, Harvester Wheatsheaf, 1989.

11 David Gauthier, 'Morality, Rational Choice, and Semantic Representation: A Reply to my Critics', in *The New Social Contract: Essays on Gauthier*, eds Ellen F. Paul, F.D. Miller, J. Paul and J. Ahrens, Oxford, Blackwell, 1988, pp. 220–1.

12 David Gauthier, *Morals by Agreement*, Oxford, Clarendon Press, 1986, p. 316. For Gauthier, Western societies have discovered how to harness the 'efforts of the individual working for his own good, in the cause of ever increasing benefit', p. 17.

13 Gauthier, *Morals by Agreement*, p. 48. For Gauthier, we might regard such a view as mad but one can be reasonable in one's preferences and mad.

14 Justice is concerned with the formal consistency between a set of general rules. Hayek draws a distinction between teleocratic and catallactic orders. The teleocratic order is directed at a specific purpose, whereas a catallactic order (which for Hayek corresponds to a free liberal society) is a spontaneous order which arises from the diverse activities of individuals. Justice is concerned with facilitating the maximum freedom of human agents to pursue their own personal interests or goods. It maintains the procedural conditions for individual freedom. It is not concerned with fair outcomes. Consequently, there is a direct antagonism to social and or distributive justice.

15 As Hayek notes: 'It has of course to be admitted that the manner in which the benefits and burdens are apportioned by the market mechanism would in many instances have to be regarded as very unjust *if* it were the result of a deliberate allocation to particular people. But this is not the case. Those shares are the outcome of a process the effect of which on particular people was neither intended nor foreseen . . . To demand justice from such a process is clearly absurd, and to single out some people in such a society as entitled to a particular share evidently unjust,' in F. A. Hayek, *Law Legislation and Liberty*, London, Routledge, 1976, vol. 2, p. 65.

16 For Hayek, the principles that generally govern the frameworks of distributive justice arbitrarily reflect the personal interests of individuals. Even if distributive principles could be found, they could not be put into practice in a society 'whose productivity rests on individuals being free to use their knowledge and abilities for their own purposes', in F. A. Hayek, *New Studies in Philosophy, Politics, Economics and the History of Ideas*, London Routledge and Kegan Paul, 1978, p. 140. If individuals were to receive benefits or burdens on the basis of needs or merits then this would also undermine efficiency of the market order. Distribution in the final analysis always implies a plan and individual planners who will attempt to impose their principles coercively upon others. This was the major theme of Hayek's well known *The Road to Serfdom* (1944).

17 Hayek, *Law Legislation and Liberty*, vol. 2 , pp. 31–2.

18 Garrett Hardin 'Tragedy of the Commons', in H. Daly (ed.) *Towards a Steady-State Economy*, San Francisco, Freeman, 1973, p.138.

19 Hardin 'Tragedy of the Commons', p. 138.

20 Hardin 'Tragedy of the Commons', p. 146. Williams Ophuls has also focused on the same point. He comments: 'it is not too much to say that the central problem for all theorizers about politics, at least in the Western tradition, is precisely the tragedy of the commons writ large: how to protect or advance the interests of the whole when men behave or are impelled to behave in a selfish, greedy, and quarrelsome fashion' (Ophuls in Daly (ed.) *Towards a Steady-State Economy*, p. 216).

21 James Buchanan, *Limits of Liberty: Between Anarchy and Leviathan*, Chicago, Chicago University Press, 1975, p. 121.

22 Wenz, in addressing the issue of distributive justice and the environment, in general, notes that 'There has seldom been disagreement in the Western world

over the principles that species membership is a difference that makes a difference, and that non-human species may be manipulated', Wenz, *Environmental Justice*, p. 28.

23 As Freya Mathews notes, atomistic individualism is a cosmology which 'has served as the unquestioned metaphysical framework both for ordinary thinking and for classical science. Its assumptions so saturate our Western way of thinking that they have scarcely been formulated, let alone challenged'. For Mathews it is, in addition, a 'bad cosmology' especially in its representation of nature as indifferent or alien to our interests (Freya Mathews, *The Ecological Self*, London, Routledge, 1991, pp. 10 and 14). Within individualistic metaphysics matter is seen as dead and inert and the individual is separated from nature. Thus, liberalism, as Baird Callicott notes, 'assumes a radical individualism or rank social atomism completely at odds with the relational sense of the self that is consistent with a more fully informed evolutionary and ecological understanding of . . . human nature', in J. Baird Callicott 'What's wrong with the case for moral pluralism', quoted in Robyn Eckersely, *Environmentalism and Political Theory: Towards an Ecocentric Approach*, London, University College of London Press, 1992, pp. 53–4.

24 Brian Barry, *Justice as Impartiality*, Oxford, Clarendon Press, 1995, pp. xi, 3 and 5.

25 Barry, *Justice as Impartiality*, p. 194.

26 Barry, *Justice as Impartiality*, p. 255.

27 Barry, *Theories of Justice*, pp. 8 and 10.

28 Impartiality is, though, a bounded notion to Barry. He remarks, 'there is always some concept available that would carry the moral burden equally well if not better' (Barry, *Theories of Justice*, p. 19).

29 Barry, *Justice as Impartiality*, p. 77.

30 The most likely explanation here is that what we have in Barry and Rawls is a moral philosophy masquerading as a political philosophy.

31 Rawls, *Theory of Justice*, Oxford, Clarendon Press, 1971, pp. 505 and 512.

32 Incorporating in Barry's terms 'inanimate nature and plant life' (Barry, *Justice as Impartiality*, p. 21).

33 Barry, *Theories of Justice*, pp. 204–5.

34 Barry, *Theories of Justice*, pp. 7, 10 and 272.

35 See W. Kymlicka, 'Two Theories of Justice' *Inquiry* 33, 1990.

36 As Robyn Eckersely remarks 'from Hobbes and Locke . . . the notion of human self-realization through domination and transformation of nature persisted as an unquestioned axiom of political inquiry' (Eckersley, *Environmentalism*, op. cit., p. 25).

37 Ironically, (and in reverse of previous points) it is arguable that the Hayekian or Gauthier arguments have more *indirect* purchase on environmental questions than distributive justice. If one considered justice as deriving from rational self-interest and if one believed that environmental health was a benefit to individual self-interest, then, certainly, on grounds of self-interest, some environmental aims could be achieved. Rules will be the outcome of bargaining and attempts by individuals to maximise their interests. This position has an unsophisticated following within the Green movement - the eco-capitalists. Proponents contend that liberal capitalism has the answers to environmental problems through consumer freedom and the free exercise of choice. The environmentalist does not need to move outside the traditional domain of liberal capitalism and self-interest. Capitalism may have been initially part of the environmental problem, but with the help of green capitalists in the future it can be part of the solution. When self-interested consumers begin to demand products that are environmentally friendly, then, capitalism will change. Instead of engaging in either Luddite sentimentalism or stricter state control, environmentalists should carefully distinguish between sustainable

and unsustainable market activity. The former adjusts to recycling, cleaner technologies and alternative energy sources – all generated by the demands of the green consumer. This might be termed 'new age capitalism'. See J. Elkington and T. Burke, *The Green Capitalists*, London, Gollanz, 1989 and D. Pearce, A. Markandya and E. B. Barbier, *Blueprint for a Green Economy*, London, Earthscan, 1989.

38 John Rawls, 'The Law of Peoples', in S. Shute and S. Hurley (eds) *On Human Rights: Oxford Amnesty Lectures*, New York, Basic Books, 1993, pp. 44 and 76.

39 As Richard Sylvan has recently remarked: 'Humans simply happen to supply, presently, prime terrestrial examples of full moral agents . . . The prominent role of competent humans in morality . . . is utterly contingent' (Richard Sylvan and David Bennett, *The Greening of Ethics: from Human Chauvinism to Deep Green Theory*, Cambridge, The White Horse Press, 1994, p. 14).

40 See Holmes Rolston III, *Environmental Ethics: Duties to and Values in the Natural World*, Philadephia, Temple University Press, 1988; Robin Attfield, *The Ethics of Environmental Concern*, Oxford, Blackwell, 1983 and *A Theory of Value and Obligation*, London and New York, Croom Helm, 1987.

41 As Kenneth Goodpaster remarks: 'nothing short of being alive seems to me to be a plausible and non arbitrary criterion [of value]' (Goodpaster, 'On Being Morally Considerable' *The Journal of Philosophy*, 75, 1978, p. 310). This particular argument is now associated with 'life-based' ethics.

42 This argument is adapted from Stephen R. L. Clark's 'Gaia and the Forms of Life', in Robert Elliot and Arran Gare (eds) *Environmental Philosophy: A Collection of Readings*, Milton Keynes, Open University Press, 1983.

43 One could add here that reason, *per se*, is sustained by the natural environment and is dependent upon it for flourishing. Thus, if reason is respected non-derivatively (or intrinsically), and the environment sustains the use of reason, it follows that the environment must also be respected intrinsically. To not respect the environment is to act against reason and is thus self-contradictory. If reason directs one to the sustenance of a natural environment (which is its essential presupposition and condition of reason's flourishing) then there are good reasons for obligatory action premised upon intrinsic value.

44 A. Naess, 'Self-Realization: An Ecological Approach to Being in the World' *The Trumpeter* 4, 1987, p. 40.

45 Naess, 'Self-Realization', p. 39.

46 Arne Naess, 'The Shallow and the Deep, Long-Range Ecology Movement: A Summary' *Inquiry*, 16, 1973, pp. 263–4.

47 Warwick Fox, *Approaching Deep Ecology: A Response to Richard Sylvan's Critique of Deep Ecology*, Hobart, University of Tasmania, 1986, p. 57

48 Arne Naess, *Ecology, Community and Lifestyle: An Outline of an Ecosophy*, Cambridge, Cambridge University Press, 1989, p. 261.

49 John Rodman, 'The Liberation of Nature' *Inquiry*, 20, 1977, pp. 103–4.

8 Democracy, rights and distributive economic justice

Rex Martin

The chapter has three main sections. The first section is concerned with sketching the idea of a democratic system of rights. The second turns, then, to constructing an idea of economic justice suitable to such a system. The chapter concludes, in its final section, with a brief reflection on and assessment of the general line of argument taken.

I BASIC RIGHTS IN A DEMOCRATIC SYSTEM

A simple idea underlies the notion of a democratic system of rights: the idea that the respective justifications of its two main elements – civil rights and democratic political institutions–stem from the same source. I want to begin by developing this idea in brief compass.

Active civil rights are ways of acting, or ways of being treated, that are specifically recognised and affirmed in law for each and all the citizens within a given political society and are actively promoted.

The background supposition here is that all rights are, in some way, beneficial to the rightholder. Thus, all proper civil rights (all universal political rights within a given society), if true to this supposition of benefit, should identify specific ways of acting, or of being treated, that are of benefit to each and all of the citizens. For these claimed ways of acting or of being treated are, arguably, part of the 'good' of each one of them, or instrumental to it.

Where this requirement (of mutual and general benefit) holds good in a given case, then, what is, legally speaking, a civil right actually is a way of acting (or of being treated) that is correctly understood to be in everybody's interest. And the right here is said to be justified on that very basis.

Active civil rights, as a special case of legal rights, require an agency to formulate and maintain and harmonise them. More specifically, they require an agency to identify and establish ways of acting, or ways of being treated, that can reasonably be supposed to be in everyone's interest. It could be argued that democratic institutions – universal franchise (on a one person, one vote basis), contested voting and majority rule – can effectively perform this job and thus provide the setting required by civil rights. For, it could be claimed that democratic procedures are a stable and relatively reliable way of identifying, and then implementing, laws and policies that serve interests common to the voters or to a large number of them, presumably at least a majority.

We can see, though, that the claim just made is problematic. For it is deeply ambiguous; it covers a number of quite distinct, even disparate, options. Thus, the claim could be read as covering and emphasising (i) those policies and laws that are in the interest of each and all or, alternatively, as covering and emphasising (ii) those policies and laws concerned, for example, with national defence or the growth of Gross National Product (GNP), that is, concerned with things that are in the corporate or collective interests of the group of which each is a member (though not necessarily in the interests of each person there) or, finally, as covering and emphasising (iii) those policies and laws that are in the interests of a large group of people (presumably a majority) though not in the interests of some others (presumably a minority). Indeed, these majority interests might even be detrimental to the interests of a given minority.

Most likely, we do not want to eliminate any of these options from our list of democratic goods altogether. The best solution, then, might be to try to rank them in some definite order. This ranking, if it could successfully be achieved, would thereby become *part* of the very justification for having and relying on democratic institutions. But if we cannot establish a plausible ranking, then we (as democrats or as citizens of a properly ordered democratic state) are stuck with unrestricted majority rule, and with whatever threat it might pose to the rights of each and all.

I think that an ordering would, in fact, emerge as we reflected on these options (while keeping in mind that further one, of unrestricted majority rule). Here it would be decided, I am suggesting, that policies or laws should conform to a definite schedule of priorities. In sum, the ordering of permissible options, put in terms of the interests involved, would be (i) the interests of each and all over (ii) the good of the corporate whole and either or both of these over (iii) a mere majority interest. And a mere majority interest would have to be understood in a very definite way – as limited to those policies and laws that concern interests the helping or hurting of which is compatible with serving interests under either of the first two considerations. For the notion of democratic goods does not include any interest of the majority that harms rather than serves such *vital* interests of a minority.

The upshot of my argument is that the setting required by civil rights can be provided by democratic majority-rule government. Democracy, in its turn, needs a suitable justification and this, I have suggested, can best be provided by giving preference to policies that serve the interests of each and all and by avoiding policies that override these interests. And such a preference would include, as a proper subset, universal political (or civil) rights.

What were initially two quite independent elements – civil rights and democratic procedures – have been systematically brought together and connected to one another, by argument. Our two key notions (accredited civil rights – of individual persons – and justified democratic government) are mutually supportive of one another. Thus, they can form the central under-girding of a distinctive political system, one in which civil rights are accorded priority. This priority does not arise from the idea of universal rights, as one might have initially supposed, but, rather, from the idea of democratic insti-tutions, as suitably justified. Perhaps, it would be clearer, though, to say that this priority arises from the connection and grounding of each of the two key elements in the same justificatory pattern, in the idea of mutual and general benefit.

Before we leave this brief account, an important background feature of the argument must be noted. The relation between the non-defective operation of democratic institutions, on the one hand, and the production of civil rights laws, on the other, is at best only probabilistic. We have merely identified a tendency here. There are other relevant considerations we could cite as well. For example, the possibility of cyclical majorities, the distortions introduced by strategic voting, the problem of constructing a 'general good' or common interest out of the perceived interests of the various individuals involved.

Thus, we will never be in a position to say that literally all civil rights laws actually are in the interest of each and everyone. But we do have adequate evidence for saying that well-accredited civil rights are in that interest. Or, at least, the likelihood is quite high that they will be. For well-accredited civil rights are rights that have passed the test of being proposed and often reconfirmed by legislative majorities and of being affirmed and, then, sup-ported, often over many years, by the other major political institutions in that society. And they are rights that have survived the scrutiny of time and experience and public discussion; they have been winnowed by the self-correcting character of the democratic process.

Well-accredited civil rights, assuming here that a highly concurrent favourable social opinion exists in their case and that convincing reasons (with wide appeal) can be offered on their behalf, are the paradigms, the exemplars of rights justifiable on the standard of general and mutual benefit. They have a peculiar title, then, to be regarded as basic rights in a democratic system of rights.

This particular conception of basic rights as well-accredited (or, in the usual case, as long established) may be the only one fully compatible with the idea of justified democratic majority rule and, hence, the only kind of basic right we can reasonably expect to flourish in a democratic system of civil rights. And given the mutually supportive character of our two key notions – civil rights and democratic government – such basic rights, like the democratic institutions themselves, will be among the institutional essentials in a democratic system of rights.

In a society modelled on such a system, well-accredited civil rights (as basic or constitutional matters) would enjoy a presumptive priority even over those justified civil rights that are not themselves similarly established or that are not yet supported by a strong social consensus. Thus, in American law (to cite one example), the right to freedom of political speech or of the press might trump a right to privacy which, absent these rights, would normally prevail. Such basic rights (as those of speech or press), at least in central cases, are not to be superseded or significantly impaired by these lesser rights or by other normative considerations (such as national security or GNP or aggregate net welfare). And certainly not by *mere* majority interests.

II DISTRIBUTIVE ECONOMIC JUSTICE

I want next to direct attention to the place of social justice within a democratic system of rights. This is an issue that has not, up to now, been effectively dealt with within the frame of this particular set of ideas.

Let us begin with a straightforward claim. Many issues of justice are captured, more or less adequately, through an analysis of the rights (in particular, the basic rights) involved. But it appears that not all issues of justice can be handled in this way. For example, standard defences of affirmative action (as it is called in the USA) are characteristically put in terms of justice – in terms of compensatory justice or of distributive justice. But, arguably, a policy of affirmative action, even when justified on such grounds, does not reduce to a question of basic rights. Why not?

For one thing such policies are understood to be temporary in nature. More important, they are not ways of being acted toward that are a means to (or parts of) the good of *each and all*. Rather, they are policies that benefit some individuals (members of some groups) but do not, unlike basic rights, benefit all individual citizens.

The issue then is whether economic justice fits this particular pattern: where it is understood to be a matter of justice, but not one readily resolvable into a question of basic rights. In order to focus discussion here let us put one well-known contemporary theory of economic justice, that of John Rawls, under the magnifying glass.

Rawls claims that inequalities among persons stem in important ways from differences in people's natural endowments and in their initial social circumstances. He claims as well that in a just or well-ordered society resultant inequalities in positions and in income and wealth can be allowed – indeed, should be allowed – subject to certain conditions. One of these conditions is that the basic political and social and economic arrangements are such that goods and services are so distributed as to improve over time the level of income and wealth of the various income groups involved. A society that met this standard would be 'thoroughly just' in Rawls' view. But to be 'perfectly just', it would also have to *maximise* the level of income and wealth of the least well-off group in particular.

This last point is not intended to identify a benefit for everyone but only for those in the bottom group. Moreover, the distributive effects enjoined by the overall operation of this principle (often called the maximin principle) are not the same for everyone; they are not even the same for everyone in the target group, the bottom one-fifth, say. The relevant effects here, rather, are the effects on a 'representative' person within that target group; they are effects on an ideal-type *average* individual in the bottom group.

Unlike the case with basic rights, then, the benefits required by economic justice cannot be reduced to a *rule* which specifies an identical way of acting or of being treated and proclaims that way as an equal matter for everyone. (Or, at least, it cannot be reduced to such a rule for everyone *if* their incomes were above a certain level.) The guarantee of a minimum income level can attach over a given period only to some. And over a lifetime only some – but not likely each and everyone – can have the benefit of this guarantee.

Such restricted beneficial effects are not appropriate to basic rights, Rawls believes. He concludes, then, that the result required by his principle of distributive economic justice – in particular, in its maximising version – is not, properly speaking, itself a basic right.

Another point is worth making here as well. It could be argued that, even if the result required by 'perfect' Rawlsian economic justice *could* be a basic right, it is not *in fact* one in Great Britain or in the rest of Europe or in the United States. Now, granted, in many European countries (for example, Denmark or Sweden) there is an extensive 'safety net' or social minimum in place, concerning such matters as health care, public schooling, housing, unemployment and retirement income. My point, though, is that this social minimum does not conform to the requirements of Rawls' maximising principle; for it does not typically pitch things at that high a level. Hence, it is fair to say that the maximin standard is not recognised and maintained in any of these places as a basic right.

Indeed, it could be further argued (as Rawls himself does) that the required result *should* not, given the precise character of the American political system, be recognised and maintained there as a basic constitutional right; instead, the required result should properly be a legitimate object of legislative policy but *not* a feature of the fundamental constitution itself. Rawls' reason for saying that the maximin principle should not be incorporated as a feature of the text (or of the understood text) of the US Constitution is that he does not want that principle to become an object of interpretation by American courts. Rather, he wants the basic determinations and principal implementations of policy to remain within the province of the legislature (in this case, of the US Congress).[1] The debate is by no means closed on this matter, but I think enough has been said to suggest that distributive economic justice (at least as Rawls conceived things) may not be a matter of basic rights at all.

Let me add another consideration here. It concerns a point of procedure in normative political theory. Let us, to focus attention, imagine a difficult philosophical issue. Say, whether speech merely as discourse (as distinct from immediate incitement) can ever be harmful, or at least harmful in such a way or to such a degree as to justifiably require its restriction or even its prohibition. German law provides an instance of such a case in its prohibition of mere speech that denies the Holocaust. When one is confronted with such a question (as the one this German law raises), I think it a good rule of procedure to *assume* the more difficult case. And then to conduct one's arguments, at least initially, on *that* ground. In the example under discussion, we would begin by assuming that mere discourse could sometimes be significantly harmful. The point, presumably, would then be (if one is an advocate of freedom of speech and the press) to argue that such speech none the less ought to be legally protected as Dworkin, for instance, has recently argued respecting the German law cited earlier.[2]

For, clearly, if mere speech were *never* harmful, then the case against ever prohibiting it by law could fairly easily be made out.

We should follow a similar line of reasoning in the issue we are presently concerned with in this chapter, distributive economic justice. Here we would assume that some important matters of justice *cannot* be reduced simply to matters of basic rights. For if the easier case were assumed (that all matters of justice are matters of rights) then we'd have relatively little problem in squaring distributive economic justice with basic rights *per se*.[3]

Accordingly, if distributive economic justice is to be fitted into our account of a democratic system of rights, we should begin (as a matter of sound philosophical procedure) by assuming the harder case. We should begin by assuming, if only for the sake of argument, that it is not itself a matter of basic rights. And we must try to fit it into our account of a democratic system of rights on some other basis.

Let me suggest how it might be accommodated there on some such basis. In our previous account of a democratic system of rights two quite distinct elements – civil rights and democratic procedures – were brought together and connected to one another, by argument. This particular systematic connection was underwritten by the intrinsic affinity each element exhibited (under analysis) for the other, based on their shared justification by the standard of mutual and general benefit. By the same token, if distributive economic justice could itself be shown to be a matter of *everyone's* benefit – or, at least, of every income group's benefit – then it might plausibly come within that same orbit.

Thus, distributive economic justice might enter the political space appropriate to a democratic system of rights on this very basis. In being concordant with the notion of mutual and general benefit, distributive economic justice shares an important feature with the main elements of that system – with basic rights and democratic political institutions, as justified.

The question is whether this particular notion of distributive economic justice is one that could gain wide acceptance or whether it is, on the contrary, simply one person's idea (say, Rawls' or mine). I think this notion could command a surprisingly wide assent; it is deeply rooted in existing theory. There is in effect already a consensus about economic justice. For we can point to a single, common, underlying idea of economic justice (or, better, to an element within that idea) which can be found in Locke, in Adam Smith, in Marx and in much recent contractarian theory – in Rawls, as I've already indicated, but also in Gauthier and in Nozick, if we count Nozick as a contractarian of sorts, though more Hobbesian than Lockean in certain respects.

The root idea here is that the arrangement of economic institutions requires, if it is to be just, that all contributors benefit or, at least, that none are to be left worse off. Thus, the root idea requires that if some individuals (say, those in the top 20 per cent) improve their standard of living (measured in terms of real income and wealth), others should do so as well; no group, not even those least well-off (say, those in the bottom 20 per cent), should be left behind. All should continually improve their lot in life together. None at least are to be left worse off.

Of course, important differences come in the way each thinker embeds this root idea in an overall theory. Locke puts it in a state of nature, and thus within the context of a theory of natural rights; Smith lodges it in an open and competitive market and then puts that ultimately within the confines of a rather utilitarian scheme of justification; and Marx embeds it in a system of proper social ownership of the means of production and that, in turn, is set within his theory of historical materialism. I've already indicated that the root idea is also one we can plausibly ascribe to Rawls. For he seems committed to the principle that every income group is to benefit or, at least, none is allowed to become worse off. Indeed, Rawls says this, quite explicitly, at a number of points.[4]

To sum up. I've made a quick but plausible case, ultimately on inductive grounds, for saying that there is a root idea of distributive economic justice. This root idea can be stated, in simplest terms, as 'every income group benefits or, at least, none is to become worse off'. And I've suggested that this root idea is not in any way idiosyncratic; for it has, historically, been supported on natural rights, utilitarian, Marxist, and contractarian grounds. Finally, I've suggested that mutual and general benefit (an idea central to the theme of justification within a democratic system of rights) can plausibly be regarded as similar, in important respects, to this root idea and, thus, with the idea of economic justice, historically conceived. Given this connection, we have a presumptive case for making the issue of justice so conceived a matter of public political policy in a democratic system of rights.

Let us next try to determine what might be a likely shape for policies of economic justice to take in such a system. The root idea (that every wage-earning group benefits, over time) will, of course, be present. Thus, people in a given democratic society are justified in moving from one set of economic arrangements to another (say, to a new tax law and attendant scheme of expenditures) if all income groups benefit (or at least none are left worse off). This idea, when carefully stated, becomes the principle of (Pareto) efficiency.[5] Often, though, several such efficient arrangements are feasible, given a single determinate starting point. What then?

In such an event, that arrangement (among those available) which minimises the difference in income between the top-most and the least well-off

group should be selected and implemented. This constraint at least seems a
plausible one to add here – that is, in the context of a democratic system of
rights. For it has the merit of recommending the selection of that one alternative which minimises the necessary inequality required to be imposed, consistent with satisfaction of the root idea that every group is to be benefited.

Thus, an 'everybody benefits' or efficiency principle constrained by some
form of egalitarianism emerges as a likely, perhaps even the preferable,
account of distributive economic justice when seen from the perspective of
contemporary democratic theory (as given in the account of a democratic
system of rights). For the root idea of economic justice – (i) that every group
is to benefit – as constrained (ii) by a reasonably vigorous egalitarianism
would appeal, in *each* of these crucial emphases, to values already central to
the idea of a democratic system of rights. Hence, it could suitably direct
democratic decision making there.

My guiding intuition throughout this section of my chapter has been that
setting the root idea of economic justice within a democratic framework
should yield a distinctive principle of economic justice, one that is peculiarly
appropriate to elements within that framework. What counts in a democratic
system of rights is what is compatible, in particular what is integral, with the
leading ideas of that system. Accordingly, I have tried to show that it would
make good sense to incorporate an efficiency-cum-egalitarian theory of distributive economic justice into the theory of democracy, to set this theory
within the justifying network that connects basic rights and the democratic
political institutions.

Now, as we have already noted throughout, economic justice (historically
conceived) is an aggregative notion and best attaches to groups; moreover,
such justice, even with the so-called egalitarian constraint, exhibits no real
commitment to the strict equality of all citizens. For it does not require that
economic benefits or offices of ownership be identically or even substantially
the same for each and every citizen (except, perhaps, at some minimum
level).[6] Thus, on this understanding, the conception of economic justice I've
recommended is, in important respects, *unlike* the case with basic rights.

Accordingly, the demands of this particular conception of economic justice
will probably not count as among the institutional essentials of a democratic
system of rights nor be accorded the highest priority there. For economic
justice, as here conceived, is neither a basic right nor a corporate good (such
as one finds, for example, in providing for a suitable level of gross national
product [GNP]). Even so, the claims of economic justice should have a
reasonably high profile in such a system (given the close kinship of the root
idea of economic justice with the formative notion of mutual and general
benefit, the notion which does in fact justify the institutional essentials in
that system).

Here, then, appropriate political policies that are themselves democratically developed would have to be designed to achieve such justice.
These policies would be, if properly constructed, policies that made every

income group better off (or at least none worse off) over some reasonably determinate period of time, subject (of course) to the egalitarian constraint. And the policies we are interested in would have to be policies that when properly constructed did not supersede or violate existing basic rights in the particular country in question. Or at least these are the main results I have argued for.

The various norms I have emphasised in this brief summary are norms appropriate to distributive economic justice when conceived within the framework of a democratic system of rights. Achieving economic justice, in this manner, is part of the democratic project. It is part of the project of identifying and then implementing policies that serve interests common to the voters.

Distributive economic justice (on the efficiency-cum-egalitarianism principle) is a standard for achievement, a standard for assessing policies in a democratic system of rights. And the goal it invokes should be part of the public understanding of such a system and should inform debate there. For distributive economic justice, as here conceived, is the kind of thing we'd expect a rights-respecting democratic government and electorate to be specially concerned with. To provide economic justice (on the efficiency-cum-egalitarianism model) is one of the things such a democracy should be doing, given its character and its justifying norms.

Achieving distributive economic justice is a matter of democratic majority rule, but it is not a matter of *mere* majority rule. For it is never a matter of sheer indifference how policies turn out as to their impact on distributive economic justice in a democratic system.

Thus, we should expect to find in the typical operation of a democratic system such things as policies of job creation and job training, redistributive taxation and income transfers and various subsidies at the lower income levels, and, finally, controls on campaign spending and policies designed to give more or less equal empowerment to voters at all income levels. For the idea here is that the total set of policies in a country modelled on a democratic system of rights should be geared to achieve distributive economic justice, as understood in the idea that everybody benefits (as constrained by egalitarianism).

III A REFLECTION AND ASSESSMENT

In concluding the argument of this chapter, and as a main part of my assessment of the project it proposes, I think it important to establish one point in particular, a point that may not be, as yet, wholly clear. The argument I have conducted in this paper is intended to show two things merely: that the meeting of the criterion set by the everybody benefits-cum-egalitarian principle has been developed as a *sufficient* condition for distributive economic justice and that the criterion, so understood, would be both acceptable and integral within a democratic system of rights.

Let me put this point a bit more precisely here. The criterion would be a sufficient condition for distributive economic justice, if certain preconditions were met. Some of these conditions are already familiar to us; they pertain to the notion of a democratic system of rights itself and were mentioned at the end of the previous section. I mean such things as the priority of basic rights and the need to rely on democratically derived policies and on democratic scrutiny in meeting the 'everybody benefits' goal. And some of these preconditions belong to the theory of justice itself. Perhaps most important here would be the meeting of the standard of fair equality of opportunity at a suitable level.[7]

My claim, then, is that if the criterion is actually met in a country modelled on a democratic system of rights, that fact would be a sufficient condition for saying that the distributive economic arrangements there were just, for rebutting claims (should such be made) that they were *un*just. The satisfaction of the criterion marks a sufficient condition for saying that the various levels of income and wealth for representative groups (say, the top 20 per cent of wage earners on down through the bottom 20 per cent) in that country were not contrary to justice.

I have not argued, however, that the meeting of this criterion is a *necessary* condition for distributive economic justice in such a system. More specifically, I have not argued that meeting the 'everybody benefits' part of this criterion is a necessary condition there. In other words, if the criterion is *not* being met in a country modelled on a democratic system of rights, or not being met on the point that every income group benefits, it does not follow (from that fact alone) that the distributive economic arrangements there are positively *un*just. Or so my argument is meant to suggest.

At least four reasons could plausibly be advanced for thinking that satisfying the relevant criterion (the criterion set by the everybody benefits-cum-egalitarian principle) should not be a *necessary* condition for distributive economic justice. They could, for purposes of reference and ready recall, be identified as: (1) historical reasons, based on interpreting the various theories of economic justice (Locke's, *et al.*) briefly mentioned in the previous section; (2) reasons of limited knowledge and of reliance on shared normative intuitions and of the indeterminacies these introduce; (3) reasons of conceptual indeterminacy in the efficiency-cum-egalitarianism criterion itself; and (4) reasons of democracy. Only the last of these crucially concerns the argument of the present paper. Let me turn, briefly then, to this particular argument from democracy.

Consistent and determined adherence to a necessary condition requirement would be inappropriate within a democratic system of rights. For to insist on such adherence would be inconsistent with the institutional essentials – in particular, those identified with the idea of democracy (contested voting, majority rule) – which constitute the theoretic system of political institutions and ideas which we must rely on to ground the idea of distributive economic justice, justificatorily, in the first place.

In a democratic system of rights, one is committed to the notion that majority rule decision-making, so long as it conforms to the main priorities established there, is itself decisive and determinative. Distributive economic justice (as we have conceived it) does not have the status of a democratically derived basic right or set of such rights in the theoretic system we are discussing. Nor is it a corporate good there. Thus it cannot control democratic decision-making in the way that these main concerns do. Indeed, a creditable profile of economic justice in such a system must itself conform, in appropriate ways, to democratic norms, norms which include (as we have noted) contested voting and majority decision among their crucial and defining features.

Consistent and determined adherence to a necessary condition requirement would take us *outside* our justifying net, and cause us to lose our moorings in the very system of institutions and ideas whence we had begun. And we would have surreptitiously turned what had been a mere historical fact, an inductive generalisation from modern discourse about distributive economic justice (as captured in the root – or everybody benefits – idea and its obvious importance), into an absolute, into the governing norm, into the very idea of justice.

It would be far better to take satisfaction of the efficiency-cum-egalitarianism criterion, not as a hard-edged, either/or, invariant rule (or, even worse, as an unvarying rule justified by metaphysical intuition), but to take it as a regulative principle, as a principle subject to interpretation. In short, my suggestion is that we treat the criterion for purposes of the present argument as a principle which has weight and consideration within a democratic polity, and thereby take it as a guide to public discussion and as a standard for assessing results and even for constructing policies there. In calling it a principle, I am also distinguishing it from a mere rule-of-thumb.

Unlike, rules of thumb, it can never be ignored. It always has normative force; for even when it does not prevail, it can none the less serve as a touchstone. Deviations from the criterion are inherently suspect in principle. And some failures of satisfaction may indeed prove to be simply unacceptable and out of character with what justifies a democratic system of rights in the first place.

The view I am disputing, that the criterion of efficiency-cum-egalitarianism is a necessary condition of economic justice, suffers from a serious flaw. It fails to see that *in*justice, like the idea of justice itself, is something that requires political interpretation. It fails to see that neither injustice nor justice is a simple, clear-cut idea. Instead it assumes without further ado that the sufficient criterion here is also a necessary one and that – within relevant parameters – all failures to satisfy it are *per se* unjust. In this respect it dogmatically begs the very question we are here concerned with.

The fact is, people may well think that not all failures to meet the criterion are unjust. And if they do think that, and if the grounds for so thinking can be made out in a principled way (and, in particular, one fully consistent with the justifying norms and the network of institutions of a democratic system of rights), then we have in hand all that is needed to settle the matter at issue.

Consider here the following two cases, which we can call paradigm case A and paradigm case B. Let us begin with A. Here all indicators (in all expert hands) show both that some groups are actually worse off (in particular, those in the bottom group, who are now much worse off) and that the disparity between top and bottom has actually significantly increased over time. Both these results are permanently irreversible.

Surely, we have here a presumptive case for saying that the distributive arrangements implicated herein are *un*just. I would agree. But the case can be conclusively made only *within* the actual operation of a democratic system of rights.

The principle we have relied on to make our judgement in case A, the principle that everybody benefits as constrained by egalitarianism, comes within the orbit of the very justification for having a democratic system of rights at all; the principle has a definite place in the priorities of any such system and draws its normative force (in the case at hand) from having that place, as located within the network of democratic institutions. Or so I have argued. This much is granted then, as background.

The judgement I've endorsed is a presumptive one. But the public debate and the ensuing votes would actually have to *reach* this very judgement, over time and given experience, for it to count as a fully conclusive one within a given democratic state.

In sum, when we say that some such judgements or conclusions can be drawn *upon reflection*, the reflection we have in mind is found in free public discourse, in contested voting, in majority decisions, in confirmation through the checking devices, in established public consensus within an ongoing democratic polity over time. Such reflective conclusions as these are authoritative in a given democratic polity and, under the conditions identified, serve to resolve otherwise ineradicable indeterminacies in the inbuilt criterion of distributive economic justice, as (for example) in determining what is positively *un*just.

Let us consider next, in concluding the argument of this section and of the chapter, a somewhat different case from paradigm A. We can call it paradigm case B. Here all indicators (in all expert hands) show both that some groups are actually worse off (in particular, those in the top group, who are now marginally worse off) and that the disparity between top and bottom has actually significantly decreased over time. The first result (expected to last, let us say, for a decade) is not permanently irreversible, though the second may well be.

These two cases, A and B, are different in many relevant respects. But they are alike in one: each represents a failure of satisfaction of the efficiency-cum-egalitarianism criterion at a crucial point, at the point of the so-called root idea (as given in the 'everybody benefits' principle). Given this important point of similarity between A and B, do we have a presumptive case (as

we did in A) for saying that the distributive arrangements implicated in case B
are *un*just?

My own intuition in the matter – shared with many other people, I would
suspect – is that we don't. But, under the terms of our present analysis, this is
at best only a presumptive conclusion. Suppose, now, this very conclusion –
the conclusion that such arrangements are not unjust – was in effect drawn
within a democratic polity (under the same conditions as in case A: free
public discussion etc.). Such a conclusion-in-effect would be drawn when
democratic policy produced or endorsed such a result under those conditions.

The argument of this section of the chapter would lead us to endorse this
conclusion, from within the confines of a given democratic polity (and ultimately from within the idea of a democratic system of rights). To endorse it
as authoritative, as reflectively sound, as a practical and principled way of
resolving one of the otherwise ineradicable indeterminacies in the inbuilt criterion of distributive economic justice we have identified, that of efficiency-
cum-egalitarianism.

If one accepts this overall conclusion – that the result given in paradigm
case B is not presumptively unjust and would not be decided to be, given
time and reflection, in a polity modelled on a democratic system of rights –
then one cannot consistently believe that satisfaction of the governing criterion is a *necessary* condition of distributive economic justice in such a system.
Or, to put the matter here somewhat differently, if one thinks the overall conclusion to be based on sound reasons, then one would not take the criterion
to be a necessary condition (in the sense that any failure to satisfy the criterion
is, under plausible circumstances, *un*just as such).

CONCLUSION

The question of distributive economic justice is one of the fundamental issues
that all democratic countries face today. The present chapter has suggested
that this issue can be confronted within the frame already established by
basic rights and by the democratic institutions. Social justice, as given in the
criterion of efficiency-cum-egalitarianism, can be on the agenda for political
programmes within a democratic system of rights. And it is important to be
clear in our understanding of the criterion we have tried to establish: it is
understood to be a sufficient, but not a necessary condition, for distributive
economic justice within any given polity modelled on a democratic system of
rights.[8]

A NOTE ON REFERENCES/SOURCES

For a characterisation of rights, in contrast to alternative accounts, and for
the grounds on which I think the one I've relied on is to be preferred, see
chs 2–5 of my book *A System of Rights*, Oxford, the Clarendon Press, 1993
(hereafter SR). For the point made about rights as beneficial, see SR, chs 2,

5, and 10. For the justification of democracy (and of the priority of the various options involved), see SR, chs 6 and 7. For the point about the fundamental compatibility of basic rights with justified democratic majority rule (the basic point developed at the beginning of the present chapter), see SR, chs 7 and 12, in particular; for the idea that well-accredited rights are not to be superseded, in central cases, by other normative concerns, see SR, ch. 5, section 4; also pp. 159–65. And, for a convenient summary of the main argument, see the short paper 'Basic Rights', *Rechtstheorie*, 1993, Beiheft vol. 15, pp. 191–201 (on which Section I of the present chapter is based). Finally, for the point about the self-correcting character of democratic procedures, see SR, ch. 7. (This idea is taken from T. L. Thorson, *The Logic of Democracy*, New York, Holt, 1962, esp. ch. 8; and also pp. 120–24.) Sections 2 and 3 of the present chapter are based in part – in particular the discussion of Rawls – on my paper 'Economic justice: contractarianism and Rawls's difference principle', in *The Social Contract from Hobbes to Rawls*, David Boucher and Paul Kelly (eds), London, Routledge, 1994, pp. 245–66. An earlier version of the present chapter was published in *Analyse & Kritik*, 1995, vol. 17, pp. 35–51. I want to thank Michael Baurmann, editor of the journal, for agreeing to the publication of the paper in its present revised and shortened form here in this collection.

NOTES

1 The argument I have just described in Rawls is a long-standing feature of his writings. It is especially evident in his recent writings and is quite explicit there. See, for one example, Rawls' Tanner Lectures (1981), reprinted as Lecture VIII, pp. 289–371, in his *Political Liberalism*, New York, Columbia University Press, 1993, at pp. 338–9 esp.; for another, see *Political Liberalism*, Lecture VI, in n. 23 on pp. 236–7.

2 See Ronald Dworkin's opinion piece, 'Should Wrong Opinions be Banned?' *The Independent* (London), 28 May 1995, p. 27.

3 Mill is widely interpreted as holding (in his *Utilitarianism*, ch. 5) that all matters of (moral) justice are matters of rights and all matters of rights (at least those that can be morally endorsed) are matters of justice. The idea that rights and justice are coincident or 'correlative' notions is, indeed, widely shared or even endorsed, as with Brian Barry (the source of the term quoted, in his book *Liberty and Justice: Essays in Political Theory 2*, Oxford, Clarendon Press, 1991, p. 187). Tom Campbell argues against any such correlation in his article 'Rights Without Justice', *Mind* 1974, vol. 83, pp. 445–8.

4 Let me add to this claim about Rawls a qualification that should be noted. At some stage (as we follow a Rawlsian pattern of reciprocal improvements), we could conceive options which, if any one were taken, would leave us at a point (on a curve, so to speak, or in a region) where no further reciprocally improving changes were possible. Here the only way members of any one class could be better off (say, the members of x_2) would be for those in another class (say, x_1) to be worse off. When this point, this 'curve' or frontier, has been reached, we have reached the 'Pareto optimal' zone. Obviously, options to *move* to such a frontier can be taken, but no further moves within it are thereafter allowed (for none could be reciprocally improving).

In short, Rawls' theory (in my view) is governed, despite his frequent invocation of the maximin ideal, not by that ideal but by the notion of reciprocal or mutual benefit. (See esp. Rawls, *A Theory of Justice*, Cambridge, Mass., Harvard University Press, 1971, pp. 79, 104–5, 585.) On this interpretation, then, Pareto *optimality* is a limiting case (in the way just described); on the 'everybody benefits' principle; one can move *to* the optimality zone but not *within* it, so to speak. Once optimality is achieved, presumably at the maximin point, the only acceptable step is to preserve a steady state, an equilibrium of sorts.

Rawls goes only so far, then, with the notions associated with Pareto's name. And here I have responded to a criticism of my paper at the 1995 Gregynog conference (in Wales), at which the argument of the present paper was initially shaped. The criticism was made by Manfreddi LaManna (and was clarified for me by Ken George and by Gabriella Slomp). For additional discussion and useful background, see 'Economic justice: Contractarianism and Rawls's difference principle', in *The Social Contract From Hobbes to Rawls*, op. cit., pp. 245–66.

5 That is, in a situation where there are two or more beneficial options for change, we should choose – where such choice is possible – that one which is 'efficient' (that is, which is *most* beneficial for *each* of the parties or groups involved). Thus, we understand the notion of everyone's continual benefit, in such a way as to be compatible with what is called Pareto efficiency. Of course, on this understanding there may be (from the perspective of a given point) *several* efficient solutions. Here we would need a tie breaker, an issue I next take up (in the text). For further clarification, see Figure 3 and the subsequent figures and discussion in the article on Rawls referred to above.

6 And the minimum level (which concerns the lifetime prospects for income and wealth of, say, the bottom one-fifth of wage earners) is one that the great majority of citizens can reasonably expect to stay above throughout their whole lives. Thus, the minimum level establishes a provision of benefit available to all, one that can be maintained, and probably will be maintained, by governmental action. But we are not contemplating here an *active* provision of benefit for everyone, one that each and all can reasonably expect to benefit from (except, possibly, in indirect ways) during their lifetimes.

Another consideration also merits attention here. The establishment of benefits at some minimum level might require, to give a possible example, that the top-most income group have *less* increased income than it might otherwise have had in order that the bottom-most group have a high enough income to meet the test of benefit for all groups. Satisfying the egalitarian constraint might require a similar result. In short, then, although nobody loses under this test, some groups may *gain* less than they otherwise would, even in roughly the same economic environment.

Two points seem salient then. (1) The achievement of a minimum level affords an active provision of benefit only for some. (2) The result of achieving this minimum may require a degree of relative loss for others.

However, something similar could be said about the right to a fair trial. Its active benefits extend only to some; achieving what the right requires may impose costs on others. None the less, it is regarded as a basic right. Thus, the facts I have cited (in particular, the fact of radically restricted actual benefit) would not support the claim that some *minimum*-level provision of benefit, if enacted into law, could *not* count as a *basic* right.

The problem, though, is that the fixing of such a level – in the strong sense that to fall below it is *per se* unjust – is itself an inherently indeterminate matter. Indeed, as I shall shortly argue, such a minimum can properly be fixed, on given occasions, only by a democratic decision. In sum, then, a usable idea of what is to count at various times as the minimum level can *result* only from democratic lawmaking but such an idea – even when it is conclusively set on a given occasion – cannot stand on its own to *direct* or *guide* such lawmaking on subsequent occasions. Thus, in this way, then, the notion of a determinable social minimum is sharply dissimilar from any well-accredited right (even the right to fair trial mentioned earlier).

Accordingly, we might say that *once set* the minimum level constitutes, for the time of its duration, a very important politically universal right. But it cannot be regarded as itself a basic right; its deep indeterminacy and its radical temporal delimitation – the fact that it must be set on each occasion by democratic decision and then set anew on subsequent occasions – bars it from that status.

7 For discussion of fair equality of opportunity in this context, see my book *Rawls and Rights*, Lawrence, University Press of Kansas, 1985, esp. chs 4, 5, and 8.

8 I want to thank a number of friends and colleagues for help and comments on various earlier versions of the present paper. Let me mention in particular Manfreddi LaManna, Ken George, Jack Bricke, Richard DeGeorge, Donna Martin, and David Reidy. And I want to thank audiences in the USA, the UK, Germany, and Sweden for their comments on earlier versions of the present paper.

The idea sketched in Section III, that Pareto efficiency is not a necessary condition of distributive economic justice, has been sharpened by discussions with Ann Cudd (and by my reading of her paper, 'Is Pareto optimality a criterion of justice', *Social Theory and Practice*, 1996, vol. 22, pp. 1–34) and with Prakash Shenoy (who is quite unsympathetic to my claim). I have used this particular idea to develop a response (in the context of a democratic system of rights) to troublesome criticisms raised earlier, and independently, by Russ Shafer-Landau and by Shanti Chakravarty.

9   Justice in the community
Walzer on pluralism, equality and democracy[1]

Richard Bellamy

Justice is conventionally portrayed as blindfold. According to this standard image, fairness and impartiality are guaranteed by the rigorous application of universal and general norms, without regard to the particular status or context of the persons concerned, or the good or bad being distributed. Indeed, many philosophers have argued that the avoidance of self-serving bias or prejudice requires that the very formulation of principles of justice must be undertaken, as it were, in the dark, and in ignorance of our own capacities and circumstances.[2]

Michael Walzer's *Spheres of Justice* challenges this approach.[3] He believes that the diversity of social norms, and related variations as to what count as goods, undermine the possibility of universal or generalisable rules of justice. It is impossible to abstract from either the particular persons to whom justice is to be applied, or the specific social settings within which judgements take place. Equitable treatment, on this view, requires that justice removes her blindfold and pays attention to the plurality of goods and principles operating both within and between different communities. If justice and equality are linked, in the sense that the former turns on treating like cases alike and dissimilar cases differently, then we need to drop a universalist for a particularist perspective which respects the importantly diverse ways in which people and societies conceive of the just and the good. Within a particularist understanding of the nature of our moral rights and obligations, the goals of fairness and impartiality come to be incorporated within, and to some degree strengthened by, a practice of reciprocity. For the tensions between one's personal standpoint and the claims of the collectivity are lessened when one is asked to identify with the particular goals and values of the community or associations to which one belongs, rather than with some set of abstract universal ideals that are said to apply to humanity as such.[4]

Walzer contends that this communitarian account of justice builds on a defence of pluralism and equality. Furthermore, he holds this view to be profoundly democratic. For it turns on taking seriously the conceptions and assumptions of ordinary people. In what follows, these contentions will be explored and to a large extent questioned. After an exposition of Walzer's thesis in Section I, Section II argues that his communitarian approach fails to offer a full account of either pluralism or equality, whilst Section III disputes the democratic credentials of his theory. The attempt to compartmentalise the different spheres of justice is not only in tension with his insistence on the socially relative nature of justice, but also incoherent and undesirable in its own terms. Pluralism, equality and democracy all have a universalist dimension that is a vital aspect of any defence of their particular manifestations. Justice may need to see and be seen in order to be done, making a contextual and more political approach desirable. However, that is at least partly because there are rival universalisms in play that operate across spheres and cannot be blocked off into discreet units.

I SPHERICAL JUSTICE

The social thesis

The central thesis of Walzer's theory of justice is that goods are conceived of, created and distributed within a social context. Goods do not have fixed and inherent 'natural' or 'ideal' meanings that are prior, and hence common, to all communities. All goods are the product of particular social relations and have no existence or value apart from the men and women who employ and fashion them.[5] Even goods that appear to have a private significance, such as a family heirloom, a pint of beer, or an esoteric invention, form part of a public culture that makes such personal appreciation comprehensible and possible. Indeed, personal identity is in crucial respects socially constructed through the use and pursuit of social goods.[6]

Because goods and their meanings are socially constituted, Walzer concludes that 'distributions are patterned in accordance with shared conceptions of what the goods are and what they are for'.[7] However, social meanings are neither immutable or universal. They change over time and differ between, and in certain cases within, societies.[8] Walzer draws a number of important consequences from this alleged fact. First, and in contrast to Rawls,[9] he insists that because societies value different goods and alter their own evaluations during the course of history, there can be 'no single set of primary or basic goods conceivable across all moral and material worlds'.[10] Some goods may be highly favoured in certain societies and marginalised or absent from others. While many categories of goods will have analogues across most societies, they will usually not be understood in exactly the same way everywhere. Much of Walzer's study is devoted to tracing these differences, notably by comparing contemporary American ideas of education, leisure, office and similar goods with those found in other places and at other times. He notes how even such a basic necessity as food can have different meanings in different contexts. Thus, 'bread is the staff of life, the body of Christ, the symbol of the Sabbath, the means of hospitality, and so on'.[11] Nor will it be clear which meaning has primacy. A group of starving devout Christians might still choose to place the religious usage over the nutritional one, for instance.

Second and relatedly, the same good will be distributed in different ways in different contexts according to how it is understood by those concerned. 'Distributive criteria and arrangements are intrinsic not to the good-in-itself', which for Walzer does not exist, 'but to the social good.'[12] He claims that 'if we understand what [a good] is, [that is] what it means to those for whom it is a good, we understand how, by whom, and for what reasons it ought to be distributed'.[13] If I wish to know how to dole out the bread, for example, I must first discover how it is valued by those concerned. When it is the 'staff of life' certain criteria will apply, when it is the 'body of Christ' others will be appropriate, and so on. Although many categories of goods will have analogues across most societies, therefore, these goods will usually not be understood in exactly the same way everywhere.

Third, universalist theories that seek to apply a single distributive principle or set of criteria across all goods and societies are doubly misguided.[14] Different communities apply different meanings to a given good, even value a good differently in different contexts and at different times, as in the case with bread in the example above, and prioritise different sets of goods. Distributive principles vary both between societies and within them, according to the good concerned, and cannot be abstracted from these specific contexts.

Fourth, and once again taking issue with Rawls, he disputes that there can be an Archimedian point, such as Rawls' Original Position, for the evaluation of any given society's distributive criteria. For 'the question most likely to arise in the minds of the members of a political community is not, What would rational individuals choose under universalising conditions of such-and-such a sort? But rather, What would individuals like us choose, who are situated as we are, who share a culture and are determined to go on sharing it? And this is a question that is readily transformed into, What choices have we already made in the course of our common life? What understandings do we (really) share?'[15] Any critique must be an immanent criticism based on the traditions and practices people are engaged in. The hypothetical arrangements of idealised agents who have been artificially shorn of their identities and allegiances have no relevance for actually existing people and societies.

Finally, any theory of justice must assume a certain political as well as a social context. Walzer believes the bounded political community constitutes the best approximation 'to a world of common meanings', which, on his view, any account of goods and their appropriate distribution necessarily presupposes.[16] Within the nation state, in particular, 'language, history and culture come together . . . to produce a common consciousness', at least to a greater degree than anywhere else.[17] As a result of this common culture, its members identify with each other and are 'committed to dividing, exchanging, and sharing social goods' amongst themselves.[18] States also possess a set of political mechanisms for this purpose, that are capable of arranging and securing distributions according to the criteria agreed on by the group.

There would be little point in elaborating principles of justice without such institutions and a commitment to them on the part of those involved.

Walzer derives two general and related norms from the above largely descriptive claims, which should guide how we think about distribution. First, he contends that since 'justice is relative to social meanings . . . a given society is just if its substantive life is lived . . . in a way faithful to the shared understandings of its members', so that 'all distributions are just or unjust relative to the social meanings of the goods at stake'.[19] Indeed, 'to override those understandings is (always) to act unjustly'.[20] Second, he argues that 'when meanings are distinct, distributions must be autonomous. Every social good or set of goods constitutes, as it were, a distributive sphere within which only certain criteria are appropriate.'[21] Consequently, 'no social good x should be distributed to men and women who possess some other good y merely because they possess y and without regard to the meaning of x'.[22] Walzer sees the second principle as following from the first. However, as I shall show in later sections, the relationship between the two is a contingent rather than a necessary one. His prioritising of the first over the second undermines the pluralist, egalitarian and democratic credentials of his theory. Unfortunately, the second principle is unable to sustain them either.

At one level, Walzer presents his principles as simple logical entailments of the social thesis and the purported intrinsic relationship between the shared meanings of goods and the criteria for their distribution. Justice, on this view, cannot be other than what a given society understands it to be. To the extent that understandings of goods and their distribution differ amongst both societies and their spheres, there are different possible accounts of justice and no way of ranking them.[23] Indeed, Walzer's thesis makes it not only unjust but also nonsensical to distribute goods in any way other than according to their relative social and spherical meanings.

Some instances of such intrinsic links between spherical justice, distribution and social understandings certainly do exist. Thus, if a prize has been established for the Politics candidate scoring the highest marks in finals, it could not be awarded to any one but the person with the best scores without changing the nature of the award. Of course, there are equally plausible criteria one might adopt, such as giving it to the individual who had tried the hardest or improved the most over the year. Choosing between them on the grounds that there exists a 'natural' or 'most just' criterion for the award of university prizes would be slightly absurd, however. It all depends on what qualities a given department or university values or is seeking to promote. In this sort of case, a just distribution is clearly relative to the social meaning of the good.

The prize example also illustrates Walzer's point about preserving the autonomy of distributional spheres. Walzer is particularly concerned at the way money invades all spheres, enabling individuals to buy goods to which they are not entitled.[24] The prize cannot be legitimately bought and sold, however, for it would be not simply unjust but ultimately meaningless to commodify it in this way. The only reason a less able student could have for bribing the examiners to give him the award, would be so he could pass himself off as the most successful candidate. The open sale of degrees is pointless for analogous reasons, since it would so undercut their social purpose as symbols of a certain level of academic achievement as to render them valueless. The difficulty, explored below, is that money is now the chief prize.[25]

At another level, a more substantive argument underlies Walzer's normative claims. He argues that persons should be equally respected in their capacity as 'culture-producing creatures', who 'make and inhabit meaningful worlds' involving 'distinct understandings of places, honours, jobs, things of all sorts, that constitute a shared way of life'.[26] Outsiders can never amend what they believe to be the unjust arrangements of another community without committing an even graver injustice. For the human ability to invent a variety of different cultures and social identities means there is no external and universal view of justice to which one might appeal to justify such interference. As with missionaries, attempts at conversion to one's point of view show contempt for people's self-understanding and tend to slide into coercion. No matter how well-intentioned, such exercises are always paternalistic, and end up offering a spurious ideological cover for some form of neo-colonial domination. The only legitimate criticism comes from inside a society in the form of an immanent critique of that society's own standards by its members.[27]

In recent writings, Walzer has conceded that this argument for particularism involves a universalist dimension that stresses the importance of communal self-determination.[28] However, he couches this thesis in communitarian/descriptive terms as a claim that certain minimal moral requirements *are* reiterated within all cultures, not as a universalist/prescriptive argument that certain conditions *ought to be* recognised, whether they are or not.[29] The assumption that all societies value some degree of individual and collective autonomy is empirically dubious, though, and at best offers a contingent defence of pluralism, equality and democracy within communities. Nor is it clear that all societies would accept that principles of justice are relative to the understandings of the people who employ them and the goods that they are applied to. For example, it is arguably a deep assumption of Western societies that correct notions of justice are objective and capable of being justified independently of any particular groups beliefs about them. We shall return to these points below.

Similar reasoning underlies his case for preserving the autonomy of different spheres. Human creativity not only gives rise to diverse cultures but also to a variety of goods within them, which reflect in turn the wide range of human talents and abilities. Just as the attempt to impose a particular view of justice across different societies involves a lack of equal respect that ultimately proves tyrannous, so too does the attempt to apply a single distributive principle across all goods within a society. Inevitably it leads to the monopolists of a particular good exploiting their advantage so as to dominate all other areas. This argument rather begs the question that people actually do perceive goods in this sphere specific manner. I shall challenge this assumption below. The contention that they can and should do so, however, is crucial to the radical political claims Walzer wants to draw from his theory.

A radical liberalism

Walzer regards the argument for different spheres of justice as 'a radical principle'.[30] He traces the respective shortcomings of capitalism and state socialism back to their failure to respect it. Capitalism allows the sphere of money to dominate, whilst socialism gives excessive weight to those who control the sphere of political power. Both systems also work with a related and defective account of equality. The former employs a purely 'formal' view, which involves merely treating everyone the same in certain specified respects. The latter advocates a 'simple' egalitarianism, that seeks to render everyone the same in respect of some good or goods. In each case, these approaches to equality merely serve to promote the tyranny of the dominant good, leading to highly inegalitarian results of an unjustified nature.

Walzer's critique of the formal equality of capitalist societies is most clearly expressed in an earlier essay, 'In Defense of Equality', that rehearses many of the central themes of *Spheres of Justice*.[31] Walzer criticises an argument by Irving Kristol to the effect that the inegalitarian 'bell-shaped' distribution of wealth and power in contemporary capitalist countries echoes the similarly 'bell-shaped' distribution of talents and abilities amongst human beings. Walzer counters that to get the full picture one needs to have a separate curve for each of the many human capacities: from intelligence, physical strength, agility and grace through to artistic creativity, mechanical skill, leadership, endurance, memory, psychological insight and so on. He contends that the ability to make money is but one more talent to place alongside these. He thinks it highly unlikely that any individual will consistently show up on the same place on each of these curves. To be consistent, Kristol ought to admire the whole range of human talents and abilities. A true meritocracy would involve valuing each of them for their own special qualities rather than for other, irrelevant, reasons. The trouble with a system of purely formal equality is that it fails to distinguish adequately between the various substantive criteria appropriate to different goods, and allows individuals or groups to exploit their success in one sphere to gain an undue advantage in another. In particular, if certain talents come to attract greater financial reward than others, the beneficiaries can 'buy' into another sphere even if they lack the appropriate qualities. Millionaires may lack good looks or a scintillating personality, features that normally are needed to attract friends and lovers, yet prove attractive to others and even be praised for their beauty and wit on account of their wealth alone. Likewise, though by and large less in need of health care than the poor, the rich can jump hospital queues and purchase immediate treatment even for relatively trivial complaints. When talent really gets its just deserts then 'many bells ring'. Money reduces this pluralism to the monotone of the cash register by acting as a universal medium of exchange that allows its possessors to purchase virtually every other sort of social good. Walzer provocatively concludes that 'a radically *laissez-faire* economy would be like a totalitarian state', since it would involve both the market and money 'invading every sphere, dominating every other distributive process.'[32]

Walzer thinks that this line of attack offers a way of rehabilitating the socialist ideal of egalitarianism by avoiding the two classic weaknesses targeted, he believes with some reason, by conservative critics such as Kristol.[33] Namely, that it involves levelling down to the lowest common denominator, replacing meritocracy with mediocrity, and requires the state constantly to deploy huge coercive power so as to check those with superior personal skills or attributes gaining any advantage from them. The pursuit of simple equality results in the tyranny of money giving way to what Walzer concedes to be the far greater, because more direct, tyranny of the state. Political power, no less than economic power, needs to be kept in its place, and Walzer endorses all the usual liberal constitutional checks and balances designed to do so.[34]

Walzer holds that his own position of 'complex equality' avoids these pitfalls whilst remaining socially egalitarian. This notion does not require either that all people be treated according to the same rules across all distributions, as formal equality demands, or that we try and realise equality in some important area by ensuring everyone receives the same shares of some favoured quality or good, as 'simple' egalitarians advocate. Rather, he argues that we should allow different goods to be distributed by different criteria, some of which will be substantive but most of which will be largely formal. Consequently, distributions will be inegalitarian so far as each good is concerned, and in most cases so will be the results.[35] However, no person or group will be allowed to use their monopoly or dominance with regard to any given social good to tyrannise over all other distributive spheres. Walzer contends that the social equality desired by the egalitarian arises as an indirect product of this scheme. No person or group of people is likely to excel in all things. So long as the distributive spheres remain autonomous, therefore, we will come to respect not only a wide range of personal qualities but also a broad spectrum of different people. Within such a system, power and status are far more likely to be equally distributed amongst the population as a whole, with all persons being valued and valuing others in turn according to their distinctive attributes. He speculates that 'complex equality' is most likely within a democratic market socialist society consisting of workers co-operatives, which disperse political and economic power.[36]

His communitarian starting point and socialist preferences notwithstanding, Walzer offers his theory as a defence and development of a prime liberal practice: what he calls 'the art of separation'.[37] He contends that his argument for the separation of spheres of justice carries forward the logic of liberal calls for the separation of powers, of state and civil society, of church and state, and of public and private life. In particular, he insists that the traditional liberal separations designed to limit state power are likely to be undermined unless the economic and social power of the market and wealth are kept to their proper sphere in the manner he proposes. In what follows, it will be argued that these conclusions can only be sustained if Walzer is prepared to take a general, society-wide perspective that challenges at least some of these distinctions.

II PLURALISM AND EQUALITY

Walzer's theory of justice aims to connect pluralism and equality. The plurality of goods and their different social meanings are linked to a conception of complex equality that aims to secure equal respect for the whole gamut of human qualities and forms of life. This section will dispute both the pluralist and egalitarian credentials of his thesis. I shall argue that both involve considerations that cut across the different spheres of justice as opposed to keeping them distinct, as he maintains.

Pluralism

Pluralists contend that human beings pursue a wide range of forms of life. These emphasise different goods, interests, goals and values, often involve differing sorts of moral claim, and reflect divergent world views or conceptions of human flourishing. These differing goods, ends, outlooks and evaluations are held to be not simply diverse but incommensurable, rendering conflicts between logically or practically incompatible goods, interests or ideals highly problematic. For pluralists argue that such clashes cannot be resolved by appealing to a common denominator or single scale against which all values or points of view might be measured.[38]

How pluralist is Walzer's argument when set against this standard account of pluralism? Walzer claims to be a radical pluralist who believes 'that the principles of justice are themselves pluralistic in form; that different social goods ought to be distributed for different reasons, in accordance with different procedures, by different agents; and that all these differences derive from different understandings of the social goods themselves – the inevitable product of historical and cultural particularism'.[39] However, his whole approach is designed to short circuit the potential for conflict between incompatible and incommensurable goods and moral codes. Each good is assigned its distinctive sphere with its corresponding distributive principle. Differing moral systems are allocated to different nation states, whose cultural homogeneity can be protected by an appropriate membership policy. As a result, conflicts between differing goods or conceptions of the good become a matter of boundary disputes. The trick is to isolate the sphere or social system within which a given principle or set of values may be said to operate.

Unfortunately, this avoidance of the prime difficulty of a pluralist perspective fails to work. As we noted above, Walzer's central thesis is that distributive principles are relative to the social meaning of goods. However, in all but the most homogeneous of societies, there are likely to be a variety of social meanings available. Moreover, what motivates such differences is unlikely to be a disagreement about the true social meaning of the good in question, but moral considerations that apply across spheres. For the moral concerns that theories of justice seek to articulate regarding equality of opportunity, individual responsibility, autonomy, harm, well-being and the like are not sphere specific, but refer to human and social relations generally. Indeed, because distributions in one sphere tend to have knock on effects for distributions in others, such general considerations are likely to prove necessary to help resolve conflicts between spheres.

These points are best illustrated by looking at a few examples. Walzer suggests that need forms the socially recognised criterion for apportioning health care resources within modern welfare states[40]. One might broadly accept this position, however, and yet believe that a number of other considerations ought none the less to be taken into account. 'The nature of a need', as Walzer admits, 'is not self-evident.'[41] Any conception of health needs or account of the relative ordering of different such needs will draw on wider social and ethical doctrines that are not themselves specific to the sphere of health.

Some theorists seek to circumvent this difficulty by sharply distinguishing needs from mere wants or desires and regarding need as a minimal requirement. Unfortunately, as Shakespeare's Lear famously observed, the 'natural' needs of human beings are indistinguishable from those of beasts, and do not offer a justification for anything like the range of care offered by a modern health system. Nor is it clear that one can have a purely 'medical' definition of need, related to the level of existing health technology. Are those with critical conditions necessarily more needy than those suffering from chronic complaints, for instance? In a world of limited budgets, to say both types of medical need ought to be satisfied simply side-steps the issue. All health-systems are forced to cash limit certain treatments. Whilst the grounds for choosing which patients to treat may be roughly medical, such as likelihood of success, they tend to be mixed with other considerations, such as favouring the young over the old, which reflect wider moral notions such as utility, fairness, autonomy and the like. Similar issues arise when weighing up the amount of the health budget which should go on heart and kidney transplants, dialysis or prolonged courses of chemo-therapy, as opposed to the removal of piles, or hip operations. The former may be more urgent for the individuals concerned, but the treatments are highly expensive, may have less chance of success and benefit relatively few people. By contrast, the latter are more common, often cause people persistent, if not life threatening, pain over many years, their treatment is more sure, and the quality of life of those concerned may well in the long run be greatly improved. Limited resources mean such choices have to be made, yet here too reference to health care need alone does not get you very far. Purely medical reasoning has to be supplemented by broader ethical judgements.

Walzer implies that we can avoid these sorts of problems with a more socially relative understanding of health need.[42] This solution offers a sleight of hand that allows Walzer to hide the fact that any social definition already incorporates a number of non-sphere specific moral considerations of the sort discussed above. As Walzer himself points out,[43] it necessarily involves a reference to the sphere of membership, which connects up in turn to the whole range of social goods. Consequently, any social definition of need will turn on how medical care relates to all the other spheres connected to citizenship, such as education, voting, employment and the like. A social understanding of 'need' will also involve some judgement as to the relative importance of health care *vis à vis* these other goods. For health provision not only supports access to them, but also potentially detracts from them. Health care advances are now such that apportioning resources on the basis of 'need' alone may well be tantamount to writing a blank cheque that will leave no money to do anything else. Spending on health, therefore, will have to be compared and weighed against the financing of other important public services, such as education. This balancing, in its turn, will necessarily involve further cross-sphere moral arguments, such as Aristotelian or utilitarian versions of the relative importance of different goods to human or social well-being. Thus, the debate will switch from an enquiry into the social meaning of a specific good, to a disagreement over which moral theory best captures the relative distribution of the whole range of goods.

Note that not only meta-ethical judgements, but also self-standing ethical values of independent weight are involved in these deliberations. Amy Gutmann has observed,[44] for example, that many would regard individual responsibility as having some bearing on the issue of how someone should be treated. Thus, those engaging in 'dangerous' sports are usually required to take out special insurance rather than relying on the public health system to pay the full amount for tending any injuries that might result. Some theorists regard heavy drinkers and smokers as similarly responsible for the increased probability of their requiring medical attention. Just as private insurers would charge them higher premiums, so, it is argued, they ought to contribute more to public funds. Analogous reasons lead Gutmann to dispute Walzer's apparent veto on people prudentially seeking to supplement state health provision by taking out private policies that allow them to queue jump and so on, on the grounds that this involves an inappropriate invasion of money into the sphere of health. Her point is that certain general moral principles, in this case the view that people ought to be partially responsible for their voluntary behaviour and reap the rewards and penalties as the case may be, influence how we think goods ought to be distributed. They belong to no particular sphere and are attached to no given good, but rather form part of the public moral culture of a community. Yet another consequence of pluralism, of course, is that these too may be contested – producing a further dimension of complexity missed by Walzer's analysis.

Health care, then, is not simply an issue of medical need alone. Other moral and social concerns provide a context within which we can evaluate different types of medical need and situate them within the general pattern of goods and values. Two important criticisms of Walzer's position emerge from the above. First, the social meaning of any good turns out to be itself more complex, and hence more likely to be contested, than Walzer appears to appreciate. Second, even where an agreed meaning exists, that in itself may not be sufficent to justify a particular mode of distribution. It is one thing for people to recognise that health care is a human need, quite another for them to believe that it must therefore be publicly provided on a non-market basis.[45] After all, food and clothing are also needs but Walzer does not argue that they should only be available on the basis of some form of public rationing scheme in state department stores and supermarkets. The reasons for having a welfare state that offers an extensive national health service that covers everyone but only provides food, clothing and housing for those on the bread line, for example, will turn on a wide range of arguments, some of which will be directly related to health and the particular type of need it represents and others (perhaps the majority) to general issues of social justice.

Walzer ignores these difficulties because his communitarianism tacitly solves them. The fact that each good is socially constituted inherently relates it to other spheres and ideals. Walzer assumes such connections so that he does not have to tackle explicitly the tricky problem of conflicts between spheres. However, this social view of goods implicitly threatens the idea of their operating within separate spheres. Moreover, the assumption of an already existing social meaning for goods also pushes pluralism to one side. The disputes across and within spheres to which it gives rise are simply taken as solved.

Equality

Keeping the spheres distinct is central to Walzer's account of complex equality. If the above argument is correct, however, this will prove impossible. Even if it was possible, this arrangement is only contingently egalitarian in the conventional sense. A great deal turns on Walzer's claim that talents are roughly evenly distributed throughout the population – that there are no renaissance men and women who happen to excel at most, if not all, things, or any complete duffers who are no good at anything, or whose only talent lies in a somewhat trivial sphere, such as the ability to recite the whole railway timetable from memory. He also assumes that by and large inequalities within each sphere will not be too great. In the event that few or none of these assumptions turn out to be true, then the relationship between people would be best described as one of complex inequality rather than equality.

In this case, Walzer simply accepts that his theory would allow 'for an inegalitarian society' but concludes 'it would also suggest in the strongest way that a society of equals was not a lively possibility'.[46] The egalitarian credentials of complex equality, therefore, rest on the largely unsupported empirical assertion that inequalities will be 'small' and 'will not be multiplied through the conversion process' or 'summed across different goods',[47] although these are all theoretical possibilities of his thesis – even if the spheres remain formally separated.

Of course, Walzer's argument is that something other than the 'simple' equalising of conditions underlies the notion of equality. He contends that 'the aim of political egalitarianism is a society free from domination',[48] by which he means individuals and groups employing their monopoly of one good to control access to another. Separating the spheres supposedly achieves this goal. His underlying purpose appears to be to engender equal respect for the manifold talents human beings possess as a whole – a view, as David Miller has recently pointed out – best captured by some notion of 'equality of status'.[49] In Walzer's words, equality on this definition means 'no more bowing and scraping, fawning and toadying; no more fearful trembling; no more high-and-mightiness; no more masters and slaves'.[50] Unfortunately, his argument for complex equality ultimately collapses because, for reasons already partly rehearsed above, the spheres cannot be kept distinct in the way Walzer desires. Although he rightly believes that equal status forms an important aspect of egalitarianism, it cannot be totally distinguished from equality of condition.

Note first that equality of status is as socially contingent on Walzer's account as rough equality of condition. He admits that in some societies social meanings may be 'integrated and hierarchical', and so 'come to the aid of inequality'.[51] Once again, his communitarian starting point can subvert the very defence of pluralism and equality it is supposed to support. Where a belief in the complete autonomy of different spheres forms no part of the public culture, insistence on the socially relative character of justice undermines the spherical separations his argument requires. Even then, as we have seen, it remains unclear quite how sharply such distinctions could (or should) be made. Walzer treats this problem as a peripheral one, citing caste societies as a singular instance of a society where the dominance of a group has been incorporated into the social meaning of goods. If gender is substituted for caste, however, then the difficulty emerges as far more pervasive and pernicious. As Susan Moller Okin remarks, 'like the hierarchy of caste, that of gender ascribes roles, responsibilites, rights and other social goods in accordance with an inborn characteristic that is imbued with tremendous significance. All the social goods listed in Walzer's description of a caste society have been, and many still are, differentially distributed to the members of the two sexes.'[52] So far as gender is concerned, social meanings infringe the autonomy of different distributive spheres to some degree in all societies. Within a gendered society, all distributive criteria are likely to have a discriminatory bias built into them in the form of a 'male comparator' test. Keeping the spheres distinct will have no critical purchase on such discrimination – only a global onslaught on the broader social context within which particular meanings are framed. That involves thinking about justice and equality in general and not merely socially and sphere specific terms.

According to Walzer, preserving equality of status merely involves preventing advantages (or disadvantages) in one sphere passing over into others. In spite of the high degree of social differentiation and stratification within modern societies, however, there tends to be a significant correlation and convertability between different modes and forms of power and position.[53] Take employment, which Walzer believes ought to be distributed according to fitness for the job. For a start, having a job of any kind in itself tends to confer a certain social status *vis à vis* the unemployed for fairly widespread general moral reasons, such as the importance of making a contribution to society and of earning one's own living to some extent. These often make it hard for the unemployed to attain much self-respect let alone that of others. Then there are the different statuses attached to different kinds of work. Walzer suggests that we can somehow compartmentalise these. We can give each person his or her due as a refuse collector, bank manager or academic, rank them against other members of their respective professions, yet not make comparisons between these different jobs when it comes to those persons having access to other goods. However, certain forms of work will, by their very nature, extend into more fields than others, giving people some advantages in those spheres. Indeed, in many cases there may be an inherent link between success and standing in certain jobs and high status in other areas. In part this arises because the qualifications necessary for some types of work necessarily involve a high degree of attainment in other spheres. Indeed, sociologists have noted causal links between distributions of some goods and those amongst others. Education, for example tends to give people access to better jobs generally, not simply academic ones, and operate as a positional good in all sorts of spheres. To preserve 'complex equality' by blocking either the possibilities for conversion or the causal linkages between the distribution patterns of different sorts of goods, would require just as much, if not more, intervention on the part of the state as the 'simple' egalitarian policies Walzer criticises on just these grounds. As Adam Swift has observed, the former Eastern bloc did achieve some elements of the separation of spheres Walzer desires, with correlations between education, income and prestige apparently lower there than in Western capitalist countries. Yet these were achieved at a high price so far as personal liberty was concerned, and even here elements of convertability took place in the form of Party contacts and political influence.[54]

In fact, the best way of ensuring 'equality of status' almost certainly remains ensuring equality of opportunity to different positions for all social classes and groups, and reducing financial differentials between different forms of employment. However, Walzer has difficulties with countenancing the forms of affirmative action programme that may be required to support the first strategy, or the redistribution of wealth necessary for the second. The first conflicts with his view that only suitability for the post fits our social understanding of office.[55] Yet bias does not result solely from external incursions into a given sphere. As feminists have pointed out, it is frequently internally present in the way certain good-specific criteria get formulated in the first place so as to reflect biases within society at large.[56] The point of affirmative action is at least partly to change the criteria we employ in selecting for certain spheres in ways that render them less discriminatory and more inclusive of difference.

The second strategy poses comparable problems, since it seems to involve allowing the sphere of money to encroach outside its realm. Walzer regards money as the chief culprit in undermining the autonomy of spheres and, in the process, complex equality. It destroys the inherent link between the meaning of a good and its criteria of distribution. Whilst it would be meaningless to steal your degree certificate unless I could convince someone I was entitled to it, your cheque for the best essay can be put to any use I please. Walzer draws two propositions from this quality of money, both of them misguided. On the one hand, it should be excluded, or 'blocked', from influencing decisions outside its sphere. On the other hand, he suggests that money itself has no determinate social meaning and hence that it is senseless to seek to redistribute it. 'Given the right blocks', he argues, 'there is no such thing as the maldistribution of goods.'[57]

With regard to the first, Walzer's analysis is too crude.[58] His main target is the commodification of goods. True, it seems perverse to think that certain goods are obtainable for money – as the Beatles memorably put it, 'money can't buy me love', although it can purchase sex. However, human beings cannot live on love alone, and even the most collective and non-monetary organisations, such as families, will need to reflect the restrictions of limited resources in budgetary terms when identifying their priorities. The problem with 'market imperialism' lies not so much in the extension of the sphere of money and commodities, inappropriate though this is in certain limited areas, as in the dominance of the market ethos. Like other supporters and critics of the market, Walzer tends to conflate the two issues. But one can clearly acknowledge the need for budgets without believing they must or should be set in a market manner.

Worries about the imperialism of the market are best seen in terms of a fear that its ethos distorts the incentive structure and nature of certain practices. Games offer a good illustration of this point.[59] Success and enjoyment can only follow from adopting a point of view that is internal to the given game. External goods and especially financial rewards may play a part in people's involvement, especially if that is how they earn their living, but the pursuit of these rewards must not come to dominate if the spirit of a game is not to be destroyed. Concern about the commercialisation of sport, for instance, has less to do with paying tennis or football players large amounts of money than with the way these games get altered to enhance their commercial value so that these fees can be paid — say by increasing their 'entertainment' qualities or by retimetabling and adding extra rest periods to fit in with television schedules and advertising breaks. Similarly, and more importantly, those who complain about the way successive Conservative governments introduced the market into the provision of certain public services over the past decade and a half, such as health and education, do so not because they spurn value for money or accountability in the delivery of these goods, but because they fear that the market ethos will destroy the internal connection between standards of performance and the type of good being delivered by focusing the attention of service providers on the acquisition of the external good of money. Pure academic research will give way to the pursuit of lucrative grants and careerism, managers will supplant doctors in the setting of priorities in the health service and so on. Non-monetary incentives, such as more research time in academia, may be more appropriate in promoting the pursuit of the good concerned.

Naturally, this does not mean that decent salaries are not important — academics have food and housing bills to pay like everyone else. Moreover, many jobs do not possess the sort of intrinsic satisfactions that research and scholarship bring, and almost all generate 'bads' as well as 'goods'. Thus, we might also think it right to compensate someone who works particularly hard not simply with greater job satisfaction but say with longer holidays and higher pay so that they can find fulfilment in other areas. Money, in other words, has a role to play in non-market spheres, even if the market ethos does not.

The market ethos proves damaging to pluralism because it renders all moral motivations the same. This aspect is reasonably well captured by Walzer's argument for different spheres of justice. However, blocking exchanges to preserve complex equality provides no answer to this situation, for the problem is not commodification or money *per se* but inequality of resources. In this respect, his second view regarding money — that it has no intrinsic value of its own to justify its distribution — simply misses the point. For a prime feature of market distributions is their tendency to generate highly inegalitarian results that need not even guarantee certain groups and individuals the most basic goods. It proves necessary, therefore, to have some method of globally distributing resources across spheres on such general grounds as fairness. Complex equality thereby comes to depend on considerations relating to equality of condition.

It will be recalled that Walzer feared that this approach would lead to undue political intervention with individual liberty. Here, as elsewhere in his discussion of the market, his argument has a tendency (contrary to his broader aims) to mirror that of the New Right. However, whereas patrolling the borders of different spheres would require both eternal vigilance and constant interference, redistribution through progressive taxation can be achieved in an entirely rule-governed and generalised manner. What becomes important in this approach is the justice of the background conditions against which individual activity, including that of the market, takes place. A concern with the justice of what John Rawls has called the 'basic structure of society' usually takes the form of state support for a number of public and cultural goods deemed necessary for different sorts of human endeavour.[60] The state steps in because the market either erodes or cannot be guaranteed to support these goods due to the absence of appropriate economic incentives, or would only make them available to those able to pay for them.

Walzer rightly reflects that societies will differ over which goods warrant public provision, although he down plays the degree to which there will be intra-societal disagreements as well. Such discussions, however, concern the justice of society as a whole rather than an enquiry into the internal meanings of different goods. Equality figures in such debates not as a matter of avoiding domination, or not directly that. The equal status of those involved is already assumed, since some recognition of the importance of certain goods to all citizens forms at least part of the justification for their public regulation or provision in the first place. Such reasoning underlies the extensive welfare provision in the fields of education, health, housing and social security of most advanced industrial societies, for example.[61] Thus, it is the simple equality of citizens as members of society that entitles them, as a matter of supraspherical social justice, to a complex array of goods, rather than the complex equality of different spheres of justice that produces the equal status of members of the community. Walzer's argument is back-to-front.

III DEMOCRACY AND THE SEGREGATION OF POLITICS

The demands of equal citizenship brings us to the role of democracy in Walzer's argument. Walzer associates his theory with a broadly democratic vision of society and of value. It is socially democratic because complex equality supposedly replaces social tyranny with a world in which citizens rule and are ruled in turn, according to their ability in the given sphere of activity in which they are engaged.[62] It is epistemologically democratic because the principles of justice are said to reflect the views of those involved in exchanging the goods that give rise to them.[63] He advocates political democracy as involving both these dimensions within a form of government in which advantages in one sphere do not give domination over others. 'Every extrinsic reason is ruled out . . . Citizens come into the forum with nothing but their arguments. All non-political goods have to be deposited outside: weapons and wallets, titles and degrees.'[64]

In spite of these claims for his theory, the democratic credentials of Walzer's position can be questioned on each of these three counts. We have already noted that 'complex equality' is only contingently socially egalitarian. Indeed, it cannot even be guaranteed to promote equality of respect. Similarly, his theory will only prove epistemologically democratic when the authority of the people is socially recognised. If priests, mandarins or an all powerful leader are regarded as the authoritative interpreters of social meanings, then the people will have at best a subordinate place in interpreting shared meanings. Moreover, where power is organised hierarchically it is highly likely that meanings will be too.

Walzer's defence of democracy as '*the political way* of allocating power'[65] seems at first sight unequivocal. Closer investigation reveals a certain ambiguity in his account. Not only does Walzer wish to keep politics to its sphere, but he is also clearly exercised by the fact that democracy does not enjoy universal support amongst all nations of the world. Both worries serve to undermine his case.

The first concern is motivated by his fear of tyranny. Walzer accepts that the boundaries of the different spheres have to be policed and defined by politics. 'Political power', therefore, 'is always dominant – at the boundaries, but not', he wants to argue, 'within them. The central problem of political life is to maintain that crucial distinction between "at" and "in".'[66] Because the various spheres cannot be kept as separate as Walzer wishes, however, this distinction also collapses. As we have seen, a sphere's meaning and hence its boundaries are tied up with general moral issues that cut across spheres and serve to define how, when and to whom goods ought to be distributed. Goods and their distributional principles have only a very limited autonomy, and are defined as much from without as from within. Walzer appears to suggest that such matters might nevertheless be discussed in terms of 'pure' political arguments, such as liberty rights, shorn of 'every extrinsic reason' – a position reminiscent of Rawls' theory of 'public reason'.[67] Yet to fully appreciate the force of the various moral considerations and interests relating to and across different spheres, they need to be voiced directly. He also tries to minimise the extent of such generalised disagreements by assuming relatively homogenous communities. However, pluralism makes this assumption unlikely in all but the most ethnically cleansed and authoritarian regimes. To the extent that democratic politics offers the means whereby these different general views can be voiced and balanced against each other, it must necessarily operate within and across as well as at the borders of the spheres.

Keeping politics 'at' the borders also overlooks the extent to which oppression operates 'within' them and may require political rectification. Feminist complaints prove instructive once more, since Walzer's argument reflects a typical ambiguity in the liberal distinction between the public and the private that they have done most to highlight. The absence of personal space may be the mark of a tyrannous regime, but unregulated that space can also be the locus of private forms of tyranny that are every bit as oppressive as those of the state. Moreover, discrimination and subordination within the private sphere can distort in their turn the character of the public. The type of influence exercised within their spheres by employers, family, friends, fellow members of a club or church and the like is a political matter, therefore, both in itself and because of its external effects. Walzer's remarks on 'The Woman

Question' show up this problem in his argument well.[68] In keeping with his spherical demarcations, he contends that 'the real domination of women has less to do with their familial place than with their exclusion from other places'.[69] Yet elsewhere, in the context of a discussion of nineteenth-century China, he acknowledges that liberation from 'political and economic misogyny' may require that 'the family itself must be reformed so that its power no longer reaches into the sphere of office'.[70] In this case, however, as well as in the tantalising hints he offers with regard to reforming the contemporary organisation of families,[71] 'social meanings' have to be challenged and a commitment to equality imposed across spheres. This may have the effect of preventing domination in the domestic sphere spilling over into others as well, and so prove consistent with Walzer's separation of spheres. But that entails prioritising his second over his first principle – something he is reluctant to do. Indeed, the autonomy of the different spheres could not provide the main rationale for this policy – more general egalitarian considerations that apply to some degree within as well as between all spheres do.[72] Nor are such changes likely to occur without the political will to politicise the personal, at least in part. Segregating politics to its own sphere cuts off these all important issues. In any case, it is doubtful that a hard distinction can be drawn between inter-spherical boundary drawing and intra-spherical interference. The outer contours of a sphere will almost certainly have some bearing on its inner character as well.

Politics assumes a public culture concerning the rights and duties of citizens. Walzer's second worry comes in here. As I noted in Section I, at least one universal principle seems to run through Walzer's argument: namely, that we should respect the cultural creations and choices of different human beings. In earlier work, he linked some such idea to the need for all social arrangements to be based on consent – a thesis that would appear to point straightforwardly to democracy.[73] Recently, however, he has been reluctant to draw this conclusion. The only valid universalism, he now contends, is the 'thin' reiterated product of numerous 'thick' particular moralities, and always bears the peculiarities of its local manifestations. From this perspective, discussion of the preconditions of democracy gets matters the wrong way around. If and when democratic principles emerge, they will be the distinctive products of the societies which give them birth. There are 'a number of different "roads to democracy" and a variety of "democracies" at the end of the road'.[74]

Quite how the 'collective' and uncoerced reflection necessary to generate such moves towards democracy could get going in the absence of certain general preconditions remains something of a mystery. After all, there are societies where it is part of the meaning of citizenship and political power that it be distributed unequally – feudalism being an example. Walzer's solution to this problem has been that societies always possess the resources for immanent self-criticism. Inside every 'thick' reactionary regime, it seems there is a 'thin' liberal one waiting to get out. This belief can best be described as a pious hope. As Joseph Raz has observed,[75] the thesis that existing morality can be interpreted so as to provide a moral criticism of itself proves incoherent. It implies the paradox that the prevailing morality contains both true and false moral propositions. Yet if morality is simply the existing morality it cannot be a source of moral error, only of truth. Likewise, any radical overhaul or even any change of the existing morality would imply that it was or had somehow become wrong. This proposition too is logically absurd, since once again the only ground for moral correctness is that self-same morality. The only possible immanent moral critique, therefore, consists of pointing out false deductions from accepted premises, uncovering duplicity and the like – a point that Walzer sometimes appears to concede.

Such reasoning may not produce the radical conclusions Walzer desires, however. As Raz pointedly remarks, neither the protestors in Tienanmen Square nor their foreign supporters, with the apparent exception of Walzer,[76] based their condemnation of the Chinese government on arriving at the correct interpretation of the relevant cultural discourse. It may well be that according to Chinese political traditions the massacre was justified. Critical purchase on this event derives from invoking principles that have a wider and not just a parochial relevance, whereby certain forms of behaviour are condemned as simply wrong.

Walzer's invocation of a 'thin' universalism was an attempt to block this line of criticism. To do any work, though, universalism has to be more than purely formal – otherwise Walzer risks the slide into relativism, the avoidance of which motivates this new twist to his thesis. However, if local cultures are to remain consistent with a more substantive universalism, they are likely to simply offer a particular 'thin' elaboration of 'thick' universal concepts, rather than differing totally from them in the way Walzer supposes.[77] Britain, France and Italy, for example, all have recognisably liberal democratic political systems that are informed by certain common 'universal' principles, such as a respect for human rights. Yet there are considerable differences in the political and legal procedures they adopt for realising them that reflect important local historical differences. Thus, Walzer is undeniably correct to say the Chinese should seek to construct a democratic system suited to China rather than simply importing American institutions. But this need not involve studying Confucian or Mandarin traditions, let alone Maoist-Leninist van-guard doctrines, for an elusive Chinese conception of democracy, as he proposes.[78] To the extent that democracy possesses certain intrinsic merits, it can be justified independently of the existence of any indigenous form. Its introduction merely entails adapting the democratic ideal and its associated rights to Chinese circumstances. That this task will be probably better per-formed by the Chinese than others, no matter how well-intentioned, is in most cases no doubt also true. Walzer suggests that such regard for the self-determination of peoples only proves consistent for an 'intepretative' approach that respects the 'thick' local moral views of others.[79] But 'thick' universalists need not be paternalistic imperialists, as Walzer fears.[80] They can believe that China will have to embrace democratic practices of its own accord for largely pragmatic reasons, such as that it will probably be more enduring and successful in that case, or because they value autonomy as an inherent aspect of democracy.

The only ways Walzer can consistently hold to an interpretative morality based on a purely immanent critique is for him either to adopt some form of progressive immanent teleology, whereby existing morality is seen as the evolution of some inherent principle that must gradually work through various stages with all their contradictions. Or he has to argue that existing 'thick' moral systems involve far more 'thin' universal elements than he usually wants to admit, but that these are shockingly poorly observed by many of those who claim to profess them.[81] On occasion, he appears to adopt the former course, as when he argues that the modern view of human equality 'grew out of the critique of a failed hierarchy' during the feudal era, and that progressive interpretations will culminate in the acceptance of egalitarianism.[82] This view, however, is hopelessly optimistic. For example, far from adopting the radical welfare and democratic socialist measures that Walzer contends are at the heart of Western liberal values,[83] the general trend is towards the ever greater extension of the market – a development for which libertarian thinkers can provide a perfectly coherent rationale. This fact does not mean that radical views cannot be defended or libertarian ones criticised, merely that appeals to contemporary *mores* are unlikely to prove the best ground for conducting a debate between these positions. In contrast, Walzer's frequent complaint that many philosophers fail to recognise the degree to which ordinary people's beliefs are moral points in the direction of the second course. However, this strategy fits ill with his assertions about the variety of moralities. Either way, he cannot avoid offering some criteria for sorting out the wheat from the chaff in any tradition.[84]

Walzer's argument here (as elsewhere) trades on confusing two levels of pluralism: namely, differences of view over the universal rules, on the one hand, and disputes as to the interpretation of those rules, on the other.[85] Certain debates of the first kind will concern differing justifications for democracy – such as discussions between utilitarians and Kantians. Moreover, both camps allow for plenty of room amongst their adherents for disagreements of the second kind. Within this range one can talk of different paths and kinds of democracy, and a diversity of policies on matters such as welfare, employment and the like. But some putatively universal moralities simply deny democracy along with any, or only minimal, concessions to pluralism and equality. At the local level, Walzer's arguments have no purchase so far as they are concerned. They can be challenged only in universal terms. Thus, it is the differences between and within a number of thick and broadly democratic universal moralities that allows for a thick politics with numerous thin local variations, not the reverse as Walzer contends. Neither the justification or sphere of operations of democracy is totally particularist, therefore. Rather, to a large degree its rationale and purpose lies in the equitable weighing of universal positions and applying them in given contexts. To fulfil this task politics cannot be squeezed into an elusive space between the spheres.

CONCLUSION

Walzer believes that the democratic socialism he supports is implicit in the public culture of modern industrial societies and develops out of the complex equality they favour. This chapter has disputed both these contentions. Contemporary societies are more plural and the meanings of goods more contested than he appreciates. The resulting fragmentation of traditional societies means that social solidarity cannot be assumed, as he does, but needs to be politically constructed. Complex equality tends to reinforce rather than challenge the social divisions between rich and poor and their tendency to live in such different spheres that the former are largely ignorant of and indifferent to the latter. In this context, arguments for social justice have to be made across and not only between spheres. Indeed, given the poverty of the third world, they increasingly need to be made across societies as well. Walzer's desire to compartmentalise different spheres of justice, and the resulting limitation of democracy, denies his approach the resources for this task.[86]

NOTES

1 I am grateful to Andrew Mason and Paul Kelly for their helpful comments on an earlier draft of this chapter.
2 A thesis encapsulated in Rawls's device of the 'original position' in his *A Theory of Justice*, Oxford, Oxford University Press, 1971.
3 M. Walzer, *Spheres of Justice: A Defence of Pluralism and Equality*, Oxford, Martin Robertson, 1983.
4 Walzer, *Spheres*, p. 5. David Miller has recently developed this point in his *On Nationality*, Oxford, Clarendon Press, 1995, pp. 49–58, where he offers a clear account of the differences between ethical universalism and particularism and their relationship to partiality and impartiality.
5 Walzer, *Spheres*, p. 7.
6 Walzer, *Spheres*, pp. 7–8.
7 Walzer, *Spheres*, pp. 6–7.
8 Walzer, *Spheres*, p. 9.
9 Rawls, *Theory of Justice*, pp. 92–5, 396–9.
10 Walzer, *Spheres*, p. 8.
11 Walzer, *Spheres*, p. 8.
12 Walzer, *Spheres*, pp. 8–9.
13 Walzer, *Spheres*, p. 9.
14 Walzer, *Spheres*, p. 10.
15 Walzer, *Spheres*, p. 5.
16 Walzer, *Spheres*, p. 28.
17 Walzer, *Spheres*, p. 29.
18 Walzer, *Spheres*, p. 31.
19 Walzer, *Spheres*, pp. 312–13, 319.
20 Walzer, *Spheres*, pp. 314.

21 Walzer, *Spheres*, p. 10.
22 Walzer, *Spheres*, p. 20.
23 Walzer, *Spheres*, pp. 312, 314.
24 Walzer, *Spheres*, pp. 10, 95–103.
25 Although I suppose one could imagine a society where degrees were simply the status symbols of the rich. For these points see Brian Barry, 'Spherical Justice and Global Injustice', in Miller and Walzer (eds), *Pluralism, Justice and Equality*, pp. 67–71.
26 Walzer, *Spheres*, p. 314.
27 *Spheres of Justice* mainly concentrated on the need to preserve the autonomy of different spheres within a community. Walzer has developed the epistemological and international aspects of his argument in later books and articles, most particularly *Interpretation and Social Criticism*, Cambridge Mass., Harvard University Press, 1987 and *Thick and Thin: Moral Argument at Home and Abroad*, Notre Dame, University of Notre Dame Press, 1994. I have addressed the epistemological arguments in my 'Walzer, Gramsci and the Intellectual as Social Critic', in J. Jennings and A. Kemp-Welch (eds), *Intellectuals in Politics*, London, Routledge, 1997.
28 E.g. Walzer, *Interpretation*, p. 24 and *idem*, *Thick and Thin*, pp. 4, 7, 15.
29 In essence, Walzer's later argument differs little from his suggestion in *Spheres* that 'it may be the case . . . that certain internal principles, certain social goods, are reiterated in many, perhaps in all human societies. That is an empirical matter. It cannot be determined by philosophical argument among ourselves – nor even by philosophical argument among ideal version of ourselves.' (Walzer, *Spheres*, p. 314, and compare *Thick and Thin*, p. 4).
30 Walzer, *Spheres*, p. 10.
31 M. Walzer, 'In Defence of Equality', in *idem*, *Radical Principles*, New York, Basic Books, 1980.
32 Walzer, *Spheres*, p. 119.
33 Walzer, *Spheres*, pp. xi–xii, 13–17.
34 Walzer, *Spheres*, p. 15.
35 The exception will be when the distributive principle is need, which Walzer believes to be the appropriate distributive criterion for welfare within Western societies. Here an unequal distribution to the most needy has the effect of reducing substantive equality by raising the well-being of those who receive it towards the level of the rest of the population.
36 Walzer, *Spheres*, p. 318.
37 M. Walzer, 'Liberalism and the Art of Separation', *Political Theory*, 12 (1984), 315–30.
38 For a recent outline of the pluralist case see J. Kekes, *The Morality of Pluralism*, Princeton N.J., Princeton University Press, 1993.
39 Walzer, *Spheres*, p. 6.
40 Walzer, *Spheres*, p. 84.
41 Walzer, *Spheres*, p. 65.
42 Walzer, *Spheres*, pp. 64–7.
43 'Distributive justice in the sphere of welfare and security has a twofold meaning: it refers, first, to the recognition of need and, second, to the recognition of membership.' Walzer, *Spheres*, p. 78.
44 A. Gutmann, 'Justice Across the Spheres', in D. Miller and M. Walzer (eds), *Pluralism, Justice and Equality*, Oxford, Oxford University Press, 1995, p. 112–13.
45 This point is well made by Barry, 'Spherical Justice and Global Injustice', pp. 72–3.
46 Walzer, *Spheres*, p. 20.

47 Walzer, *Spheres*, p. 17. Some supporting empirical evidence is provided by David Miller, 'Complex Equality', and Adam Swift, 'The Sociology of Complex Equality', both in Miller and Walzer (eds), *Pluralism, Justice and Equality*.
48 Walzer, *Spheres*, p. xiii.
49 Miller, 'Complex Equality'.
50 Walzer, *Spheres*, p. xiii.
51 Walzer, *Spheres*, p. 313.
52 S. M. Okin, 'Justice and Gender', *Philosophy and Public Affairs*, 16 (1987), p. 57.
53 Swift, 'Sociology of Complex Equality', surveys the relevant literature. His analysis inspires the argument of this paragraph.
54 Swift, 'Sociology of Complex Equality', pp. 255, 265.
55 Walzer, *Spheres*, p. 154, although Gutmann rightly points out the contentiousness of this argument, noting that jobs are also viewed as a welfare good (Gutmann, 'Justice across the Spheres', pp. 103–11). As usual Walzer tries to dodge these issues by saying that there ought to be a commitment to full employment and a policy of reparations to disadvantaged groups such as Blacks. Even so, the redistribution of resources would be hard to justify without engaging in inter-spherical comparisons and evaluations.
56 For a useful summary of this literature, see B. Brown, 'Feminism', in R. Bellamy (ed.), *Theories and Conecepts of Politics*, Manchester: Manchester University Press, 1993, ch. 7.
57 Walzer, *Spheres*, p. 70.
58 The next few paragraphs draw on R. Keat, 'The Moral Boundaries of the Market', in C. Crouch and D. Marquand (eds), *Ethics and Markets*, Oxford, Basil Blackwell, 1993, pp. 6–20 and R. Bellamy, 'Moralising Markets', *Critical Review*, 8 (1994), pp. 341–57.
59 Alasdair MacIntyre develops a similar point to Walzer's employing precisely this analogy. See his *After Virtue: A Study in Moral Theory*, London, Duckworth, 1981, pp. 175–6, 221, and the discussion of his thesis by Andrew Mason, 'MacIntyre on Modernity and How it has Marginalized the Virtues', in R. Crisp (ed.), *How Should One Live? Essays on the Virtues*, Oxford, Clarendon Press, 1996, pp. 191–209.
60 J. Rawls, *Political Liberalism*, New York, Columbia University Press, 1993, Lecture VII.
61 T. H. Marshall, *Citizenship and Social Class and Other Essays*, Cambridge, Cambridge University Press, 1950, remains the *locus classicus* of this argument.
62 Walzer, *Spheres*, p. 320.
63 See M. Walzer, 'Philosophy and Democracy', *Political Theory*, 9 (1981), pp. 379–99 for his clearest statement of this argument.
64 Walzer, *Spheres*, p. 304.
65 Walzer, *Spheres*, p. 304, emphasis in original.
66 Walzer, *Spheres*, p. 15 n.
67 Rawls, *Political Liberalism*, Lecture VI. S. Mulhall and A. Swift have suggested a Walzerian reading of Rawls on this point in their *Liberals and Communitarians*, 2nd edition, Oxford, Basil Blackwell, 1996, pp. 206–10.
68 Here I follow Okin, 'Justice and Gender', pp. 61–2.
69 Walzer, *Spheres*, p. 61.
70 Walzer, *Spheres*, p. 240
71 Walzer, *Spheres*, pp. 174–5, 233n.
72 On this point I disagree with Okin, 'Justice and Gender', p. 64.
73 M. Walzer, *Obligations*, New York, Simon and Schuster, 1970.
74 Walzer, 'Introduction', *Thick and Thin*, p. ix.
75 J. Raz, 'Morality as Interpretation', *Ethics*, 101, (1991), 392–405.
76 Walzer, 'Maximalism', pp. 59–60.

77 Walzer, 'Moral Minimalism', in *Thick and Thin*, ch. 1, pp. 1–19.

78 Walzer, 'Maximalism', pp. 59–61.

79 A similar argument has recently been put forward at some length by David Miller in his *On Nationality*, Oxford, Oxford University Press, 1995, ch. 4. I have criticised this position in a review of Miller's book entitled 'National Socialism: A Liberal Defence', in *Radical Philosophy*, 80, Nov/Dec 1996, pp. 37–40.

80 Which is not to deny that they have been, usually (though not always) with disastrous results.

81 In a recent critique of Charles Taylor, Ronald Beiner has noted how he too oscillates between these two positions. See his 'Hermeneutical Generosity and Social Criticism', *Critical Review*, 9 (1995), 447–64.

82 Walzer, 'Maximalism', p. 45.

83 Walzer, *Spheres* of Justice, p. 318.

84 The above criticisms are developed more fully in my 'Walzer, Gramsci and the Intellectual as Social Critic'.

85 I owe this observation to Martin Hollis.

86 Although in fairness one should acknowledge that he has been forced to recognise this difficulty. See his 'Exclusion, Injustice and the Democratic State', *Dissent*, 40 (1993), pp. 55–64.

10 Contractarian social justice

An overview of some contemporary debates

Paul Kelly

My concern in presenting this survey of some recent debates in liberal political theory is to offer speculations about why contractarian theories of distributive justice have persisted for normative theorising about social or distributive justice. My claim will be that there is an affinity between the process of justification of norms of distributive justice and the character of some problems facing modern democratic states. This does not imply that the conclusions of contemporary normative theories are of only local concern,[1] but it does show that the motivational force of any possible justification requires the equal recognition of those to whom the reasons are addressed, and this equal recognition must rule out certain conceptions of political philosophy as viable alternative ways of addressing the problem of justice.

Rawls has not merely bequeathed us a set of issues concerning how best to distribute the benefits of social cooperation, but has also bequeathed us a method for political theory, which radical critics have been unable to displace. I will not make the strong claim here, that it cannot be displaced, but will instead show, in my survey of recent criticisms of contractualist liberalism based on a politics of *identity*, that the alternative theories advocated by such critics are not sufficient to displace the primacy of distributive justice. Indeed I will suggest that the recognition of problems of identity politics gives a renewed significance to impartialist contractarian theories of distributive justice.

By focusing on the politics of *identity* I will provide a survey of some of the most contested issues in normative political philosophy without merely rehearsing yet again the communitarian critique of foundationalist liberalism.[2] My argument will commence with an account of the Rawlsian paradigm of rules of justice as principles providing for fair cooperation between individuals who disagree about the good or about fundamental ends. This will involve a brief discussion of how Rawls' hypothetical contractarian theory of the 'original position' and the veil of ignorance has given way to a modified Scanlonian contract in the work of Brian Barry.[3] My concern will be to trace criticisms and developments of contractarian justice from within that tradition, leaving aside the much discussed communitarian critique, and to give some account of what contractarians think is still vital within that tradition. This will be followed by an account of two key strands of criticism, the first connecting issues of identity with a critique of the primacy of distribution, will cover the criticisms of Michael Walzer and Iris Marion Young, and second, I will discuss the related political challenge mounted by advocates of multiculturalism and group rights.

DEVELOPMENTS WITHIN CONTRACTARIANISM: FROM THE 'VEIL OF IGNORANCE' TO REASONABLE AGREEMENT

John Rawls in his *A Theory of Justice*[4] uses the traditional Kantian idea of the social contract as a reasonable agreement, as his metaphor for a just society: a just society is a fair system of social cooperation.[5] As well as adopting the contract device as a metaphor for political society, Rawls also uses it to legitimise the two principles of justice which he argues should determine the basic structure of society (its basic rights and institutions) and ensure that it is fair, and therefore, a possible basis for consent. His defence of the content of the two principles is given independently of the contract device, but he is left with the issue of what special authority his two candidate principles have, and why they should claim our allegiance? The two principles are: first, that each person is to have the most extensive set of basic liberties compatible with the equal liberties of others: and second, that social and economic inequalities be arranged so that they are both to the advantage of the worst off and that they are attached to positions open to all on the basis of fair equality of opportunity. The problem of legitimacy is solved by showing that they are principles which would be chosen in an initial fair choice situation. To demonstrate this part of his argument he constructs a hypothetical contract in which the participants are to choose in an 'original position' those principles which should govern the basic structure of their society. However, this choice cannot simply be an unrestricted bargain or else the principles chosen would merely reflect the unequal power and bargaining positions of individuals in existing society; these have no claim of justice and could not, therefore, be the basis of free uncoerced consent. To rectify this problem Rawls introduces the 'veil of ignorance'. This is a constraint which denies the participants in the 'original position' specific knowledge about their goals and life plans, knowledge about their social position and all but general information about their society. The 'veil of ignorance' is intended to have the effect of turning a rational calculation of advantage into a situation of impartial and fair choice, as no one will be able to seek her advantage at the expense of others. Inequalities may well be justifiable in such an agreement, but only in so far as they are to the benefit of the worst off in that society.

Rawls' argument has been the subject of extensive criticism and comment,[6] so much so that it would hardly be an understatement to claim that the subsequent development of normative political theory in the English speaking world has been so many footnotes to Rawls. Three issues are particularly relevant from the perspective of critics within the contract tradition, as problems with Rawls' account of the hypothetical contract: first, whether the 'veil of ignorance' does not actually undermine the separateness of persons which is a central part of his critique of utilitarianism; second, whether choice behind the 'veil of ignorance' would result in Rawls' two principles and not average utilitarianism; and third, whether the contract device does any real work.

One of the main objectives of Rawls' *A Theory of Justice* was to challenge and displace utilitarianism as a possible basis for distributing the benefits of social cooperation and regulating the basic structure of society. A utilitarian theory, it was argued, was unacceptable because it could countenance the sacrificing of some to the good of others. This lack of respect for persons had roots in its method of social and political decision-making. The impartial spectator model of utilitarianism functioned by summing all the preferences of each individual in a society and then choosing that policy or rule which maximised utility, however conceived. This impartial spectator model was an extension of individual prudential rationality to society as a whole.[7] The problem with such a view according to Rawls is that it collapses impartiality into impersonality, whereby the distinction between persons actually disappears. Without maintaining the distinction between persons as a constraint on social rules it is possible to sacrifice some for the good of others. Whilst Rawls' assault on utilitarianism's failure to take seriously the distinction between persons, has had a significant impact on the subsequent development of utilitarian scholarship,[8] the charge of impersonality has been turned back on his own conception of the 'original position'.[9] If the contractors in the 'original position' lack any knowledge of the individuating features of their personality, then they become indistinguishable and this violates the 'separateness of persons'. This matters in Rawls' case for it means that his own contractarian model gives rise to the difficulties he tried to overcome in utilitarianism. However, a full-knowledge contract was ruled out, because given the motivation of Rawls' contractors it would merely result in a mutual advantage contract reflecting conventional inequalities of bargaining position.

As well as the problem of maintaining the 'separateness of persons' there is also the problem that Rawls' attempt to preclude the bargainers in the 'original position' adopting some version of the utility principle, such as average expected utility, undermines the point of the 'original position'. The claim is made that in the situation of ignorance, it is not unreasonable for the contractors to gamble that they would be better off under an average expected utility rule, than if they were to be the worst off under Rawls' difference principle which is a 'maximin rule' (one designed to maximise the position of the worst off). Rawls attempted to rule out such a possibility by arguing that the contractors are 'risk averse' and, therefore, inclined to take the least risky strategy, which is the maximin rule of the difference principle where the worst off will always do as well as possible. But how can Rawls just rule out the possibility of rational risk-taking? He does this by appeal to the 'strains of commitment' argument. Rawls says of the parties: 'They are rational in that they will not enter into agreements they know they cannot keep, or can do so only with great difficulty.'[10] An average utilitarian outcome might impose great burdens on some for the benefit of others and this according to Rawls is overburdensome because the parties in the contract situation will also know that the maximin rule was also a candidate principle. Any choice in the 'original position' which could not be accepted as a reasonable burden once one comes out from behind the 'veil of ignorance' has to be ruled out by the 'strains of commitment' argument, because those to whom the rule applies would find it particularly difficult to comply with the distribution created. Given that Rawls expects the choice behind the 'veil of ignorance' to be a once and for all choice, it cannot be one that the parties will want to defect from once the 'veil of ignorance' is removed.

The 'strains of commitment' argument will provide a reason for excluding the choice of average expected utility or any other utilitarian principle, but only at considerable expense to the whole of Rawls' theory of the 'original position'. The problem with the 'strains of commitment' argument, as Brian Barry, has pointed out is that it is not merely a modification to the psychology of the contractors, rather it is the incorporation of a moral principle that has the effect of making Rawls' whole account of the 'original position' and choice behind the 'veil of ignorance' redundant.[11] The real force of this criticism is that the incorporation of a free standing moral test for the outcomes of the 'original position', the authority of which is derived external to the specification of the 'original position' does appear to make the whole contractarian device redundant. This takes us to the third criticism of Rawls' theory.

As Barry points out, the problem with the 'strains of commitment' as an argument against the choice of utilitarian principles is that it only works because it assumes that it is unfair to place burdens on some to be worse off than they could be under the 'difference principle' so that others can be better off. If there is nothing wrong with this situation other than that it tends to instability, then one response might merely be the creation of efficient institutions of public order which could ensure compliance. However, Rawls' is not merely concerned with stability in this sense, as it has no moral bearing on the issue. Instead he wants compliance to be the outcome of our sense of justice. But this has the effect of confirming Barry's claim that the 'strains of commitment' argument is an illegitimate moral constraint that is actually doing all the work. Rawls' claim can only be that it is morally unacceptable to place burdens on the worst off (who ever they are) because they cannot be given a reason to accept those burdens other than that they are to the advantage of others. What kind of reason is it to say to the worst off, that they are as badly off as they are so that others can benefit? The 'difference principle' gives the worst off a justification for inequalities, in that they could only be made better off by making the worst off group under a new distribution less well off than the current worst off are now. It is unreasonable to expect the worst off (whoever they should be) to accept that they become worse off still in order that some become better off. This is precisely the sort of trade-off that utilitarians wish to make and which contractarian theories of justice wish to rule out. But what all this actually shows is that the 'strains of commitment' argument is doing all the work in deciding what principles can or cannot be candidates for principles of justice, and that the rest of the complex edifice of the 'original position' with the 'veil of ignorance' is doing no work at all.

Given that the 'strains of commitment' argument raises the issue of reasonable rejection as the appropriate test for principles of justice, Barry concludes in his recent reworking of the Rawlsian position in *Justice as Impartiality*, that a more appropriate justificatory model is that provided by T. M. Scanlon.[12] Scanlon's theory is not a theory of justice, but rather a contractualist account of the concept of moral wrong. For Scanlon the criterion of moral wrongness is: 'An act is wrong if its performance under the circumstances would be disallowed by any system of rules for the general regulation of behaviour which no-one could reasonably reject as a basis for informed, unforced general agreement'.[13] Barry, takes this contractualist account of moral wrongness, as a more fruitful justificatory model for a theory of justice than Rawls' theory of the 'original position'. He claims that it can incorporate the basic components of Rawls' theory of justice as fairness without its unnecessary complexities: it assumes that reasons must be given for treating people differently – this is the premise of fundamental equality; it assumes that those reasons must be acceptable to those who get the least in any distribution of rights, liberties or the benefits of social cooperation; and it incorporates the idea of preserving the 'separateness of persons' on the grounds that a worsening of one person's position cannot simply be justified on the basis of an improvement in another's position.[14] The advantage of the Scanlonian model is that it is a full knowledge contract, in that the parties know who they are. The difference between it and a mutual advantage contract which assumes the validity of outcomes based on existing inequalities of advantage, is that it gives all the participants a formal equality in that they can veto the unreasonable imposition of the burdens of mutual advantage.

Two things should however, be made clear about Barry's version of the Scanlonian contract; first, it is not intended to provide an account of moral wrongness as Scanlon intends. Barry's concern is political, in that the point of a theory of justice as opposed to a complete morality, is to provide terms of reasonable cooperation between those who disagree about fundamental ends. As such the agreement is intended to give rise to a second-order conception of justice as impartiality which is concerned with the institutions and structures of social decision-making, and with the distribution of the power to determine how to settle contested issues between those who disagree fundamentally. It is not a first-order morality, in which judgements of strict impartiality are intended to be applied to each case of moral decision-making, as some claim is intended by strict act utilitarianism.

Barry's argument also avoids a problem that plagued Rawls' theory of the 'original position' in that Rawls' had difficulty in giving an account of why persons who are self-interested in the way in which he describes them in the specification of the 'original position' would want to adopt the perspective of impartiality it entailed. This problem is avoided by Barry, in that he assumes the existence of the 'agreement motive', that is the desire to seek agreement on reasonable terms. This he takes to be fortunately widespread. Whether it is or not is of course an empirical matter that cannot be determined by political philosophy, but it seems less implausible an assumption than that individuals are narrowly self-interested. The important thing to note here is that the justification of second-order impartiality as an account of distributive justice is based on a hypothetical contract, not a real interpersonal agreement. As such it does not have to propose that this motivation is universal or near universally recognised. All that Barry and Scanlon need to ground their theories is the view that there is a human motivation which this kind of theory can rely on. If such a motivation was wholly absent, then the theory would obviously collapse as no one would have a reason to accept it, but equally there would be no reason for individuals to be interested in issues of justice either, and clearly there is evidence that a good many people are.

The crucial issue however, is not simply whether the 'agreement motive' exists but whether it can have priority in the hierarchy of individual practical reasoning. The motivation for reasonable agreement assumes the desire to accept reasonable terms of social cooperation and to regulate public disagreement by appeal to open public debate and justification. The motivation to accept the burdens of reasonable justification in part comes from the recognition of the alternative which is the coercive imposition of public rules on the basis of majority or even minority will. Of course this might merely result in a *modus vivendi* whereby parties agree to seek reasonable terms of cooperation on the basis of equality of recognition, until such time as one of the parties is in a strong enough position to impose its will or values on others. Once again however, this assumes a strong motivation to disregard the status of those who disagree fundamentally which is perhaps no more of an unproblematic motivation than the agreement motive. Ultimately these are issues of motivational psychology that political philosophy cannot settle.

A remaining ambiguity in Barry's version of the Scanlonian contract concerns the issue of reasonableness. Scanlon's own account of moral wrong employs an extremely rigorous epistemological constraint on the idea of reasonableness. He assumes that the agreement must be fully informed, and this entails that an informed agreement must preclude any controversial or insupportable claims about the world. Given that the process of justification, employing such a rigorous criterion, must be potentially open ended it does not provide a good model for Barry's theory of justice as impartiality. That said, Barry recognises the need to place some constraint on the content of reasonableness, otherwise someone could accept the burdens of public justification, whilst denying that the rules which they propose, but others oppose, are being *reasonably* rejected. If someone believed for example that homosexuality is a form of psychological disorder then she might claim that those who reject coercive medical treatments of this condition, are not *reasonably* rejecting the policy, and therefore, they cannot veto it.[15] This issue becomes particularly acute when a person's conception of what counts as *reasonableness* draws on substantive moral commitments, such as the view that homosexuality is morally deviant behaviour, or that because all life is a gift from God there can never be any justification for terminating a pregnancy. Barry, attempts to overcome these problems by appealing to a weak form of scepticism, one that does not deny the truth claims derived from controversial conceptions of the good, but does merely assume that there is no conception of the good *so certain* that it can reasonably be imposed upon others irrespective of their views. This is a scepticism aimed not at the beliefs held, but rather at the degree of certainty with which they are held: a scepticism concerning certitude as a psychological attitude. In this way Barry is concerned to maintain a broadly liberal position without making controversial claims about the nature and content of morality which would in effect be imposing a conception of liberalism as the good.

Although both Scanlon and Barry retain the title of contractarians, neither are particularly concerned with the issue of how far their own perspectives are consistent with classical contract theorists such as Locke and Kant, or with the issue of whether the idea of reasonable agreement is sufficiently analogous to the idea of a contract (in law for example) for their theories to be genuinely contractarian. Why then do they persist with the idea. The point seems to be that the contract metaphor remains the best way of describing the three basic components that they wish to salvage and defend from Rawls' theory. Rawls' contractarian critics are more or less unanimous in abandoning the contraption of the 'original position', but what inspired it remains important. And that is, a commitment to fundamental equality; a recognition of the need to justify inequalities to those who do least well by them and finally the idea of the 'separateness of persons'. Taken together these three components form part of a particular moral stance, and it is in virtue of subscribing to these and not some particular device that post-Rawlsian contractarians such as Barry remain contractarians. Ultimately what inspires Barry – though only indirectly Scanlon – is a concern to defend a substantive theory of justice and not a method or contraption. But even Rawls is primarily concerned with principles of justice and not the device of the contract. Nothing much should be taken to hang on the use of a word.

The idea of the contract brings together a distinctive moral position. The defence of that position is ultimately provided by its articulation in a particular theory and its ability to expose and undermine rival views whilst withstanding internal criticisms. One of the chief ways in which the contractarian method has been claimed to be of continuing relevance is in relation to the issue of justifying inequalities or disadvantages to those who will do least well by them. This not only has relevance in matters of economic redistribution but increasingly in terms of the potential burdens or harms of imposed cultural and political identities. It is the growth of identity politics out of communitarianism that in part demonstrates the relevance of contractarian theories of distributive justice.

THE POLITICS OF IDENTITY

Theorists of the politics of identity take up a communitarian concern with the idea of the liberal subject as being either too thin, or else as denying the social constitution of personality and its consequent implications for moral and political philosophy. This can take either of two forms: the first abandons the communitarian advocacy of traditional social practices and identity-conferring institutions; the second is favourable to traditional identity-conferring practices and institutions though acknowledging their plasticity. Using the idea of personality and identity as a social creation, they extend this to a criticism of the character of contemporary theories of justice with their implicit individualism and tendency to universalism and cosmopolitanism. I will commence with an assessment of a radical attack on the idea of distributive justice that has its roots in the work of Michael Walzer, but is developed in the work of Iris Marion Young.

Walzer and Young: against the distributive paradigm

Michael Walzer's work has an ambiguous character in that he can be conceived of both as a narrow communitarian, in his attempt to replace political philosophy with situated social criticism,[16] and as a more radical critic of the concern of post-Rawlsian political theory with issues of distributive justice. It is in his latter guise that Walzer has had such a profound influence on the work of Iris Marion Young.[17] Hence I will discuss the two together.

Walzer's *Spheres of Justice*,[18] is an attempt to displace the so-called 'distributive paradigm' which has come to hold centre stage since Rawls' *A Theory of Justice*. The 'distributive paradigm' assumes according to Walzer, that the fundamental issues of political theory are distributive in character; they involve some group giving something – rights, basic liberties, etc. – to another group who do not have them. The goods that are being distributed are also supposed to have a universal character, like Rawls' 'primary goods'. They are things people must want whatever else it is that they want. For Walzer, conceiving all fundamental political issues as primarily distributive has certain consequences. First, it assumes that there is some set of goods which all people want whatever else they want. This in turn entails a uniformity of human nature and moral agency. Second, it assumes that the character and value of the goods that are to be distributed are uncontroversial. And, third is assumes a need for a distributive agency whose responsibility it is to maintain this distribution.

Walzer challenges the first two implications of the distributive paradigm by contending that men are not passive recipients of goods that have their origin elsewhere, but rather that they are active in the sense of creating social meanings for objects which are then distributed in accordance with those social meanings. What this means is that the value attached to any particular good or object to be distributed is not something that can be abstracted from the conditions which gave rise to its creation, and the identities and self-understandings of those involved in the creative process. For Walzer, our identities as subjects or persons cannot be given independently of the processes and contexts in which we create and discover our identities. Furthermore, these identity-conferring institutions and practices which give rise to the social meanings of those things which we create, embody within them appropriate localised standards or criteria of distribution. The appropriate distributive criteria for any good is not some absolute egalitarian standard, but rather a criterion internal to the distributive sphere constituted by the social meaning of the object. For Walzer this explains why we use terms of disapproval to describe prostitution or the sale of political or ecclesiastical office. These are goods the like of which should not be sold, but distributed in accordance with affection and intimacy in the case of sexual activity, or with piety in the case of ecclesiastical office. Each sphere of distribution of a good that has a determinate social meaning should be kept autonomous from any other; thus wealth should not become the sole distributive criterion for all goods, such as health care, education, sexual favour or political office.

Focusing on the distribution of some determined set of universally valued primary goods obscures the real problem which modern theories of justice fail to acknowledge, and that is the need to maintain the autonomy of each distributive sphere. The 'distributive paradigm' focuses on the problem of monopoly rather than on that of dominance. What this means is that the 'distributive paradigm' focuses on one set of social goods and claims that these are the goods, possession of which is a condition of owning any other goods. The problem is that the dominant good is held in the hands of one particular group, and it needs to be redistributed. The requirement to overcome monopoly leads to a conception of simple equality. Tackling monopoly only leaves the dominant good in its position of dominance. If we take the dominant good to be money, then the requirement of justice is to redistribute wealth within a society so that all are not denied the goods that are dependent on the possession of wealth, rather than to deny wealth's position as the criterion for distributing social goods such as education or health care. Complex equality on the other hand is not concerned with the simple equalisation of holdings, but rather with the need to challenge any particular good's position of dominance. In this way Walzer attempts to alter the focus of attention from who has what, to the issue of who has the power to transform the social meaning of a good into an instrument whereby that good holds a position of dominance over the distribution of others. By attacking the issue of dominance, the monopolistic holding of any particular good becomes far less of a pressing political issue.

Walzer's critique of the 'distributive paradigm' is taken up by the feminist difference theorist Iris Marion Young in her criticism of impartialist theories of distributive justice. Young is particularly concerned to employ Walzer's account of dominance as the primary issue of political theory to support her argument for the idea of 'difference' in post-modern feminism. The problem that Young addresses is one which reduces the political concerns of feminists to requests for a certain kind of good, which they do not have, and which they need in order to become equal. This idea of equality assumes a gender neutral standard or norm against which women's disadvantage can be measured. Such a standard is not possible due to the persistence of patriarchal domination. Women are not merely asking for the opportunity to compete fairly in the race of life, as some earlier feminist thinkers had assumed, because this race of life is itself distorted by the gender structured distribution of power in society. Obtaining equality of opportunity would, in effect, merely be obtaining the opportunity for women to become more like men. Women do not need to be equalised with men, that is, brought up to a level at which they can be like men in male gendered political and social structures. Women and other oppressed groups need to be empowered in order to be able to create institutions and opportunities that are determined by those groups' own priorities and self-understandings.

Young couples her critique of the 'distributive paradigm' with a conception of the person that borrows from communitarianism. For Young, individual identity is not something that is pre-given, rather it is something that we acquire from membership of different identity-conferring institutions and practices. However, whereas many communitarians use this kind of argument to reinforce traditional social and political structures, Young takes a more radical view. Our identities, she claims, are much more fluid than these communitarians recognise, consequently we can be members of a whole variety of identity-conferring institutions at any one time.

The problem with the 'distributive paradigm' is that it attempts to impose a false identity on people by bringing them under an egalitarian norm. This has the effect of marginalising the genuine identities of individuals because in so far as these are inconsistent with the egalitarian norm they are effectively silenced and ruled off the agenda of liberal political philosophy. These marginalised identities and the groups bearing them are also disempowered by the 'distributive paradigm' for it does not take account of the oppression and marginalisation they feel as a result of being excluded by the norm of liberal society. Rather the 'distributive paradigm' reinforces that marginalisation by excluding the possibility of challenging the dominant conceptions of personality and well-being that are operationalised within liberal political theories.

The appropriate response to this problem, according to Young, is not the redistribution of some set of primary goods from those who have them to those who do not, instead it involves a challenge to the dominant conception of personality that underlies the basic norm of liberal theories of distributive justice. This involves not the distribution of equal rights, but a substantial departure from egalitarianism in order to secure political representation of difference. In this way, the presence of different identities will be able to disrupt the 'distributive paradigm' and exercise power in ways that allow these systematically oppressed groups to articulate their own political agendas. In other words, Young wants to take Walzer's conception of social meanings and apply it to the identity of political groups and the issues of political representation. What needs to be equalised is group identities and this requires group representation in a democratic forum. The groups to be represented are social groups as opposed to interest or ideological groups. Social groups are identified by an 'affinity' through a shared form of life, rather than identification via some particular cause or set of beliefs which serve as the criteria for interest and ideological groups.

Both Walzer and Young mount a vocal assault on what they consider to be the 'distributive paradigm' but how seriously should we take these identity based criticisms? Do their theories make any sense as alternative prospectuses for the character of normative political theory?

Walzer and Young begin their assault on the 'distributive paradigm' by assuming that it imposes some egalitarian norm which coerces difference into a kind of uniformity. As we saw in the discussion of Rawls, Scanlon and Barry a commitment to fundamental equality is at the heart of their theories, but does that cause the problems claimed by Walzer and Young? Not necessarily, if we see the impartialist norm that emerges from liberal contract theories as applying at a second-order level, not to the distribution of all goods directly, but to the distribution of power at the constitutional level to determine how contested political issues should be decided. It is only if the impartialist norm is interpreted as a first-order principle applying to particular cases that it would necessarily undermine the autonomy of distributive spheres, and there is no good reason why a liberal theory of justice need be wedded to a first-order impartialist theory. Indeed, given the role of the 'separateness of persons' in constituting the contractarian perspective, it is not clear that an unrestricted conception of first-order impartiality could emerge as a justified distributive rule.

Second-order impartiality would seem to be needed in order to secure the integrity of distributive spheres and preclude the possibility of any one good becoming dominant. A just constitutional settlement on the basis of second-order impartiality provides the best security against any existing distribution of advantage transforming its monopoly of wealth or political power into a permanent system of domination. Much of the force of the critique of the 'distributive paradigm' depends upon an assimilation of dependency arguments that are common in 'new-right' critiques of the welfare state. The increased bureaucracy of the welfare state furthers a culture of dependency among those who are the recipients of welfare, which has the consequence of further entrenching the inequality they suffer and completely disempowering them. There is much justice in the critique of the tendency to bureaucratise the delivery of welfare as merely another opportunity for the state to extend its powers of control over the subject many, but it is not at all obvious that any of this is telling against the liberal concern with distributive justice. Second-order impartiality can take some account of the need for a variety of distributive principles pertaining to different goods. There is nothing in second-order impartiality that entails that higher education places should be distributed on any grounds other than merit, or certain medical treatments on proven medical need. But certain goods should be distributed on a strict egalitarian basis, and these things include basic civil and political liberties and possibly also the material conditions of minimal welfare such as an equal basic income.[19] Again the Walzerian argument does not preclude the need for an impartialist egalitarian principle at a basic level of constitutional design, though his theory does not provide the theoretical resources for providing it. Were he to preclude such a principle then he could be in the awkward position of allowing as a matter of justice that a political community could deny political rights to Jews, Women or Blacks merely because it is part of that society's self-understanding of political rights that they are distributed on the basis of gender or ethnicity. Of course in the past this was the way many societies distributed such goods, and many still do. But all this shows is that history and anthropology have only limited value as bases for thinking about justice. The appeal of second-order impartialist theories of justice, and the motive behind post-Rawlsian political philosophy, is that it attempts to provide criteria of justice that enable us to assess which conventional rules and practices have any authority as genuine sources of obligations of justice. Furthermore, Walzer's whole characterisation of what is wrong with dominance assumes that there is a form of equality of recognition that is denied by dominance. But again this case can only be made by appeal to a criterion other than that given for the distribution of the good in terms of its social meaning. After all the issue is really one of who says what the social meaning of a particular good is – is it a minority caste, an economic class, or something that should be settled by majority decision? The question of which procedure we should appeal to in order to settle this issue is precisely that within which second-order impartiality theories apply: they are concerned with the distribution of decision-making power.

Similar problems arise with Young's argument. She also sees the problem as one of an oppressive distributive framework imposing a single egalitarian norm which has the effect of silencing difference and disempowering oppressed groups. But again this is because she conceives of impartiality as universal first-order impartiality, which is inimical to particular relationships in the same way as simple act utilitarianism. Her account of the problem of systematic oppression and lack of recognition of difference in modern political theory still refers to a claim for basic equality of recognition. This basic egalitarian norm can only be presented as significantly different from that of second-order impartiality by characterising the norm implicit in the 'distributive paradigm' in such a way that it involves the coercion of difference.

Yet as we have seen already, this is not the only way in which we need take account of fundamental equality. A further problem which Young does not adequately address, but which goes to the very heart of her defence of group rights on the basis of recognising identity-conferring groups, has to do with the selection of groups who should be allowed additional special representation, and which conceptions of identity should be marginalised and prohibited. Not all identities are due public recognition as many of them are the basis of coercive relationships and oppression. So presumably Young only wants to empower those identity-conferring groups which are non-coercive in some way, presumably because they acknowledge the equal status of others. She clearly excludes what she calls ideological groups such as Nazis and racists[20] on the grounds that these identities are not based on shared experience but rather on a set of beliefs. This is a precarious strategy, for very many racists are of a peculiarly unreflective cast of mind, and their racism has as much to do with simply being with a group of similarly placed individuals as with sharing any curious late twentieth-century theory of race. Young must employ a principle of inclusion which can discriminate among identity groups, but this raises the question of what principle of inclusion. If she denies a foundational commitment to equality as the basis for her principle of inclusion then she will have a problem justifying its status to those to whom it is to apply. If, on the other hand, she adopts an inegalitarian principle favouring arbitrarily some groups at the expense of others, merely on the basis of some preference, then she will not have a principled response to those who reject her preferences. Adopting an egalitarian norm as the basis of group recognition does not entail a commitment to second-order impartiality without the introduction of further premises, but it does at least undermine the perception that Young's argument is actually employing a radically distinct method of political theory to the form of post-Rawlsian justice theory that she mistakenly caricatures as the 'distributive paradigm'.

Both Walzer and Young criticise liberal contractarian theories on the grounds that they operate with a thin egalitarian norm that grounds a conception of justice which is dominating and insensitive to identity-conferring practices. However in criticising contractarian justice and advancing a thicker conception of equality they open themselves to the very problem that modern contractarian theories of second-order justice address. The tyranny of liberal social justice argument only works if such principles are seen as operating at the first-order level in specifying how everything should be distributed. As we have seen this version of justice is almost certainly precluded by the contractarian variant of liberal social justice. If however, Walzer and Young wish to advance an egalitarianism of groups without a second-order distributive principle setting the framework within which they can function, then they are in danger of allowing the identity-conferring groups to have a dominating effect over each other and over their members. If they wish to resist that then they must appeal to a prior second-order rule which gives members a veto on whether or not aspects of identity can be imposed. What second-order contractarian theories rule out is that identity-conferring groups can impose identities on their members, as this would be a case of expecting members to accept the worsening of their condition for the benefit of others. Contractarian justice does not rule out the value of identity-conferring practices or group membership. What it does rule out is the idea that groups can maintain their identities by coercing their members.

Clearly Walzer and Young do not wish to allow group identities to be coercively imposed as this would undermine the egalitarian and democratic aspirations of their theories. But they are left with the problem of how they address the issue of coercion without retreating back to some contractarian form of second-order justice.

Multiculturalism and group identity

The issue of multiculturalism and group rights is an obvious candidate for a test of contractarian second-order impartialist theories of justice, because it connects the issue of identity and group representation with the issue of whether or not second-order impartiality is a fraud in failing to be genuinely neutral between conceptions of the good. This issue connects with the issues of multiculturalism, toleration and group rights because in modern democratic societies with significant immigrant or aboriginal populations, the fundamental disagreement which second-order impartiality has to address is not merely between individuals' different conceptions of fundamental values, but also between distinct and incommensurable conceptions of society. If liberals fail to accord some degree of respect to such communities' internal autonomy, then, it is argued, this is merely liberal culture imposing its values on people who do not share them – not the triumph of impartial reason but merely a version of intolerant cultural imperialism. In effect liberalism is merely imposing its controversial conception of the good on one group, whilst disallowing other societies to regulate themselves according to their own norms on the grounds that these are controversial. If the liberal replies that he is not imposing a conception of the good, but merely allowing individuals the freedom to determine their relationship to their sub-communities, the multiculturalist argues that this appears to be a neutral stance only because the liberal does not take seriously that his prioritisation of individual choice embodies a controversial conception of the good.

But why should the liberal not merely disregard the claims of group membership altogether? Part of the argument as to why he cannot simply ignore such claims goes back to issues of the politics of identity. It is argued by Will Kymlicka,[21] amongst others, that group membership is important because it provides the context in which individual identities can be formed. These identities are much richer and more sustaining than the kind of desiccated personalities that emerge from an atomistic liberal society. Kymlicka, though a liberal, bases his commitment to liberal values on the basic value of autonomy, so responsibility for self or identity is much more important in his theory than it is in impartialist theories in which autonomy is of questionable fundamental value. Given that community membership can make possible valuable life choices, these communities have a claim to respect and recognition according to Kymlicka, and this means that we should accord them group rights against external intervention – though he is against rights that preclude exit from the community or internal dissent. Many societies that have to deal with significant ethnic and cultural difference have taken account of such arguments in considering the protection of such minority groups.

The problem with Kymlicka's compromise theory is that it weakens the standing of these identity-conferring communities and it fails to deliver a true reconciliation between liberalism and multiculturalism because of his basic commitment to the value of autonomy. If identity-conferring communities are valuable because they are the source of valuable identities then they might have a claim to special protection within a framework of just rules prohibiting coercion, but this does not necessarily lead to liberalism as autonomy. But if autonomy is the ultimate criterion of liberal value then only those identity-conferring communities which foster and protect autonomy can have a value. This seems to collapses into saying that liberalism will accord special respect to only those communities which are consistent with liberalism. This advantages liberalism and does not take seriously the groups who contribute to identity formation, so it is unlikely to persuade the members of minority cultures.

The politics of identity seeks to accord respect to groups within a multicultural society, but how far can it go in endorsing the toleration of any practice that any particular group takes to be constitutive of its identity? The problem posed by multiculturalism is acute, because the forms of life that are raised by it are not reducible to some abstract norm of empowered difference, but can include societies and cultures that are based on false beliefs and unjustifiable power structures and influence. The problem collapses back into either a kind of relativism which just allows different people to behave differently on whatever terms they wish, however illiberal or repugnant those terms might be, or else we are left with the problem of identifying those forms of identity which we wish to cultivate and those we wish to discourage in the cause of emancipating difference. The latter course involves appealing to some kind of norm which is inevitably going to conflict with a particular group's self-understanding. If this norm is not based on some process of public justification such as a Scanlonian contract, what possible reason can it offer to those to whom it is to apply?

This of course raises the question of how neutral such impartialist theories are. It is clear that they do wish to defend some outcomes as better than others and therefore they have to take a stand on the values that may be integral to a particular community or culture. However, the language of neutrality is not wholly perspicuous in this context. Some contractarians such as Barry reject it in favour of the idea of impartiality, which does not deny that the contractarian perspective is free of any value commitments. For such second-order theories the issue is not a direct engagement with the value of cultures and practices, but the indirect one of whether they should be able to impose their values coercively on their members and possible non-members. The contractarian approach gives members a veto against the imposition of harmful practices by identity-conferring groups and cultures. It does not ask members the direct question of whether such cultures are valuable, which an appeal to autonomy must do. For perfectionist liberals such as Kymlicka and Joseph Raz[22] only those cultures which incorporate the priority of autonomy can be valuable and deserving of protection. For the contractarian the approach is indirect: it concerns the justification of coercion and not the justification of values and beliefs. Contractarian second-order impartialist theories only preclude the idea that a person can have the burdens of cultural membership imposed on them by forcing them to accept inferior rights and civil disabilities, for the maintenance of an advantage or benefit for others.

Of course this can still have the same outcome in threatening the long term viability of a culture or community. And of course it doesn't answer the culture which sees no need to justify the coercive imposition of its values on its members in terms that both they and non-members cannot reasonably reject. But short of conceding all authority to that culture or group there is no other position for egalitarians to adopt.

What the appeal to identity-conferring groups and practices by advocates of the politics of identity leaves unaddressed are issues of just how significant group membership is for individual psychology and group stability, what the political costs of both are, and whether these are a price worth paying. The politics of identity theories makes great play of the need for roots, belonging, membership and such like,[23] but they also want to deny a strict communitarian thesis which would take the sociological fact that existing groups contribute to social stability and order as a ground for political efforts to protect those institutions and practices. A lot of important work in psychology is being traded in all these claims as if either such theories were definitive in the case of political theory, or political theory can simply substantiate such psychological claims a priori. This is not to deny that some claims about identity being a social artefact influenced by membership of groups are true, but this is a long way from specifying how far we should take this thesis and what its implications for political theory are.

THE RESILIENCE OF CONTRACTARIAN JUSTICE

One of the primary reasons for adopting an impartialist perspective and more importantly for seeing issues of justice as of central political concern is the need for those of fundamentally different views to live together on reasonable terms. The assumption is the existence of irreducible disagreement within modern societies. One consequence of acknowledging this as a cause of the primacy of justice, is that such issues of justice will only be felt acutely in heterogeneous societies such as the modern Atlantic democracies. In relatively homogeneous societies these issues, though still present, are going to appear less urgent.

What this suggests is a connection between issues of distributive justice and democratic polities. In the face of such fundamental disagreement, the regulation of the public realm and of public social cooperation can either be by coercion or by consensus. It is a choice, and there seems no good reason that we can offer those who do not see the value of consensus which would make them change their minds. But in the context of multicultural societies the practical requirement to survive as a culture, along with others, might inspire some basis for consensus. However, as long as one rates highly the need to justify political actions, and not merely impose them – this, if nothing else, is what democratic politics assumes – then it is clear that we are on the agenda that leads to the primacy of only certain conceptions of political morality. Earlier in the chapter I suggested that what explains the persistence of the primacy of contractarian distributive justice is an affinity between its conception of reason giving, and public justification in democratic societies. In justifying a principle of justice that distributes the benefits and burdens of social cooperation the aim is not to coerce agreement but to find common ground. This entails searching for reasons that all can accept whatever else they might believe and this involves equal recognition as potential beneficiaries of a reason. It also gives each a veto on the imposition of burdens on them unless they can be given a reason to accept those burdens. In other words the fundamental egalitarian premise of contractualist liberalism is built into the idea of public justification. Why is there this connection? The answer seems to be that in order to justify departures from equality we need to give those who are not treated as equals a reason that can justify the inequality and this entails equality of recognition. Ater all there is no great skill in offering reasons which merely reflect the advantage of interest groups, social classes or racial groups. The alternative is not to justify actions at all but merely to impose them, but this ceases to be a problem for political theory and more a practical problem for democratic politicians.

The problem with those theories which wish to displace the primacy of liberal theories of distributive justice is that they do not recognise the constraints of public justification in societies where reasonable disagreement is ubiquitous. If we think of the identity theories we have explored above, all have assumed that the problem of difference does not give rise to the sort of fundamental disagreement that liberal theories of justice assume. If they allow for disagreement, as in the case of Young, they take it to be relatively benign. But when serious disagreement is introduced into their theories in terms of applying norms of inclusion or exclusion, these are seen as either matters merely of political will, or else they cannot but avoid returning to the kind of proceduralism which they have criticised as an aspect of the liberal 'distributive paradigm'. Once the requirement for the justification of inclusion and exclusion is raised, then the issue of what constitutes a public reason is brought to the fore and appeals to identity are seen as having no fundamental significance.

None of the above is supposed to suggest that contractarian theories of distributive justice cannot be criticised, or that the contractarian paradigm is the only possible way of theorising about politics. However, what I have shown is that the current resilience of the contractarian variant of liberal justice is in part attributable to its response to the very problems which identity theorists and multiculturalists claim are so devastating to social contract theories of justice traditionally conceived. Contractarian variants of distributive justice ask for reasons why individuals should accept coercively imposed burdens wherever they arise. The recent communitarian inspired turn to a politics of identity, as an alternative to contractarianism, has merely shown that these problems also arise acutely in the context of group membership whether it be cultural, ethnic, political or lifestyle group.

NOTES

1 Despite Rawls' early work, it does seem to be an implication of his *Political Liberalism*, New York, Columbia University Press, 1993, that issues of distributive justice are of only local concern.
2 I have provided a survey of the communitarian critique of liberalism in my 'Justifying "justice": contractarianism, communitiarianism and the foundations of contemporary liberalism', in D. Boucher and P. J. Kelly, eds, *The Social Contract From Hobbes to Rawls*, London, Routledge, 1994, pp. 226–44. See also S. Muhall and A. Swift, *Liberals and Communitarians*, revised edn, Oxford, Basil Blackwell, 1996.
3 Brian Barry, *Justice as Impartiality*, Oxford, Clarendon Press, 1995. For a critical assessment of Barry's theory together with an extended reply by him see P. J. Kelly, ed., *Impartiality, Neutrality and Justice*, Edinburgh, Edinburgh University Press, 1998.
4 John Rawls, *A Theory of Justice*, Cambridge Mass., Harvard University Press, 1971.
5 For a rejection of the view that Kant has a contract theory see O. O'Neill, *Constructions of Reason*, Cambridge, Cambridge University Press, 1990.
6 Arguing from two different perspectives see B. Barry, *The Liberal Theory of Justice*, Oxford, Clarendon Press, 1972, and M. Sandel, *Liberalism and the Limits of Justice*, Cambridge, Cambridge University Press, 1982.
7 This argument is advanced in *A Theory of Justice*, ch. 1. For an example of this form of utilitarianism see R. M. Hare, *Moral Thinking: Its Method, Levels and Point*, Oxford, Clarendon Press, 1982.
8 On Rawls's impact on the interpretation of the utilitarian tradition see, P. J. Kelly, *Utilitarianism and Distributive Justice: Jeremy Bentham and the Civil Law*, Oxford, Clarendon Press, 1990; F. R. Berger, *Happiness, Justice and Freedom*, Berkeley, University of California Press, 1984, and on utilitarian theory more generally see D. Parfit, *Reasons and Persons*, Oxford, Clarendon Press, 1984 and J. Griffin, *Well-Being*, Oxford, Clarendon Press, 1987.
9 See both Sandel and Barry, note 6 above.
10 *A Theory of Justice*, p. 145.
11 Brian Barry, *Justice as Impartiality*, pp. 65–7.

12 T. M. Scanlon, 'Contractualism and Utilitarianism', in A. Sen and B. Williams, eds, *Utilitarianism and Beyond*, Cambridge, Cambridge University Press, 1982, pp. 103–28.
13 Scanlon, 'Contractualism and Utilitarianism', p. 110.
14 Brian Barry, 'Contractual Justice: A Modest Defence', *Utilitas*, vol. 8 (1996), p. 358.
15 It is interesting to note that in Britain until the decriminalisation of homosexuality between consenting males over the age of 21 in the mid 1960s, courts had the option of imposing so-called drug treatments for homosexual behaviour. Such a sentence was a contributory factor in the suicide of Alan Turing, the eminent mathematician and father of the computer.
16 M. Walzer, *Interpretation and Social Criticism*, Cambridge Mass., Harvard University Press, 1988.
17 I. Marion Young, *Justice and the Politics of Difference*, Princeton, Princeton University Press, 1990.
18 Michael Walzer, *Spheres of Justice*, Oxford, Martin Robertson, 1983.
19 See P. Van Parijs, *Real Freedom for All*, Oxford, Clarendon Press, 1996, and Brian Barry, 'The attractions of basic income', in Jane Franklin, ed., *Equality*, London, IPPR, 1997, pp. 157–71.
20 Young, *Justice and the Politics of Difference*, p. 186.
21 W. Kymlicka, *Liberalism, Community and Culture*, Oxford, Clarendon Press, 1989, and *Multicultural Citizenship*, Oxford, Clarendon Press, 1995.
22 J. Raz, *The Morality of Freedom*, Oxford, Clarendon Press, 1986.
23 This is particularly true of nostalgic communitarians such as Robert Bellah, Amitai Etzioni and Michael Sandel, but this nostalgia is less plausible as a basis for grounding moral principles, though it might help in the field of social policy.

11 Racial equality

Colour, culture and justice[1]

Tariq Modood

In the 1970s and 1980s the central topic of academic political philosophy in the English-speaking world was distributive justice. The focus was very much on economic or material goods; the question being whether people were entitled to have what they had, or did justice require that someone else should have some of it. That the arguments about justice led to investigating the conceptions of self, rationality and community which under-pinned it meant that the debate was far from governed by economics and welfare, and was capable of moving in many directions and far from its starting-point. Yet that many of the leading participants in the 'liberalism vs communitarianism' debate should now have come to place diversity, pluralism and multiculturalism at the centre of their theorising, with the emphasis being on the justness of cultural rather than economic transactions, is surely not just a product of 'following the argument to where it leads'. The change in philosophical focus is also determined by changes in the political world; by the challenges of feminism, the growing recognition that most Western societies are, partly because of movements of populations, increasingly multiethnic and multiracial, and the growing questioning of whether the pursuit of a universal theory of justice may not itself be an example of a Western cultural imperialism. The politics I am pointing to is various and by no means harmonious, but a common feature perhaps is the insistence that there are forms of inequality and domination beyond those of economics and material distributions. An insistence which can highlight the multidimensional nature of some forms of oppression, for instance when social relations are simultaneously structured by economic, gender and racial inequalities, but which can also point to forms of inequality even when economic parity is achieved, as in some of the relations between men and some women.

This emphasis on 'difference' is a genuine advance in our conceptions of social justice. But it is quite mistaken to suppose that economics, and the opportunities and rewards that a socio-economic system offers to minorities, is not central to social justice. We sometimes take a too narrow view of economics and equal opportunities. Economic relationships and opportunity structures are not just 'given' but are constituted by cultural norms – and not just by the norms and practices of those in power, as the case of Asian self-employment demonstrates (Metcalf, Modood and Virdee, 1996). This complicates our understanding of equal opportunities – perhaps more so than we have yet realised – but it should not obscure the fact that participation and performance in the world of work is decisively determinant of life chances, and of relations between groups, including those that social policy understands as 'races'.[2]

RACIAL INEQUALITY IN THE UNITED KINGDOM

Racial discrimination is an important contributor to economic, social and political injustice in the UK today. It works in a number of direct and indirect ways, wastes talent and potential, and by creating bitter feelings of resentment and alienation undermines respect for, and desire to participate in, the political system. Discrimination is a brake on the material and social progress of the country as a whole, and while not an absolute bar to the progress of minorities it prevents success on equal terms or in proportionate numbers to that of the white majority.

The groups that suffer from the cumulative disadvantages of historical and current racism in Britain today are in the main those whose origins are from outside Europe. Such minority groups are diverse, originating as they do from different parts of the former British colonial world and shaped by different aspects of its history. While their presence in Britain pre-dates the large postwar immigration, it is only in the last few decades that they have become a feature of life in the UK, above all in England. While primary immigration was effectively stopped by the mid-1960s, family reunification and natural growth have created communities that now form over 6 per cent of the population of England (and about 1.5 per cent in Scotland and Wales), with much higher proportions in urban areas (over 20 per cent in London and Birmingham). The growth rate of some minority groups is declining to a level comparable with the rest of the population, but other groups, being younger and having larger families, are still growing.

Ethnic minorities entered British society at the bottom. The need in Britain was for cheap, unskilled labour to perform those jobs in an expanding economy which white people no longer wished to do, and the bulk of the immigration occurred in response to this need. Research from the 1960s onwards established quite clearly that non-white people had a much worse socioeconomic profile than white people and that racial discrimination was one of the principal causes. Anti-discrimination legislation was introduced in 1965 and strengthened in 1968 and 1976. While this eliminated the open discrimination that was common up to that time, there is much evidence that racial discrimination is a persisting feature of our society today (see, for example, Brown and Gay, 1985).

Despite the persistence of racial discrimination, the ethnic minorities in Britain are reversing the initial downward mobility produced by migration and racial discrimination.[3] All ethnic minority groups, however, continue to be employed and to earn below the level appropriate to their educational qualifications and continue to be grossly under-represented as managers in large firms and institutions. Moreover, while the Chinese and African Asians have achieved broad parity with whites, the Indians and Caribbeans are relatively disadvantaged and the Pakistanis and Bangladeshis continue to be severely disadvantaged.

The qualifications, job-levels and earnings spread in 1994 are roughly what one would have predicted from the spread of qualifications in 1974, if racial exclusion was relaxed but not absent. Those groups that had an above-average middle-class professional and business profile before migration seem to have been able to re-create that profile despite the occupational down-grading that all minority groups initially experienced.

The progress of ethnic minorities has also depended on their studying harder and longer than their white peers, and their working harder and longer in their jobs. The high representation of most of the Asian groups in self-employment may represent the same phenomenon. Certainly, self-employment has been critical to the economic survival and advancement of some groups, and to narrowing the earnings gap with whites.

There is severe and widespread poverty amongst Pakistani and Bangla-deshi households, with more than four out of five having an income below half the national average – four times as many as white non-pensioners. This is related to their poor qualification levels, collapse of the Northern manu-facturing industries in which they were employed, large families, poor facility in English amongst women, and the very low levels of economic activity amongst women.

While many Caribbean people seem to have escaped from disadvantage, others are probably worse off in some ways than their equivalents 20 years ago. Young black men are disproportionately without qualifications, without work, without a stable family life, disproportionately in trouble with the police and in prison. Many young black women are in work, with earnings higher than white women's; but others are disproportionately likely to be lone parents, unemployed and in social housing – with all that implies for poverty. While for most groups disadvantage may be diminishing across the generations, this is less clearly the case for the Caribbeans.

These inequalities, then, are produced by a plurality of factors, interacting in a complex way. Race relations, discrimination and disadvantage cannot be satisfactorily analysed in terms of a simple black–white divide. The situa-tion of non-whites now is sufficiently varied that aggregate statistics about 'black' unemployment, or, say, under-representation in a particular occupa-tion or economic sector, or rate of homelessness, are blunt tools for the analysis of comparative deprivation or need. They are sometimes worse than mean-ingless, because by aggregating together groups whose condition is dissimilar they mask the true extent of the disadvantaged condition of some ethnic groups. Compound statistics about Asians too ought to be met with suspicion, because the differences between, for example, East African Asians and

Bangladeshis, are much greater than between Asians and non-Asians. Where data is not available or not made available except in terms of 'black' and 'white' populations, or in terms of black, Asian and white, serious mapping of racial equality is impossible.

By uniting all those who suffer from white racism into a single category of *blackness* the race egalitarians of the 1980s provided a sharp political focus and achieved a partial mobilisation of the oppressed groups. But they failed to appreciate that the ethnic pride of various groups, necessary for a confident and assertive participation in a society from which the groups had been excluded and held as inferior, could not be built out of the mere fact of common inequality. Excluded groups seek respect for themselves as they are or aspire to be, not simply a solidarity on the basis of a recognition of themselves as victims; they resist being defined by their *mode of oppression* and seek space and dignity for their *mode of being* (Modood, 1992). Hence, however disappointing it has been to the egalitarians, it is not all that surprising that most Asians have not positively embraced the idea of themselves as 'black' (Modood, 1988 and 1994a) and that many Asian Muslims have mobilised around a Muslim rather than a 'black' identity (Modood, 1990 and 1992). The narrow focus on colour racism and the development of a unitary non-white political identity has not only been politically short-sighted but has obscured important dimensions of racism.

DISCRIMINATION, DISADVANTAGE AND DIFFERENCE

Discrimination can be based on colour racism in the direct form of discriminatory behaviour, or in the indirect form of policies and practices which have a disproportionate, even if unintended, unfavourable impact upon some or all non-white groups. The cumulative effects of this discrimination, especially when inter-generational, is what is meant by 'racial disadvantage', namely a socio-economic gap between white and (some) non-white groups which would persist even if discrimination were to disappear tomorrow. Racial discrimination, however, is not a discrete form of disadvantage (it is connected to other disadvantages); it is not a unitary form of disadvantage (it takes various forms); it is not necessarily linked to racial disadvantage (despite discrimination, some groups can achieve significant socio-economic mobility).

Racial discrimination is not a discrete form of disadvantage because many forms of indirect discrimination ('institutional discrimination') and racial disadvantage are closely related to structural inequalities better understood in terms of class. Ostensibly colour-blind recruitment policies – for example those that give first preference to people from elite universities – will none the less have a racially exclusionary effect, but through the conditions of disadvantage and their effect on educational attainment, rather than racism itself. It perpetuates racial disadvantage but the discrimination is effected through what the disadvantaged have in common across racial boundaries, rather than what separates them.

In this case, to attack the class bias of the policy is in effect to attack the racial bias and vice versa; a policy aimed at removing the conditions of racial disadvantage would make little headway if it did not challenge the existing structure of opportunities created by class divisions. Hence, an attack on certain kinds of racial inequality is only possible within a much more extensive commitment to equality and social justice. In so far as race-specific policies can provide opportunities for education, training, employment and social mobility, restrictions upon which can all be forms of indirect racial discrimination, they can only be wholly effective as refinements of broad social programmes to improve the relevant opportunity-structures for all racial groups. The race dimension of such programmes would be designed to ensure that those most disadvantaged were not overlooked by the programme and got the particular kind of assistance they needed in a culturally appropriate way; it could not be a substitute for a social equality programme – even in respect of disadvantaged racial groups (Wilson, 1987).

Racial discrimination is not, secondly, a unitary form of disadvantage because not all non-white groups are discriminated against in the same way or to the same extent. Colour-racism may be a constant but there are other kinds of racism at work in Britain. Colour racism is the foundation of racism rather than the whole edifice. Direct discrimination depends upon stereotypes and there are no stereotypes about 'blackness' as such: the stereotypes are always about specific groups or quasi-groups ('Jamaicans are lazy', 'Asians don't mix', 'Muslims are fanatical', etc.). Hence, different groups will be affected differently, and some groups can become or cease to be more 'acceptable' than others. Moreover, stereotypes, like all social generalisations, allow for counter-examples, so that individuals of any group who are able to demonstrate, for example in an interview, that they are a counter-example to the stereotype, will receive less unfavourable treatment.

Indirect discrimination depends on policies and practices which (unintentionally) disproportionately disadvantage one group compared to others. Groups whose language, religion, customs, family structures, and so on are most different from the white majority norm will experience the most disadvantage and exclusion. So, just as colour-blind class discrimination can be a form of indirect racial discrimination, so membership of a minority community can render one less employable on the grounds of one's dress, dietary habits, or desire to take leave from work on one's holy days rather than those prescribed by the custom and practice of the majority community.

This direct and indirect discrimination, taken together, constitutes 'cultural racism' (in contrast to colour racism) and is targeted at groups perceived to be assertively 'different' and not trying to 'fit in'. It is racism which uses cultural difference to vilify or marginalise or demand cultural assimilation from groups who also suffer colour racism. Racial groups which have distinctive cultural identities or community life will suffer this additional dimension of discrimination and prejudice. This form of racism is least acknowledged, debated or repudiated, and is not properly outlawed (the courts have deemed discrimination against Muslims to be lawful) and yet is the racism that is on the increase, has the greater impact upon Asians and is an important cause of the rising levels of racial violence in Britain and Europe. Contemporary attacks upon Muslims are not a case of straight-forward religious bigotry nor of colour racism but of the phenomenon I am calling 'cultural racism'. It is because of its complex character that it cannot be properly defeated by the politics of religious harmony or by anti-colour racism, but only by a movement that understands the pluralistic phenomenon of cultural racism. This approach can also explain some of the contradictions in contemporary racism, such as the observation that white working class youth culture is incorporating, indeed emulating, young black men and women while hardening against groups like South Asians and Vietnamese (Cohen, 1988: 83; Back, 1993). Survey evidence does indeed suggest that young white people are more prejudiced against Asian than against Caribbean people: while those over 34 years old are only slightly more likely to say they are prejudiced against Asians and Muslims than Caribbeans, those under 35 years old are half as likely again to say they are prejudiced against Asians and Muslims than Caribbeans (Modood *et al.*, 1997; see also Sachdev, 1996; Dawar, 1996 and Alibahai-Brown, 1997).

One way to understand the emergence and growth of cultural racism is to see it as a backlash against the emergence of 'public ethnicity'. Minority ethnicity, albeit white ethnicity like that of the Jewish community, has traditionally been regarded in Britain as acceptable if confined to the privacy of family and community, and if it did not make any political demands. However, in association with other socio-political movements (feminism, gay rights, etc.) which challenge the public–private distinction or demand a share of the public space, claims are increasingly made today that ethnic difference is not just something that needs 'mere' toleration but needs to be publicly acknowledged, resourced and represented. Thus there is a vague multiculturalism as a policy ideology and it has perhaps contributed to a new ethnic assertiveness, so that many of the race relations conflicts today arise out of a demand for public space, for public respect and public resources for minority cultures and for the transmission of such cultures to the young. Yet, because our racial equality legal and policy framework is premised on colour racism, rather than cultural racism, there is no clear view from any part of the political spectrum (except perhaps from the nationalist Right) about to what extent these political demands are justifiable, especially in relation to religious communalism, and how cultural racism should be tackled.

Prejudice and antipathy against ethno-religious groups poses a challenge the seriousness of which is only just beginning to be appreciated. While a secular framework need not necessarily be insensitively hegemonic, I think that contemporary secular multiculturalists are unaware of the contradictory signals that they are sending out. Multiculturalism which states that public recognition of minority cultures is essential to equal citizenship, combined with a denial of an equivalent public recognition of religion, can only convey the message that religious identity has and ought to have less status than other forms of group identity (Modood, 1994b). Yet, why should it be the case that groups proclaiming themselves to be 'black' are to be empowered and given distinctive forms of political representation, but equally or more disadvantaged groups that mobilise around a religious rather than a colour identity are to be discouraged? While such questions are not answered, non-white religious groups may rightly complain of double standards.

DISCRIMINATION AND OUTCOMES

Racial discrimination is, thirdly, not necessarily linked to racial disadvantage because some groups migrate with skills and capital, and because some discri-minated groups put in extra time and energy, work and study harder, develop self-help and/or other networks to compensate and, therefore, avoid the socio-economic disadvantages that would otherwise result from discrimina-tion. There is now growing evidence that some Asian groups experience discrimination in selection processes *and* are over-represented (in the sense of appearing in greater proportion than their share of the overall population) in higher education admissions and in entry to prestigious professions such as medicine, accountancy and law (Modood and Shiner, 1994; Modood *et al.*, 1997). This may be a confusing development, even though it is not unique to Britain, and the signs of it happening have been there for some years. In con-sidering the implications of such developments for re-thinking racial equality, the following in particular need to be borne in mind.

First, it is not necessarily the case that the upwardly-mobile groups experi-ence less discrimination than the less mobile groups; on the contrary, in the opinion of all ethnic groups Asians suffer more prejudice than any other group (Modood *et al.*, 1997), and it is not obvious that the successful Asian groups experience less discrimination or hostility than the others. Moreover, it is not the case that as a group is perceived to be successful and separated out from other minorities, it will attract less prejudice and discrimination: as the Jews know, those considered to be 'too successful' can suffer more prejudice than those thought to be inferior. Second, if measures to eliminate discrimination are successful, it will mean that groups like Indians or Chinese may increase their 'over-representation' in higher education, the professions, and management for some of those presently kept out will get in. At whose expense should this be? Is it clear that it should be at the expense of whites rather than, say, Pakistanis? As ethnic monitoring becomes more extensive, this argument about over-representation will force itself into debates. It has already done so at prestigious US universities, at a number of which Chinese and other Asians have complained that making entry easier for some minori-ties has the effect of imposing a ceiling upon them. The universities do not deny the charge but say it has to be offset against the wider goal of 'pro-portional representation'.

An alternative egalitarian defence might be that equal opportunities is about process not outcome, about fairness in selection, not numbers in outcomes. If so, this would mean a major shift or retreat as most equality policy statements (sex as well as race) currently say the opposite. It is therefore important to see why egalitarians currently think of equality in terms of outcomes. Ethnic origin data collection was first introduced on the basis of the reasonable assumption that differential statistics would be prima facie evidence of discrimination, of practices that needed to be investigated and justified. Where justification was not possible, the practices were to be eliminated. Yet even where this was done, further monitoring revealed that there was still an inequality in outcomes. Moreover, arguments about the fairness of procedures were proving to be time-consuming and intractable and were perceived as too academic or formalistic by both egalitarians and recruiters alike. The simple goal of 'mirroring' the population, or achieving proportionality in outcomes as the definition of absence of discrimination, cut through this knot, and made possible the setting of numerical targets or quotas. While this has now become the understanding of equal opportunities at policy level (for gender even more so than for race), Bhikhu Parekh has argued that to commit policy to proportionality is 'to ignore (the disadvantaged groups') diversity of talents and aptitudes, to control and curtail their right of self-determination, and to mould them in the image of the dominant world' (Parekh, 1992: 270).

If one accepts that different groups legitimately have different norms, priorities and cultural commitments, it is difficult to see why the measure of equality should assume that all groups equally pursue the same experiences, education, occupational and other personal goals and make the same compromises between work, family and recreation. Without such an assumption, equality has to be interpreted in a more complex way as outcomes that are the product of free choices. Yet this surely, especially on a macro-societal level, is even more difficult to measure than fairness in procedures at an institutional level. Hence it is difficult to see how we can altogether give up on equal opportunities as proportionality in outcomes. It must at least figure at the start of equality debates, even if it does not tell the full story. In talking of racial disadvantage we must necessarily be talking about comparative outcomes, about socio-economic profiles. What we cannot assume is that racial discrimination is the effective cause of racial disadvantage or that the elimination of discrimination will of itself eliminate the conditions of disadvantage, let alone produce freely chosen outcomes. Conversely, the commitment to the elimination of discrimination cannot be put aside just because the discriminated group has managed to avoid relative disadvantages. The right to not be discriminated against by public institutions and in civil society is fundamental.

It is worth spelling out one important corollary of this. To pursue a more vigorous US-style affirmative action approach to achieve equality of outcomes (inevitably based on soft or hard quotas) will create prima facie cases of injustice to individuals (for example, individuals denied entry onto a university course because of a policy which prefers others with lesser qualifications) not just against whites but also some minorities. Such a policy is not likely to be considered just or necessary unless it can be demonstrated that it is the only way to overcome racial disadvantage, but this would be difficult to sustain at a time when some minorities were being visibly successful. A broad class-based attack on socio-economic disadvantage is more likely to win public support and avoid racial and ethnic conflict.

POLICY DILEMMAS

Racial equality thinking, where it reduces racial discrimination to colour discrimination, and/or fails to think through the implications of public ethnicity, and/or assumes too close a linkage between discrimination and disadvantage, fails to keep up with the socio-cultural developments that are taking place. At the very least, these changes challenge the assumptions of political 'blackness': the view that colour racism is the most important determinant in the outcomes of non-white people who, therefore, form a quasi-class with a common socio-economic position and interests. They should also challenge the view that the only remedy for their disadvantage is through political power. For the reality is that those groups who evidence social mobility (Indians and Chinese) have no special access to state power and have assiduously kept a low political profile (in so far as they seek political power, it is to consolidate rather than to initiate social mobility). This should encourage sober reflection on the nature and extent of state intervention in this area. Yet the first conclusions one may come to are hardly unproblematic.

Ethnicity – that is, norms, group solidarities and patterns of behaviour which are not merely the products of majority exclusion, and which may be valued by the community in question and which may inculcate them in its young – can clearly be a resource. It can provide the strength to cope with racism and majority contempt, to instil group pride, to organise forms of welfare and cultural needs-satisfaction, to create business opportunities and enclaves, to maintain across the generations the discipline of deferred gratification needed to climb educational, business and career ladders, and so on. It may, therefore, be thought that sound policy should endorse ethnicity and encourage communities to use their own traditions to develop themselves. Not only would this be in keeping with multiculturalism but it would mean less direct state intervention and state management of services, and would therefore be one extension of the idea of the 'enabling state'.

Two problems, however, immediately suggest themselves. First, some communities may be too fragmented or too resourceless to benefit from this approach. Second, the legitimising of 'difference' that this approach involves might increase group consciousness and therefore encourage the potential for group competitiveness rather than inter-group social solidarity. Moreover, it would tend to harden boundaries that may otherwise become fluid, and strengthen intra-group authority in ways not wholly consonant with a political culture of individual rights. Perhaps we should bite the bullet and simply recognise that multiculturalism is a legitimate limit on individualism.

This, however, is not as simple an idea as it might sound, or easy to use as the basis for political consensus. Consider equal opportunities recruitment policies. The principle often enunciated is that of overcoming stereotypical bias by treating everyone the same: but how can one do that if people have different norms, sensibilities and needs? It is not possible to treat someone as an individual if one is ignorant about their cultural background and the things that matter to them, for the greater the ignorance about a group of people by an outsider or observer, the greater the reliance on a stereotype. To decrease the use of unfavourable stereotypes one has to increase the level of knowledge about the groups and to make sure that the knowledge used is not only of the outsider's generalising type but includes some understanding of how the group understands itself, of what it believes to be some of its distinctive qualities or virtues, its circumstantial difficulties and so on.

An abstract culture-blind individualism will necessarily impose majority norms and expectations upon all candidates and, therefore, discomfort and disadvantage some minority candidates. On the other hand, to treat the latter differently can be very difficult to justify in any particular case, let alone to institutionalise through policies and procedures and to build the necessary consensus amongst managers, staff, etc. Where active multiculturalism contradicts such a basic (if partial) intuition of fairness as uniformity of treatment, it will be very difficult to get public support for differential policies that are not merely about tolerating difference but involve large-scale resource commitments. A debate about the implications of cultural difference for equality is therefore unavoidable if multiculturalism is to mean more than tokenistic recognition of minority cultures.

Not only is there a clash between some of our intuitions about fairness and equality, but well-meaning policies may well collide. Some have expressed concern that policies of multiculturalism which, say, allow Asian girls to be withdrawn from certain activities at school (for example, sex education, sport, dance,) or to not be entered for certain subjects, collude with traditional views on gender difference and sex roles. Similarly, though less noticed as an example of how tackling some forms of discrimination actually reinforces other forms of discrimination, is how many racial equality policies currently act as a barrier to recognising the needs of, say, Muslims. An example is the same-race adoption and fostering policies which place black Muslims with black Christians, and Asian Muslims with Hindus and Sikhs.

The Muslim example is not simply illustrative but urgent. By the usual socio-economic measures of disadvantage Asian Muslims are among the very worst-off groups, and yet, unlike religious groups such as Sikhs and Jews, they are not deemed to be an ethnic group and so are outside the terms of existing anti-discrimination legislation (UKACIA, 1993). Their low level of representation in mainstream institutions and fora in Britain is chronic: no

Muslim had ever sat in either House of Parliament or even been chosen by a political party to fight a winable seat till the 1997 election. Given that they may form nearly half the non-white population in Britain and over 60 per cent in the EU (Anwar, 1993), it is difficult to see how there could be a race relations settlement without the Muslim communities. Combining as they do the facets of being a socio-economic underclass, targets of colour racism and victims of cultural racism, they combine in their person the 3 'Cs' of race: colour, class and culture. The treatment of Muslims, especially Pakistanis and Bangladeshis, is an important test of whether racial equality policies can be extended to meet the new challenges.

A NEW CONCEPT OF EQUALITY

The concept of equality has been under intense theoretical and political discussion, especially in the English-speaking world; what is often claimed today in the name of racial equality is more than would have been recognised as such in the 1960s. Iris Young expresses well the new political climate when she describes the emergence of an ideal of equality based not just on allowing excluded groups to assimilate and live by the norms of dominant groups, but based on the view that 'a positive self-definition of group difference is in fact more liberatory' (Young, 1990: 157). She cites the examples of the black power movement, the gay pride assertion that sexual identity is a matter of culture and politics, and the feminism which emphasises that women's experiences should be celebrated and valued in their own right. These movements have not had the same impact in Britain as in parts of North America, but are certainly present here. In particular there is an ethnic assertiveness in Britain which has parallels with North America. It has been less evident amongst recent migrants and their descendants in other European Union countries, where cultural assimilation is still regarded as essential to citizenship and political equality. This assertiveness counterposes positive images against traditional or dominant stereotypes, and projects identities in order to challenge existing power relations or to negotiate the sharing of physical, institutional and discursive space. Anti-racists have challenged the presumed stigma associated with not being white or conventionally British (Modood, Beishon and Virdee, 1994).

The shift is from an understanding of equality in terms of individualism and cultural assimilation to a politics of recognition, to equality as encompassing public ethnicity. Equality is not having to hide or apologise for one's origins, family or community but expecting others to respect them and adapt public attitudes and arrangements so that the heritage they represent is encouraged rather than contemptuously expected to wither away. There seems, then, to be two distinct conceptions of equal citizenship, each based on a different view of what is 'public' and 'private'. These two conceptions of equality may be stated as follows:

1   The right to assimilate to the majority/dominant culture in the public sphere; and toleration of 'difference' in the private sphere.
2   The right to have one's 'difference' recognised and supported in both the public and the private spheres.

These are not, however, alternative conceptions in the sense that to hold one, the other has to be rejected. Multiculturalism requires support for both conceptions. For the assumption behind the first is that participation in the public or national culture is necessary for the effective exercise of citizenship, the only obstacles to which are the exclusionary processes preventing gradual assimilation. The second conception, too, assumes that groups excluded from the national culture have their citizenship diminished as a result; offers to remedy this by accepting the right to assimilate; yet adds the right to widen and adapt the national culture and the public symbols of national membership to include the relevant minority ethnicities.

CONCLUSIONS

Despite the various tensions and dilemmas discussed above, some of which cannot be resolved without considerably more thought and debate than they have received so far, I offer the following six conclusions as the basis for re-thinking racial disadvantage in the context of the new pluralism.

The first principle of racial equality should be anti-discrimination, that is to say, the right of the individual to full participation in all the major aspects of the common social life without being penalised for their racial, ethnic or religious identity, regardless of the socio-economic standing of the group to which the individual may belong. In failing to protect groups such as Muslims, existing anti-discrimination law in Britain is in need of urgent extension; in many other European countries, anti-discrimination law of any kind is in need of creation. A new offence of racial-religious violence and harassment will assist the urgent task of raising these matters up the political agenda. The Northern Irish incitement to religious hatred law also has potential for application in Britain and elsewhere (Modood, 1993b).

Second, colour is a factor in the total analysis of social disadvantage and inability to achieve full citizenship, but it is a weak indicator of need over and beyond the elimination of discrimination, for while some non-white groups may have more members in need of assistance, others may have less, and the needs in question will not always be based on race but will sometimes be identical to those of white people.

Third, some aspects of racial disadvantage can only be tackled within wide-ranging needs-based or class-based programmes, though the knowledge that non-white groups have been overlooked or discriminated against in the past, and as a result may be sceptical about provisions of new opportunities and benefits, may mean that explicit monitoring and outreach are required to ensure take-up by all individuals with the relevant needs.

Fourth, because racism is wider than colour racism, we need to be far more informed and sensitive to cultural and religious differences in both identifying 'racial' discrimination and in strategies for its elimination. This will include training for relevant professionals in the complex character of racial inequality and difference, and in the appropriate cultural backgrounds; and also the recruitment, training, and promotion of individuals who can positively relate to one or more of the marginalised minority groups and can infuse their understanding into the policy-making and implementation processes.

Fifth, we need to allow communities to use their traditions and values to meet their problems and disadvantages. Communities should be involved as partners at the level of strategic planning (for example, of an urban development programme) as well as in the provision of services (for instance, housing associations, community centres, social and health services). This has to some extent been happening in the development of black and Asian housing associations; it is time that non-European traditions of medicine and therapy were taken more seriously and that social work was able to incorporate the kinds of family-oriented counselling services that are developing in the Asian voluntary and private sector.

Sixth, where supporting ethnic community structures is not a viable approach effective ethnic monitoring should ensure that action is *targeted* to those who are actually disadvantaged (for example, in the labour market) and not simply to those who are not white. To this end it is essential that racial equality monitoring goes beyond the use of a black–white analysis or even a black–Asian–white analysis. It would be a step backwards to reduce the plural findings of the census into a frame of just two or three categories. Above all, it would be to let down those who are 'the truly disadvantaged' and on whom policy must be targeted.

Among European countries, Britain has been at the forefront of recognising and dealing with racial inequality. But racism remains a major barrier to social justice in the UK, and our concern must go beyond narrow colour racism. We now need to re-emphasise the connections between issues of race and other concerns of social justice, in particular that racial disadvantage compounds class inequality, social deprivation and exclusion. To make these connections is at the same time to recognise that racism has different dimensions and affects different groups in different ways and to different extents. Moreover, given the nature of the most prominent forms of racism in Europe, where hostility to lighter-skinned Maghrebians and Turks can be greater than to culturally integrated and darker-skinned Africans and Caribbeans, some notion like cultural racism must be a precondition of effective anti-racism.

To emphasise any 'difference' may perhaps seem to make social justice and social cohesion more difficult, yet these multiple factors of inequality are integral to the challenge of achieving social justice. Multiculturalism is not just about the appearance of society; it is about refashioning concepts of equality to take account of the ethnic mix that exists in most European cities today. Ethnic and religious diversity has the potential to make society more interesting, more dynamic and more enriching for all its members, but will only do so when its complexities are understood and made integral to social justice.

NOTES

1 This chapter is based on my Issue Paper of the same title published by the Commission on Social Justice and the follow-up volume, J. Franklin (ed.) *Social Policy and Social Justice: An IPPR Reader*, Polity Press.
2 The eclipse of the economic is even more evident amongst (ex) Marxists than social democrats.
3 The evidence for the factual claims in this and the next four paragraphs is in Modood *et al.*, 1997.

REFERENCES

Alibhai-Brown, Y. (1997) *A Report on a Survey Conducted by NOP*, London: Institute of Public Policy Research.
Anwar, M. (1993) *Muslims in Britain: 1991 Census and Other Statistical Sources*, Centre for the Study of Islam and Christian–Muslim Relations Papers, Birmingham.
Back, L. (1993) 'Race, Identity and Nation within an Adolescent Community in South London', *New Community* 19(2): 217–33.
Brown, C. and Gay, P. (1985) *Racial Discrimination: 17 Years After the Act*, Policy Studies Institute.
Baldwin-Edwards, M. (1991) 'Immigration After 1992', *Policy and Politics* 19(3): 119–211.
Cohen, P. (1993) 'The Perversions of Inheritance: Studies in the Making of Multi-Racist Britain', in Cohen, P. and Bains, H. S. (eds) *Multi-Racist Britain*, Macmillan.
Dawar, K. (1996) *Racism in Britain: a survey of the attitudes and experiences of Black, Asian and White people*, BBC, unpublished.
Metcalf, H., Modood, T. and Virdee, S. (1996) *Asian Self-Employment: the Interaction of Culture and Economics*, Policy Studies Institute.
Modood, T. (1988) '"Black", Racial Equality and Asian Identity', *New Community* 14(3): 397–404.
Modood, T. (1990) 'British Asian Muslims and The Rushdie Affair', *The Political Quarterly* 61(2): 143–60; also in Donald, J. and Ratansi, A. (eds) *'Race', Culture and Difference*, Sage, 1992, pp. 260–77.
Modood, T. (1992) *Not Easy Being British: Colour, Culture and Citizenship*, Runnymede Trust and Trentham Books.
Modood, T. (1993a) 'The Number of Ethnic Minority Students in British Higher Education: Some Grounds for Optimism', *Oxford Review of Education* 19(2): 167–82.
Modood, T. (1993b) 'Muslims, Incitement to Hatred and The Law', in Horton, J. (ed.) *Liberalism, Multiculturalism and Toleration*, Macmillan.
Modood, T. (1994a) 'Political Blackness and British Asians', *Sociology* forthcoming.
Modood, T. (1994b) 'Multiculturalism, Establishment and British Citizenship', *Political Quarterly* 64(4), January.
Modood, T., Beishon, S. and Virdee, S. (1994) *Changing Ethnic Identities*, Policy Studies Institute.

Modood, T., Berthoud, R., Lakey, J., Nazroo, J., Smith, P., Virdee, S. and Beishon, S. (1997) *Ethnic Minorities in Britain: Diversity and Disadvantage*, The Fourth National Survey of Ethnic Minorities, Policy Studies Institute.

Modood, T. and Shiner, M. (1994) *Ethnic Minorities in Higher Education: Why Are There Differential Rates of Entry?*, Policy Studies Institute.

Parekh, B. (1992) 'A Case for Positive Discrimination', in Hepple, B. and Szyszczak, E. (eds) *Discrimination: The Limits of Law*, 1992.

Sachder, D. (1996) 'Racial Prejudice and Racial Discrimination: Whither British Youth?' in H. Roberts and D. Sachder (eds) *Having Their Say: The Views of 12–19 Year Olds*, Young People's Social Attitudes Survey, London: Barnardos.

UK Action Committee on Islamic Affairs (UKACIA) (1993) *Muslims and the Law in Multi-Faith Britain: Need for Reform*, A Memorandum to the Home Secretary, London.

Wilson, W. J. (1987) *The Truly Disadvantaged: The Inner City, The Underclass and Public Policy*, Chicago: University of Chicago Press.

Young, I. M. (1990) *Justice and the Politics of Difference*, Princeton: Princeton University Press.

12 Democracy, freedom and special rights[1]

Carole Pateman

In the 1990s, democracy and rights have achieved unprecedented prominence. The United Nations and numerous non-governmental organisations monitor human rights, and issues about democratisation and rights even enter into foreign relations and international economic policies. The language of democracy and rights is now spoken in the remotest parts of the world, but is heard most loudly in the USA where the Constitution has ensured that rights have always been central to politics and where claims made in terms of rights have proliferated in recent years. In other Western countries rights talk (as it is sometimes called) has also increased as anti-discrimination measures and other reforms since the 1970s have enlarged the scope of rights.

But this is only part of the picture. In the last twenty-five years, rights of all kinds have become a major domestic and international battle ground. Opposition comes from a wide range of sources, and certain rights, particularly those that concern women or religion, provoke particular hostility. The charge is frequently now heard in international forums and academic circles that rights are a Western invention and an imposition that threatens the integrity of other cultures. Within Western countries, the charge is also made that over-emphasis on rights creates serious social problems. Supreme Court Justice Clarence Thomas, for instance, has blamed the 'rights revolution' for helping to foster crime and the breakdown of order.[2] The assertion that rights talk has gone much too far is heard today from a broad spectrum of political opinion.

At least since the French Revolution, both conservatives and radicals have attacked rights as unacceptably individualist, and so as a threat either to the social fabric or as an inadequate basis to create a new society. The difference in the 1990s is that, at the very time when democracy is so popular, deep suspicion about, or outright rejection of, rights seems more widespread than ever. For example, although feminism is often presented as being nothing more than the extension to women of the rights of man and the citizen, rights are a controversial matter within contemporary feminism. Some feminists have rejected rights as part of an abstractly individualist and masculine conception of political life, others emphasise needs rather than rights, and a number of feminists have expressed severe doubts whether the achievement of equal rights improves women's social position.

Opposition to, or doubts about, rights are confounded by a major intellectual challenge to universalism that has been underway for some time. Advocates of a variety of philosophical and theoretical perspectives look to the local, the particular and the culturally specific, rather than the universal. For three hundred years, rights have been conceptualised in universal terms – natural rights, the rights of man, human rights, and, more recently, the rights of sentient beings – so the challenge strikes at the heart of rights talk. However, the practical implications for rights of extremely abstract philosophical arguments against universalism remain unclear; leading anti-universalist philosophers still seem to accept universal suffrage and other familiar democratic rights, at least in their own countries, and prominent figures have recently begun to write about human rights.[3] But I shall not pursue these general issues here. I am going to concentrate on a narrower set of questions about democratic rights, citizenship and the welfare state in Britain and the USA.

In so far as rights are separated from universalism, it would seem to follow (assuming that rights talk can still be carried on) that rights must be specialised and specific to various categories and groups of citizens. The idea of rights special to certain groups has been at the centre of the battleground over rights in the USA and Great Britain during the last quarter-century. One of the most heated clashes in a number of different contexts is between, on the one side, the advocates of equal, general, formal or universal rights, applicable in the same way to everyone within a given jurisdiction; and, on the other side, those who also advocate rights that are special to certain groups within, or categories of, the population, by virtue of a particular characteristic or circumstance.

Affirmative action measures are a well-known example of these controversies. From one perspective, measures that give preference to qualified candidates, or, more strongly, less qualified candidates, from certain groups, or to women, in employment or admission to university, are seen as extending equal opportunity and equal rights of access to education or employment to the whole population. From another perspective, such measures are seen as unjust, as giving special treatment or a privilege, an illegitimate advantage, to certain groups over the rest of the population, or to women at the expense of men. Another way of making the latter argument is that these rights are unjustified because they give advantages or privileges to some rather than maintaining the freedom of all.

Such debates are carried on using a variety of terms, but I shall use the term *special rights* for four reasons. First, in order to emphasise the fundamental importance of freedom in debates about rights. Second, to draw attention to a certain view of freedom that is too rarely challenged in the political and philosophical disputes over welfare rights. Third, to argue that many so-called special rights are nothing of the sort, but are necessary for the creation of a more democratic citizenship. Fourth, to highlight another set of special rights that remain largely unacknowledged in discussions of rights. These are rights that uphold power, domination and privilege rather than freedom and therefore truly deserve the designation 'special'.

Rights and freedom are so closely interwoven that the phrase 'civil and political rights' is used interchangeably with 'civil and political liberties'. Such usage is possible because of the mutual inter-relationship between freedom, rights and democracy that began about three hundred years ago when the idea that men were born free, equal and rational, or were naturally free and equal to each other, and thus self-governing, first gained wide currency. If the premise of individual self-government was not immediately to be under-cut, an equal political standing with the rights necessary to maintain freedom and to participate in political life was required. Or, that is to say, democratic citizenship was necessary. More precisely, in principle, the premise of freedom as a birthright led to democratic citizenship; in practice, all those who were dependent on others for their subsistence were held to fall outside the company of those who were born free. Anyone held to be dependent was thus excluded from the category 'man' which signified those who could possess and exercise rights.

'Dependence' has become a fashionable term recently in controversies about welfare rights and is intimately linked to claims about freedom. The provision of public benefits, and the associated rights that T. H. Marshall called social rights in his famous essay, *Citizenship and Social Class*, have been under concerted attack since the 1970s. In the USA, the term welfare rights has now become little more than a synonym for a certain form of special rights. And even Marshall's social rights, though very different from 'welfare rights' in American usage, are now being seen in a similar way.

In some recent discussions of Marshall's very influential classification of citizenship into the three elements of civil, political and social rights, doubts are raised whether social rights can, or should, have the same status as civil and political rights. Social rights, it is claimed, are, at best, merely secondary rights of citizenship, or not even rights at all.[4] Civil and political rights, it is argued, constitute a formal, universal, legal status; they are unambiguously part of equal citizenship and democracy. Social rights, in contrast, are particular and substantive, concerned with the circumstances and needs of individuals, especially those in poverty. Since the extent to which poverty can be alleviated and individual needs met depends on the fiscal and economic health of the state, social or welfare rights are, according to this line of argument, either secondary rights, or merely benefits contingent upon economic prosperity. Welfare rights are not needed to maintain free citizenship. They are, therefore, quite unlike the fundamental civil and political rights of the suffrage or free speech; they are special rights.[5] Such an interpretation of Marshall's argument is indicative of the extent to which a very large part of popular and official opinion, both critics or defenders of the welfare state, including political philosophers, see welfare as a matter of the relief of poverty and discuss welfare rights from the perspective of the nineteenth century British Poor Law.[6]

Welfare rights as special rights compensate for the poverty that arises through the operation of the labour market. They provide compensation for the accidents of fortune that leave some citizens without a buyer for their labour power or services, or unable, through illness or old age, to participate in the labour market. Defenders of welfare rights regard them as justified special rights and want to see generous compensation. The harshest critics of the welfare state reject anything but the basic minimum of benefits required to relieve destitution – and even that minimum is being questioned. After the Republican Party gained control of the US Congress in 1994, for instance, pronouncements were made comparing private charity favourably to public relief. For these critics, welfare rights are unjustified special rights, not so much because they confer privilege, although in popular discourse they are also seen in this fashion, but because they undermine individual freedom and create dependence. The critics of welfare rights see dependence as the anti-thesis of freedom, so that freedom is identified with *independence*. In a further crucial step, independence is then exemplified by the ability to enter into transactions in the labour market.

Although this is a remarkably narrow view of freedom, independence in this sense is now at the heart of much public policy in Britain and the USA. The introduction of 'workfare' into welfare policies in both countries – the requirement that paid work must be undertaken in return for receipt of bene-fits – is justified as enlarging individual freedom and reducing dependence. Discussions of welfare and announcements of policy changes have begun more and more to resemble the arguments of one fervent advocate of workfare who wrote a decade ago that the poor must be 'forced to be free', to regain their independence by being compelled to take low paid jobs.[7]

A striking aspect of current controversies is how seldom defenders of the welfare state couch their arguments in terms of an alternative idea of freedom. They have, so to speak, allowed the market in the discourse of freedom and rights to be cornered by the critics of welfare rights. The typical response of the defenders draws on a long history of argument about rights and citizen-ship that focuses on class inequality. Marshall's essay provides a splendid example of this tradition of argument, and the revival of interest in his work tends to reinforce the concentration on inequality and poverty. This does little either to counter the claim that welfare rights have, at best, a merely contingent status, and, at worst, are inimical to individual freedom, or to combat the charge that increased equality is always obtained at the expense of freedom. Economic policies pursued on both sides of the Atlantic over the past twenty years have led, of course, to a very marked increase in social inequality and to serious social problems. But the failure to provide an alter-native view of freedom makes the task of fashioning policies to ensure a decent life for all citizens, and to enhance democracy, even more difficult.

I shall come back to the issue of welfare or social rights. I now want to turn to another example of the debate over equal and special rights, and to another reason why the challenge to freedom as independence is so muted. The neglect and misinterpretation of feminist arguments means that the importance of freedom in the history of feminism remains unacknowledged.

As I have already noted, feminism is frequently declared to be about equality, or, more precisely, equal rights. A popular perception of feminism is that it is about the extension to women of the Rights of Man and the Citizen proclaimed in the *Declaration* of 1789. Feminists, it is held, demand that civil and political rights should be shared by women. This view ignores the work of early feminist theorists writing in England from the 1690s to the 1790s, and so misunderstands the history of, and vastly underestimates the complexity of, feminist argument about rights. The major insight of the early feminists was that natural rights, or the rights of man, embodied special rights. These rights are 'special' in a very different sense from the special rights that I have discussed so far.

To be sure, feminists have long been interested in and claimed the rights of men and citizens – indeed, women in England petitioned Parliament on a number of occasions from 1642–51 on various matters, including their rights or liberties. In 1649 they declared, 'have we not an equal interest with the men of this Nation, in those liberties and securities contained in the Petition of Right and other good laws of the Land?'.[8] By the early 1790s, Mary Wollstonecraft was arguing for civil and political rights for women, including the suffrage. In revolutionary France, the Marquis de Condorcet was a prominent supporter of the extension of the rights of man to women, and Olympe de Gouges issued a *Declaration of the Rights of Woman and Citizen*, modelled on the more famous *Declaration* of 1789. But this is only one aspect of the early feminist argument about rights.[9]

Feminists both demanded, *and* criticised and rejected, the rights of man. Their crucial, but neglected, insight was that rights were two-dimensional. The first dimension consists of the familiar civil and political rights. The second dimension consists of the rights that men enjoy by virtue of their sex. The rights of man, that is to say, include both the civil and political rights that uphold the freedom of citizens, and the special rights that men exercise over women, rights that deny freedom to women.

Men's rights in the second sense are not written down in famous declarations of rights, but some of them are enshrined elsewhere. They can be found, for example, in the English common law of coverture, under which husband and wife became one legal person and a married woman lost any independent civil standing; and, after the French Revolution (during which, in 1791, women were excluded from the franchise), in the Code Napoléon (1804). Both these legal codes presupposed not only that men alone ('independent' beings) could exercise the public rights of citizens and so take part in government, but that men should govern women ('dependent' beings) in the private sphere. None of this, nor the broader beliefs, institutions and relationships which still maintain women's subordination to men, are usually mentioned in standard discussions of rights. The battles over equal and special rights, over freedom, dependence and privilege, typically remain within the confines of a one-dimensional view of rights. The second dimension remains in obscurity, yet rights that bestow power (in the case of men) and deny freedom (in the case of women) are indeed *special* rights.

The earliest feminists, such as Mary Astell (1666–1731), were aware of the two dimensions of rights long before the rights of man were proclaimed in 1789. The fact that many of the writers in the late seventeenth and early eighteenth centuries were conservatives, in Astell's case a political absolutist and high Anglican, who rejected ideas of natural freedom and rights, illustrates the complexity of the relation between feminism and rights. These writers displayed little interest in the public rights of man, with the important exception of men's monopoly of access to education and educational institutions, which they roundly attacked. Much of their attention was directed at men's private rights, especially their despotic powers as husbands.

Astell's political and religious views and her ironical, often sarcastic, style, make her inclusion in the ranks of feminism and interpretation of her writings a somewhat contentious matter. But she shared with her political adversaries, the proponents of freedom as a birthright, the belief that political arguments must be judged by the light of Reason. She was influenced by Descartes, and she turned reason and rational argument to some very unexpected uses for someone with her political affiliations. Paradoxically, precisely because she advocated hierarchy and submission, not individual freedom, she was more aware of the sweeping political implications of, and of the limits to, claims about natural rights than many present-day upholders of the doctrines of the English, American and French revolutionaries.

In a witty and frequently caustic manner Astell pointed out, in her *Reflections Upon Marriage*, that none of the charges of women's natural intellectual inferiority withstood rational analysis. Even more importantly, she had no difficulty in exposing the inconsistencies of the political radicals who attacked absolute monarchy in the state but were only too willing to support it in the household, and thus to deny their wives the freedom they claimed for themselves. It was Astell who asked the question that lies at the heart of feminism, but that is almost always ignored in discussions of rights: 'If all *Men are born Free*, how is it that all Women are born Slaves?'.[10] But Astell rejected the idea that either sex was born free. The problem, as she saw it, was not that husbands were absolute rulers, but that they were arbitrary tyrants. Their demand for obedience from their wives had no rational basis, but rested on physical strength and the fact of their masculine sex. Astell believed that once a woman became a wife she must obey, but the absolute submission required of wives was an arduous and difficult undertaking. If a woman had doubts about her capacity to submit to her domestic sovereign, then, Astell implied, she had better remain single.

Astell's sharp mind and dislike of domestic tyranny led her to skate on some very thin political ice for a supporter of absolute authority. When she asked, 'If absolute Sovereignty be not necessary in a State, how comes it to be so in a Family? Or if in a Family why not in a State; since no Reason can be alleged for the one that will not hold more strongly for the other?'[11] she must have known full well that the political argument cut both ways. By the end of her *Reflections*, Astell's premise of a wife's obedience begins to ring rather hollow to late twentieth-century ears.

By the 1790s, feminist advocates of natural freedom and equality were wielding the weapon of Reason both for and against the rights of man. Mary Wollstonecraft (1759–97) stood at the opposite political pole from Astell; she was a political radical and a friend of the leading English (male) advocates of the rights of man, including Tom Paine. She published a *Vindication of the Rights of Men*, in reply to Burke's attack on the French Revolution, two years before her *Vindication of the Rights of Woman* of 1792. Wollstonecraft's demand for education and civil and political rights for women is much better known than her argument that women's political exclusion was linked to men's special rights. That is, the rights men exercised in their capacity as husbands, in their control of education, and in their control of the means of economic independence and monopoly of citizenship and political power.

Wollstonecraft agreed with Rousseau, her favourite author, that the family was the foundation of the state and that public and private virtue were interdependent. She was also his vigorous critic, but her criticism is still largely ignored by political theorists and philosophers of rights. Wollstonecraft used the doctrine of natural liberty to show that the special rights of men undermined republican political virtue and free citizenship, including the version found in Rousseau's theory.

She argued that a tyrant in the home could not develop the capacities needed for political liberty and equal rights, and nor could a domestic slave develop the qualities needed to exercise citizenship. The problem for women was not that they were dependent or lacked reason and political capacities by nature, but that they were systematically denied their birthright of freedom. Their apparent inability to participate in public life arose because they lacked the freedom necessary to develop private and public virtue; the special rights of men, and women's subordination, were the obstacles to women's rights. Wollstonecraft, therefore, argued for radical social and political changes, not only the extension of the rights of man (in the first sense) to women, but for women's education, their economic independence from their husbands, and the transformation of marriage and sexuality – in short, for elimination of the special rights enjoyed by men.

Very curiously, Wollstonecraft has been presented as 'helping to define'[12] what contemporary feminist historians have called republican motherhood. This doctrine held that women, by nature, were unfit for citizenship, yet eminently fit for the political task of maintaining the republic by giving birth to (male) citizens. While Wollstonecraft highlighted women's work as mothers, she also argued that women had to be strong, educated, economically independent citizens if they were to be good mothers. Her view of citizenship was very different from our own. Writing before the household was completely separated from the workplace and deemed irrelevant to public life, Wollstonecraft treated motherhood, fatherhood, and work performed in the household as integral to citizenship. Moreover, to place Wollstonecraft in the camp of republican motherhood presupposes men's special rights – the very rights that Wollstonecraft was so vigorously opposing in her writings.

Feminists have engaged in a very long political struggle against men's special rights. The last vestiges of coverture and other legal embodiments of these rights have been abolished only in the last few years. But the legacy of the second dimension of the rights of man is still very visible in social expectations, particularly in sexual relations, in men's avoidance of 'housework', in the continuing male monopoly of authoritative positions in major institutions, and in the structure of citizenship in the Anglo-American welfare state. Men's special rights are also very obviously entrenched in the rest of the world. In recent years, feminist legal scholars have begun to expose how 'human rights' have also been interpreted in a one-dimensional fashion,[13] without, however, recognising some close parallels between their arguments and the insights of early feminists about natural rights.

The determination with which many men still cling to their special rights in Britain and the USA has led to policies (for example, affirmative action for women) that have sparked off some of the conflicts about special rights – in the sense of special versus universal rights with which I began. I now want to come back to this question. Feminists have engaged in their own skirmishes over these special rights for most of this century, but, as in the much better known controversies, the question of freedom again tends to get lost.

The clash over equal or universal and special rights has its own starting point within feminism. Just as the rights of man is an ambiguous rallying call, so is the claim for women's rights. Does 'women's rights' refer to the rights women must share with men, or rights that women require because of their difference from men? The argument from Reason and appeals to women's rationality went only so far. By the 1790s, the question of bodily difference between the sexes had become central to the politics of rights. In Paris, the revolutionary proponents of the rights of man justified women's exclusion from the suffrage on the grounds that women's bodies, made for motherhood, entailed that only men could be citizens. A similar argument for men's republican citizenship and women's republican motherhood had already been made during the American Revolution. Both sets of revolutionaries resolutely upheld men's special rights. They proclaimed that nature had manifestly endowed women for a vital political task, but the endowment meant that women's' contribution to the state could not form part of citizenship.

Well into the twentieth century, feminists countered the doctrine of republican motherhood by insisting that women's distinctive contribution, and sacrifice of their lives as mothers, a service to the state that only women could give, was just as valuable as the contributions and sacrifices made by men as soldiers. Their work as mothers thus added to women's claim to the rights of citizens. The claim foundered against the insuperable obstacle that citizenship had been established as a special right of men; motherhood stood as the antithesis to citizenship.[14] Nevertheless, one aspect of this feminist argument spilled over into broader controversies about the welfare state and welfare rights. Feminists also argued that women should receive the assistance from the state necessary to enable them to provide their valuable and distinctive contribution as mothers.

Some of the first welfare provisions were, in fact, concerned with maternity. In Germany, for instance, as part of health insurance legislation in 1883, women factory workers obtained three weeks optional maternity leave, and, in Norway, insurance legislation in 1909 provided maternity benefits in cash for insured women and for the wives of insured men. The British National Insurance Act of 1911 included similar benefits. In the USA, thirty-nine states established mother's pensions, usually for widowed or deserted mothers, between 1911 and 1919, and in 1921, following the passage of the Sheppard-Towner Maternity and Infancy Act, a national welfare system for mothers and children began to be established.[15] Such measures, however, were not enacted to enhance women's citizenship, but as support for their private duties as mothers, and, above all, as a means of relieving poverty and its deleterious effects on the next generation. The American political climate did not allow the development of a policy like British family allowances, but throughout this century the prevailing assumption has been that mothers raising children, including mothers undertaking this work on their own, require assistance. An historic shift is now taking place in the USA, and young lone mothers are being brought into workfare policies.

But to turn back to the 1920s; the Sheppard-Towner Act and other so-called protective legislation was at the heart of a major rift within the women's movement. On the one side, there were the defenders of protective legislation, or special rights, for mothers or working women; on the other side, the defenders of equal rights, symbolised by the Equal Rights Amendment, introduced into Congress in 1923. The lines between the two sides were not drawn quite so clearly as is often suggested, because some prominent opponents of the ERA had been just as prominent in the fight for the suffrage, that earlier symbol of the equal rights of citizens, won nationally in 1920. The defenders of protective legislation feared that its abolition would harm those already in a disadvantageous position in the labour market and the home. Their opponents supported the ERA because, in their view, while women were singled out as a special case, as in need of privileges or protection, they could only be seen as dependent, as less able than men to take their place as citizens.

More recently, much the same feminist disputes, now fought out under the banners of equality versus difference, have flared up again in the USA and

Britain. Despite the efforts of the Thatcher and Major governments to shift British society and welfare policies nearer to the American model, the conflict between the two sides, as was the case in the inter-war years, is less sharp than in the more individualist political culture of USA. American feminists, for example, have clashed over the issue of whether women in paid employment should be granted leave of absence, unavailable to men, explicitly labelled 'maternity leave', or whether pregnancy, along with illness or accidents, should be brought under the broader heading of 'disabilities', so that leave is available equally to both sexes. Opponents of equal rights have claimed that the unacceptable, masculine individualism of rights talk is revealed in the refusal to admit that women have special requirements precisely because they are different from men. One philosopher once even drew the conclusion from such cases that, for women to demand equal rights as individuals, is 'an exercise in futility'.[16]

The common feature that unites the numerous disputes over special and equal rights, whether between feminists or between the protagonists in the more familiar wrangles about welfare rights, is that the terms in which they are conducted mean that a resolution is impossible. The very notion of 'special rights' ensures that these rights must be seen as an addition to, and so occupying a different status from, equal rights. One side then claims that the addition is justified because of special circumstances, such as poverty or pregnancy; the other side claims that the addition cannot be justified because it confers privilege, and freedom is turned into dependence. Neither side pays any attention to the consequences for democracy of the special rights of men.

The long-standing stalemate over special rights has been greatly exacerbated since discussion of welfare policy became dominated by the doctrine of freedom as independence. The failure to develop an alternative view of freedom has reinforced an old, very narrow and abstract view of rights that, ironically in the era of rights talk, is precisely the view that has led radicals, conservatives and feminists to reject, or, at least, to be very wary of, rights. To see freedom and rights as independence, and independence as exemplified by participation in the labour market, entails a particular conception of the individual: namely, the conception of the individual as an owner of property in the person, or a self-owning, self-subsistent entity (an idea that, as I have argued elsewhere, is a political fiction).[17] When individuals are seen as self-subsistent, then rights must form part of property in the person, something that individuals 'have'. Individual independence is exhibited when part of that property – services or labour power – is rented out in exchange for wages. Civil and political rights are required to allow transactions of this kind to proceed in an orderly fashion.

To see freedom and rights from the perspective of this brand of individualism leads directly to the impasse over equal and special rights, and to the claim that welfare rights are not genuine rights. Individuals are said to 'have' rights if civil and political liberties have been established. Critics of abstract individualism, including feminists who point out that this individual is bestowed with masculine characteristics, then invariably make one of two moves. Either special rights are introduced to bring back individuals as social beings, with specific characteristics who live in specific circumstances. Or special rights form part of an argument that 'having' rights is meaningless in a context of social inequality – an argument summed up in the famous aphorism that rich and poor alike have the right to sleep under the bridges of Paris. The debates then continue along the familiar trajectory. Attention is thus deflected from one of the most important aspects of the 1990s; the way in which policies advocated by the critics of welfare rights have created conditions in which independence collapses into lack of freedom.

Under the British Poor Law until 1918, to become destitute and have to enter the workhouse meant the loss of civil and political rights. Citizens are no longer stripped of their rights, but, over the past two decades, the freedom and standing of many citizens has been significantly diminished or undermined altogether in the name of independence. The consequence of policies that have increased social inequalities is that many people have been pushed to the margins of citizenship. Reductions in public support at a time when the global restructuring of capitalism has led to a rapid increase in low paid and casual employment, means that many of the employed now lead a precarious existence. Mass unemployment has returned, and many thousands of people are homeless.

The poor conditions in which so many are now living makes it all too easy for them to be seen as less than citizens. In the case of the homeless, their condition '*consists* in unfreedom'. The homeless lack the very basis for freedom of action, a place, or guaranteed access to a place (their access to public parks and buildings has been restricted), in which they can perform their ablutions and other tasks that must be undertaken daily if human beings are to have a healthy and dignified life. Without these basic amenities, individuals are rendered unfree.[18] In addition, without an address they are also effectively cast out from citizenship.

The homeless are often dependent on private charity or individual beneficence but this hardly makes them free. The consensus that individuals who rely on public payments for all or some of their subsistence are dependent is curious to say the least. It rests on the assumption that source of income is sufficient to distinguish dependence from independence. If income is obtained through employment, then citizens are independent. But this assumption does not stand up to even cursory scrutiny. Only certain categories of welfare beneficiaries are called dependants – for example, old age pensioners, recipients of social security and veterans are not – and other recipients of vast amounts of public funds are rarely so labelled, or seen as participants in a system of welfare. Historically, the term 'dependence' has been a euphemism for subordination, and today it refers, more often than not, to chronic insecurity – a condition, as Hobbes showed long ago, that is far removed from freedom.

When T. H. Marshall gave his lecture on citizenship in 1949, he, along with many others in Britain, believed that such insecurity would not be seen again. His conception of social rights was predicated on the assumption that, in the mid-twentieth century, the conditions that bring loss of civic standing would be eliminated once and for all. Sadly, it is necessary to restate Marshall's arguments over again in the 1990s – but in the spirit not the letter. He was, for example, oblivious to coverture and men's special rights. He thus based his classification of rights on a mistake; on the incorrect assumption that civil rights were universal in the nineteenth century. Marshall also equivocated about the status of social rights, and so left a way open for the claim that they depend on the fiscal health of the state and are in a different category from civil and political rights.

But civil and political rights also depend upon the expenditure of considerable public resources and the existence of numerous, specialised public agencies.[19] For a system of universal suffrage and free and fair elections to work properly, or for the judicial system to operate fairly, requires a complex set of institutions and regular expenditures. That outlays on elections and law courts are taken for granted, whereas the welfare budget is controversial, is indicative only of the acceptance of a particular view of democracy. Political judgements and decisions and economic nostrums determine how all public funds are allocated, whether used to maintain civil and political rights, spent on schools or weapons, on medical facilities and houses, or sent up in space, used to underwrite privatisation, bail out failed banks, or to entice private investment to certain cities or regions.

To move discussion of rights on to a new footing, Marshall's classification of rights is best abandoned, together with talk of special rights – except where it is warranted in the case of men's rights. Much of what was called special protection and is now called special rights is a necessary step in the creation of free and equal citizenship. The step is required because citizenship has been developed around men's special rights and in a context of enduring social inequality. The problem needs to be tackled at its source. That is to say, 'affirmative action' cannot *substitute* for policies aimed at democratisation, at reduction of the inequalities and subordination that diminish the citizenship of so many.

The current movement in the USA to eliminate affirmative action for designated ethnic groups and for women[20] is no doubt fuelled in part by reaction to the (still limited) achievements of women in entering previously male bastions, and the changes in the ethnic composition of the undergraduate intake at universities such as UCLA, where 'minorities' have been a majority of freshmen in the past few years. But in part it is also fuelled by the insecurity and unemployment affecting such a large proportion of the workforce, and the replacement of jobs for male breadwinners by 'junk jobs' that pay extremely low wages. The assertion that privileges for some stand in the way of equal rights for all has an immediate appeal, but also glosses over the tenuous connection between such 'privileges' and the problems that would remain if they disappeared overnight. Neither the presence nor absence of affirmative action can in itself solve the problems generated by global restructuring, company 'downsizing' and the lowering of living standards, or, for example, illiteracy, lack of medical insurance, the prevalence of weapons in schools, shattered neighbourhoods and families, and homelessness.

The endless conflicts over special rights serve to distract attention from the unfinished business of democracy in Britain and the USA. The process of democratisation needs to be continued and strengthened; it is not, as we are encouraged to believe, a process relevant only to other countries. Paradoxically, democracy is being invoked across the political spectrum along with a narrow view of freedom and rights that is inimical to democratisation. Rights talk has hardly gone too far. Rights talk has not yet been transformed into the language of *democratic rights*; that is to say, rights that are *enjoyed* by, or are of *equal worth* to, all citizens.

The equal standing made possible by a system of rights is the keystone of democratic citizenship, but a major difficulty in the creation of democratic rights that maintain the equal worth of citizenship is the entanglement of rights with employment and the idea of property in the person. The notion that individuals 'have' rights, and the assumption that freedom is independence, have to be replaced by an understanding of rights as relations that structure institutions. Institutions are one manifestation of the *interdependence* that, as anthropologists and sociologists have reminded us for a very long time, characterises human social life. A conception of rights must be developed in which freedom is secured through recognition of the interdependence of all citizens, rather than the independence of some in the labour market. Democratic rights are thus integral to freedom as *autonomy*, the autonomy that allows all citizens to participate fully (or as fully as they wish) in all aspects of social and political life.

In current conditions where men's special rights still remain, and many citizens lack the security required for participation, the worth of rights is much diminished. Marshall's discussion of citizenship was informed by the generosity of spirit exhibited in the great British social reforms of the 1940s. Today, the mean spirit of the Poor Law has seeped into and eroded the political culture in Britain, and the USA, where little is left of the spirit that animated the New Deal. In contrast, Marshall's argument was based on the premise that all vestiges of the Poor Law had been abolished. He stated that the significance of the removal of the punishment of disenfranchisement for receiving public relief, 'has, perhaps, not been fully appreciated'.[21]

Nearly fifty years later, his statement is as relevant as ever. The complete abolition of the Poor Law means that freedom as independence is transformed into freedom as autonomy. It entails that citizens in a democracy cannot be allowed to fall below the standard of life and culture which enables them to make use of and enjoy their citizenship. Or to make this important point another way, receipt of public benefits no longer signifies dependence or loss of standing. On the contrary, a system of public expenditure – an expenditure that does not have to be made through highly bureaucratised and centralised methods – becomes a major means through which interdependence is recognised, freedom is enhanced, citizenship is enriched and democratisation furthered.

In short, democratic rights (as Marshall wrote of social rights) enable everyone 'to share to the full in the social heritage and to live the life of a civilised being according to the standards prevailing in the society'.[22] In the 1990s, the terminology of 'the social heritage' and 'civilisation' cannot be used so confidently, now that the exclusionary character of such terms is so well documented. But, as I have said, it is the spirit, not the letter of Marshall's argument that is relevant. The import of his statement is that, if everyone who wishes to do so is to be able to participate as a citizen, a wide array of public provision and facilities is required. Marshall argued that citizens should be assured of education, housing and health care, family allowances, a living wage, access to the legal system, and, by implication, access to all the cultural amenities required to take part in civilised life. It follows that the democratic rights of citizens are an entitlement, exactly like that emblem of equal rights, the suffrage.[23]

To establish democratic rights, as Marshall recognised, meant that the principle of the sanctity of contract had to be relinquished. Marshall stated that 'rights are not a proper matter for bargaining', and, he continued, 'to have to bargain for a living wage in a society which accepts the living wage as a social right is as absurd as to have to haggle for a vote in a society which accepts the vote as a political right'.[24] Acceptance of a universal franchise has been a far more difficult process than is generally suggested. The difficulties are obscured because male suffrage is so often identified with 'democracy'.

Consider, for example, this recent statement: 'the United States was the first country in the world to democratise. A mass white, adult male franchise became established during the 1830s. Before that decade the United States was a kind of halfway house between a wholly elite dominated regime and a democratic one.'[25] If a 'democratic regime' includes slavery, the exclusion of native peoples and all women, then the United States in the 1830s qualifies for the title. But New Zealand, where universal suffrage was achieved in 1893 when women were enfranchised (the Maori people had four reserved seats in the legislature from 1867) is a much better candidate as the first democracy. In Britain one person one vote has existed only since 1948; Black people could freely exercise the suffrage in the USA only from the 1960s; women won the vote in Switzerland in 1971; the first election on a universal franchise in South Africa was 1994; and women still are excluded from voting, for instance, in Kuwait.

In light of these difficulties in establishing universal suffrage 'as a political right', it is perhaps not surprising that the creation of a standard of living for everyone that is adequate for democratic citizenship is still a very contentious matter. Marshall assumed that a living wage – for most able-bodied men, at least – would be obtained through full employment. That remained a fairly reasonable assumption for male workers for about three decades after Marshall gave his lecture. However, the assumption is no longer tenable, not only does it ignore the position of those without employment, but, in itself, is now a very dubious basis for public policy. Ironically, the proponents of workfare still assume that some kind of jobs, in sufficient numbers not just for men, but women too, including young mothers, will be available. The restructuring of capitalism is one reason for uncoupling living standards from employment, but not the most important reason. Democratic rights, taken seriously, mean that it is also inappropriate to bargain about the material resources of those paid less than a living wage or not in paid employment.

To put rights talk on a new footing, to drop the language of special rights except in the case of the aptly named special rights that are a barrier to women's equal standing, would help open the way for the development of policies that assist rather than work against democratisation and free citizenship. To focus on freedom is not, let me emphasise, to deny the importance of equal or universal rights; on the contrary, a secure background of equal rights has, so to speak, to be taken for granted if the standing of all citizens is to be secured. Symbolically, equal rights are a permanent reminder of democratic principles. Substantively, these rights structure the institutions within which freedom is exercised. Some rights will be the same for all; for instance, all citizens must have the same number of votes. The content of other rights will differ according to the circumstances of individuals and groups, to ensure that the worth of citizenship is not eroded. The difficult policy decisions are about this content, about the best means to uphold and enhance citizens' standing and participation.

In my book *Participation and Democratic Theory* I referred to a comment made by G. D. H. Cole earlier this century. He claimed that, if people were asked what was the greatest evil in our society, most would refer to poverty. This, for Cole, was the wrong answer; he saw subordination as a greater problem. My arguments about special rights assume that his insight is still valid, but, as I have indicated, I would now modify my argument, shared with Cole, that the workplace holds the key to greater freedom and democracy. I still believe, however, that there are sound arguments for the democratisation of major institutions, including workplaces. The arguments need to be formulated in terms of freedom and in terms appropriate to conditions at the close of the twentieth century. It is unfortunate that, because of the persistence of men's special rights, and the fact that current conditions include the revival of nineteenth-century economic dogmas and an updated Poor Law, a necessary preliminary task is to consider again some basic questions about democratic rights.

NOTES

1 This chapter, with some minor revisions, was presented as the John C. Rees Memorial Lecture, the University of Wales Swansea, January 1995.

2 Cited in David S. Savage, 'In the Matter of Justice Thomas', *Los Angeles Times Magazine*, 9 October 1994.

3 Notably Richard Rorty, 'Human Rights, Rationality, and Sentimentality', and Jean-Francois Lyotard, 'The Other's Rights', both in *On Human Rights: the Oxford Amnesty Lectures 1993*, Stephen Shute and Susan Hurley (eds), New York, BasicBooks, 1993.

4 See, for example, J. M. Barbelet, *Citizenship: Rights, Struggle and Class Inequality*, Milton Keynes, Open University Press, 1988, pp. 67–72; Daniel Zolo, 'Democratic Citizenship in a Post-Communist Era', in *Prospects for Democracy*, David Held (ed.), Cambridge, Polity Press, 1993, p. 264.

5 This argument follows the older claim that the rights listed in the International Covenant on Economic, Social, and Cultural Rights (1966, in force from 1976) are not genuine human rights. That status is reserved for the rights contained in the International Covenant on Civil and Political Rights (1966, in force from 1976). For a well known statement of this claim see Maurice Cranston, 'Human Rights, Real and Supposed', in *Political Theory and the Rights of Man*, D. D. Raphael (ed.), London, Macmillan, 1967.

6 Brian M. Barry, 'The Welfare State Versus the Relief of Poverty', *Ethics*, vol. 100, 1990, pp. 503–29.

7 Lawrence Mead, *Beyond Entitlement: The Social Obligations of Citizenship*, New York, The Free Press, 1986.

8 Cited in Patricia Higgins, 'The Reactions of Women', in *Politics, Religion and the English Civil War*, Brian Manning (ed.), London, Edward Arnold, 1973, p. 217.

9 This section draws on Carole Pateman, 'The Rights of Man and Early Feminism', in *Schweizerisches Jahrbuch für Politische Wissenschaft*, Bern, Editions Paul Haupt, 1994.

10 Mary Astell, *Some Reflections Upon Marriage*, New York, Source Book Press, 1970, [1730, 4th edn] p. 107.

11 Astell, *Reflections*, p. 106.

12 Joan Landes, *Women and the Public Sphere in the Age of the French Revolution*, Ithaca and London, Cornell University Press, 1988, p. 129.

13 Hilary Charlesworth, 'What are "Women's International Human Rights"', in *Human Rights of Women*, Rebecca Cook (ed.), Philadelphia, University of Pennsylvania Press, 1994.

14 These points are drawn from Carole Pateman, 'Equality, Difference, Subordination: the Politics of Motherhood and Women's Citizenship', in *Beyond Equality and Difference*, Gisella Bock and Susan James (eds), London and New York, Routledge, 1992. Let me emphasise here that neither in the latter chapter, nor in my other work, have I argued for 'two different forms of citizenship' for men and women, or that women have been, are, or should be, citizens as mothers (Chantal Mouffe, 'Feminism, Citizenship and Radical Politics', in *Feminists Theorize the Political*, Judith Butler and Joan Scott (eds), New York and London, Routledge, 1992, p. 375). My argument, presented in more detail in this earlier paper, is that, as a matter of history, motherhood has been a major vehicle of women's incorporation into the state, analogous to that of soldiering or employment for men. The difference is that, for women, motherhood was *not* a vehicle for citizenship – which is precisely why feminist arguments that motherhood was a contribution of citizens cut little political ice. The zeal with which many feminist theorists have been hunting out and condemning 'essentialism' has led to almost any argument concerned with motherhood being dismissed as 'essentialist', irrespective of its content.

15 Gisela Bock, and Pat Thane, (eds), *Maternity and Gender Policies: Women and the Rise of the European Welfare States, 1880s–1950s*, London and New York, Routledge, 1991, 'Introduction'. See also Barbara J. Nelson, 'The Origins of the Two-Channel

Welfare State: Workmen's Compensation and Mother's Aid', in *Women, the State and Welfare*, Linda Gordon (ed.), Madison, University of Wisconsin Press, 1990.

16 Elizabeth Wolgast, *Equality and the Rights of Women*, Ithaca and London, Cornell University Press, 1980, p. 156.

17 See, Carole Pateman, *The Sexual Contract*, Cambridge, Polity Press: Stanford, Stanford University Press, 1988. I might remark here that an abstract (and masculine) view of the individual is often mistakenly identified with 'liberalism' in general instead of contract theory, a distinct tradition of argument with which I was concerned in *The Sexual Contract*.

18 Jeremy Waldron, 'Homelessness and the Issue of Freedom', in *Liberal Rights: Collected Papers 1981–1991*, Cambridge, Cambridge University Press, 1993; the quotation is from p. 320.

19 Raymond Plant, 'Social Rights and the Reconstruction of Welfare', in *Citizenship*, Jeff Andrews, (ed.), London, Lawrence and Wishart, 1991.

20 As is often pointed out, veterans have a very large and well-established welfare and 'affirmative action' system, and admissions policies to universities have long given special accommodation to athletes and children of alumni, but these are not popularly seen as illegitimate privileges.

21 T. H. Marshall, 'Citizenship and Social Class', in *Sociology at the Crossroads*, Heinemann, London, 1963, [1950] p. 83.

22 Marshall, 'Citizenship', p. 74.

23 This interpretation of Marshall can be challenged from other parts of his argument. A critical and more detailed discussion is presented in my 'Democratisation and Citizenship in the 1990s: the Legacy of T. H. Marshall', the Vilhelm Aubert Memorial Lecture, the University of Oslo, 1996.

24 Marshall, 'Citizenship', p. 116.

25 Alan Ware, 'Introduction: Special Issue, Democracy and North America', *Democratisation*, 1996, vol. 3, p. 1.

13 Beyond social justice and social democracy

Positive freedom and cultural rights[1]

David West

I INTRODUCTION

In recent years, and particularly in the English-speaking world, the notion of social justice has come under sustained attack from neo-conservative thinkers. In its conservative and libertarian variants the 'new right' both questions the value of social justice and alleges deep-seated problems with the functioning of welfare states.[2] At the same time, in a number of countries the characteristic institutions of social democracy and the welfare state have been cut back or dismantled by governments espousing the new right's agenda. Even social democratic and labour parties have made significant concessions to the free market, small government nostrums of 'economic rationalism'. On the other hand, for many on 'the left', who are unconvinced by the new right's agenda, both social justice and the welfare state must be defended against these attacks.[3] However, there are reasons to attempt something more than a purely defensive strategy. In the first place, a defensive response unnecessarily accepts the burden of proof. It is not obvious that principles of social justice stand more fundamentally in need of justification than, for example, the private property rights of individuals so cherished by the right, yet much of the theoretical debate now takes place on the neo-conservatives' terms. But secondly, a defensive strategy too easily concedes much of the political battleground as well. The recent 'modernisation' of a number of 'new' labour parties, such as those in Australia and Britain and the Democrats in the United States, promises no more than an unsatisfactory compromise between economic rationalism and social justice with, at best, the preservation more or less intact of what remains of the welfare state and little prospect of a serious counter-attack or compensating gains. Finally, an exclusively defensive strategy fails to acknowledge some real problems facing the social democratic project. By contrast, systematic inadequacies and even 'crisis tendencies' of the welfare state have been identified by a number of theorists with little sympathy for the neo-conservative agenda. Such critical analyses also help to account for social democracy's currently lukewarm support in several Western electorates. An approach hoping to combine theoretical resistance with political prospects must surely seek to explain rather than dismiss popular misgivings.

In what follows I shall attempt to draw together some strands of a more ambitious response. The approach adopted here is self-consciously synthetic and even schematic, aiming to identify the broad contours of an alternative response and leaving many aspects and interrelationships unexplored. The main focus highlights the part played by cultural factors in right and left critiques, with the suggestion that neglect of these factors helps to explain both some of the problems facing social democracy and the political and theoretical weakness of its response to the right's attack. The following section briefly reviews some of the cultural or, in other words, ideological, moral, psychological and motivational effects alleged by critics of social democracy. Both right and left critics accept that the institutionalisation of social democracy has effects within the sphere of culture, which create problems for the realisation of its moral and political ideals. As a response to these allegations, the final section proposes a systematic extension of social justice to incorporate a notion of cultural citizenship rights or rights in the sphere of culture. This category of rights is presented as a further stage in the evolution of conceptions of rights classically described by T. H. Marshall.[4] According to Marshall's account, the rise of capitalist liberal democracies created problems of poverty and inequality not addressed by existing civil and political citizenship rights. These problems eventually led to the introduction of the social welfare rights characteristic of twentieth-century social democracies. Analogously, it is argued here, the cultural deficiencies of contemporary social democracies call for the systematic extension of citizenship rights to the sphere of culture. Far from countenancing further erosion of the moral and institutional fabric of social democracy, this response to neo-conservatism argues for its enrichment and extension in the name of a conception of justice *beyond* social justice.

II CULTURAL DEFICIENCIES OF THE WELFARE STATE

In this section the problems and crisis tendencies attributed to welfare state societies are briefly reviewed, with the aim of identifying one significant convergence on a broad range of cultural effects. The right's critique is well known.[5] However, it is worth emphasising that it encompasses at least four dimensions. At the level of political philosophy, the right's *moral* critique typically argues that there is no philosophical basis for social justice claims not already implicit in existing social practices or, in effect, that there is no such things as social justice.[6] Further, attempts to meet such claims are themselves liable to be unjust, because they violate what libertarians, at least, tend to see as inviolable (sometimes natural) private property rights.[7] Second, at the level of what might be called *socio-cultural* critique, the right argues that welfare provision in response to social justice claims erodes individualist or 'Victorian' values of self-reliance, responsibility, enterprise and the work ethic.[8] This effect is not only intrinsically undesirable, it also causes increased dependence on the state with escalating and ultimately unsustainable demands for even greater welfare provision. Third, these effects are exacerbated at the *economic* level, because the increased burden of taxation necessary to finance the welfare state diverts resources from more productive and profitable private investments and so reduces the fiscal basis for further provision.[9] Finally, the *political* process is distorted by public sector unions and bureaucracies, who promote ineffective or even counter-productive welfare programmes in their own interest as providers rather than for the sake of their clients.[10] In the end, the state's diminishing ability to satisfy escalating demands may threaten its authority in an impending 'crisis of governability'.[11]

For the purposes of the present argument, it is the socio-cultural critique that is most relevant. The welfare state is alleged to erode inherited cultural values in such a way that its effectiveness and even its survival are seriously in doubt. Perhaps surprisingly, as we shall see, the right's socio-cultural critique is echoed on the left. Of course, left-wing critics of the welfare state refuse to accept the neo-conservative proposal simply to dismantle the institutions of social democracy. For them liberal capitalism in its unmitigated form was morally indefensible and its evolution towards social democracy provides historical evidence that it was also socially unsustainable. Still, these left critics are critical of the welfare state. However, two major strands of left critique must be distinguished. The first strand, stemming from more traditional socialists, focuses on the incomplete or imperfect realisation of largely unchallenged social democratic principles. A second strand, characteristic of what Claus Offe calls the 'new politics', is critical of both the principles and functioning of welfare state societies.[12] As we shall see, both strands attribute cultural deficiencies to the welfare state.

To consider the first strand, then, more radical and revolutionary socialists always feared the 'pacifying' intentions and effects of 'reformist' welfare states. On this view, the main function of the welfare state is not so much to relieve working-class hardship as to shore up capitalism by mitigating some of its more unpleasant and potentially revolutionary effects.[13] Certainly, state-funded education, health care and social security alleviate some of the uncertainties and vicissitudes of working-class life; they offer more equal opportunities in a competitive market economy. But these gains are bought with declining levels of political radicalism, as those relieved of hardship turn their attentions from revolutionary and even further reformist activism toward self-advancement and the comforts of consumerism. As a result, the successes of the welfare state may ultimately serve to erode its social and political basis of support. The beneficiaries of welfare are liberated into an individualist lifestyle and, in some cases, delivered to the conservative cause.[14] Thus, where conservatives once bemoaned the feckless indolence of the 'undeserving poor' and the new right now complains of welfare dependency, traditional socialists see selfishness and *political* (as opposed to economic) apathy as possible outcomes of the welfare state.

Further criticisms from the traditional left point to the incomplete realisation of social democratic principles. This is evident, first, in the stubborn persistence of material inequalities and elusiveness of real equality of opportunity. Attempts to guarantee equal opportunities through access to health, education and housing have reduced but certainly not eliminated inequalities in life chances, health and longevity.[15] If the welfare state is more effective than neo-conservatives suggest, it has achieved far less than its founders hoped. But this shortfall is compounded, secondly, by bias in the content of welfare provision. State education is dominated by middle-class values and linguistic codes; working-class children 'learn to labour' or learn to fail.[16] Education at all levels is subject to the functional imperatives of markets, which require, above all, that schools instil in children the willingness and the ability to contribute to profitable production.[17] Nor are such effects confined to class or the effects of capitalism. Parallel criticisms are levelled by feminists, lesbians and gays, and members of ethnic, 'racial' and indigenous minorities. Women contest the patriarchal assumptions of health care practitioners.[18] Gays have objected to medical approaches to the 'cure' of homosexuality and, more recently, state policy and practice in the response to HIV/AIDS.[19] Aboriginal activists in Australia have castigated culturally genocidal policies of compulsory adoption specifically directed at aboriginal children gradually abandoned only in the sixties.[20] The 'caring' welfare activities of the state, in other words, are distorted by systemic inequalities of power between social groups. Overall, the welfare state not merely fails to eliminate material inequalities, it serves to reproduce both these inequalities and related cultural assumptions about class, gender, sexuality, race and ethnicity.

The second, anti-statist strand of the left's critique represents a more fundamental challenge to the welfare state, because it implies that there are problems with any traditional left strategy seeking simply to complete the welfare state. This strand draws on antipathy to bureaucratic and statist forms of socialism from a variety of radical ideological sources, including anarchism, situationism, the New Left and, more recently, poststructuralism, postmodernism and the politics of 'new social movements'. Its suspicion of statist and bureaucratic solutions implicates not so much the biased content as the paternalistic form of welfare state provision.[21] The welfare state's reproduction of social inequalities is compounded by its paternalist mode of operation, whereby allegedly objective needs are bureaucratically rather than democratically defined and satisfied. Bureaucratic definitions of need are liable to reflect functional market imperatives, powerful interest groups and dominant cultural assumptions rather than the culturally specific wants of the supposed beneficiaries of welfare.[22]

For other critics suspicious of statist solutions, there is evidence that the welfare state faces an impending crisis, again at least partly as a result of deep-seated cultural and psychological effects.[23] Thus, in *Legitimation Crisis* Habermas argued that the further expansion of welfare states involves the fourfold risk of 'economic', 'rationality', 'legitimation' and 'motivation' crises. According to Habermas the interventions of the welfare state, which include not only the mitigation of poverty, inequality and insecurity but also the Keynesian management of levels of demand and unemployment, have succeeded (for the time being, at least) in countering the economic crisis tendencies of liberal capitalism. But its expanded role only exposes the state to further dangers. As the welfare state is held responsible for socio-economic outcomes which, under liberal capitalism, could be blamed on indolence, fate or misfortune, political and administrative systems are increasingly overloaded by escalating demands and so threatened by 'rationality' crisis. If the political system fails to meet the demands placed upon it, it also risks losing popular support or legitimacy. Evidence of an impending 'legitimation' crisis of that kind is provided by falling levels of party and trade union membership, increasingly unstable party affiliations and declining levels of conventional political participation. The prospects of complementary legitimation and 'motivation' crises, finally, are increased to the extent that previously unquestioned moral and psychological 'premises of politics', such as the work ethic, the bourgeois family and religion, are eroded by the continued expansion and ever deeper penetration of market and state systems into the cultural 'lifeworld' that ultimately sustains them.[24]

Rejecting the neo-conservative response to these political and cultural crisis tendencies (essentially a return to liberal capitalism with its economic crisis potential), Habermas looks instead to 'new social movements' for a potentially progressive resistance from the lifeworld against invasive state and economic systems. In these terms, both the women's and green movements resist the 'colonisation of the lifeworld', though only the women's movement represents an 'offensive' struggle 'deeply rooted in the acknowledged universalist foundations of morality and legality'.[25] According to Claus Offe's congruent but more empirically grounded analysis, new social movements consist predominantly of agents marginal to the 'old politics', which was constructed around the interests of capital and labour and played out mainly within and between the systems of money and power. The agents of the 'new politics' include decommodified groups such as the unemployed and the retired, 'new middle class' professionals such as teachers and social workers, as well as some marginalised and disenchanted members of the old middle class, particularly farmers, shop-owners and artisan producers. Still, though activists can be shown to come disproportionately from certain class locations, the new politics is more concerned with non-material issues – it 'is typically a politics *of* a class but not *on behalf of* a class'.[26] Environmental movements aim not to secure greater benefits for themselves but to restrict overall levels of consumption for the sake of the longer-term interests and quality of life of society and even humanity as a whole. The characteristic issues of the new politics concern people in their roles 'as citizens, as consumers, as clients of state-provided services, and as human beings in general' rather than as workers or employers.[27] Although economic issues remain relevant, movements of greens and women, lesbians and gays and ethnic minorities are more distinctively concerned with culturally sensitive values of autonomy, personal fulfilment and identity. They manifest what Offe calls a '"modern" critique of modernization', responding to the now unmistakable defects of the modernising projects of capitalism and the nation-state but, in contrast to the new right's projected restoration of traditional practices and values, in the name of unashamedly modern values.[28]

Theorists like Habermas and Offe provide useful social-theoretic tools to understand the politics of contemporary welfare state societies. This is not the place for an extensive discussion of their more positive proposals. However, both Habermas and Offe emphasise the importance of a reactivated civil society as the condition of a more deliberative and participatory democracy. Social movements constitute what John Keane calls 'spheres of autonomous public life'.[29] David Held and John Keane have argued in similar vein for a renewed synthesis of socialist and liberal democratic principles. Whilst continuing to advocate socialist transformation in order to secure economic rights and social justice for all, they emphasise the importance of retaining the civil and political rights of 'bourgeois' democracy, if an autonomous civil society is not to be suppressed once again by a bureaucratic state socialism 'mobilised against the formation of independent centres of power'.[30] Held and Keane advocate a complementary 'politicisation of civil society' and 'civilisation of the state'. Not only must existing state institutions be made more genuinely democratic, democratic forms must also be extended beyond the state throughout both economy and civil society. This complementary reinforcement of political and economic rights would amount to a 'double democratization' of both state and civil society.[31]

However, although proposals for the reinforcement and extension of existing liberal and democratic principles are certainly attractive, they represent arguably only a partial response to the problems of social democracy. Although democratisation of the institutions of the welfare state might benefit some constituencies, it is doubtful whether democracy in itself represents a reliable bulwark against the pacifying and paternalistic practices of the state. In the first place, the difficulties of achieving a genuinely participatory democracy are well known. There is no guarantee that those who most need to exercise greater control, such as women and members of ethnic minorities, will have the necessary resources and motivation to participate effectively.[32] Again, the principle of majority rule is of little use to vulnerable minorities. No doubt, in the nineteenth century the prospects of a tyranny of the majority did not greatly concern a burgeoning working class ruthlessly exploited by a minority of capitalists.[33] But the principle of majority rule is less appealing in the context of an explicit politics of cultural and ethnic diversity. By implication, even a socialist politics reinforced by a wide-ranging and deepened commitment to democratic decision-making cannot be relied upon to address adequately the cultural politics of social democracy. As we shall see, the complementary and more traditionally socialist reinforcement of liberal liberties that theorists such as Held and Keane also propose – supplementing formal liberties and 'negative' rights with social justice and 'positive' economic rights – is also likely to prove inadequate. In sum, even a socialist politics reinforced by commitments to more effective bourgeois liberties and a democratised civil society neglects an essential dimension of social justice. In the following section it will be argued that what is required in addition is a substantially enriched commitment to 'positive' freedom and justice in the sphere of culture through the recognition of cultural citizenship rights.

III CULTURAL CITIZENSHIP RIGHTS AND POSITIVE FREEDOM

The proposal to enrich social democratic interpretations of social justice with a commitment to rights in the sphere of culture implies a further stage in the evolution of citizenship rights outlined by T. H. Marshall. Marshall describes how, with the rise of capitalism, the particular but amorphous rights and privileges of feudal society were gradually replaced by universal and functionally differentiated civil and political rights of citizenship. He defines civil and political rights as follows:

> The civil element is composed of the rights necessary for individual freedom – liberty of the person, freedom of speech, thought and faith, the right to own property and to conclude valid contracts, and the right to justice. . . . By the political element I mean the right to participate in the exercise of political power, as a member of a body invested with political authority or as an elector of the members of such a body.[34]

By 'social rights', on the other hand, Marshall refers to a range of rights 'from the right to a modicum of economic welfare and security to the right to share to the full in the social heritage and to live the life of a civilised being according to the standards prevailing in society'.[35] In these terms, the move from the unequal 'status society' of feudalism to a capitalist 'contract society' based on the equal status of citizenship involved the gradual introduction of civil and then political rights. In the process the complex tissue of social rights and obligations implicit in traditional customs and regulations controlling prices, wages, products, methods of production and so on, was gradually eroded.[36] The social rights implicit in feudal society had served to mitigate, at least partially, its stark inequalities of status, wealth and power. Contract society dispensed with social rights in that sense and left the poor, powerless but formally equal citizens with little protection from the ravages of early capitalism. In Britain the high-point of contract society was reached early in the nineteenth century with the final elimination of wage regulations and the Poor Law reform of 1834. The latter recognised minimal social rights only in exchange for what amounted to renunciation of citizenship. As Marshall puts it, 'paupers forfeited in practice the civil right of personal liberty, by internment in the workhouse, and they forfeited by law any political rights they might possess'.[37]

The contemporary social welfare state begins to emerge with the gradual introduction of universal and functionally differentiated social welfare rights in the late nineteenth century and the twentieth. This development was spurred both by the appalling conditions endured by the working classes during the Industrial Revolution and later their growing industrial and political power. Major advances included abolition of property qualifications for the vote, payment of members of parliament, the introduction of legal aid, pensions and social security provisions, as well as measures to redistribute wealth through progressive taxation and inheritance taxes, free universal education and state-funded health-insurance schemes. Social rights of this kind helped to moderate the extreme inequalities of liberal capitalism. However, as Marshall observes, they simultaneously legitimated them. The ambivalence of the social rights of contract society is apparent in social democracy's core conception of equal opportunity, which implies 'the equal right to display and develop differences, or inequalities; the equal right to be recognised as unequal'.[38]

The significance of considering a fourth dimension of *cultural* rights can best be clarified by linking Marshall's three categories of citizenship rights with corresponding conceptions of freedom. In these terms, civil rights correspond to liberalism's core conception of negative freedom understood as the absence of coercive interference by other individuals or the state. An individual is free in terms of negative freedom, if she is not subject to coercive interference or is allowed to do what she wants. Negative freedom depends on laws enforcing 'negative' rights; these rights are negative, because they demand only that others refrain from interference. Political rights, on the other hand, correspond to the democratic understanding of freedom as self-determination. A citizen is free in terms of political freedom, then, if the actions of the state (including those required to enforce a regime of negative liberty) depend in some way on his or her own will. Where negative freedom implies limited government, political freedom implies some form of democracy.[39] Nowadays, the liberal democratic amalgam of negative and political freedom is commonly taken for granted. Taken together, negative and political freedom define freedom within the 'politico-legal' sphere that has been the main concern of liberal democratic theories of justice.

A third conception of freedom, associated with the 'social liberalism' of Hobson, Hobhouse and T. H. Green, is one important source of social democratic ideology and corresponds to Marshall's third category of social welfare rights.[40] An agent is free in terms of what I shall call 'effective' freedom, if she is not only free from outside interference or *allowed* to do what she wants, but also has appropriate resources, information and capacities, such that she is *able* to do it. The notion of effective freedom seeks to capture the insight that merely formal negative and political freedoms (and corresponding civil and political rights) are systematically undermined and may even be rendered worthless by social and economic inequalities.[41] Effective freedom requires so-called 'positive' rights, which in contrast to negative rights require not only the enforced absence of interference by others but also the active transfer by government of economic resources to relatively deprived social groups.[42] Whereas negative freedom is classically understood to imply economic *laissez-faire*, the notion of effective freedom justifies government regulation of the economy, including for example legal protections for both employees and consumers, government measures of redistribution, welfare provision and so on. Effective freedom extends the notion of justice beyond the politico-legal into the economic or productive sphere. In other words, effective freedom implies social welfare rights and *social* justice.

In these terms, the proposal to enrich social democracy and move beyond its core conception of social justice involves a fourth conception of 'positive' freedom and a corresponding conception of 'cultural rights' or rights in the 'sphere of culture'. For a person to be free in terms of positive freedom it is not sufficient for her to be both allowed (negative freedom) and able (effective freedom) to do what she wants. Beyond that positive freedom requires that her wants are, in some sense, genuinely her own or 'authentic' wants or wants that reflect her 'real interests'.[43] Positive freedom thus corresponds to the notion of autonomy, whereby an individual is not merely free to do whatever she wills, but her willing this or that is also free from heteronomous determination (whether from the individual's own irrational impulses or another's overt or covert interference). As the variety of formulations may lead one to suspect, specifying a precise conception of positive freedom is a difficult task that is certainly beyond the scope of the present chapter. None the less, a strong argument for the necessity of such a conception is provided by the recognition, prominent within Hegelian, Marxist and communitarian social philosophies, that a person's wants are socially and culturally formed. Even apparently biological needs for food or shelter must be interpreted in culturally specific terms defining, for example, what is edible or what counts as shelter. Because wants are culturally formed, they must also be regarded as potentially *de*formed. Interpretations of need are always vulnerable to distorting effects. A variety of ideological perspectives suggest examples of such effects: wants may be imposed or manipulated in the interests of some dominant social group or class (as alleged by some versions of Marxism and feminism); inappropriate or constricting wants may be inherited from unreconstructed cultural traditions (as alleged by the critique of homophobia); wants may be manufactured in the interests of profitable capitalist accumulation and so on. The salient point here is that such distorting effects are in principle compatible with negative, democratic and effective forms of freedom: someone whose wants are distorted may still be free to act in order to fulfil them. By contrast, a positive conception of freedom requires a systematic demarcation between distorted and undistorted, authentic and inauthentic wants.

Within the liberal democratic and even social democratic traditions positive conceptions of freedom in the sense just defined are typically regarded as dangerous, because they are thought to encourage the paternalistic imposition of goals considered to be in someone else's 'real' interests. Such interference may even be regarded as compatible with its victim's 'real' or 'genuine' freedom if, in the classically totalitarian phrase, it forces him to be free. However, as I have argued elsewhere, positive freedom can be defined so as to reinforce rather than undermine resistance to paternalism. Briefly, it is the tendency to reify someone's interests – to treat a person's interests as objective entities knowable as reliably by others as by that person – which does indeed encourage paternalistic interference for the sake of someone's 'real' interests.[44] But positive conceptions of freedom need not reify interests in this way. It is possible to maintain both the corrigibility of wants or interests (that our wants may be distorted and so less than ideal) and their necessary self-ascription (that only we can ultimately know what our real interests really are). Others may help us to come to know our real interests, but they cannot know them on our behalf. In fact, the claim that an individual's wants are socially or culturally formed and so potentially deformed (which, as we have seen, provides one important justification for a positive conception of freedom) tends to support rather than undermine the necessary self-ascription of interests, because it undermines reifying notions of objectively ascertainable real interests. If interests are always defined within particular cultural traditions, supplying a variety of principles for the interpretation of need and identity, there can be no uniquely correct or objective specification of a person's interests independently of such a context.[45] At most there might be thought to be a single definitive interpretation of interests *within* a particular culture. But, as I argue below, there are reasons to question the view of culture as a single, all-encompassing medium that a definitive interpretation of that kind would seem to presuppose. The principle of the necessary self-ascription of interests also means that positive freedom should be understood as supplementing rather than overriding other rights and freedoms. Far from justifying the paternalistic curtailment of someone's negative freedom, a positive conception of freedom implies simply that negative freedom is no guarantee of genuine autonomy.

As I have argued elsewhere at greater length, the corrigibility and necessary self-ascription of interests can be reconciled, if positive freedom is understood not as the realisation of objectively ascertainable and fixed real interests but rather as a culturally relative and unfinishable process of 'free formation'.[46] On this view, authentic (or more authentic) interests correspond to the wants individuals would adopt under ideal (or more ideal) conditions for the formation of wants. Conditions of free formation might include, for example, the absence of manipulative interference and the availability of significantly differing possible interpretations of need. This approach suggests not a single fixed standard of 'positively free' as opposed to unfree action, but rather an ongoing formative process in which ever-improving interpretations of interest become possible. Because this formative process is irreducibly cultural and social, other individuals will typically be involved in some capacity, however indirect. But clearly, an important condition of free formation is the setting of limits to the legitimate involvement of others in this process, limits implied by the principle of the necessary self-ascription of wants. Thus, for example, any account of the free formation of wants must establish the value but also the limitations to the role of advice and influence from parents and friends, counsellors, psychologists or psychoanalysts, shamans, priests or teachers. Overall, a positive conception of freedom is concerned not to provide a fixed criterion of real interests that might be exploited by paternalists or tyrants, but rather to define and help protect the integrity of those processes in which our wants are formed.

By now it should be clear that positive freedom extends notions of freedom and justice beyond both politico-legal and economic spheres to the sphere of culture. It can accordingly be explicated in terms of a conception of cultural rights. In simple terms, every individual has the right (subject, of course, to legitimate legal constraints designed to protect the rights of others) to interpret her interests in terms of her own cultural tradition, to act according to her own world-view. Specific cultural rights can then be derived as the basis of institutional guarantees promoting aspects of this generalised right. The complementary notions of positive freedom and cultural rights can, perhaps, be clarified best in relation to some of the problems of social democracy reviewed in the previous section. In this context, the notion of cultural rights will correspond to the idea of an active citizen, sustained by one (or more) cultural communities, who is engaged in securing the satisfaction of autonomously formed rather than externally (for example, bureaucratically) defined needs. As corollary, the institutionalisation of social rights should enhance rather than diminish the autonomy of citizens. This idea of the autonomous citizen is clearly not compatible with paternalistic forms of welfare provision, which disrupt the relationship between individuals and their distinctive cultural orientations. From the perspective of positive freedom these cultural orientations are essential but vulnerable resources for the interpretation of interests, for the sustenance and reform of otherwise fragile identities. As such they are essential to any satisfactorily non-reductive conception of welfare as human flourishing or 'well-being'.[47]

The implications of this notion of autonomy and cultural rights can be illustrated with two examples. First, it would support the now widely accepted claim that the active involvement of people living with AIDS is essential in the development of HIV/AIDS education campaigns. Changes in sexual or drug-taking behaviour depend on voluntary and culturally mediated changes of life-style, which neither compulsion nor mere information (however frightening) are likely to catalyse. Education campaigns displaying scant understanding of the lives of gay men and drug-users have been correspondingly ineffective.[48] To consider a second example, an important concern of the women's movement of the last decades has been the struggle against patriarchal and paternalistic medical models and the attempt to promote forms of childbirth and healthcare compatible with women's conception of themselves as active and autonomous citizens.[49] In general, the lesson to be drawn from these examples is that the fulfilment of social rights should be understood not as provision by an active state on behalf of the objective needs of passive 'clients', 'claimants' or 'recipients' but as a reciprocal relationship between government and an active and culturally autonomous citizenry.

Obviously, the more detailed policy implications of a conception of welfare modified by recognition of cultural rights represents a large topic beyond the scope of this chapter. Certainly, any provision of services by the state implies some degree of objective and potentially paternalistic definition of need.[50] State education presupposes the value to all citizens of certain kinds of knowledge; Western health systems presuppose the value of scientific medicine for our health. Paternalism of this order may be acceptable and indeed inevitable in any political order incorporating social welfare rights. At the same time, considerations of autonomy and the cultural specificity of needs may argue in favour of greater emphasis on the 'portability' or 'abstractness' of benefits. Portable benefits permit greater choice in the take-up of services that are otherwise conceived generically so that, for example, entitlement to healthcare is interpreted more flexibly to include a variety of alternative forms of medicine. The currently unfashionable ideal of material equality would represent the most radical interpretation of the emphasis on abstractness in the institutionalisation of social welfare rights.[51] Short of this extreme, the consideration of cultural rights argues for forms of provision more sensitive to citizens' own interpretations of need.

It is perhaps important, in order to avoid at least one possible misunderstanding, to emphasise that the notion of cultural rights should not be allied with a dogmatic conception of culture as a single, fixed and all-encompassing medium. Communitarianism, for example, is sometimes associated with a conservative and potentially authoritarian interpretation of culture as inherited and inevitably shared by all members of 'the' community. In that case, the individual is effectively disbarred from criticising inherited cultural assumptions supposed essential to his or her very identity. Notions of community and citizenship may then also be defined in socially, ethnically, sexually or racially exclusive ways: in diverse societies cultural unanimity is bought at the cost of xenophobia, even 'ethnic cleansing' or genocide. A less dogmatic conception of culture is able to recognise a diversity of cultural contexts and associated interpretations of need and identity within the same political community or state. As Marilyn Friedman puts it, 'The problem is not simply to appreciate community *per se* but, rather, to reconcile the conflicting claims, demands, and identity-defining influences of the variety of communities of which one is part'.[52] In similar vein, we can recognise the activities of new social movements as attempts, in Habermas's words, 'to put reformed lifestyles into practice'.[53] The gay and lesbian communities, for example, can be understood as cultural communities, which make available to their members more authentic interpretations of need, more adequate conceptions of self or identity than those supplied by the dominant culture. By the same token, a reformed welfare state would presumably involve more reciprocal relationships with the constellation of social groups, associations, organisations, movements and associated cultural forms constituting civil society.[54]

The cultural conditions of positive freedom are arguably also crucial to any politics designed to overcome persisting distortions of the welfare state by inequalities of class, gender, sexuality, race and ethnicity. Although well-intentioned changes to the objective material content of welfare provision could in principle eliminate some of these distortions, only the active involvement of those affected is likely to ensure that one paternalistic regime of provision is not simply replaced by another. The experience of 'actually' and now 'previously existing socialisms' suggests that a political organisation claiming to act on behalf of the objectively conceived 'class interest' of its constituency is likely to institute a new form of class rule.[55] The emphasis of some new social movements on autonomous organisation, consciousness raising and empowerment offers a more promising route to positive freedom. Liberation is something that, in the final analysis, people must do for themselves – though, as the experience of these movements suggests, not *by* themselves. However, this experience also points to potential dangers of what has become known as the 'politics of identity'. Sometimes one 'radical identity' has been regarded as the universal and compulsory 'essence' of the 'liberated' member of the oppressed constituency.[56] For example, the feminist challenge to traditional patriarchal roles in the name of the 'liberated woman' has encouraged hostility to women choosing the traditional and 'unliberated' role of mother. Lesbians and women from ethnic minorities and indigenous communities have felt excluded from an identity promoted mainly by white, middle-class, heterosexual women. In other words, as postmodernist and 'difference' feminisms emphasise, the politics of identity is dangerous in the absence of a complementary commitment to difference and otherness. In effect, essentialising one radical identity reifies interests in a way parallel to the reification of 'objective class interests' in some versions of communism.[57]

A further context for complementary notions of positive freedom and cultural rights is provided by the more specifically cultural politics of contemporary social movements. Certainly, many activities of the women's, lesbian and gay and anti-racist movements aim for the extension of civil, political and social welfare rights to previously disadvantaged or excluded groups. Earlier waves of the women's movement fought for the extension of full political and civil rights to women; equal pay legislation and state support for child care have been significant issues in 'second wave' feminism. Similarly, the gay movements in Western countries have fought for and, for the most part, only just achieved basic (and not always equal) civil rights for homosexual men.[58] But from the 1960s radical feminist, Black, gay and lesbian activists have pursued a politics of liberation beyond these more narrowly political, legal and economic struggles. This 'politics of oppression' points to the irreducibly cultural dimension of entrenched forms of social domination. Legal, political and economic forms of subordination are invariably reinforced by cultural assumptions manifest in the prejudice of the oppressor, the absence of pride and disempowerment of the oppressed. The politics of consciousness raising, identity and pride directly confront these cultural components of oppression, which may survive even after the demise of legal, political and economic subordination.[59]

Nor can the politics of oppression be safely ignored even by partisans of more restricted conceptions of justice, as an important dimension of cultural domination concerns the unfair application of existing civil, political and economic rights. There is considerable evidence from contemporary western societies that the policing and adjudication of formally non-discriminatory laws is systematically distorted by cultural prejudices of race, ethnicity, sexuality, gender and so on.[60] The cases of Rodney King and O. J. Simpson in the United States provide contrasting and complex examples of the interaction between a formally neutral legal system and a racially fractured society. Employers' decisions about hiring and promotion are similarly affected by bias, even when they are formally committed to equal opportunities and anti-discrimination policies. Thus even if the conventional array of liberal and social democratic rights were regarded as sufficient in principle, the fair implementation of these rights in practice cannot be guaranteed in the absence of justice in the cultural sphere. In fact, we must assume that a substantial remainder of oppression will always be reproduced. The suggestion being pursued here is that the elimination of this remainder of oppression requires additional (but not necessarily special) cultural rights beyond those currently recognised within contemporary social democracies.

However, even when considered in isolation the existence of oppression in its various guises is incompatible with a fully just society. The notion of cultural rights implies a 'private sphere' for the free formation of interests and identity. Invasions of this sphere by oppressive cultural formations such as racism, patriarchy and homophobia threaten positive freedom in the same way that physical harm and coercion violate the negative liberties of citizens. In fact, by disempowering its victims cultural oppression also affects individuals throughout the civil, economic and political spheres of their lives as well. Undoubtedly the protection of a private sphere of free formation raises serious difficulties for conventional liberal theory with its suspicion of government intervention in the cultural and ideological domains. For example, the principle of free formation might be taken to justify anti-racist, anti-sexist or anti-homophobic education programmes within schools as attempts to modify the cultural prejudices of dominant social groups in order to protect cultural (including sexual or 'lifestyle') minorities from the effects of prejudice. Recognition of a private cultural sphere also seems to be implicit in 'anti-vilification' legislation recently passed in Australia for the protection of ethnic, racial and sexual minorities.[61] Such state interventions in the cultural sphere create difficulties for conventional liberal interpretations of the appropriately distanced relationship between government and culture. Certainly, state propaganda and indoctrination are unacceptable and, to judge by the experience of previously existing socialisms, highly ineffective intrusions on the free formative processes of persons. Of course, providing precise criteria to distinguish indoctrination from education is no easy task.

On the other hand, the emphasis on positive freedom, cultural rights and the empowerment of citizens need not imply a more intrusive state overall. Contemporary social movements demonstrate the potential impact of *non*-state initiatives for cultural change within civil society.[62] There will often be good reasons for stopping short of direct legislative intervention. Government intervention is sometimes counter-productive in practice: it may entrench prejudice by lending it the glamour of resistance; it may provide helpful publicity to a small, bigoted minority. Government intervention is at best a catalyst for processes of cultural change that must, in democratic societies at least, be initiated elsewhere. But even if some provisional and hopefully self-eliminating legislative interventions *are* justified in the short term, the emphasis on empowerment and active personal involvement in emancipation ultimately points to a declining role for government.

In any case, the dangers of government interference should always be considered in relation to dangers stemming from other centres of power, persistently ignored or minimised by liberal theorists. In this context, complementary notions of cultural rights and positive freedom argue against neo-conservative proposals to substitute free market mechanisms for existing forms of bureaucratic welfare provision. In the first place, consumer choice represents a decidedly reductionist account of personal autonomy. The consumer is only autonomous in a limited way as someone who chooses whether to save or to buy from a given range of commodities. But as Charles Taylor has argued, it is possible to distinguish between more and less important (shallow or deep) purposes or goals. Genuine 'freedom . . . involves my being able to recognise adequately my more important purposes, and my being able to overcome or at least neutralise my motivational fetters, as well as my way being free of external obstacles'.[63] In these terms, capitalist markets constrain the qualitative range of choices even when they furnish a seemingly endless array of products. Economic rationalism imposes a covert choice for marketable and profitable products backed by 'effective demand', with the result that the market furnishes far greater and more meaningful choices to the wealthy than to the poor. Overall, market systems exclude choice as much as they provide it, and the choices excluded may be more significant than those provided. Other features of the 'consumer society' compromise personal autonomy even more directly within the sphere of production. Commercial advertising and marketing treat consumers as manipulable objects, who must be goaded into performing appropriately energetic and profitable acts of consumption. The wants that consumers are encouraged to develop are only accidentally related to real needs. In the current variant of capitalist society individuals are enticed into consumption, where previously they were hectored into work. As Jean Baudrillard puts it:

> Modern man spends less and less of life in production, and more and more in the continuous production and creation of personal needs and of personal well-being. He must constantly be ready to actualise all of his potential, all of his capacity for consumption.[64]

To earn pleasure through consumption rather than work is our prime duty according to the 'fun morality' of consumer society. Overall, free market capitalism is not obviously more sympathetic to the genuine autonomy of citizens than the bureaucratic welfare state.

In order to ward off a further possible misunderstanding it is worth emphasising that cultural rights are not *ipso facto* collective or 'group' rights.[65] Cultural rights can be conceived, at least initially, as rights possessed by individuals just like the civil, political and social citizenship rights already institutionalised within welfare state liberal democracies. Obviously, the culturally defined context of free formation that cultural rights are designed to secure is itself irreducibly collective. But rights of association, trade union membership and religious worship are in the same way individual rights with collective implications and conditions.[66] Provision for social welfare rights typically has a collective dimension too: for example, the right of individuals to education and healthcare is normally translated into provision for communities of a certain minimum size. For a number of reasons the collective interpretation of cultural rights is best avoided in social democracies founded on liberal conceptions of individual rights. Criteria of group membership may be controversial, vague or subjective; competing groups may propose conflicting criteria.[67] The granting of group rights may provoke matching or escalating claims from other groups; it may encourage the formation of previously unrecognised groups. Still, notions of cultural rights and positive freedom, whether individual or collective, *are* clearly involved in the increasingly frequent demands for cultural autonomy and self-determination raised by minority indigenous, ethnic and national groups. The demands of indigenous peoples for land rights highlight the interdependence of economic and cultural dimensions in social justice.[68] Obviously related are claims for language rights within education, welfare and judicial institutions. Once again, clearly, the fulfilment of such rights inevitably has a collective dimension: there are practical limits to the degree of recognition that can be accorded to extremely small language communities; traditional land rights are normally granted to groups rather than individuals.[69] But it is not immediately obvious that collective claims cannot usually be translated into individual rights.

Obviously, any extension of rights into the sphere of culture raises difficult moral and theoretical questions scarcely touched upon here. The value of any form of rights discourse is open to doubt. The preceding discussion has ignored the question of the appropriate balance between rights and duties. Even within the terms of a discourse of rights there are serious difficulties to be faced. Most obviously, cultural rights will sometimes conflict with existing civil, political and economic rights. However, as classical liberals and libertarians have long argued, even the pursuit of a narrower conception of social justice involves conflict between the values of equality and liberty (or, in the terms employed earlier, between effective and negative freedom). More positively, recognition of cultural rights may even help to defuse some other value conflicts: if the welfare state can be redesigned so as to activate and empower its citizens, then both its expense and intrusiveness will be reduced. No doubt the resolution of conflicting demands for cultural autonomy will involve difficult decisions even within the sphere of cultural rights. The protection of one group from vilification restricts another group's expression of prejudice or 'deeply held conviction'. State intervention in the sphere of culture will be justified only when it serves to prevent a more significant invasion of autonomy from elsewhere. However, the difficulties raised by cultural rights and positive freedom are no reason to ignore them, for they offer some prospect of advancing beyond the current impasse of social democracy.

NOTES

1 For comments on earlier drafts of this chapter I am grateful to David Boucher, John Charvet, Gwen Gray, Glenn Worthington and Bob Goodin as well as to participants at a conference on Social Justice at Gregynog, University of Wales, in 1995.

2 There are, of course, various types of welfare state. Here the main focus is on the values underlying a range of welfare states from 'liberal' to 'social democratic': see Christopher Pierson, *Beyond the Welfare State: The New Political Economy of Welfare*, Cambridge, Polity Press, 1991, p. 187.

3 For convenience I refer to theorists hostile to conservative and libertarian agendas simply as 'left' or 'left-wing', even though there are good reasons to question any such straightforward 'left–right' opposition.

4 T. H. Marshall, 'Citizenship and Social Class', in *Sociology at the Crossroads, and Other Essays*, London, Heinemann, 1963.

5 On the new right see, for example, N. Bosanquet, *After the New Right*, Aldershot, Dartmouth, 1983 and R. Levitas (ed.), *The Ideology of the New Right*, Cambridge, Polity Press, 1986.

6 See F. A. Hayek, *Law, Legislation and Liberty: A new statement of the liberal principles of justice and political economy*, London, Routledge & Kegan Paul, 1982, vol. 2, esp. ch. 9.

7 See R. Nozick, *Anarchy, State, and Utopia*, Oxford, Basil Blackwell, 1974, esp. chs 7–8.

8 F. A. Hayek, *Law, Legislation and Liberty*, vol. 2, p. 99.

9 See M. Bleaney, 'Conservative Economic Strategy', in S. Hall and M. Jacques (eds), *The Politics of Thatcherism*, London, Lawrence and Wishart, 1983, p. 135

and I. Gough, 'Thatcherism and the Welfare State', in *The Politics of Thatcherism*, pp. 159–63.

10 On the 'economics of politics' see N. Bosanquet, *After the New Right*, ch. 4.

11 See S. P. Huntington, 'The United States', in M. Crozier *et al.*, *The Crisis of Democracy*, New York, New York University Press, 1975 and J. O'Connor, *The Fiscal Crisis of the State*, New York, St. Martin's Press, 1973. For a reply to the right's crisis predictions see C. Pierson, *Beyond the Welfare State*.

12 On the 'new politics' see C. Offe, 'New Social Movements: Challenging the boundaries of institutional politics', *Social Research*, vol. 52, no. 4, Winter 1985, pp. 825–32.

13 See, for example, R. Miliband, *The State in Capitalist Society*, London, Weidenfeld & Nicolson, 1969, pp. 72–6.

14 Miliband, *The State in Capitalist Society*, pp. 99–100 and see Pierson, *Beyond the Welfare State*, pp. 190–3.

15 For a survey of class inequality at the height of the welfare state in Britain, see J. Westergaard and H. Resler, *Class in Capitalist Society*, Harmondsworth, Penguin Books , 1975.

16 See I. Reid, *Sociological Perspectives on School and Education*, London, Open Books, 1978, ch. 6 and P. Willis, *Learning to Labour: How working class kids get working class jobs*, Westmead, Saxon House, 1977.

17 See S. Bowles and H. Gintis, *Schooling in Capitalist America: Educational reform and the contradictions of economic life*, London, Routledge & Kegan Paul, 1976, esp. Part II. Of course, conservatives too are critical of the utilitarian imperatives of state education, but they usually go on to champion private schools as havens of traditional morality, family values, academic excellence or humanistic self-cultivation.

18 For some feminist perspectives on the welfare state see Diane Sainsbury (ed.) *Gendering Welfare States*, London and Thousand Oaks, Calif., Sage Publications, 1994.

19 See J. A. Ballard, 'Sexuality and the State in Time of Epidemic', in R. W. Connell and G. W. Dowsett (eds), *Rethinking Sex: Social Theory and Sexuality Research*, Melbourne, Melbourne University Press, 1992, pp. 111–16 and Dennis Altman, *AIDS and the New Puritanism*, London and Sydney, Pluto Press, 1986.

20 See P. Read, *The Stolen Generations: The removal of Aboriginal children in New South Wales 1883 to 1969*, Sydney, NSW Ministry of Aboriginal Affairs, 1984.

21 C.f. John Keane's analysis of the limits of state action in *Democracy and Civil Society*, London, Verso, 1988, ch. 1.

22 A powerful demonstration of this claim in the area of education is provided by Samuel Bowles and Herbert Gintis, *Schooling in Capitalist America: Educational Reform and the Contradictions of Economic Life*, New York, Basic Books, and London, Routledge & Kegan Paul, 1976.

23 But whilst these critics agree with neo-conservatives that the welfare state is unsustainable, they regard capitalism as similarly unsustainable without it. As Claus Offe puts it, 'The contradiction is that while capitalism cannot coexist *with*, neither can it exist *without*, the welfare state'. C. Offe, *Contradictions of the Welfare State*, J. Keane (ed.), Cambridge, Ma., MIT Press, 1984, p. 153.

24 See J. Habermas, *Legitimation Crisis*, Thomas McCarthy (trans.), London, Heinemann Educational, 1976, part II, sections 4–7.

25 J. Habermas, 'New Social Movements' *Telos*, 49, 1981, p. 34.

26 C. Offe, 'New Social Movements', p. 833. C.f. John Keane's related account of crisis tendencies of the welfare state in *Public Life and Late Capitalism*, Cambridge and New York, Cambridge University Press, 1984, esp. ch. 1.

27 C. Offe, 'New Social Movements', p. 836.

28 Offe, 'New Social Movements', p. 850.

29 J. Keane, *Public Life and Late Capitalism*, p. 2.
30 J. Keane, *Civil Society and the State*, London, Verso, 1988, p. 2. Cf. Russell Keat, 'Liberal Rights and Socialism', in K. Graham (ed.), *Contemporary Political Philosophy*, Cambridge and New York, Cambridge University Press, 1982.
31 See D. Held and J. Keane, 'In a fit state' *New Socialist*, March/April, 1984, pp. 36–9.
32 For a discussion of some of these problems see Anne Phillips, *Engendering Democracy*, Cambridge, Polity Press, 1991, ch. 2, esp. pp. 38 ff.
33 Of course, it did greatly concern conservatives and 'aristocratic liberals' such as de Tocqueville and J. S. Mill.
34 Marshall, 'Citizenship and Social Class', p. 74.
35 Marshall, 'Citizenship and Social Class', p. 74.
36 Marshall, 'Citizenship and Social Class', pp. 90–1. C.f. R. L. Heilbroner, *The Worldly Philosophers*, New York, Simon and Schuster, 1967, ch. 1, 'The Economic Revolution'.
37 Marshall, 'Citizenship and Social Class', p. 83.
38 Marshall, 'Citizenship and Social Class', p. 114.
39 Classical liberals and contemporary libertarians emphasise the distinction between 'genuine' or negative liberty and political freedom. See for example, F. A. Hayek, *The Constitution of Liberty*, Chicago, University of Chicago Press, 1960, pp. 13–15.
40 For example, see the discussion of 'social' and 'economic' liberty in L. T. Hobhouse, *Liberalism*, Oxford and New York, Oxford University Press, 1964, pp. 21–4. For a more recent account of social democracy in these terms see R. Hattersley, *Choose Freedom: The Future of Democratic Socialism*, London, Michael Joseph, 1987.
41 Compare Rawls's discussion of the 'worth of liberty', in J. Rawls, *A Theory of Justice*, Cambridge, Ma., Harvard University Press, 1971, pp. 204–5 and N. Daniels's criticism in 'Equal Liberty and Unequal Worth of Liberty', in N. Daniels, *Reading Rawls*, Oxford, Blackwell, 1975.
42 This conception of freedom is sometimes called positive freedom, because it involves positive as opposed to negative rights. Here the term 'positive freedom' is reserved for a conception of freedom which concerns the content rather than merely the satisfaction of wants (see below).
43 For a classic exposition (though not defence) of positive freedom in this sense see I. Berlin, 'Two Concepts of Liberty', in *Four Essays on Liberty*, Oxford, Oxford University Press, 1969, esp. pp. 131 ff.
44 See my 'Spinoza on Positive Freedom' *Political Studies*, vol. 41, no. 2, June 1993, p. 288. Significantly, it is the same conception of interests that is implicated in bureaucratic forms of welfare provision.
45 See 'Spinoza on Positive Freedom', pp. 294–6.
46 D. West, *Authenticity and Empowerment: A Theory of Liberation*, Hemel Hempstead, Harvester Wheatsheaf, 1990, esp. ch. 3.
47 More recently, there has been greater recognition within the liberal tradition of the importance of cultural membership for meaningful individual choice. See for example W. Kymlicka, *Liberalism, Community and Culture*, Oxford and New York, Clarendon Press, 1989, esp. ch. 8.
48 See my 'AIDS and morals' *Interlink*, Autumn, 1987, pp. 15–16. See also *National AIDS Bulletin* (Sydney, Australia), vol. 10, no. 2, March–April 1996 on 'Gay Men and HIV/AIDS Education'.
49 See Lesley Doyal, *What Makes Women Sick: Gender and the Political Economy of Health*, London, Macmillan, 1995, esp. ch. 8, and Dorothy H. Broom, *Damned If We Do: Contradictions in Women's Health Care*, Sydney, Allen & Unwin, 1991, esp. chs 2–3.
50 I am grateful to John Charvet for this point.

51 For a plausible defence of the ideal of material equality see G. W. Mortimore, 'An Ideal of Equality' *Mind*, vol. 77, no. 306, 1968.

52 Marilyn Friedman 'Feminism and modern friendship', in S. Avineri and A. de-Shalit, (eds), *Communitarianism and Individualism*, Oxford and New York, Oxford University Press, 1992, pp. 101–19, 108.

53 J. Habermas, 'New Social Movements', p. 33.

54 An attempt at a politics of this kind was practised by the late and (by some still) lamented Greater London Council under Ken Livingstone. The role of a rapidly growing 'third sector' of voluntary groups, associations and organisations within civil society is also receiving greater recognition by both theorists and politicians.

55 A classic account of this process is M. Djilas, *The New Class: An Analysis of the Communist System*, London, Unwin Books, 1966.

56 See S. Rowbotham, 'The Women's Movement and Organising for Socialism', in S. Rowbotham *et al.*, *Beyond the Fragments: Feminism and the Making of Socialism*, London, Islington Community Press, 1979, p. 20.

57 On the importance of opting for a 'relational' rather than 'essentialist' politics of identity see I. M. Young, 'Together in Difference: Transforming the Logic of Group Political Conflict', in W. Kymlicka, (ed.), *The Rights of Minority Cultures*, Oxford and New York, Oxford University Press, 1995, pp. 155–76, esp. pp. 157–61.

58 A prominent exception is, of course, the Australian state of Tasmania.

59 In the case of homophobia, cultural oppression is the main focus of resistance in countries with little politico-legal or economic discrimination. See my *Authenticity and Empowerment*, pp. 61–2 and *passim*.

60 See Fiona Williams, *Social Policy: A Critical Introduction, Issues of Race, Gender and Class*, Cambridge, Polity Press and Blackwell, US, 1989; and Christopher Pierson, *Beyond the Welfare State*, ch. 3.

61 See *Australian Journal of Human Rights*, December 1994 and in particular M. Jones, 'Racial Vilification Laws: A solution for Australian racism', pp. 140–8. See also K. E. Mahoney, 'Hate vilification legislation with freedom of expression: where is the balance?', Ethnic Affairs Commission of NSW, Ashfield, NSW and Ethnic Affairs Bureau of Queensland, Woollongabba, Queensland, 1994.

62 For a good overview of the politics of new social movements, see C. Offe, 'New Social Movements'.

63 C. Taylor, 'What's wrong with Negative Liberty?' *Philosophical Papers*, Cambridge, Cambridge University Press, 1985, vol. 2, p. 228.

64 J. Baudrillard, 'Consumer Society', in *Jean Baudrillard: Selected Writings*, M. Poster (ed.), Cambridge, Polity Press, 1988, p. 48.

65 This issue is addressed in a number of contributions to W. Kymlicka (ed.), *The Rights of Minority Cultures*, Oxford and New York, Oxford University Press, 1995.

66 An argument against the necessity of recognising collective rights, even where collective goods are involved, is provided by Michael Hartney, who claims that 'conceptually, there are no moral rights which inhere in collective entities': M. Hartney, 'Some Confusions Concerning Collective Rights', in W. Kymlicka (ed.), *The Rights of Minority Cultures*, pp. 202–27, 219.

67 Similar problems are raised by attempts to provide guaranteed group or associational representation within systems of parliamentary democracy. However, if such guarantees are limited to a narrow range of activities (such as voting and representation), they are less problematic than collective rights, which may be invoked in relation to a wide range of contexts and practices.

68 In Australia Aboriginal land rights and abandonment of the doctrine of *terra nullius* have recently been recognised in the High Court's so-called Mabo decision. See M. A. Stephenson and Suri Ratnapala (eds), *Mabo, A Judicial Revolution: The Aboriginal Land Rights Decision*, St. Lucia, Qld, University of Queensland Press, 1993.

69 In fact, indigenous land rights seem to be the strongest candidates for collective or group rights. They are demanded on behalf of particular communities rather than individuals and any land obtained is usually regarded as indivisible and inalienable. See W. Kymlicka, *Liberalism, Community and Culture*, ch. 9 and the useful discussion in W. Kymlicka (ed.), *The Rights of Minority Cultures*.

14 Social justice in theory and practice

Kenneth Minogue

I

'Social justice' is an idea without a precise referent. It is one way of pointing to a family of ideas, and our first business must be a bit of genealogy.

Socialism is perhaps the ancestor: the aspiration to turn the modern European state into an equal partnership of workers all living largely the same mode of life. (No rich, for example.) *Social democracy* is a term which attempts to bridge the problem – a problem for those who support both socialism and democracy – that democratic politics will not always generate socialist policies. It is the attempt to determine not only the will of the people but also the content of that will. Social democrats believe that they know what the people ought to think, and sometimes exhibit a certain disdain for the actual opinions of the *demos* itself, opinions often redolent with the prejudices which intellectuals pride themselves on rejecting. *Marxism* is another member of the family, influential partly because it was socialism dressed up as if it were academic, a science in fact. Marxism's operational wing, *communism*, dropped any serious claim to democracy by indulging in a taste for violent, indeed murderous, social transformation. These two members of the family are currently in disgrace and have been relegated to the attic of oblivion. Lastly we might mention (though our list is far from complete) the *welfare state*, which is the way in which modern states have implemented many policies recommended in terms of social justice.

For my present purpose, *social justice* is an abstract term referring to the pure ideal which underlies these various projects. It refers to a society in which everything currently and conventionally regarded as a benefit or an advantage (or a 'privilege' – these are all technical terms of the family's discourse) available in modern life is freely available to all.

Let me advance as a first proposition, then, the view that *social justice is an abstract universal*. I mean by this, partly, that it is not concrete, as for example, is justice itself, or the state. These latter ideas refer to actual practices; they are presuppositions of how we actually live. The term 'justice' is not merely an admired norm, but also stands for a vast complex of practices spelled out in the law of the land. Quite what the content of justice is varies, of course, from place to place. Four wives count as no injustice in some Islamic states, but we don't hold with it. To cane a youth convicted of vandalism is just in Singapore, but not in Anglo-Saxon countries. *Autres pays, autre moeurs*. But it is rare to the point of non-existence to find any society without some idea of justice, however odd its details may seem to our judgement. Justice everywhere derives from religious beliefs, and our Western ideas of justice emerge from Christianity. But Western ideas of justice have equipped themselves with a philosophical foundation which has persuaded Europeans that our practices instantiate justice *tout court*. Claiming to be rationally rather than parochially grounded, our Western idea of justice has become part of the package of global modernisation and sought to supersede other forms of justice – abolishing slavery, for example, and demanding female participation in the work force. This universalism is often seen by outsiders as a form of domination. Social justice is derived from it.

Social justice is thus abstract and universal in the following sense: it is grounded (according to its protagonists) not on a concrete way of life but on rationality and need. This universalism is often formulated in terms of rights. Social justice is the belief that it is the duty of government to redistribute the wealth of a society so that each person enjoys at least the right to a basic minimum and so that, poverty having been abolished, certain equalities prevail. Those who write of social justice seldom specify who would be the agent of this redistribution, but it can only ever be the state, which alone has the immense power needed to compel people with wealth to hand some of it, or perhaps all of it, over to those without. In fact, concealment of this agency – what it is hard at times not to regard as a certain furtiveness about realities – is so instinctive to social justice theorising that it invents another concept to be the surrogate bearer of agency: namely the thing called 'society'. But as the philosopher Thatcher once famously remarked, there is no such thing as society, by which she meant that the expression 'society' cannot, except in the mouths of very confused people, ever refer to a causal condition. The Bishop of Oxford recently committed the Thatcher fallacy when he wrote a short piece accurately entitled 'Praise be to taxes, the sign of a truly civilised *society*' (my italics).[1] It is not of course 'society' which taxes people. It is the state.

The propositions of social justice are universal in the sense that they are not advanced as policies suitable merely for a modern European state such as Britain, but as being *desiderata* for the whole of mankind. It has to be said that the rest of mankind seems to be in no hurry to sign up. It is not merely that the economic and civil superstructure in many places is not in place. It is that 1,200 million or so Confucians in China are deeply attached to the principle of the iron ricebowl; that 800 million Hindus think a good deal more about caste than about equality; that a billion or so Muslims have a complete and apparently satisfying way of life which bears little relation to social justice; that Latin America is sunk in *machismo* and Africa pretty unsound on issues of social responsibility. Even in Western countries, there are many thinking people who reject social justice.

We therefore begin with the paradox that social justice is in one sense an abstract universal applying to all mankind, and in another sense a remarkably limited, particular and parochial doctrine, largely found among political activists in Western countries. It would take great ingenuity to exaggerate the blinkered character which results from this contrast. One might mention, merely, that there are some believers in social justice for whom their theory is so much the absolute standard that they judge not only present and future in its terms, but the past as well. They have discovered that the history of all hitherto existing societies is one of exploitation and oppression – of women, of workers, of peasants, of other races, of homosexuals, of . . . but the list is endless. How fortunate we are to live in the first age of enlightenment, in which at least some people understand the imperative of social justice.

It is necessary to make these points strongly, in order to convey the remarkable unreality in which the whole idea of social justice is embedded. There is on the one hand, the logical pretension of an abstract theory claiming mankind for its domain, and on the other hand, the concentration on the operation of justice purely in terms of the *distribution* of wealth, without any concern, in all the talk of rights and utility, for the costs and conditions of its production. The emblem of this unreality is perhaps the figure of Anthony Crosland, who charmingly believed that socialism could be fun, but also thought that modern society had produced the economic equivalent of a perpetual motion machine.[2] It would be no surprise to a sociologist of knowledge to discover that the social location of belief in social justice was in academic and civil bureaucracies: basically, that is, among a set of people who (until recently) hardly knew how difficult it is to create wealth, and who understood an economy as a static structure in which entrepreneurs make unfair profits out of the sweat of the worker.

We need further to make clear that social justice is a *telos*. Those who affirm it are much given to metaphors drawn from the construction industry, metaphors which adumbrate a future time when we shall have built a society without poverty, injustice and inequality, as an achieved condition of things. It is a bourgeois dream, like the last chapters of Dickens' novels in which the survivors retire to a life of country leisure. For cynics like myself, it is easy to imagine the paralysing boredom of such an impossible condition, and the undoubtedly nasty way in which it would fall apart – indeed the way in which very much less developed adventures of the same kind have *already* fallen apart. It is enough, on this particular point, I think, to remember Pascal's observations on the fatal restlessness of the human race.

We might also remember another significant reality: twentieth-century communists were keen to struggle against capitalism, but hardly one of them wanted to emigrate to Communist countries and live the detail of building such perfection. The means were found more amusing than the end. That it is better to travel than to arrive might tell us that such aspirations contain a large element of illusion.

II

I now wish to analyse the idea of social justice in terms of its emergence: to provide a kind of conjectural history of the idea.

I must begin, then, with the idea of justice itself. This has been well-elaborated in the social contract theories found both in Plato and in the early modern political philosophers. A set of independent magnates, patriarchs no doubt, disposing of certain rights and properties, establish a government which will sustain a set of laws under which each of them can pursue whatever project he pleases.

This doctrine has often been criticised as a civic myth; and construed as a theory of origins, it does no doubt commit, as Hume argued, a *petitio principi*. None the less, it gets to the heart of the matter. Civil associations have always rested upon a balance between a ruler having restricted powers, on the one hand, and a set of magnates disposing of independent power, i.e. property, on the other. Even when they begin in conquest, as the Anglo-Norman regime of 1066 began, they rest upon this balance, and the magnates have a recognised right to bring the ruler to book if he should exceed his powers.

King and barons share, then, a common idea of justice, which is giving to every man what is his own. And although we are talking here of magnates, the principle of justice, like other abstract principles, cannot be bounded. It runs all the way down to the humblest subject, and the king will enforce the rights of such a subject against exploitation. Not always effectively in rough times, no doubt – but it will become the rule.

Contrast this idea of justice with that found in other civilisations, and in earlier times also in the West. Where conquest is not merely the origin but also the ruling conception of a regime, the ruler exercises total power and understands himself to be the source of all order within his territories. This order is what is called justice, and it can easily be distinguished from oppression, even in despotisms. On the tomb of Darius the Great is inscribed the motif: 'Because I am the thing I am, I am the friend of justice.' The ruler, like a Solomon, declares what is just in terms of some pre-ordained and generally divinely inspired system of ideas.

We have, then, two conceptions of justice: the Western one with which we are familiar, which we may call a posteriori because it derives from the pre-established fact of independence among the subjects and responds to their evolving inclinations; and the despotic one, which we may call a priori because although in fact its workings are capricious, it depends upon a conception of society as a harmonious set of roles and relations forever likely to fall into confusion because of human weakness. It is a portentous fact of intellectual history that the philosophers, following Plato, have often found perfection in the unchanging character of a priori justice. The reason is that justice a priori arises, as its name suggests, from an idea. In an actual despotism, the idea of the tradition of the civilisation itself – a harmony between castes, for example – is the ideal built into the practices of a people. Philosophers spin their idea out of reason and other concepts. Both are profoundly static.

Justice a posteriori is clearly a conservative kind of justice, because it depends entirely upon a set of power relations such as have been actually established. It responds to interests as they change from time to time, and what has in fact happened in Western history is that increasing numbers of people have moved out of a condition of tutelage or clientship to become disposers of property in their own right. Modern politics has responded to their aspirations, and justice has, as a result, become increasingly complicated. And precisely because it responds to the conservative strand in Western politics, justice a posteriori has been extraordinarily dynamic. It has changed, without any of the rhetoric of change, in every generation – a fact which may lead us to suspect that those who use the rhetoric of change in favour of some ideal (the good society, socialism, social justice, etc.) actually nourish dreams of *changeless* perfection. This is an important paradox of radical rhetoric.

Justice a priori is in its philosophical form detached from the forms of contemporary society: that is precisely its *critical* point. This directly generates a definition of radicalism, which is any project of change which refuses to be tethered by the actual inclinations and activities of the society in question. Justice a priori rests upon an idea: Plato's idea that a city is a device for sharing the scarce resource of rationality, for example; or the idea that society reflects the changing lives of endlessly recycled individuals allocated to castes; or that there is a divinely sanctioned order in which subject must obey ruler, son father, little sister obey elder sister, etc.; or indeed, that there is a right social order in which everyone is equal. All these cases reject the Western responsiveness to the activities of the people themselves, and demand conformity to some fixed ideal. And the ideal must be backed by immense, despotic power, because the people often have other things on their mind.

But why do I invent new names for this contrast? It is the familiar distinction between the dynamic Western idea of justice as process, as applying the rule of law, on the one hand, and the traditional idea of justice as a fixed and determinate state of affairs, as envisaged by King Solomon, Harun al Raschid, Chinese Emperors, to which list, with some exaggeration, we might add Lord Beveridge, John Rawls,[3] Jacques Delors, and many others, on the other.

III

Social justice is, of course, an a priori notion of justice and that is why it is so remarkably parochial. Our concern now, however, must be to ask: what distinguishes it from the justice we ordinarily enjoy?

Justice in the courts is the adjudication of disputes in terms of property: People go to court in order to secure what is (as they believe) their own. It therefore depends upon history, upon the question of who owns what, and upon evidences of the past. It also reflects a world of conditionalities: i.e. free individuals may acquire money and goods by working for them successfully or by inheriting them from their parents. Inheritance sounds easier than work, and no doubt it is, but that does not affect the immense variability and dynamism of modern society. Enjoyment of benefits is essentially *conditional*, and a just order is constantly changing.

A *need* (or a social and economic right), by contrast, is not conditional. It results from one's status as a human being. It almost seems to be something for nothing. The consequence is that the concept of need in ethics and politics rejects one of the central features of human life: reciprocity, mutuality, trans-action – all forms of conditionality. This is highly significant because the needer, as it were, is thus construed as a passive thing to be provided with some schedule of needed things. Membership of society is constituted by his (or her) pure dependence, and socialist theory is the attempt to persuade us of the false proposition that we are *all* socially dependent in just the same way. Man is a social animal, we keep repeating after Marx, but the mantra does not erase the difference between the beggar and the entrepreneur.

This is a point of immense significance. The model of someone who is construed in terms of his or her needs is a beggar, or at best a client. To be unable to participate in reciprocal human transactions has commonly been thought to be a reason for shame, except where some form of disability oper-ates. In those cases, what the needer receives is charity, and to be a recipient of charity is not honourable. This point is well-recognised by exponents of social justice thinking, who attempt to disguise the reality of this situation rhetorically by the device of redescribing charity in terms of rights. Indeed, so as entirely to erase the mark of shame, the aim of social justice must be to make all these rights universal, thus reducing the entire population to depen-dence upon the state. Such a right is thus a Greek gift, because it is an instru-ment of subjection. The state becomes the manager of all enterprise within the society.

The project of social justice is thus the attempt to break any connection between what property (including abstract rights) people may have, on the one hand, and their energies and abilities on the other. At any given moment, there is in Britain a certain distribution of houses, money, swimming pools, foreign holidays, consumer goods and all the rest, and this actual distri-bution is, in social justice terms, wrong. It results from what fifty odd million Britons have been doing with themselves over the last few generations, and social justice requires that these things should, as it were, be thrown into the melting pot and redistributed. (According to one ingenious solution, by lottery.)[4] The redistributors will be politicians and their officials, guided, no doubt by expert normative political philosophers.

The current distribution of things has resulted from the operations of individual self-interest in the proper sense of the term (which is, of course, quite distinct from selfishness). Yet since individual self-interest, or individualism, has produced a maldistribution (in these ideal terms) of goods, it must be a bad thing. Indeed, individual action and judgement must be seen for this very reason as essentially selfish. The project of social justice thus requires an Altruistic Redistributor to remedy such selfishness, and this must, of course, be the state, for that is where the power lies. Hence one remarkable implication of social justice thinking is that governments are altruistic, while individuals are selfish. You might think this a miracle, the transformation of selfish individuals into an altruistic corporation by the gift of total power, but belief in such a miracle has been swallowed not only by Marxist thinkers, whom one might expect to be superstitious, but even by bishops of many Christian churches, who ought not to be. As we have seen, the Bishop of Oxford takes high taxing governments to be a sign of civilisation. The paradox of moral government and selfish citizens is generally evaded by attributing contemporary distributions to the abstraction called 'the system', alias capitalism.

Even theologically, the bishop is on pretty unsound ground. We may observe, for example, that St. Paul told the Thessalonians 'if any would not work, neither should he eat'.[5] In those times of vastly greater scarcity, lack of reciprocity was a serious matter. It is not that these Christian communities were uncaring or unsharing; they were simply not sentimental. But these considerations must not lead us to detour from our task of specifying a political idea. We must consider two related actualities.

IV

First, a political idea like social justice finds its most complete expression in normative political thought, and would consequently be 'merely academic' were it not for the fact that when such ideas escape from the study and start living a life of their own on the streets, they can also become an instrument of social transformation. They can tap into a powerful human disposition.

The disposition arises from merging (or perhaps confusing) charity – love of our neighbour – with justice, thus muddling both ideas. Justice involves reciprocity, while charity is something we give to those who need it but may not deserve it; indeed, perhaps especially to such people. The offspring of this is a curious political virtue, in which rights and solidarity seem – but only seem – to be detached from any duties at all. The beneficiaries must be understood as purely passive, things of a system, the theory of which we may illustrate by an entirely typical formulation. It is: 'You cannot minister to the alienated youth on the streets of London without addressing yourself to the causes of that alienation, and asking fundamental questions about the economy . . . about the prevalent hopelessness.'[6] Now you might think that a feeling of hopelessness is merely subjective, but this is not really so. The thesis is that hope on the one hand and the victims of such hopelessness are separate entities, and that hope is something – a commodity perhaps – which should be given to them. They should be set up, unconditionally, with food and shelter. As people think these things, new abstract ideas become detached to lead a life of their own, and in another connection entirely I have found reference to a basic human right 'to hope'. Now hope is not, of course, something people can be supplied with. Except in extreme situations, it is largely a matter of temperament. And if people are not given hope, what should our reaction be? Bishop Huddleston thinks it should be anger, which has become a very fashionable social justice emotion. We should be angry at 'a society that lets these things happen'. What this actually means is sometimes actualised in the anarchist slogan: 'Kill the rich.'

The point of this detour is, then, to observe something of the emotional trajectory of social justice . And anger can generate remarkable beliefs about Britain. Will Hutton, writing in the *Guardian*, for example, tells us that wealth has become so skewed in Britain that 'over half the population is unable to save more than £10 a week'.

Social justice, then, is a form of normative a priori in which conditionality disappears, and our basic standards of moral judgement are taken not from the capable majority of the population, but from the supposedly incapable minority, and that minority as presented in the most hopeless and atomised terms.

V

Our second detour is to remark that the poor, in this sense, have always had a certain social visibility. In the middle ages, they were the province of the Church. The Tudors created the Poor Laws, and from the nineteenth century onwards regulation of industry and provision for the poor (up till 1909, when pensions began to be introduced, often self-provision) increased greatly, leading to the present welfare states and their analogues throughout the Western world.

The expression 'welfare state' thus plays two roles in our political understanding. The first is as a portmanteau expression for changing forms of governmental provision for people who cannot afford such provision for themselves. There is very broad agreement these days that such provision is necessary: what that provision should be, how much it should be, how it should be organised, what its relation should be to the remarkably tenacious continuation of non-governmental charities – all these issues and many others are the stuff of politics, in which socialists, liberals and conservatives may be found engaged in a perpetual dialogue. It is an arguable point as to whether the concept of justice is at all relevant to these discussions, except in terms of their detail. That the poor should be provided for is one thing; that they should be allocated a set of *rights* is another. Arguably, this second move makes the whole area undesirably rigid.

The second role played by the 'welfare state' is as the highly partial achievement of some of the aims of social justice, by which it is encased in a kind of Brezhnev doctrine, or perhaps a doctrine similar to the *acquis* in European Community affairs: what we have we hold. It may be extended, but it must not be changed or diminished. The Labour MP Peter Hain was recently on record as supporting universal benefits on the ground that they were necessary to persuade the middle class to fund the welfare state by taxation – as good an example of the attempt to bribe people with their own money as one could find.

It matters, then, in talking about the welfare state, that we should be clear which of these two meanings is being discussed, i.e.: the political meaning, by which the government responds to the poor in terms of current sensibility; or the meaning found in normative political philosophy, as the adumbration of an ideal which still needs a lot of work.

VI

I now wish to block in a further feature of the idea of social justice: namely, its supposed causal relations with other social characteristics. Here again, the best source for understanding what social justice means is not the writings of normative political philosophers but the point at which philosophy touches social policy. I take my bearings from what Bernard Williams wrote when the Social Justice Commission (of which he was a member) published its report in October 1994.

Inequalities, he argued, must be eliminated as much as possible, and 'everyone is entitled, as a right of citizenship, to be able to meet their basic needs of income, shelter and other necessities'. We are clearly some distance from St Paul's 'if any would not work, neither should he eat'. Such is the principle, and it leads on to one version of the causal hypothesis generally incorporated in social justice thinking: '. . . a vision of social justice does not conflict with economic success. It is an ideal in its own right, of course, but the economic success of this country, and even its economic survival requires a greater measure of social justice.'[7]

And in these terms, the Commission unrolled what it remarkably called 'strategies' for social justice. I say 'remarkably' because the metaphor here is from warfare. In America the slogan 'war on poverty' soon produced the comment: 'Poverty won.'

Now what is remarkable is that this demand for more measures of welfare, as part of the project of social justice, comes half a century after the first attempt to implement a priori justice in Britain. The Attlee government of 1945 took over the commanding heights of the economy. It nationalised basic industries, set up a health service 'free at the point of demand' and began a process of slum clearance in order to create council estates in which accommodation would be distributed by local authorities rather than rented from landlords or owned and managed by those who lived in them. It could not be said that this Labour government did not have a strategy. It had, we may vulgarly say, strategy coming out of its ears. The succeeding Conservative governments did not disagree with the strategy. Later came tower blocks (many soon fell down) and incomes policies (wages were soon rising faster than ever). Reality's revenge was brutal, and hardly any of this strategy is now taken seriously. My difficulty is to understand how a notable philosopher such as Bernard Williams can, with a straight face, say just the same things as used to be said in the 1940s, yet without the slightest recognition of how such bright ideas have failed in the past. The very terminology echoes the past: what sort of solutions? Well, radical, of course. And what is the basic problem? Poverty, in the abstract.

The central point, however, lies in the causal hypothesis. Social justice, of which the welfare state is a part, will lead to economic success; or perhaps negatively, without social justice, there will be no economic dynamism. Correspondingly, inequality causes economic paralysis and (if we take professor Williams seriously) threatens our very economic survival. Sometimes other hypotheticals will be floated. If lack of social justice causes crime, then provision of social justice will diminish it. Or perhaps if we live in a more equal society, we shall be happier, or more at ease with ourselves. Is any of this at all plausible?

My view is not. If anybody wishes to try and establish a connection between social equality and economic dynamism, I should like to hear it. In fact, Britain exploded with economic dynamism when unequal during the industrial revolution, and has been slowing down to a large extent in proportion to the amount of welfare redistribution. The history of social justice projects is almost universally a history of disillusion. In the 1960s, for example, the expansion of higher education was to bring us into line with other countries and generate the required dynamism. All it did was to create the mass campus. Every so often governments fall in love with the idea of industrial strategies (sometimes imitating MITI or French indicative planning, or whatever tickles the fancy of intellectuals because it seems to be working abroad). They are never, at least in Britain, very good at it. Subsidy and central direction, which assume that governments are wise and that subjects are both passive and stupid, have a bad record everywhere. But projected on the future and fuelled by hope, they have a delusive rationality which convinces simple people. And it is a constitutive feature of rationalism that every time a big idea fails, it is plausible to say that it failed because we didn't have enough of it. When central planning produces anomalies, the obvious solution is more power to the planners so that they can deal with the anomalies.

Surely, it may be said however, governments must intervene to bring social justice in some areas – race relations, for example. In the United States, for example, Black youth unemployment at the end of the 1970s was nearly

40 per cent, that of Whites 16 per cent. The remarkable fact, however, is that in 1948, before wars on poverty and such like, the Black unemployment rate was actually lower than that of white males – 9.2 per cent against 10.4 per cent. The economist Walter Williams from whom I take these figures thinks that this merely corresponds to evident economic reality: Blacks are the victims of minimum wage and other welfare legislation, much of which serves those already established in jobs by making younger unskilled workers unviable. And the evil is not merely that workers rendered uneconomic by well-meaning legislation lose such jobs, but that they also lose the experience and self-discipline needed to fit them into a workforce.[8]

Social justice policies involve open-ended redistribution of wealth which becomes an increasing charge on the national wealth. Between 1949–50 and 1992–3, social security spending rose in real 1992 pounds from £10.3 billions to more than £80 billions and it is rising faster than ever. A great fuss has been made in social justice circles about the damage done by fifteen years of government by Margaret Thatcher and her successors. Welfare spending between 1979 and 1992 rose by £31 billions or 67 per cent. As the financial journalist Bill Jamieson remarked when commenting on Sir Gordon Borrie's Social Justice Commission: 'Among millions of young people the psychological damage of the dependency culture is rampant: illiteracy, cynicism, defeatism and near total demotivation. For this Borrie has a solution: more.'[9]

These considerations are worth rehearsing because they make it unmistakable that any abstract theoretical discussion of social justice is exiguous to the point of fraudulence. Social justice is, remarked Bernard Williams, 'an ideal in its own right' but he then proceeded to claim actual benefits for it. If ideals do not have benefits, what value *do* they have?

One might go further. Social justice is an idea which, because it proselytises, has come to be noticed beyond the Western world. The Chinese, in particular, are derisive of it, and regard it as an attempt by a decadent West to involve everybody else in the same decadence, for they believe that social justice can only lead to a fatal decline in Western power – of its population, of its ability to compete economically, of its harmony and cohesion.

VII

What I have sought to do, then, is to lay out what is to be understood by the idea of social justice. It is an ideal, a morality, a political project and a powerful movement engaging the passions and thoughts of many peoples. I want finally to make some remarks on its significance.

The first point arises merely from the fact that it is an idea. Political projects which seek to transform a real living breathing society on the basis of an idea may be called rationalist or ideological. Their common characteristic is that they largely reject historical knowledge, which is disabled by the argument that history is merely a tale of blind exploitation and oppression. Abuse of the past is a clever device for preventing us from learning from it. It makes us stupid. Burke, it will be remembered, thought politics must in large measure be tied to interests, because they involved at least some element of reality which put some limits on human folly, whereas ideas might have limitless consequences. Ideas inevitably change with the generations. Today the bright idea which commonly dominates rationalist projects is equality. Yesterday, it was racial purity and in some places today it is ethnic cleansing. Who knows what it will be tomorrow? It would seem wise to fear rationalist politics.

Consider the following protest: 'Of the fifteen thousand prisoners shut up with me, three thousand no longer have whole bodies. About two hundred have no legs at all . . . Twelve hundred prisoners have only one leg, others are one-armed. A few have both arms missing. . . . These fractions of men who retain only a given proportion of their bodies receive the same quantity of food as prisoners in possession of their full quota of limbs. This is a great injustice. I propose that these prisoners should receive rations in proportion to the amount of body still in their possession.'[10]

You are horrified? You are meant to be. This is from a satire. But remember that Political Correctness began as a joke, indeed to some extent remains a joke. Remember witch trials. Hitler's new order was a piece of a priori justice which not only ignored past and present in favour of a bright idea, but proceeded to take the corrupt present apart by killing those who did not belong in it. Rejecting conservatism, rejecting the past embedded in the present for the sake of justice has very worrying risks.

We may put this another way: rationalist politics are categorially defective in that they can find no place at all for *conservatism*, which is inextinguishably one of the central strands of the Western political tradition. Sometimes these days it is called 'pragmatism' but what it must involve, by either name, is rejecting the rationalist idea that the experience of the past is hopelessly corrupted by oppression and false ideas. You do not have to be a conservative to value the role of conserving in politics. To reject it altogether, to be radical, is to embrace the world of bright ideas, of ideology.

Second, the idea of social justice has no proper place in political philosophy because it is monistic. We reject Platonic monism because, if it *were* intended in any way to be practical, it would be totalitarian. Social justice is a form of ethical fundamentalism designed to be imposed on culture, the economy and society. Rationalist projects generally *are* monistic, because having two or more ideals makes impossible conflicts between them inevitable. Real politics is a succession of just such conflicts.

In politics as we know it, nothing at all has a single significance. The most ideal project has implications for power, and every power move has moral characteristics. In our generation, social justice and similar rationalisms have fatally corroded our sense of legality and constitutionality. Most people are content to be persuaded merely that a proposal is desirable or undesirable in order to support or reject it. In our decadent times, many seldom consider that what is desirable may be constitutionally destructive. In other words, the real ancestor of the social justice family of ideas is despotism, which is free-dom from constitutional limitations – benevolent, perhaps, or perhaps not, but certainly despotism.

For social justice is, if I may borrow a phrase, the ghost of scientific social-ism sitting crowned on the grave thereof.

As such, it corrupts not only political practice, but also political philosophy by turning it from an explanatory activity into being a kind of surrogate, blinkered politics.

VIII

I leave till last the most important point. It is that the idea of social justice, like other forms of rationalism, is transforming our conception of the point of human existence.

The ideas we have about this are different from those of other civilisations, and they derive from Christianity. They remain fundamental for us even amid the collapse of Christian belief. The point of a human life lies not in the satisfaction of needs, however important that may be, but in meeting the chal-lenges of life; each day challenges us not to be found wanting, and happiness lies in our success or failure in this respect. This is the theological transposition of the profound passion for adversariality which lies at the heart of our civil-isation: it determines the way we deal with crime in law courts, the way we produce commodities, our party political system, our passion for competitive sport, and much else. It is an implication of this view of life that success and failure are vitally important to us, and that both pain and failure are impor-tant ways in which we construct our identity. This is why we are almost cease-lessly to be found locked in transactional reciprocities.

Treating human beings as creatures with needs to be managed assumes that the point of human life is to enjoy a succession of pleasant experiences – a good quality of life as it is often called. Social justice which guarantees food shelter and an adequate income leaves open to the challenge of life little except the moral equivalent of pocket money. In fact, hardly that, because on the horizon of social justice lies a completely de-moralised and therapeutic conception of human life.

Is there, then, such a thing as social justice? Well, yes: there is a reactionary project for a managed society. But has this project any relation to justice? I believe not. Rather, it is the employment of a noble rhetoric in the service of a servile state.

NOTES

1 *The Times*, 15 October 1994.
2 Anthony Crosland, *The Future of Socialism*, London, Cape, 1956.
3 As Rawls elaborates his view of justice, for example, even natural propensities, such as intelligence or industriousness, are up for political grabs. Distribution of good

things, he judges, should no more be settled by 'the distribution of natural assets than by historical and social fortune'. *A Theory of Justice*, Oxford, Oxford University Press, 1972, p. 74.

4 See Barbara Goodwin, *Justice by Lottery*, London, Harvester Wheatsheaf, 1992.

5 2 *Thessalonians*, 3, 10.

6 Kenneth Leech, interviewed by Valerie Grove in *The Times*, 23 December 1994. The Reverend Leech runs Centrepoint near Euston Station in London.

7 'Radical solutions needed for a society disillusioned by poverty and crime' *The Times*, 24 October 1994.

8 Walter Williams, 'The Poor as First Victims of the Welfare State', the Ludwig von Mises Lectures series, *Imprimis*, vol. 9 no. 7, July 1980.

9 'Borrie's panacea is a suicide pill' *The Sunday Telegraph*, 30 October 1994.

10 C. Virgil Gheorghiu, *The Twenty Fifth Hour*, New York, Knopf, 1950, pp. 276–7. Also quoted in Chain Perelman, *The Realm of Rhetoric*, London, University of Notre Dame Press, 1982, pp. 66–7.

15 Why social justice?

Raymond Plant

The aim of this chapter is to argue for the continuing salience of the idea of social justice for democratic politics. This view may now be regarded as rather quaint: first of all on the economic liberal right in politics which has adopted Hayek's view that social justice is an illusion and that a politics built upon it is a fatal conceit; secondly on the contemporary Left there are assumptions shared with the neo-liberals as well as views about the nature and responsibilities of government which do not fit at all well with a positive commitment to the idea of social justice. The first part of my argument will be in essence a statement and critique of the ideas of Hayek and the New Right in respect of social justice. This does mean unfortunately the repetition of some arguments I have developed elsewhere, but this is unavoidable since this critique underpins the rest of my argument.

I shall take various elements of the economic liberal critique and subject them to criticism. At this stage however, it might be worth saying that the core idea of the economic liberals which underpins a good deal of their critique is that the 'distribution' of income arising in a free market is fair and legitimate if it arises out of individual acts of free exchange whatever the degree of inequality which it may embody. The job of government in relation to fairness or justice is to provide a framework of rules within which each individual act of free exchange is uncoerced so that the distribution of income and wealth which arises out of these uncoerced exchanges is fair. They want to block the possibility of the moral critique of that outcome in terms of social justice and to block the idea that government should act to correct it. We need now to look at each element of the argument which underpins this view.

(1) It is often argued by the economic liberal that we do not bear moral responsibility for the distribution of income and wealth in a free market since we are only responsible for the intended outcomes of our actions. However, the overall pattern of income and wealth at any point in time in a free market economy is not the result of anyone's intentional action. In a market individuals buy and sell for all the individual reasons they have and this leads to a particular pattern of distribution, but this is not really a distribution since no one intended it. Indeed the term 'the distribution of income and

wealth' is a misnomer since there is no distribution: it is an outcome which just happens as a result of all the individual intentions of all the millions who participate in markets. It is not intended by anyone. Hence we bear no moral responsibility for market outcomes, so long as they are uncoerced and there can be no moral basis for the critique of market outcomes since these are unintended.

This argument is flawed. We bear responsibility not only for the intended but also the foreseeable outcomes of our actions. If it is foreseeable that those who enter the market with least are likely to leave it with least, then we can be said to bear responsibility for that. If people's capacity to participate in markets is influenced by class, by opportunity, by schooling, by race and by gender, so that disadvantage may led to a limitation on effective market participation, then this is something for which we bear responsibility. It is incoherent for economic liberals to argue that market outcomes are not fore-seeable otherwise they would have no basis for arguing for the extension of markets. It is only because of the beneficial effects that markets are supposed to bring that they favour deregulation and privatisation and therefore at the heart of their project must lie an account of what they take to be the foresee-able effects of markets. However, if market outcomes are foreseeable we can bear responsibility for them, and with this goes the possibility of a moral critique of the outcomes of markets.

(2) It is argued by the economic liberals that injustice can only be caused by intentional action. This is why we do not think that natural disasters such as floods or earthquakes cause injustice. They are matters of misfortune or bad luck, not injustice. Similarly, we do not regard physical disabilities which are caused for example by genetic defects as injustices since they are not intention-ally caused. The political rub here is that we do not normally think that the state has a duty to compensate for bad luck or misfortune. So if market out-comes are not intended, but are the unintended consequence of millions of acts of buying and selling then those at the bottom of the pile have not suffered an injustice so much as misfortune and bad luck and it is not the duty of the state, and fellow citizens to try to rectify that position by policies governed by ideas of social justice. The response to bad luck or misfortune is altruism or charity; not coercive collective action by the state.

This argument is false for two reasons. The first is implied in what was said under (1). We are normally held to be responsible for the reasonably foresee-able consequences of our actions as well as those consequences which are intended. If the relative position of the poor is worsened by an unregulated free market (assuming for the moment that we believe that relative positions matter) when there is an alternative, namely a more just distribution of resources than that produced by a market, then we can be said to bear moral responsibility for that outcome. Market outcomes are not, *pace* Hayek and his followers, like acts of God, they can be foreseen and because of that moral considerations have a purchase on them.

Second, as John Rawls has argued, we do not normally think that the justice or injustice of a state of affairs has been settled once we settle how it arose – whether by intentional action or not; rather justice and injustice are also rooted in our response to a situation. If we can compensate people who suffer disadvantage at no comparable cost to ourselves, then not to do so can be regarded as unjust. To put the point very starkly in terms of an example: imagine that a small child has been blown over face down into a pool of water, I am the only person in a position to pluck the child out of the water before it drowns. Would we really believe that if I failed to do so when there was no comparable cost to myself then the question of the justice or injustice of my failure to act would be settled by claiming that after all the child was the victim of a non-intentional process namely the action of the wind. Most people (outside of philosophy journals) would believe that I had acted unjustly however the circumstances had arisen. So it is with the outcomes of markets. If there are ways of compensating those who have fallen victim to market outcomes, then the failure to do so can be regarded at least prima facie as an injustice.

(3) Critics of social justice argue that they want to place the idea of freedom at the centre of their beliefs and then go on to argue that the possession of resources and opportunities has nothing to do with liberty. Freedom is the absence of *intentional* coercion; market outcomes are unintended, hence the lack of resources as the result of market outcomes is not an infringement of liberty, or as Sir Keith Joseph put it in his book on Equality (with J. Sumption) 'poverty is not unfreedom'.[1] The argument is backed up by drawing a sharp distinction between being free to do something and being able to do something. I am free to do whatever I am not intentionally prevented from doing; whether I am able to do what I am free to do is quite a separate question. No human is able to do all that he is free to do – we all in different ways lack the resources, the abilities and the opportunities to do all the things which we are not intentionally prevented from doing. Hence, the argument that it is necessary for government to secure resources and opportunities to people to enable them to do more than they otherwise could and to see this as an extension of liberty is false since liberty has nothing to do with ability. The lack of resources is not a restriction on liberty and thus poverty is not unfreedom.

This is coupled with the argument that the rule of law limiting acts of intentional coercion is something which a free society can secure to every individual. This can be done by a framework of law which prescribes mutual non-interference which can be applied to all with impartiality. Once, however, freedom and ability are mixed up then there is no way in which a government can secure equal liberty since equalising abilities, resources and opportunities is an unattainable ideal and one which threatens freedom, properly understood as the absence of coercion. The political rub to all of this is that so long as individual acts of economic exchange are uncoerced, that is not the result of intentional coercion, then the aggregate outcome of such acts, i.e. the 'distribution' of income and wealth is legitimate, whatever the degree of inequality it may embody.

This argument about the relationship between freedom, ability, resources and opportunities is dubious for three reasons. In the first place it is arguable that there is a closer link between freedom and ability than the critic will admit. It is surely the case that a general ability to do X is a necessary condition of settling whether someone is free to do X. If I asked: were people free to fly before the invention of aeroplanes? I think the question would be meaningless. An individual is only *free* or unfree to fly if people generally are *able* to fly. If general ability to do X is a necessary condition of A's being *free* to do X then there cannot be a categorical distinction between freedom and ability.

Second, if one were to ask the critic why freedom understood as the absence of coercion is valuable, the most likely (indeed perhaps the only) answer is that in the space within which I am free from the coercion of others I am able to do things which I would not be able to do if I was being coerced. If this is true, then the value of the very kind of liberty which the critic endorses will depend on some account of what liberty enables me to do and is thus associated with ability.

Finally, to borrow an argument from Charles Taylor,[2] if freedom is seen as wholly negative, as the absence of coercion, then it would follow that the judgement as to whether one society is more free than another will depend on the number of coercive rules in a society. That is to say it will be a quantitative judgement based on the number of rules prohibiting action which a society has, rather than a qualitative judgement about what people are able to do in a particular society. This will however, lead to paradoxical results, in that if one asked say in 1985 whether Britain was a freer society than Albania, then on the critic's view the answer would depend on how many laws circumscribing action there are in the two societies. Because Britain is a more complex society – for example, in terms of traffic or in terms of financial complexity, it is quite likely that there are more rules prohibiting action in Britain than Albania. Of course, this will not wash and the reason why it will not wash has to do with ability. It is because in Britain we are *able* to do things like criticise the government, or emigrate that we believe that Britain is a *freer* society. However it cannot then be claimed that freedom and ability are different in a categorical way since the judgment that Britain is freer than Albania is rooted in some account of the valued abilities which we have and the Albanians do not.

What is essential then is that we have a clear account of what are these valued abilities within a particular society, and within our society I would have thought that these would include not only political and civil forms of ability, but also economic and social ones such as access to income, education and health care for example.

(4) The next criticism of the idea of 'social justice' takes up this last point. The argument here is that the term 'social justice' is purely rhetorical. It is an appeal to the idea that the social product should be divided according to just principles, but in the view of the critic there are many competing distributive principles each of which would lead to a different distribution of the social product: need, desert, merit, entitlement, equality, contribution, etc. In a morally diverse society we have no way of agreeing on what the basic principle should be, and even if we had ideas about needs or merits for example, they would be so subjective as not to be able to provide a clear guide to policy formulation and the ability to define rules of distribution. Many people will want to be sensitive to the claims of several principles, say to both need and desert, and, in the distribution of some goods, to equality. But how do we put these in order and how do we weight them? When do we stop meeting needs say and turn to desert? What would be the economic consequences of meeting needs as our priority and neglecting desert? To see the point at stake here let us take a very simple, homespun example. Imagine that a family is sitting down to afternoon tea and there is a cake to be divided up between members of the family. The prima facie principle of dividing the cake is in terms of equality: each should get an equal share. But there might be all sorts of reasons for moving away from this principle: if one member of the family has missed lunch his or her need might be greater; one person may have done very well at school and we feel that a bigger slice might be a reward for desert; if it was a family which had read the works of political philosophers we might ask who baked the cake? Does labour and contribution merit a specially large share? We might even ask who owned the ingredients, whose money purchased the flour and the eggs? These debates can be settled around a table within a family because there are common values, common experiences, common expectations. The critic will, however, argue in a morally diverse society we have no way of settling such issues and if we wish to be sensitive to most of the principles at stake there will be irresolvable conflicts about when we move from one principle to another, particularly in the economy between the claims of need, desert, contribution and the rights of ownership and investment. We do not possess a rational way of resolving these issues. To settle them by the exercise of political power is not satisfactory because this will ride rough shod over the fact of moral disagreement in society.

This leads to further difficulties. In the view of the critic, it will be the socialist and the social democrat who will place most emphasis on the idea of distribution according to need, but in the critic's view need is essentially highly subjective: we do not possess a clear account of what needs are and how the urgency of one set of needs is to be set against another. Because of the vagueness and subjectivity of need, the claims to need can be bid up by interest group pressures and by the power of professionals such as doctors, teachers, social workers and so forth whose professional scope and responsibility is increased as needs are increased – so they have an incentive to discover, or create new needs which then have to be satisfied, thus continually expanding the range of need and crowding out our concern for other principles which also have moral force (as well as pushing up public expenditure to meet needs). Equally, we have no way of limiting the claims of need, particularly for example medical and educational needs which expand inexorably with the growth of technology. All of this has to be considered against the background of scarcity of resources, so that we are faced with potentially unlimited needs and a lack of resources to meet them.

In the critics view, this leads to two politically baleful consequences. The first is that distributive politics, far from being based on the moral principles of social justice, are in fact a matter of interest group and professional pressure and government is likely to fund those needs which are sponsored by the most powerful interest groups in society or coalitions of such groups. Social justice pursued against a background of scarce resources is going to turn politics into a bleak zero sum game in which gains for one group as the result of interest group pressure is going to mean losses for other groups. A government pursuing 'social justice' will fall victim to coalitions of interest groups pushing their own particular interpretations of what they need/deserve in respect of justice.

The second consequence is that because the principle of need is so vague it cannot be the basis of clear distributive rules and those charged with meeting needs out of public expenditure are bound to act in arbitrary and discretionary ways as they seek to ration the limited resources at their command to meet needs. This means that a regime of social justice is bound to entrench arbitrary and discretionary power in the hands of public sector officials and professional groups and this arbitrary power is incompatible with the rule of law.

In the view of the critic it is therefore best to prefer market to political distribution. People in markets are able to define their own needs and seek to meet them as best they can in markets. In any case, as we have seen already, any lack of resources is, in the critic's view, neither a restriction of liberty nor an infringement of social justice. This also has the advantage for the critic in that a market can avoid irresolvable questions of needs, merits and desert in that in a market these are left to individual preference. What I am worth depends on what other people are prepared to pay for what I have to offer, and this is a matter of their subjective preference. Also a market and its inequalities will recognise incentives in a way that a need oriented view of distributive justice will not. Incentives will create a dynamic economy which through the trickle down effect will mean that even the worst off groups will be able to meet more and more of their subjectively defined needs through markets.

In my view some elements of this argument are quite powerful. Unless the idea of social justice is further specified into distinct principles of need, desert, equality, etc. it actually means very little. It is also true that different principles can lead to quite different bases of distribution, and if we believe in social justice it is no good just invoking the principle; we have to look very hard at the relative weightings of different principles. The point about interest group pressures also follows from a point which I made earlier, namely without a distributive consensus around a view of social justice which goes beyond rhetoric, then a government pursuing social justice is likely to fall victim to such interest group pressures. These difficulties cannot be solved in a short study such as this. However the following points are worth making.

The critics arguments seem persuasive enough on these specific points if we were all thoroughgoing libertarians, that is to say believing that governments have no duty to establish a welfare state even of the most minimal sort. An argument of this sort is to be found in Robert Nozick's influential *Anarchy, State and Utopia*.[3] However, in fact most of the economic liberals believe that there is a case for a limited welfare state which does meet basic needs and that these should not be left entirely to market forces. However, once this is admitted, as it surely is in the realms of practical politics, then the differences become much less sharp. If critics of social justice accept that there are needs which the state should meet then we face the same difficulties about defining needs, about the ways in which needs can be bid up by interest groups, and about problems of meeting needs against a background of scarcity. It is just not possible to draw a sharp distinction between a minimal welfare state which is supposed to meet basic needs or residual needs and a welfare state which is based on the idea of a just distribution according to need. If the critic is right, we do not possess a clear idea of basic needs and a set of limited resources which will meet them. If we do not, then we cannot draw a clear distinction between a minimal or limited welfare state and one which is animated by the idea of social justice or just distribution. If this is so, then we have to be in the business of trying to settle the idea of the scope of distribution according to need by political negotiation and not looking either for the libertarian's idea of abolishing a need based pattern of distribution altogether, or the limited government approach which was to draw a sharp distinction between a minimal welfare state and a distributive welfare state.

There is no Platonic Idea of distributive justice which will act as a kind of philosophers' stone here: it is a matter of political judgement, and then trying to create a consensus around that judgement. The judgement will however, have to be based on a recognition of a limit to resources, and this is likely to mean that we have to try to develop some view of the range of needs which should be met by public expenditure and in the case of health for example. This is going to mean that some hard decisions have to be faced. It also means that issues about universal and selective benefits will have to be faced (about which I say a little more later) because if we believe both in meeting needs and that there are scarce resources we have to be sensitive to the extent to which some groups are in fact able to meet their needs through the market.

(5) The critic of social justice will argue that distributive politics will lead to conferring rights or entitlements to resources at particular levels to

individuals. However, in the view of the critic there cannot be enforceable rights to scarce resources and it is a piece of socialist and social democratic rhetoric to believe that there can be economic and social rights of citizenship conferred by an appeal to social justice. If resources are scarce, then there cannot be rights to them. The scope of rights should be restricted to rights which secure non-interference. A right to life is the right not to be killed, not a right to the means to life; the right to security is a right not to be assaulted, raped, coerced, not a right to income; a right to work is a right not to be prevented from going to work (for example by pickets) not a right to a job. These rights are essentially negative, they imply a duty of forbearance on others. Forbearance is costless, it does not run out and therefore these rights can be enforced. However, the social rights of citizenship are necessarily rights to resources, and rights to a so-called just share in the social product, which because of scarcity, cannot be enforced and are meaningless. Therefore, in view of the critic, we should abandon the idea of such rights. This goes back to the earlier point about the rule of law. Negative rights can be held by all and their protection is impartial. Social rights fail this test.

This argument is false, or at least the strictures apply as well to negative rights. Negative rights, the rights not to be interfered with, coerced, assaulted, etc. have to be protected and enforced, because forbearance is in fact limited by people's motivation. In a community of saints there would be no problem about forbearance; in the real world, there is. This enforcement involves costs and resources. Enforcement is not just an accidental, a side issue, or contingent feature of rights just because a right is distinguished from other sorts of claims, interests, preferences, etc. and we believe that rights should be capable of being enforced. Thus if the idea of a right is tied conceptually to enforceability, then all rights involve costs. Or to put it another way if there is a right to the protection of rights (and without it how would the rights be rights?) then these rights involve the commitment of resources. Take a specific example: my negative right to physical security is protected and enforced by the police and the police have limited resources in the same way as the health service does. The Chief Constable has to make a decision based on professional judgement about how to deploy his resources in the same way as a consultant has to do in the health service given that neither has the resources necessary to protect all rights simultaneously. This has not led critics of social rights to say that we do not have rights to the protection of civil and political rights. We seem to accept that the extent of protection of negative rights is secured by political negotiation and political consensus and what we have to do in the field of social and economic rights, as I have argued already, is to recognise the fact of scarcity and try to achieve a consensus over what is a reasonable level of provision to protect social rights in the same way. This is not easy, and it is no good just assuming that the resources are there to protect all such rights equally any more than they are with the police service. We have to think hard about what is a reasonable level of provision and what is a fair distribution of provision to protect what we believe to be the most important rights in the social and economic field and then try to carry people along with that. Indeed, there are large questions about distributive justice to be faced in relation to the protection of civil rights. This clearly applies to Legal Aid. It also has wider ramifications. Do the poorest sections of our society have an appropriate degree of protection against crime given that they are not in a position to pay to defend themselves against it?

The critic might accept the justice of most of these points and still say correctly that all I have done is to justify a role for the state in securing resources to the worst off but that this falls a long way from the more traditional socialist and social democratic ideal of equality as that tradition's preferred form of social justice. In the rest of this chapter I want to say a little about the case for equality, while at the same time insisting on some qualifications. The point at issue is this: why do inequalities matter? If either the market economy or, on my arguments, the state secures to the poor basic resources, why does further inequality matter?

The first has to do with liberty. If one accepts that liberty does indeed involve ability and the associated resources and opportunities, then radically different resources and opportunities will have a close bearing on liberty. This is not so for the economic liberal as we have seen for whom liberty is the absence of coercion, not the possession of resources or opportunities. However, we have seen reason to doubt this. Historically Western societies have held out the ideal of equal liberty and thus if there is a link between liberty and resources, then a fairer distribution of resources and opportunities is necessary for a fairer value of liberty in society. However, we have to be careful about how this argument is handled, because this does not mean equality of outcome as it has done for some socialists, nor does it mean procedural equality of opportunity as it does for the liberal, that is removing intentionally erected barriers to advancement. The concern with fairness is with what Rawls[4] and Crosland[5] called 'democratic equality' that is to say that social institutions should be concerned with a fair distribution of resources as a way of securing a fair value for liberty. We cannot equalise outcomes even if this were desirable without the most extravagant acts of government intervention and likely mutual impoverishment. It would be irrational to prefer a more equal distribution of resources which left everyone, including the poor, worse off than they would be under a system under which there would be some inequalities, but which would also benefit the poor. We cannot get an equal value for liberty without threatening to destroy it, but we can get a fairer distribution of resources and opportunities which bear most directly on the capacity for action. Our distributive concern is with fair conditions for the exercise of liberty, not equalising outcomes and because of the link between the rent of ability and wealth creation this must allow for sensitivity both to the concerns of the worst off and what economic incentives are necessary to pay the rent of ability. This has to be a matter of political judgement and market realities. But, the critic might say, what are these opportunities and resources which bear most directly on liberty? This is a complex issue and there are a variety of answers to it. I believe, however, that the most rigorous answer has been supplied by Alan Gewirth in his books *Reason and Morality* and *A Community of Rights*.[6] I cannot go into the details of Gewirth's argument here, but it is essentially concerned with what he calls the generic conditions of agency. That is to say, in order to be able to act at all, certain conditions have to be in place. If I am going to pursue my conception of the good I must be first of all free from the coercion of others, but equally I have to have access to those goods which will satisfy my basic needs as positive aspects of the generic conditions of agency in order for me to act autonomously. These needs will be focused on physical security, health and education. Without having these conditions and skills in place as generic conditions of action, I shall not be able to act at all efficiently. Social justice is therefore concerned with a fair distribution to meet such generic conditions of agency.

The second reason why we should be concerned with relativities as well as the absolute position of the poor in society has to do with the idea of citizenship. The economic liberal wants to define citizenship in purely civil and political terms, not in social and economic terms. However, as I have already suggested free democratic citizenship goes beyond civil and political rights vitally important though these are, to citizenship in the social and economic sphere as well and this involves trying to make sure that the terms of social and economic citizenship embody some idea of the fair value of liberty. If we are concerned only with the absolute rather than the relative position of the worst off they can still be effectively marginalised from participation in which those higher up the ladder of unlimited equality take for granted as part of what it is to be a citizen in our sort of society.

Finally there is a further central, but more difficult point. Since the mid 1970s economic liberal thinkers have made a good deal of the idea that the market empowers people. The trickle down effect of the market economy is held to improve the absolute position of those in work and that this distribution is a form of empowerment. This is however, difficult to accept, because it implies that the power of one group in society can increase while its relative position declines because of inequality. There is quite a deep reason why this surely cannot be so. Power is a positional good in the sense that its value depends on some other people not having it. In fact it might be regarded as a pure positional good in the sense that if power were to be distributed equally then it would disappear altogether. If this is so then power has to be connected to relative positions and power cannot be increased like the supply of washing machines which may be subject to the trickle down effect. Empowerment cannot therefore be secured by the market mechanism alone through the trickle down effect and the improvement of the absolute position of the worst off. Empowerment has to be concerned with relativities and not just absolutes. If we believe in a fair distribution of power as well as liberties, then we cannot avoid distributive questions and have to move beyond the economic liberal's concern with absolute levels.

This section on fairness may be the place to say something about universal versus selective benefits. This is the field of the social policy expert which I cannot claim to be, but I believe that our thinking on these matters should be guided by some general principles. This is an important issue because if fairness is to be concerned with the securing of the generic conditions of agency, then we have to have some idea of appropriate distributive principles.

The debate over selectivity produces a clash of three values all of which have been historically important. The first has to do with need as a distributive principle. If we take the view that the principle of need lies at the basis of social policy, then it would, at least in principle, be relatively easy to justify selectivity in the distribution of benefits. Only those with the needs should receive the benefits. It would be better to target benefits if we believe that underlying social policy is the principle that it should respond to identified need. Of course it might be argued that in fact a universal benefit like Child Benefit is best paid on a universal basis because this is the best way of getting it into the pockets of those who need it. This is partly because of stigma, and partly because the take up of selective benefits is less high. This however, is not an argument about the principle, it is rather one about the best means of delivering the benefit to the needy. For those who believe in social justice according to need, therefore, the focus should be on whether there are in fact ways of delivering benefits to the needy without universalising them (involving huge costs) if there is a more efficient way of delivering them. Indeed the point is stronger than this. It would prevent benefits being allocated on the basis of other inappropriate principles of allocation than that of need.

The second principle which favours universality is to see benefits as a right of citizenship so that one gets them merely through the fact of citizenship irrespective of whether one needs them. A benefit should be no more selective than the right to vote, both are a right of citizenship, not based upon a more specific or sectional claim. Of course there is another way of formulating the citizenship argument which would move us away from this and that would be to say that the right of citizenship is not a right to benefit as such but a right to have one's needs met, when one cannot do so for oneself. Given that the social and economic rights of citizenship probably depend on a need based argument anyway (as I have tried to argue elsewhere)[7] then this restriction of the citizenship argument seems quite plausible.

The final principle which would favour universality is the one which links benefits with contributions, a relationship which has become opaque over the years. However, on this view because one has paid in to a scheme of social insurance, one should be able to benefit proportionately from that. In the same way as a private insurance company pays out on a claim because one has insured for it and does not take into account the question of whether one needs the money, so in a scheme of social insurance, one should have the benefit whether one needs it or not. Some have argued[8] that it is essential for socialists to restore the idea of social insurance to meet these issues whereas at the moment we have a very confusing mixture of need oriented criteria along with insurance principles. Of course, this is not a clear-cut matter in that one might move to an explicitly insurance based view for some benefits and a need oriented view for others. I shall come back to some of these issues.

I want now to turn to questions of political motivation and social justice. It has been argued by some that distributive justice is actually in people's self interest if only they would realise it. Taxation funds various institutions such as health, education, unemployment benefit, etc. which are in people's own self interest. The argument here is that politics creates and funds public goods which everyone wants, but which cannot be funded by individuals separately, or can be done only with great inefficiencies. So it is in every individual's interest to pay tax to fund these public goods since they never know when they might need them. A health service, a social security system, public parks and so forth are in everyone's interest, but they cannot be funded by individuals separately. The production of these goods and fair access to them as a part of distributive justice can be justified in terms of self-interest.

One way of fleshing out this kind of view would be to go back to the idea of social insurance. On this view social policy should not be about meeting publicly defined needs of the worst off, thus raising the good Samaritan problem, but rather should be seen essentially in terms of social insurance. On this view the benefits system should be seen as a mechanism for proportionate income replacement so that individuals can enjoy different levels of benefit covering a proportion of their income depending on what they have contributed. On this view a move to a social insurance model, as is the case in many European countries, will address the motivational issue by making differential levels of social insurance a matter of self-interest.

However, as an overall response to the issue of social justice the self interested argument will not do the work that is required of it. First of all in terms of its public goods form it will not necessarily provide a rationale for funding public goods which, from a social justice perspective, are supposed to be perhaps of the greatest advantage to the least advantaged. That is to say the self interest argument might provide a rationale for a safety net approach to the public funding of health, education and welfare, but it will not justify a more egalitarian approach to public provision or a conception of the welfare state which is supposed to fund social justice either through the direct provision of services or through cash transfers. This does not mean we should reject the argument because there are of course a number of public goods from public parks, roads, clean air, defence, etc. which are in everyone's self-interest and cannot be provided individually, but it is clearly a very limited argument in that it cannot by itself be used very clearly to fund public services or cash transfers which have a redistributive or social justice dimension to them.

The same considerations apply to the social insurance model despite its obvious attractions. It is not a redistributive form of public policy at least in the sense that its defenders set it out. It is rather a way of securing income replacement in times of hardship which replicate existing inequalities of income. Nor can it avoid arguments about needs in the sense that a compulsory form of social insurance would have to be in terms of an argument about those needs which we regard as most important and the costs of insuring them. Again though, we do not necessarily want to see all of public provision as being concerned with social justice and with diminishing inequality and thus, for those parts of the benefit system which we do not want to see as having this intention, there might be a strong case for this being assimilated to an insurance model.

The second argument that has become fashionable recently has been to emphasise the idea of community. We belong to a community, or even a family writ large and therefore as members of a community we want to pay attention to the needs of the least advantaged as well as to our own aspirations and advancement. It has been argued that in the 1990s we are moving into a period when the idea of community is much more salient than the 1980s when we were taught that there is no such thing as society, only individuals and their families, and that we should try to link a concern with social justice to the growing salience of the idea of community.

It is perhaps worth commenting at this point that this appeal stands in very stark contradiction to the image of society presented by the economic liberal. In place of the idea of society as a community or as a family, they sometimes suggest that their alternative model is that of a hotel. In a hotel there is a framework provided for individuals to pursue their own ends – people come to hotels for different purposes and to achieve different things. Their relationships are anonymous. Within the hotel they are bound by a framework of rules, but that is all: they do not have goals or purposes in common. If people in hotels come to share things it is from choice and not from obligation. Contract and anonymity are the hall marks of relationships in such a society. They do not have common obligations or common purposes beyond mutual non-interference, unless people choose to belong to groups and choose to assume the obligations of such groups. On this view the idea that we belong to a community of common fate, common purposes and common aspirations which can ground positive obligations to one another is naive and potentially totalitarian and furthermore in their view it is an image of society which is being constantly undermined by economic change and social mobility, as well as changes in morality, the growth of divorce and so forth.

Few socialists or social democrats would find this attractive as a vision of society. However, we do have to avoid being sentimental about community as a possible basis for our values. First of all, it is easy to be sentimental about working-class communities and the accompanying senses of solidarity and neighbourhood which now perhaps have very little salience to people.

Second, people appeal often to the sense of solidarity in 1945 which provided a basis for a greater degree of consensus about the distribution of collective resources. However, that sense of national community and solidarity was fuelled by the war and it is not clear that it persists in any rich way today. It is important to remember as a matter of history rather than philosophy that these values underpinned the Beveridge Report and they received a ready echo in society at large. It is very doubtful indeed whether we are able to assume such a consensus about values as a basis for a contemporary account of distributive motivation.

Apart from this we have to be careful about the appeal to community as a basis of distributive politics because people belong to different communities which impinge on them in different ways. For example, I have a house in a middle-class area of a large city and the poor areas of Southampton impinge very little on the neighbourhood community in which I live. I suspect that for most of my neighbours the area in which I live provides a more direct sense of community than belonging to the wider community of Southampton, or for that matter the UK does. People can, as it were, buy into communities in suburbs which are both physically and psychically very separate from the communities whose needs the supporter of social justice wants these people to address. It is not clear that appealing to their sense of community which may be very circumscribed will do the trick. If we invoke community as a basis of moral concern then it might turn out to be surprisingly limited and may not serve well as a basis of common concern and common obligation. One has to doubt the realism of basing an appeal to social justice and a concern for the worst off on a sense of community which either might not exist or where it does exist may do so to the exclusion of other communities with which social justice should be concerned.

The final possibility is that altruism and a sense of duty can be the basis of social justice. As with community no advocate of social justice would want to deny the importance of the idea of altruism and mutual aid as important motives in human life which should be encouraged and sustained. An appeal to altruism has been important in some parts of the socialist tradition particularly with the kind of communitarian anarchism favoured by people like Kropotkin in his book *Mutual Aid*.[9] It has also been important in Britain through the work of Richard Titmuss on *The Gift Relationship*[10] in which he shows that a nation-wide institution like the blood donor system can be operated on the basis of free gift. It works more efficiently than market systems of blood provision and provides a significant outlet for altruistic concern. However, as with community there are dangers in being too sentimental about altruism. This is so for several reasons. Those socialists like Kropotkin who invoked altruism posited a general transformation of human consciousness and motivation as a basis for a cooperative society. In this sense his appeal to altruism was highly Utopian. Second, while Titmuss does a good job in *The Gift Relationship* in accounting for the motivation of blood donors and the efficiency of the donor system compared to the market, it is very difficult to know what general conclusion to draw from his work. First of all, blood is a highly peculiar commodity invested with a range of meanings which do not apply to other things, and second, while the donor system is very important, it does not really involve all that many people relative to the population as a whole and I think we can learn very little from it in terms of the general organisation of social policy. Finally, it is at least arguable that altruism is nurtured by community, by a sense of belonging and common obligation. If as I have argued a sense of community is becoming less salient, then it is possible that altruism is a rather insubstantial basis for an appeal to social justice.

In many respects the more traditional social democratic approach to this particular problem still has its appeal, namely that a concern with social justice in the tax and benefits system and in the provision of services should be linked to plausible policies for economic growth. Otherwise we are thrown back entirely on the motivational issues already discussed. What I think we need is a commitment to both economic growth and expounding the moral case set out earlier. The moral case is however more likely to prove acceptable if people can feel confident that it is not going to impede their own ambitions and aspirations.

NOTES

1 J. Sumpton and K. Joseph, *Equality*, London, John Murray, 1979.
2 C. Taylor, 'What's wrong with negative liberty', in C. Taylor, *Philosophy and the Human Sciences: Philosophical Papers*, vol. 2, Cambridge, Cambridge University Press, 1995, pp. 211–30.
3 Robert Nozick, *Anarchy, State and Utopia*, Oxford, Basil Blackwell, 1974.
4 John Rawls, *A Theory of Justice*, Cambridge, Mass., Harvard University Press, 1971.
5 C.A.R. Crosland, *The Future of Socialism*, London, Jonathan Cape, 1956.
6 A. Gewirth, *Reason and Morality*, Chicago, University of Chicago Press, 1978, and *A Community of Rights*, Chicago, University of Chicago Press, 1996.
7 R. Plant, H. Lesser and P. Taylor-Gooby, *Political Philosophy and Social Welfare*, Basingstoke, Macmillan, 1981.
8 Brian Barry, 'The continuing relevance of socialism', *Democracy, Power and Justice*, Oxford, Clarendon Press, 1989, pp. 526–42.
9 P. Kropotkin, *Mutual Aid*, London, Heinemann, 1915.
10 R. Titmuss, *The Gift Relationship*, London, Allen and Unwin, 1970.

Index